W9-DDL-423

WITHDRAWN

F.V.

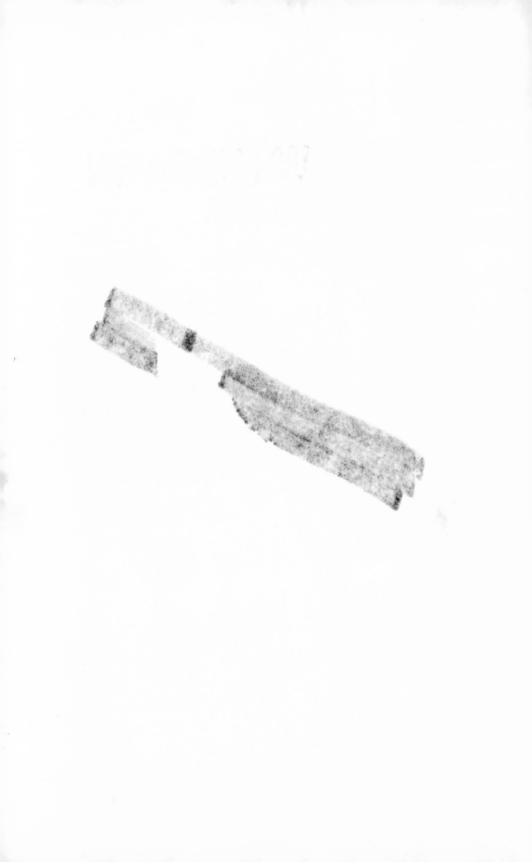

A PIECE OF THE PIE

A PIECE OF THE PIE

BLACKS AND WHITE IMMIGRANTS SINCE 1880

STANLEY LIEBERSON

UNIVERSITY OF CALIFORNIA PRESS
Berkeley   Los Angeles   London

UNIVERSITY OF CALIFORNIA PRESS
Berkeley and Los Angeles, California

UNIVERSITY OF CALIFORNIA PRESS, LTD.
London, England

Library of Congress Cataloging in Publication Data

Lieberson, Stanley, 1933–
  A piece of the pie.

  Bibliography: p. 395
  Includes index.
  1. Minorities—United States. 2. Afro-Americans—
Social conditions. 3. Afro-Americans—Economic
conditions. 4. United States—Ethnic relations.
5. United States—Race relations. I. Title.
E184.A1L49   305.8'00973   80-12772

PRINTED IN THE UNITED STATES OF AMERICA

1 2 3 4 5 6 7 8 9

To Becky, David, Miriam,
and Rachel

Contents

4
Government: The New European Groups 77

5
Legal and Political Issues 100

Part II: Socioeconomic Conditions

6
Education 123

7

Education in the North 159

8

Further Analysis of Education in the North 200

9

Residential Segregation 253

Preface

The origin of this book lies in a question that I often encounter when teaching undergraduate college courses on race and ethnic relations. My lectures on the "new" immigrant groups, those who began to migrate in sizable numbers from South, Central, and Eastern Europe after 1880, frequently lead to questions about why these groups fared so much better in the United States through the years than did blacks. I have always argued that the handicaps faced by blacks were more severe than those encountered by the new Europeans. The latter, notwithstanding their foreign tongues and broken English, their clothing, alien ways, non-Protestant religions, and the like, were after all *white* and a generation or two later it was possible for their descendants to shed as many of these markers as necessary. Blacks on the other hand were blacks no matter how anglicized their surnames, the absence of ties to distant lands, their language, their clothing, or their Protestantism. Besides the new Europeans got to the Northern cities in sizable numbers first, before the demand for unskilled workers declined. Anyway there were the unions and discrimination of all sorts in the North as well as in the South of a magnitude never experienced by the Europeans.

This was a satisfactory answer, at least for classroom purposes. First, all of my statements were certainly true. Second, it seemed to be an acceptable response for both blacks and nonblacks in the class. If any students were not convinced, they were not inclined to say anything.

But I had a nagging dissatisfaction with the answer. If what I said was true, was it all of the truth? Were the differences between South—Central—Eastern Europeans and blacks merely a question of differences in the opportunity structure? I did not know the answer.

I discovered that I was not alone; among my sociologist friends there were others who had one answer for public purposes but privately were not at all sure about it. There was the reluctant suspicion held by many that some unknown part of the gap between the new Europeans in America and blacks was a reflection of something else. I got to thinking about one of my colleagues at the time, who in his midsixties was completing an enormously successful career accompanied by virtually all of the highest honors possible in the scholarly path that he pursued. What would this American-born offspring of new immigrants, who faced poverty and other obstacles as a child, be doing if his skin pigmentation were different? I did not know the answer, but I was determined to find out as best as I could through whatever quantitative and qualitative clues were obtainable. This volume is the product.

Stanley Lieberson

Pima County, Arizona

Acknowledgments

This study was supported by a generous grant from the National Science Foundation as well as through a Guggenheim Fellowship. In addition, part of my work was aided by funds obtained from the Population Research Center, University of Chicago. I benefited from helpful conversations with Rudolph M. Bell, Albert J. Bergesen, Charles E. Bidwell, Edna Bonacich, James T. Borhek, Vernon Carstensen, Richard F. Curtis, Beverly Duncan, Otis Dudley Duncan, Neil D. Fligstein, John Hope Franklin, Avery Guest, Philip M. Hauser, Charles Hirschman, Michael Hout, Morris Janowitz, Evelyn M. Kitagawa, Patricia L. MacCorquodale, Jerry L. L. Miller, S. Frank Miyamoto, Donnell M. Pappenfort, Donald Weinstein, William Julius Wilson, and Wendy C. Wolf. Most important of all, several superb graduate students helped out, not merely by digging up references and running the data, but also by giving me their ideas and commenting on mine. My deepest appreciation is extended to Donna K. Carter, Guy C. Dalto, Mary Ellen Marsden, and Joan Talbert. Much of the manuscript was typed by Sandy Goers who, as always, contributed useful suggestions while doing an outstanding job. Additional computing help was provided by David Craigie, Irene Rubin, Theodore Shen, Mark Warr, and Christy Wilkinson. Jacqueline Adams-Thomson was largely responsible for the index.

1

The Problem: Black–New European Differences

The source of European migrants to the United States shifted radically toward the end of the last century; Northwestern Europe declined in relative importance, thanks to the unheralded numbers arriving from the Southern, Central, and Eastern parts of Europe. These "new" sources, which had contributed less than one-tenth of all immigrants as late as 1880, were soon sending the vast majority of newcomers, until large-scale immigration was permanently cut off in the 1920s. For example, less than 1 percent of all immigrants in the 1860s had come from Italy, but in the first two decades of the twentieth century more migrants arrived from this one nation than from all of the Northwestern European countries combined (Lieberson, 1963b, p. 550). These new European groups piled up in the slums of the great urban centers of the East and Midwest, as well as in the factory towns of those regions, and in the coal-mining districts of Pennsylvania and elsewhere. They were largely unskilled, minimally educated, poor, relegated to undesirable jobs and residences, and life was harsh.

The descendants of these South–Central–Eastern (SCE) European groups have done relatively well in the United States. By all accounts, their education, occupations, and incomes are presently close to—or even in excess of—white Americans from the earlier Northwestern European sources.[1] To be sure, there are still areas where they have not quite "made it." Americans of Italian and Slavic origin are underrepresented in *Who's Who in America*, although their numbers are growing

(Lieberson and Carter, 1979, table 1). Every president of the United States has thus far been of old European origin. Likewise, a study of the 106 largest Chicago-area corporations found Poles and Italians grossly underrepresented on the boards or as officers when compared with their proportion in the population in the metropolitan area (Institute of Urban Life, 1973).[2] There is also evidence of discrimination in the upper echelons of banking directed at Roman Catholics and Jews, to say nothing of nonwhites and women generally (United States Senate Committee on Banking, Housing and Urban Affairs, 1976, pp. 218—219, 223). For example, as of a few years ago there were only a handful of Jews employed as senior officers in all of New York City's eight giant banks and there were *no* Jews employed as senior officers in any of the nation's 50 largest non-New York banks (Mayer, 1974, p. 11).

Nevertheless, it is clear that the new Europeans have "made it" to a degree far in excess of that which would have been expected or predicted at the time of their arrival here. It is also equally apparent that blacks have not. Whether it be income, education, occupation, self-employment, power, position in major corporations, residential location, health, or living conditions, the average black status is distinctly below that held by the average white of SCE European origin. Numerous exceptions exist, of course, and progress has occurred: There are many blacks who have made it. But if these exceptions should not be overlooked, it is also the case that blacks and new Europeans occupy radically different average positions in society.

Since the end of slavery occurred about 20 years before the new Europeans started their massive move to the United States and because the latter groups seem to have done so well in this nation, there are numerous speculations as to why the groups have experienced such radically different outcomes. Most of these end up in one of two camps: either blacks were placed under greater disadvantages by the society and other forces outside of their control; or, by contrast, the new Europeans had more going for them in terms of their basic characteristics. Examples of the former explanation include: the race and skin color markers faced by blacks but not by SCE Europeans; greater discrimination against blacks in institutions ranging from courts to unions to schools; the preference that dominant whites had for other whites over blacks; and the decline in opportunities by the time blacks moved to the North in sizable numbers. Interpretations based on the assumption that the differences in success reflect superior new European attributes include speculations regarding family cohesion, work ethic, intelligence, acceptance of demeaning work, and a different outlook toward education as a means of mobility. Not only is it possible for both types of forces to be operating but that their relative role could easily change over time, since a period of about 100 years is long enough to permit all sorts of feedback processes as well as broad societal changes which have consequences for the groups involved. Hence the problem is extremely complex. As one might expect, those sympathetic to the difficulties faced by blacks tend to emphasize the first factor; those emphasizing the second set of forces tend to be less sympathetic.

The answer to this issue is relevant to current social policies because an understanding of the causes would affect the ways proposed for dealing with the present black—white gap. In addition, there is the related issue of whether the SCE groups provide an analogy or a model for blacks. Finally, the historical causes of present-day circumstances are of grave concern to all those who are enmeshed in these events. Is the relatively favorable position enjoyed by the descendants of new European immigrants to be seen as purely a function of more blood, sweat, and tears such that easy access to the same goodies will in some sense desecrate all of these earlier struggles—let alone mean sharing future opportunities with blacks? If, on the other hand, the position held by blacks vis-à-vis the new Europeans is due to their skin color and the fact that blacks experience more severe forms of discrimination, then the present-day position of blacks is proof of the injustices that exist and the need to redress them.

Because there is a big stake in the answer, not surprisingly a number of scholars have addressed the question already. But as we will see, many of the answers have been highly speculative. It is one thing to note the sharp present-day differences between the new European groups and blacks and then to speculate about the causes of these differences. A far different task is the search for data that might help one determine in at least a moderately rigorous way what was going on earlier in this century and at the tail end of the last. Indeed, there are moments when I empathize with both the frustrations and challenges archaeologists must feel as they try to piece together events from some ancient society. To be sure, the overlap with the efforts of contemporary quantitative historians is both obvious and not insignificant. But there is more going on here than merely a historical question. An attempt to determine the crucial earlier events that led to the current situation also involves the application of a wide variety of theoretical notions about racial and ethnic contact and the forces generating shifts in the positions of such groups. Whether it be the use of queuing theory in dealing with occupational opportunity (chapter 10), or the linkage between political power and ethnic position (chapters 3 and 4), or a new approach to the forces affecting residential segregation (chapter 9), various theoretical issues must be confronted and modified in seeking an answer to the question at hand.

CURRENT INTERPRETATIONS

Before discussing the past causes of present black—new European differences suggested in the literature, it is important to recognize that nearly all authors identify a set of diverse causes before turning to what they see as the most significant one. Hence, the statements are to some degree taken out of context, being used here as an illustration of the existing speculations about the primary factors rather than as a comprehensive review of each author per se. Moreover, I use the term "speculation" quite intentionally because nearly all of the conclusions thus far have been made with virtually no empirical evidence. Glazer (1971), for example, in contrasting the "internal colonialism" model of Blauner (1972) with his own influential position, is at one point forced to argue that: "Unfortunately, the data, neatly arranged to prove this point, are simply not available. We do not for example have good studies of the economic and educational status of Polish Americans and other Slavic groups by generation and length of residence" (p. 454). He goes on to discuss what he thinks the data would show if there were any on home ownership, occupation, family, economic power, and schooling differences between blacks and the SCE groups. One of the pleasures for the author in reviewing the existing statements is knowing that in later chapters the reader will be able to evaluate some of them with relevant data rather than merely leave matters at the level of speculation, conjecture, and—not surprising given the touchy nature of the topic— polemics. Recognizing that these interpretations have served important functions in stimulating further work, it is now necessary to begin to evaluate them through more rigorous examination. In doing so one must recognize that it is not simply a question of whether the assertions are true empirically, but whether they are causally linked to the differences under consideration. For example, it is one thing to say that blacks differ from the SCE European groups because the former were classified as racially distinct from the dominant white groups, it is another matter to show that this difference accounts for a substantial part of the gaps under consideration here.

Race

In one form or another, race is widely recognized as an obvious and central difference between blacks and the new Europeans (Appel, 1970,

p. 340; National Advisory Commission on Civil Disorders, 1968, pp. 143–144; Silberman, 1967, p. 511; Stone, 1970, p. 107; Taylor, 1973, pp. 33–34). Skin color serves as a marker, making it much easier to distinguish blacks from the remainder of the population. By contrast, after a generation or two, it is much harder to distinguish the various new European groups from other whites. There are, of course, *aggregate* physical differences between white ethnic groups in complexion, eye color, hair, stature, and the like, but there is so much overlap between groups that these markers do not work as sharply as do white-black distinctions (albeit the latter is less complete than many think). Hence, assimilation could mean more options for the new Europeans than comparable behavior would open up for blacks.

Perhaps more critical than this matter of merger and identification is the notion that blacks in the United States were more severely discriminated against than the SCE groups simply because the latter were, after all, whites. To be sure, in keeping with the biological approaches common at the turn of the century, the SCE groups were themselves considered distinctive races, such that there was an Italian race, a Roumanian race, a Polish race, and so on. Nevertheless blacks were physically more distinctive and therefore, it is argued, less desirable than even the new Europeans. If a ranking existed for any of the goodies society had to offer, blacks were therefore placed behind the newcomers from SCE Europe. The commission formed by President Lyndon Johnson after the widespread race riots of the mid-1960s describes this difference very well: "Had it not been for racial discrimination, the North might well have recruited southern Negroes after the Civil War to provide the labor for building the burgeoning urban-industrial economy. Instead, northern employers looked to Europe for their sources of unskilled labor. . . . European immigrants, too, suffered from discrimination, but never was it so pervasive. The prejudice against color in America has formed a bar to advancement unlike any other" (National Advisory Commission, 1968, pp. 143–144).

On the other hand, there are some bothersome features to this argument. In one of the few studies that actually brings empirical data to bear on the problem, Taeuber and Taeuber (1964) note that it is very difficult to assess the impact of visibility because no group can be matched with blacks on all factors except the visibility factor. But they do show that "non-white skin color, by itself, is not an insurmountable handicap in our society. The socioeconomic status of the Japanese population of Chicago in 1950 substantially exceeded that of the Negro population; and their residential segregation from whites, although high, was considerably lower than that between Negroes and whites" (p. 380). In addition to Japanese-American successes, Sowell (1975) also notes that black immigrants from the West Indies have done much better than American-born blacks. Accordingly, he suggests that the influence of race per se needs further refinement and reconsideration in interpreting the black outcome in the United States (1975, pp. 96–102). Although handicapped by very deep forms of discrimination, the descendants of both Japanese and Chinese immigrants occupy much more favorable positions presently than do blacks. This is a puzzle, along with the results for black migrants to the United States, but it does not necessarily mean one has to go as far as Banfield (1968, pp. 69–72), who argues that the importance of race is exaggerated, that most white-black differences are due to background and that, indeed, such gaps can be explained by nonracial factors. He goes on to argue that what is taken to be race prejudice is often really class prejudice. Although this no doubt does occur, the evidence persistently indicates that the standard background controls do not adequately account for the observed differences between the races for a wide variety of important phenomena, ranging from income to residential segregation. Moreover, insofar as the new Europeans were initially on the aggregate extremely poor, such thinking would not help one understand why the shifts occurred so favorably for the white groups because the same class factors would have been operating. At any rate, Banfield (1968, p. 70) is concerned more with the current forces rather than with uncovering the factors operating earlier.

Finally, just to indicate how difficult the race interpretation really is, bear in mind that there were once other very severe subdivisions within the society, cleavages that are much milder now. An excellent example, because so many of the new Europeans were Roman Catholic or belonged to other non-Protestant religions, is the intense antagonism and suspicion of those who were disparagingly described as "papists." This is illustrated in an 1871 Thomas Nast political cartoon, "The American River Ganges," described by Higham as possibly the most terrifying anti-Catholic drawing in the nation's history (shown in Higham, 1955, illustrations between pp. 210 and 211). Numerous crocodile-like figures, clearly adorned with Catholic symbols, are shown leaving the water for a beach to prey on defenseless small children who have been dropped there from a bluff by Irish Catholic politicians bent on destroying the public school system. If race seems to matter more now than religion and other characteristics that distinguished the new Europeans from older dominant white groups in the nation, we do not know whether this was always the case. At the turn of the century, was it worse to be a Roman Catholic or a black in the urban North? If the disadvantage Catholics faced in 1880 declined more rapidly than the disadvantage of race, why was it so?

On the other hand, if being a nonwhite in the United States is a surmountable, albeit added, obstacle—and this is the significance of the widely cited example of the Japanese in the United States—it could simply mean that the Japanese had enough special resources to enable them to overcome this disadvantage, but not necessarily that the new Europeans and blacks were any different from each other aside from the race factor. In other words, it may be that the success of some nonwhite groups tells us something about their special resources that enabled them to overcome the disadvantage of race; but at the same time it is possible that race was the key factor differentiating black and new European outcomes in the nation. In short, race is an exceedingly complex matter that has to be approached with great care as we seek an explanation of the gaps observed between the groups of interest here. This is, of course, one of the central empirical questions to consider in the chapters ahead.

The Legacy of Slavery

The overwhelming majority of blacks in the United States are descendants of slaves who first experienced their freedom a little more than 100 years ago. The new Europeans were extremely poor and included large numbers of peasants, but they were not slaves. The contrast is even sharper because slavery was especially severe in the United States as compared with other parts of the New World. Particularly prominent in discussions of slavery is the deleterious impact many believe it had on the family. The family is normally an extremely important force in the socialization of children, the provision of their necessities, supervision with respect to behavior ranging from school attendance to obeying laws, and adults also provide important role models. Moreover, illegitimacy and broken families in which husband or wife is absent are both far more common among blacks than among whites. Given these two key facts, the importance of family and the higher rates of family disorganization, one can see why a number of scholars have concluded that a key SCE European advantage over blacks stemmed from the latter's period of slavery (Hauser, 1965, p. 854; National Advisory Commission, 1968, pp. 144–145; Novak, 1973, p. 42).

But there are several features to this argument that are not entirely felicitous. The Moynihan (1965) analysis of the causes and consequences of black family deterioration stimulated an elegant set of historical studies dealing with black families both before and after Emancipation and in both the North and the South which culminated in the 1976 volume, *The Black Family in Slavery and Freedom, 1750–1925* by Herbert G.

Gutman. The results are extremely important for the present purposes because they indicate that the black family was not particularly disorganized either during slavery or in the early years when blacks were first migrating to the North. If this was the case, then there are two important consequences for the issue at hand: First, the lesser frequency of black husband-wife family units presently is not due to the direct heritage of slavery but must reflect more recent forces; second, any differences between black and new European progress earlier in this century cannot be so blithely attributed to this factor. There is certainly no question that there are important statistical differences between black and new European family structure presently, but the magnitude of that difference earlier as well as the consequences, both presently and in the past, are empirical questions open to study. More generally, the Gutman results warn us of a serious danger, to wit, the tendency to assume that the forces operating presently were operating in earlier periods as well— as contrasted with the alternative possibility that the patterns observed now were at least in part created by earlier events.

Cultural and Normative Differences

Closely linked to discussions of the impact of slavery and the family are speculations that blacks compare poorly with the new Europeans in terms of motivation, disposition toward education, willingness to sacrifice, and other attributes affecting the achievement of long-run goals (Appel, 1970, p. 341; Hauser, 1965, p. 869; Kristol, 1966, p. 124; National Advisory Commission, 1968, pp. 144–145; Sowell, 1975, pp. 100–102; Taylor, 1973, p. 30). It is very difficult to find even rough quantitative measures of such cultural and normative matters, but quite a bit can be done about the educational orientation of blacks both in the South after the Civil War (chapter 6) and in the North for a number of decades (chapters 7 and 8) such that we can see whether this is much of a force. I might add that the cultural and normative explanations often rest on a deceptive form of circular reasoning, not at all uncommon in race and ethnic studies. Why are two or more groups different with respect to some characteristic or dependent variable? Presumably, they differ in their values or in some norm. How do we know that they differ in their values or norms? The argument then frequently involves using the behavioral attribute one is trying to explain as the indicator of the normative or value difference one is trying to use as the explanation. A pure case of circular reasoning! Obviously racial and ethnic groups may differ from one another in their values and norms, but an independent measure of such values and norms must be obtained to justify such an explanation. It is particularly dangerous to use circular forms of reasoning because they do not allow us to consider the alternative hypothesis that forces outside of the groups' own characteristics are generating these gaps: in particular, forms of discrimination or differences in opportunity structure rather than differences in either desire or goals or values. Fortunately, one can do a certain amount of reasonably rigorous work with respect to education.

Timing

Although the presence of blacks in the North goes back to the pre-Revolutionary period, much of the black migration to the North (I include here the West and use the term to mean non-South) occurred in recent decades. When the new European movement first began, 90 percent of all blacks lived in the South. Twenty years later, in 1900, the black percentage living in the South was still 90 percent—the number moving northward being relatively small. In 1920, only a few years before massive new European immigration was to end, 85 percent of all blacks lived in the South. Three-fourths were still in the South when the United States entered World War II. This figure decreased in succeeding decades, thanks to the massive changes during and after the war, but in 1970 a bare majority of blacks was still living in the South. Since, until relatively recently, the situation for blacks was extremely difficult in the South with respect to such bread and butter issues as education, occupation, and income, clearly the timing of black migration puts them at a distinct disadvantage vis-à-vis the new Europeans. The greatest black movement to the North occurred only after the new European flow had declined radically. For example, the number of Italians migrating to the United States went from 222,000 in 1921 to 56,000 in 1924 and then never even reached the latter figure through 1970. Likewise, the figure for yearly immigration from Russia and the Baltic states (combined) was one-quarter million in both 1913 and 1914, but it then dropped to a post-World War I high of 21,000 in 1923, with less than 1,000 coming in most years through 1970.

Although the timing of black and new European migrations to the North is clearly different, there are two radically dissimilar conclusions about the long-term consequence. It is argued that the black movement to the North occurred too late, that is, after the opportunities and need for unskilled people had declined. As such, it would mean that it is harder for blacks to repeat the movement of new Europeans from the bottom into a stronger position (Appel, 1970, p. 340; Banfield, 1968, p. 69; Novak, 1973, p. 42; Rustin, 1965, pp. 409—411; Willhelm, 1970, p. 17).

The second argument is a generational one, to wit, much of the change for new Europeans took a certain amount of time, involving several generations. If analogous changes occur for blacks, it is not going to be visible yet, but will take more time (Glazer, 1971, p. 458; Kristol, 1966, pp. 50, 128; National Advisory Commission, 1968, p. 145). Because a generational distinction is crucial for understanding new European progress and because blacks have on the aggregate been in the North for a shorter span, a generational approach is called for even if the first position is also true. Indeed, one must first apply a generational perspective in order to determine if blacks are making an analogous move. (Witness, for example, the generational comparison between blacks and white immigrants used by Thernstrom [1973, pp. 183–190] to disprove the "late arrival" hypothesis.) Unless generational-specific comparisons are made between blacks in the North and the new Europeans, it will also be easy to gloss over how hard it was for the new Europeans and how many generations it took.

This is easier to preach than to practice because there is remarkably little information known about blacks in the North classified by generation (Lieberson, 1973). In many instances I have been unable to apply this distinction, but fortunately there are some valuable educational and occupational data that can be approached from a generational perspective. Although my concern is not with making policy recommendations, the question of whether blacks in the North are presently undergoing a set of changes analogous to what immigrants experienced in decades past is not a trivial one. Also important is gaining an understanding of how blacks in the North earlier in the century fared when compared with the new Europeans of that time. Although relatively few blacks migrated, it was a period during which there was a strong demand for unskilled labor. In these circumstances, as well as others, it will be important to deal with generational effects as contrasted with societal changes in trying to understand black—new European differences.

Residential Segregation

We know that black residential segregation is very high, much higher than that experienced by various white groups in the same cities. This is extremely important because residential isolation is of consequence for a wide variety of other events, such as school isolation, restriction of opportunities because of minimal contact with whites, marking the black population as distinctive and different, and the restricted opportunities to live near all sorts of employment found at great distances from the black ghettos. Through residential isolation blacks also learn over and over again of their differences from whites and the low way in which they are regarded by them—indeed isolation may intensify an ethnic bond (Yancey, Ericksen, and Juliani, 1976). But segregation is also of importance not only as a causal variable that affects life chances but as a dependent variable that reflects the general position of the group and hence serves as an indicator of the standing of blacks relative to the new European ethnic groups.

It is well known that all of these new European populations were also segregated at the time their settlements began. So there are two basic questions involving comparisons between the SCE groups and blacks: First, how do the groups compare with respect to the absolute magnitude of their segregation and the rates of change over time; second, are the forces affecting new European segregation the same as those affecting black residential isolation? I have looked at this problem in an earlier work (Lieberson, 1963a) and found grounds for viewing black segregation as, indeed, different from that experienced by the new European groups. Working with data for at least five new European groups in each of ten large northern cities over a 40-year span, I found in all cases a sharp drop in the average new European immigrant group segregation from native whites during the ten-year span between 1910 and 1920. (I would call it rather sharp when we consider the short period covered.) A downward thrust is also observed between 1930 and 1950, although the magnitude of the change is not as great in absolute terms as in the preceding period when one considers that the second comparison covers a 20-year span (Lieberson, 1963a, pp. 66–67, table 13.)[3] By contrast, black segregation from native whites increased between 1910 and 1920 in all but one of these ten cities (a slight decline occurred in Pittsburgh), and likewise between 1930 and 1950 segregation increased in eight of the cities (a very slight decline is observed in Syracuse and a somewhat more substantial one is found in Chicago) (Lieberson, 1963a, p. 122, table 38). The divergence in segregation trends had some striking consequences. In nine of the ten cities in 1910 the Italian immigrant group was more segregated than were blacks from the native white population; in a number of these cities, other immigrant groups also were more segregated from native whites than were blacks. This was reversed in most cases by 1920, with the others reversed by 1930 (Lieberson, 1963a, pp. 128–129, table 42).[4]

Given these patterns, there is good reason to conclude that black and new European segregation have been radically different in this century, even if, at the outset, some of the new European groups were more segregated than were blacks. To be sure, new European segregation was not trivial even in 1950 (a matter that has been noted with good justification in a review of my findings by Kantrowitz [1973, pp. 16–17]). Although Kantrowitz was focusing on the levels of segregation between the groups, a similar conclusion could be made with respect to the immigrant-native white levels considered here. Nevertheless, the patterns for blacks and new Europeans are still in sharply different directions during this period and do not justify the claim that there is no sharp break between the black and white ethnic residential experience (cf. Kantrowitz, 1973, p. v).

For the record, one should note that Glazer (1971) minimizes the differences in segregation between the groups. Although recognizing that black ghettos seem to have more of an involuntary character to them than do the white immigrant ghettos, he cites data from an article by Kantrowitz (1969) on New York City segregation which lead him to conclude that "the degree of segregation of blacks in New York City, while high, seems to be at one end of a continuum, one shared by Puerto Ricans, rather than radically different from white ethnic segregation" (Glazer, 1971, p. 452). The figure cited in support of this assertion is the 70.7 index of dissimilarity between Swedes and Russians (largely Jews), a value that is clearly not much higher than the indexes between blacks and various white groups. However, inspection of the original Kantrowitz article does make one wonder. It turns out that the 70.7 index (which refers actually to Norwegian–Russian segregation, not the index between Swedes and Russians) is the *highest* of any of the 55 indexes of segregation between white ethnic groups within the New York–Northeastern New Jersey Standard Consolidated Area in 1960. In point of fact, the black indexes of segregation from the 11 white groups range between 78.6 and 87.7; whereas the indexes between white groups range from 21.4 and 70.7 (Kantrowitz, 1969, p. 693, table 6). The six new European groups included have, on the average, segregation indexes of 40.8 from one another, compared with 80.1 versus blacks (Kantrowitz, 1969, p. 692, table 5). Whether these differences are grounds for suggesting a continuum is, in my estimation, questionable. Regardless, more should be done about the earlier decades to see where and when the segregation patterns of the new Europeans and blacks diverged and to learn what this tells us about the issue at hand. I think that denial of the existence of such differences is not a serious issue; the big problem is why they exist. Perhaps one should put it even more forcefully: Why was there greater resistance to residential proximity with blacks than with the new European groups?

There are two main lines of argument: One is that the housing obstacles and difficulties blacks encounter are uniquely severe; the other is that blacks have not been in northern centers in massive numbers until recently and hence comparisons are misleading until length of residence is taken into account. It is important to recognize that the two positions are not entirely contradictory because it is possible for both factors to be contributing to the higher levels of black segregation presently found.

An important article by Taeuber and Taeuber (1964) on Chicago makes a strong case for viewing black segregation as uniquely severe rather than simply a function of timing. They observe significant generational improvements for European immigrant groups in education, income, and white-collar employment that seem to accompany declines in residential segregation. By contrast, improvements in black socioeconomic status do not appear to lead to a decline in residential isolation. Appropriately cautious about the results—among other factors they do not have adequate generational data for blacks—the Taeubers suggest that the forces generating black segregation are different from those operating on the new Europeans. Updating the Taeubers' study with recent data on trends in segregation and socioeconomic progress for blacks in the Chicago metropolitan area, Roof (1978, p. 462) found little reason for modifying their conclusions because black socioeconomic advancement is still not accompanied by changes in black segregation. Consistent with these results is the observation that upwardly mobile blacks found it much harder to escape their ghetto than did the new Europeans (National Advisory Commission, 1968, p. 145; Spear, 1967, p. 26; Weaver, 1948, pp. 41–43).

Although giving such notions as voluntary segregation among blacks and the positive consequences of isolation their due, Spear (1967) has likewise concluded that the black ghetto was different.

> The Chicago experience, therefore, tends to refute any attempt to compare Northern Negroes with European immigrants. Unlike the Irish, Poles, Jews, or Italians, Negroes banded together not to enjoy a common linguistic, cultural, and religious tradition, but because a systematic pattern of discrimination left them no alternative. . . .
>
> The persistence of the Chicago Negro ghetto, then, has been not merely the result of continued immigration from the South, but the product of a special historical experience. From its inception, the Negro ghetto was unique among the city's ethnic enclaves. It grew in response to an implacable white hostility that has not basically changed. In this sense it has been Chicago's only true ghetto, less the product of voluntary development within than of external pressures from without. [Pp. 228–229]

It will be important to discover the sources of this distinctive black residential position because they may help us understand generally the ways in which the disposition toward blacks differed from that toward the SCE European groups.

Occupational Opportunities

The importance of earning a living and of upward occupational opportunities is so great that it is quite appropriate to pull together some of the issues touched on earlier. Involved here, of course, is just the North—for like so many of these events, the situation was so glaringly bad for blacks in the South until recently that relatively little has been seen as problematic about the socioeconomic differences between blacks in the South and the new European groups. (As it turns out, a North—South comparison in chapter 10 leads to a rather surprising and significant result.) As for the North, there are really four different approaches, none being mutually exclusive, although they are frequently discussed as if just one could have operated.[5] One position is based on the assumption that a differential opportunity structure operated such that new Europeans were preferred over blacks with respect to jobs and opportunities for advancement. This is part of the "racism" perspective that would argue that bad as the situation may have been for the SCE European groups, it was even harder for blacks to get a share of the action. Second, there is the position that timing was a key factor. As observed earlier, it is a fact that most of the black migration from the South occurred after the new European flow had become no more than a trickle. Accordingly, the argument runs, much of the black migration occurred in a period after the demand for relatively unskilled work had diminished. Under these circumstances, blacks would be disadvantaged even if the dispositions toward them were not especially unfavorable. A third position approaches the more recent migration of blacks differently, emphasizing the fact that new European—black comparisons are inappropriate because the latter have not been in the North as long and will, after a few generations, do as well as the other "immigrant" groups. Finally, some have argued that personality, orientation to work, and expectations about work all affect a group's chances. In turn, it is claimed that blacks on the aggregate have less favorable characteristics · than did some of the new European groups.

In attempting to resolve this issue, it is important to remember that these interpretations are not mutually exclusive; although obviously one wants to know if one is the dominant force. It is also important to recognize that they may shift over time during this century, if only because of the possibility of feedback processes such as the impact of employment barriers on attitudes and dispositions. The earlier part of this century is especially interesting because there were some blacks in the North at a time when the new Europeans were migrating in large numbers; it was also a period when clearly there were substantial demands for unskilled workers and hence some of the timing issues raised above can be avoided. Under these circumstances, were there substantial employment differences between the groups? Chapters 10 and 11 will help answer this question.

THE STEPS AHEAD

This study is divided into two major parts. Part I compares blacks and new Europeans in terms of the conditions of settlement in the United States, and the various ways in which the government, politics, and legal issues have affected their pathways in the nation. The second part deals with socioeconomic conditions, particularly education and occupational matters, with a chapter also devoted to some of the intriguing questions raised about segregation.[6] The final chapter sets out an answer to the questions posed here (based on the data gathered) and deals with broader theoretical issues raised in the course of the study.

At the outset, the reader should recognize that the volume focuses largely on past events rather than current popular issues. So much has happened in the last few decades that one could easily devote the entire book to these developments. As much as possible, the reader should avoid the temptation to rely on glib phrases and interpretations of the events because it is all too easy to slip into very facile and oversimplified explanations. If sympathetic to blacks, then skin color or racism can be quickly used to explain most any difference imaginable. On the other hand, there is no difficulty dredging up memories of the struggle faced by the new Europeans when they first settled, or perhaps invoking explanations in which the new European groups' personalities or cultural attributes play a specially strong role. None of these interpretations are too happy for me—not because they are necessarily false— because they are too readily used when, at least for my taste, they are extremely hard either to prove or disprove. On the other hand, there is nothing so pathetic as the avoidance of crucial issues simply because less critical ones more readily lend themselves to empirical study or because the data behave better. So we will have to deal with these matters, but only after exhausting various alternative explanations as well as devising appropriate indicators.

With these cautions in mind, let us begin.

PART I
Structural Background

2

The Initial Conditions

A comparison between black and new European immigrant experiences in the United States must begin with both their initial conditions of contact and the impact on these groups of forces from outside the United States. Only then will it be possible to examine these groups in terms of the developments within specific institutions. Despite the considerable earlier settlement history for blacks, their entry into American society as ostensibly free competitors at the end of slavery occurs not too many years before the new European groups began to arrive in sizable numbers in the 1880s.

Largely relegated to unskilled work in the northern urban centers, the settlement conditions for the new immigrant groups were less than ideal. They faced an incredible array of difficulties including poverty, slum housing, tedious and often unhealthy employment, and discrimination on a variety of social and economic dimensions. Many whites of Northwestern European origin, because of antipathy and/or fear, sought to avoid these alien peoples and to constrain them. Not only were the vast majority of newcomers initially unable to even speak English but their ignorance of the social structure made many easy victims of exploitation by both ethnic compatriots and others. Unacquainted with the political system, the newcomers provided the votes necessary for the maintenance of corrupt urban machines.

However, to talk of hardships, without considering degree and magnitude gets us nowhere. Full appreciation of the handicaps faced by the new immigrants and their descendants should not prevent recognition of substantial differences from blacks in the basic underlying conditions of their contact. The goal of this chapter is precisely to consider the ways these conditions were different from those faced by blacks. Examination of developments in particular institutional domains such as government is postponed for later chapters. Here, the sole concern is with the underlying conditions of contact.

THE NEW IMMIGRANT GROUPS

Long before the 1880s, except for certain minimal restrictions based on health, criminal records, and the like, the United States stood prepared to receive unlimited numbers from any and all parts of Europe and the New World. But for reasons that are beyond the purview of the task at hand, the numbers migrating from South–Central–Eastern Europe had been minimal until late in the nineteenth century. The dramatic nature of these increments is shown in table 2.1.

The waves of new immigrants represented a variety of cultures and forms of social organization that were totally alien to the whites of Northwestern European origin who had preceded them. To be sure, these new groups had been represented in America long before the

TABLE 2.1
IMMIGRATION FROM SOUTH, CENTRAL, AND EASTERN EUROPE, 1820–1919

Decade	All South, Central,[c] and Eastern Europe	Italy	Greece	Eastern European Jews
1820–1829	3,343	430	17	
1830–1839	5,758	2,225	49	
1840–1849	4,275	1,476	17	7,500[a]
1850–1859	20,063	8,110	25	
1860–1869	26,522	10,238	N.A.	
1870–1879	172,655	46,296	209	40,000
1880–1889	836,265	267,660	1,807	200,000
1890–1899	1,753,916	603,761	12,732	300,000
1900–1909	5,822,355	1,930,475	145,402	1,500,000[b]
1910–1919	3,937,395	1,229,916	198,108	
1920–1924	1,114,730	460,644	52,144	

SOURCES: Carpenter, 1927, pp. 324–325; Rischin, 1962, p. 20; Willcox, 1929, p. 393.
  [a]Between 1800 and 1869.
  [b]Between 1900 and 1914.
  [c]Persons born in Germany are not included.

Revolution, but they were now arriving in unprecedented numbers. Xenophobia was hardly novel to the history of the United States. The arrival of Irish immigrants beginning in the 1830s and Germans in the 1840s helped to stimulate the formation of the Know-Nothing and Native-American movements of the midnineteenth century (Lieberson, 1963a, p. 62). An earlier settlement of Germans in Pennsylvania had aroused Benjamin Franklin's suspicions about their loyalties (Jones, 1960, p. 48). But the response this time was more severe, ultimately leading to the demise of one of America's most distinctive ideological themes, namely, a virtually unrestricted receiver of Europe's poor and oppressed masses.

What accounted for the exceptionally unfavorable response to the newcomers from these more distant parts of Europe? Several new forces were operating: religious issues; concentration in urban centers; implicit and often explicit racial notions; anxiety about assimilation; and the threats to existing institutions and traditions posed by the enormous numbers arriving. These concerns, later aggravated by domestic issues during World War I as well as the social and political tumult that followed, eventually led to the end of an unrestricted migration policy in the 1920s.

Religion

Although Roman Catholics had long been present in the United States, the nation was overwhelmingly Protestant in its religious composition and anti-Catholic in its outlook. "Certainly the anti-Catholic bias brought to this country with the first English settlers has proved one of the sturdiest and most lasting of these qualities," writes Ellis (1956, p. 20) in describing the laws against Catholics in colonial America. This attitude was to remain even after the laws against Catholics were eliminated and despite the fact that they were not a substantial proportion of the population. Maryland, which had been settled initially under Catholic leadership, was somewhat less than 10 percent Catholic in 1708 and had completely disfranchised Catholics from 1718 to the Revolution (Ellis, 1956, pp. 21, 27). In 1790, about 1 percent of the population was Catholic. Even in 1850, the 1.6 million Catholics in the United States amounted to only 7 percent of the population. By 1900, thanks in no small way to the new sources of European migration, the 12 million Catholics amounted to 16 percent of the population and were growing yearly with each new influx.[1]

It is important to recognize that antagonism between Catholics and Protestants in this period was much more intense than in contemporary

America. As a consequence, the fact that a substantial part of the new immigrant streams coming after 1880 were Roman Catholic was seen by many as a great threat to the existing political, educational, and religious climate of the nation. The substantial influx of believers in "Rum, Romanism, and Rebellion" created fears among many native white Americans that are hard to exaggerate. Nearly a century later there remained anxiety among some Americans about the election of a Catholic president.

Many of the immigrants from these new sources were neither Catholic nor Protestant, but represented religious denominations equally strange to the earlier groups. A substantial number of the newcomers were eastern Orthodox (for example, Greek and Russian Orthodox) or were Jewish. One of the most distinctive and advanced features at the time of the formation of the United States was the constitutional guarantee of religious freedom. As is commonly the case, the practice was not entirely as pure as the ideology, but nevertheless the United States was far more tolerant of religious differences in this period than were many other nations. However, the numbers involved in the new waves were to challenge deeply some of the relatively advanced policies. Jews, for example, whose history in North America dates back to settlement in New Amsterdam under the Dutch in the 1650s (Wirth, 1928, pp. 132–133), long enjoyed privileges and opportunities that were denied them in many parts of Europe. But the substantial numbers coming from Eastern Europe beginning in the 1880s were to increase anti-Semitism in the United States both for themselves and for the earlier Sephardic and German Jewish settlers.

Urban Concentration

A second feature of this new migration wave was their concentration in the urban centers. Whereas many of the earlier immigrant groups had previously settled in agricultural areas, albeit often in clusters, the newcomers were piling up in the urban centers, particularly those found in the industrial belt. To be sure, the Irish in an earlier period had concentrated in urban centers and Northwestern Europeans arriving during this period were also settling in the cities. For example, sizable numbers of Norwegian immigrants were located in Minneapolis-St. Paul, Seattle, Chicago, and in parts of Brooklyn (Adamic, 1954, p. 256). But the most striking feature of the new movement was the rapid shift in the ethnic composition of most urban centers. It was as if the very nerve centers of the United States, the metropolises, were about to fall into foreign hands.

A good part of this shift was due to the changing industrial structure of the nation; agricultural opportunities had diminished as the vast expanses of rich farm land and in the Middle West were filled by earlier immigrants and their descendants. On the other hand, there is some evidence that immigrants from the new sources were less likely to farm than Northwestern Europeans. In 1930, among immigrants who had arrived in the United States during the first decade of the century, 12 percent of those from Northwest Europe (and Germany) were residing on farms, compared with 3 percent of those from Southern Europe (Lieberson, 1963a, p. 64).[2] But the key factor was their arrival at a time when opportunities to settle in agricultural areas had declined. In 1930, for example, among immigrants who had arrived during the preceding five-year period, only about 1 percent of the Southern Europeans and a meager 4 percent of the Northwestern Europeans were living on farms (Lieberson, 1963a, p. 64). The enormous shift in the United States from an agricultural-extractive economy to an industrial and urban society was underway; indeed, these industrial needs were significantly responsible for the substantial flow of immigrants into the nation.

By 1920 one out of every five urban residents was a white who had been born in a foreign country and three out of ten were second generation (the American-born children of immigrants). Essentially half of all urban residents in 1920 were either immigrants or the children of immigrants. This concentration was even greater in the larger cities; immigrants from all sources alone amounted to nearly 30 percent of the residents in places of 500,000 or more and, including the second generation, they accounted for two-thirds of the population (Carpenter, 1927, table 15). Actually, several decades earlier, the percentage of residents who were either first or second generation was even higher. But the big shift was in the tremendous piling up of South–Central–Eastern Europeans into these cities.

The new immigration sources alone were becoming a substantial component of the population residing in many of the nation's largest cities (table 2.2). In Chicago, fully one-third of the residents were either immigrant or second generation members of these groups; approximately 40 percent of the residents of both Cleveland and Newark belonged to these groups. In New York City, the newcomers were less than 7 percentage points away from claiming an absolute majority of the population. In other leading industrial centers of the era, Boston, Buffalo, Detroit, Philadelphia, and Pittsburgh, one-quarter of the population were South–Central–Eastern European immigrants or their immediate descendants. To be sure, there were a number of other major cities, for example, Indianapolis, Washington, D.C., Kansas City, Cin-

TABLE 2.2
"New" European Groups in Major Northern and Western Cities, 1920

City	New European Groups		Percentage of total population
	Foreign-born	Second generation	
Boston	96,243	84,418	24
Buffalo	62,625	59,206	24
Chicago	453,714	421,926	32
Cincinnati	14,993	11,642	7
Cleveland	170,064	154,793	41
Detroit	146,557	97,440	25
Indianapolis	5,416	4,156	3
Kansas City	10,434	10,655	7
Los Angeles	29,562	22,777	9
Milwaukee	12,209	36,781	11
Minneapolis	20,330	18,972	10
New York	1,330,628	1,119,807	44
Newark	80,694	80,857	39
Philadelphia	232,600	209,409	24
Pittsburgh	71,884	72,369	25
St. Louis	49,000	42,473	12
San Francisco	48,302	36,218	17
Seattle	14,509	8,802	7

cinnati, and Seattle, where the new groups were a less substantial percentage. But clearly the enormous numbers coming from these parts of Europe, coupled with the economic opportunities available in the industrial centers of the Northeast, created fear among the older white settlers about the maintenance of the American Society.

Current changes in the black-white composition of major central cities are by no means novel. If anything, the percentage of foreign white stock in many of these cities fifty years ago is far greater than the percentage of blacks currently in these centers. Not only are the patterns repeated but the current anxiety shown in some quarters about the racial composition of cities is also nothing new.

Race and Assimilation

Racial interpretations of behavioral differences, far more widespread and readily accepted in intellectual circles than now, was another force working to the disadvantage of the new groups. It was assumed that immigrants from each European source were members of distinct biological races and that the various behavioral and cultural attributes found among these groups could be at least partially interpreted as reflecting inherent differences between them. The quotations below are from the chapter on "American Blood and Immigrant Blood" by the well-known American sociologist, E. A. Ross, in his 1914 volume, *The Old World in the New*.

> The conditions of settlement of this country caused those of uncommon energy and venturesomeness to outmultiply the rest of the population. Thus came into existence the pioneering breed; and this breed increased until it is safe to estimate that fully half of white Americans with native grandparents have one or more pioneer breed being swamped and submerged by an overwhelming tide of latecomers from the old-world hive. [P. 282]

> It is fair to say that the blood now being injected into the veins of our people is "sub-common." . . . You are struck by the fact that from ten to twenty per cent are hirsute, low-browed, big-faced persons of obviously low mentality. Not that they suggest evil. They simply look out of place in black clothes and stiff collar, since clearly they belong in skins, in wattled huts at the close of the Great Ice Age. [Pp. 285–286]

> "The Slavs," remarks a physician, "are immune to certain kinds of dirt. They can stand what would kill a white man." [P. 291]

> That the Mediterranean peoples are morally below the races of northern Europe is as certain as any social fact. Even when they were dirty, ferocious barbarians, these blonds were truth-tellers. [P. 293]

> The Northerners seem to surpass the southern Europeans in innate ethical endowment. Comparison of their behavior in marine disasters shows that discipline, sense of duty, presence of mind, and consideration for the weak are much more characteristic of northern Europeans. . . . Among all nationalities the Americans bear the palm for coolness, orderly saving of life, and consideration for the weak in shipwreck, but they will lose these traits in proportion as they absorb excitable mercurial blood from southern Europe. [Pp. 295–296]

These racial notions received official government support through the Immigration Commission formed by Congress in the first decade of the century. Freely using the term "race" to refer to a variety of specific groups, the commission concluded that the various European groups could be ranked superior or inferior in terms of their inherent biological capacity. Handlin's (1957) review of *A Dictionary of Races*, one of 42 volumes from the commission, concludes that the men responsible

> agreed that there were innate, ineradicable race distinctions that separated groups of men from one another, and they agreed also as to the general necessity of classifying these races to know which were fittest,

most worthy of survival. The immediate problem was to ascertain "whether there may not be certain races that are inferior to other races . . . to discover some test to show whether some may be better fitted for American citizenship than others." [p. 83]

A general distinction began to develop between the old and new immigrants; a distinction that sought to put a variety of characteristics together. The old immigrants were from Northwestern Europe, had come to the United States in significant numbers before 1880, were more industrious, more likely to assimilate, were closer to the native white Americans in general outlook and cultural characteristics, and were of inherently more desirable stock. The new immigrant groups, those from the remaining parts of Europe, were placed on the opposite end of the continuum with respect to all of these characteristics.

How valid was this distinction? The nation was far too torn by the polemics involved to provide much in the way of an objective answer at the time. Any superficial comparison would prove most damaging to the new groups rated lower than the old. There is little doubt that the immigrants arriving from the new sources were at a disadvantage when compared with those from Northwestern Europe.

Part of this disadvantage was simply a reflection of differences in their timing of arrival. The immigrants from Northwestern Europe showed up well on some comparisons simply because they had a longer average length of residence in the United States. In the case of citizenship, an important step toward Americanization, the Northwestern Europeans appeared far more favorable. With the exception of those residing in the United States for less than one year, the data shown in table 2.3 clearly indicates an orderly decline in the proportion alien as length of residence increases. In 1900, because the average immigrant from new sources had been in the United States for a shorter period than the old, a simple comparison of citizenship rates will be unfavorable to the new groups. But when comparisons are made between immigrants with comparable periods of residence in the United States, there is some reason to believe that the Northwestern Europeans were slower than the new groups to become United States citizens (Gavit, 1922, chapter 8; Lieberson 1963a, pp. 141–146).

Northwestern European immigrants arriving after 1880 enjoyed certain advantages over SCE Europeans arriving at the same time because relatively few of the early settlers in the United States were of Southeastern European origin. Due to the previous waves from Northwestern Europe, later migrants from these sources found relatives and townspeople who had arrived earlier and were in a position to offer some help;

TABLE 2.3
CITIZENSHIP STATUS BY LENGTH OF RESIDENCE, 1900

Length of residence (in years)	Percentage alien
Less than 1	71
1	77
2	77
3	74
4	70
5	63
6-9	41
10-14	24
15-19	14
20 and longer	7

SOURCE: Lieberson, 1963a, pp. 141-142.
NOTE: Based on foreign-born males 21 years of age and older residing in cities of at least 25,000 population in 1900.

a generally more favorable attitude on the part of earlier settlers; the availability of ethnic institutions that provided services ranging from medical to recreational; and added employment opportunities available from established ethnic compatriots. Hence the fact that many of the native whites were of the same ethnic origin as later immigrants from Northwestern Europe meant a generally easier situation for these immigrants around the turn of the century.

An examination of residential segregation reveals the way in which the origins of the native white population affected the later immigrant groups. Irish immigrant residential segregation in 1910 was greatest in those cities where relatively few compatriots had settled in earlier periods. Similar patterns, although less striking, also exist for later immigrants from some of the other Northwestern European groups (Lieberson, 1963a, pp. 80–83).

Reflecting the fact that industrialization had started in Northwestern Europe before it reached the SCE European nations, immigrants from the latter sources were less skilled than those arriving at the same period from Northwestern Europe. The percentage of skilled workers among the new immigrants during the first decade of this century was roughly comparable to the percentage among immigrants from old sources who had arrived in the 1870s (Thomas, 1954, pp. 153–154). Likewise, the new immigrants had less money and less education than the old immigrants. In many cases, from one-third to one-half of the immigrants coming from new sources in 1910 were unable to read or write in any language, whereas in many cases 1 or 2 percent of the old immigrants in the same period were illiterate (see table 2.4). Only one out of every 32 Polish immigrants arrived with more than $50 in comparison with 50 percent of the Scottish.

It was easy for the earlier white groups to assume that the SCE Europeans were inferior to the Northwestern groups. And, if they were inferior, the intellectual spirit of the time was harmonious with deriving this inferiority from basic, biological causes.

Demographic Factors

Antipathy toward the new groups, and ultimately the imposition of restrictions on their continued migration into the United States, was

TABLE 2.4
CHARACTERISTICS OF OLD AND NEW IMMIGRANT GROUPS AT TIME OF ARRIVAL, 1910

Origin	Percentage illiterate	Percentage with less than $50
Old		
Dutch and Flemish	2.7	65
English	0.5	49
French	10.8	52
German	5.7	66
Irish	1.4	81
Scandinavian	0.1	86
Scottish	0.4	56
Welsh	0.6	47
New		
Bohemian and Moravian	1.1	82
Croatian and Slovenian	33.5	96
Dalmatian, Bosnian, and		
Herzegovinian	39.3	93
Greek	24.0	93
Hebrew	28.8	87
Italian (north)	7.2	84
Italian (south)	51.8	92
Lithuanian	50.0	95
Magyar	11.8	90
Polish	35.0	97
Roumanian	36.5	94
Russian	38.1	93
Slovak	21.3	94

SOURCE: Lieberson, 1963a, Table 16.

deeply affected by the arrival of new migrants in such substantial numbers. In this respect, demographic factors undoubtedly interacted with the forces described earlier to intensify the difficulties faced by South—Central—Eastern Europeans. As table 2.1 indicated, a substantial number of immigrants flowed into the nation and huge numbers appeared ready and eager to come. The ethnic composition of the white population had changed radically; about 40 percent of all whites were of either British or north Irish origin in 1920, compared with 75 percent in 1790 (Kiser, 1956, p. 311). Whites descending from the area that is now the Irish Free State increased from 4 to 11 percent; with Germans increasing from under 10 to over 15 percent during the same period. Although barely represented in 1790, the Southern and Eastern European nations were about 10 percent of the white population in 1920 and likely to increase under conditions of unrestricted immigration. A fear began to develop that the great metropolises would become alien to America as their slums were filled by the new immigrants and their children.

Because of these demographic changes, efforts were made to reverse the traditional open-door policy for European immigrants. A literacy test was introduced in 1917 to reduce the flow and improve the level of immigrant skills. But the resumption of substantial immigration from the new sources after World War I led to the passage of more stringent laws in 1921 and 1924 (the Johnson Act and revisions) that definitely limited the numbers who could be admitted from these and other sources.

There are two key facets to these laws: First, numerical limits were placed on the total number of immigrants to be admitted each year; second, quotas were established for each group that were based on the population composition determined in the census of 1910. This meant that relatively larger numbers from Northwestern Europe would be admitted compared with the new European sources. The 1924 law moved the base year to the 1890 census, thereby establishing even smaller quotas for the new immigrant sources (Handlin, 1957, pp. 74–80). It is clear that ethnic biases among the dominant white population played a central role in influencing the procedures used to set the quotas for each European nation.

Developments since the end of the heyday of immigration in the 1920s require only brief mention. Restrictions were relaxed from time to time—for example, the admission of some displaced persons after World War II and after the unsuccessful uprising in Hungary—but basically the policy of controlling the number of newcomers remains in effect today. The McCarran-Walter Act of 1952 sought to preserve the national origins of the nation by minimizing the numbers of South—Central—Eastern

Europeans who could be admitted. During Lyndon Johnson's presidency, the quota approach was finally eliminated such that no particular nation—European or otherwise—would be officially favored. However, there is a ceiling on the total number of immigrants that can normally be admitted.

BLACKS AND THE NEW IMMIGRANTS

What does this brief review of the initial responses to the new European groups tell us about the issues at hand? How was the position of blacks, released from slavery only about 15 years before the 1880 turning point, different from—and similar to—the situation faced by the European newcomers? Both groups labored under incredible hardships, poverty, suffering, and discrimination. Likewise, both were initially viewed by the dominant white population as inferior and undesirable. But this apparent similarity is rather superficial, overlooking certain key differences in the conditions faced by these groups. At the very outset, in several respects, blacks were in a substantially weaker position than the new ethnic groups.

Desirability: A Continuum

Although all of these groups were viewed as inferior, the conception involved was not an absolute one, but rather implicitly placed these groups on a continuum such that the new European groups were not as inferior as Orientals, and the latter were still relatively more desirable than blacks.

The immigration policies themselves reveal a continuum with regard to the different groups. Some 13.5 million of the new Europeans had been admitted between 1880 and 1924 when the major immigration restrictions were enacted. Contrast this to the policies with respect to Orientals (Simpson and Yinger, 1958, pp. 127–134) and blacks. Chinese began migrating to the United States in the midnineteenth century, responding to the labor needs of the railroads and the economic demands created by the gold boom. The decline in demand coupled with an intensification of their competition with white workers in the West led to the suspension of Chinese immigration by Congress in 1882 for a ten-year period that was later renewed several times. The 1924 quota law provided for no new immigration from China. Agitation about Japanese immigration led to the "Gentlemen's Agreement" of 1907 with the Japanese government in which Japan agreed to severely restrict migration to the United States. As with the case of the Chinese, the 1924 act provided for no immigration from Japan. It is of importance to note that the thrust to repress migration from Asian sources required a much lower demographic threshold than did the pattern for SCE Europeans. According to the 1880 census, there were only 100,000 Chinese in the United States two years before immigration from China was cut off. Likewise, there were only 75,000 Japanese in the nation three years after the 1907 understanding was reached with Japan's government and less than 150,000 in 1924.

As for blacks, there was virtually no voluntary migration from either Africa or some of the areas of black settlement in the New World. The 84,000 foreign born Negroes in the United States in 1900, primarily from the West Indies (Myrdal, 1944, p. 165), amounted to less than half of 1 percent of the total Negro population. In short, these differences in the numerical threshold suggest that immigrants from SCE Europe were still relatively more acceptable to the dominant native white population of the United States than were the various nonwhite peoples.

Attitudinal surveys administered in the 1920s confirm the notion that the groups were implicitly ranked on a continuum of inferiority rather than simply placed into a dichotomy of "good" and "bad." In a variety of surveys, the American population ranked Northwestern Europeans highest, then the South−Central−Eastern Europeans, in turn the Japanese and Chinese, and finally blacks (see, for example, Simpson and Yinger, 1965, pp. 113−114).

Visibility

The visibility of blacks due to their skin color and other physical features, compared with the role of cultural characteristics in distinguishing European immigrant groups, is perhaps the most widely recognized factor influencing black−immigrant differences. Even if prejudices and discriminatory practices directed against the new immigrant groups and blacks were identical, the latter would still be under a greater disadvantage simply because they were more visible. To be sure, at the outset the distinctive dialect, dress, and customs of the new Europeans marked them almost as effectively as skin color, but their descendants could shed many of the features that distinguished their parents and grandparents from the older white stocks. Not only was it *possible* but in many ways it was *encouraged* by the dominant white population as a device used to generate assimilation and loyalty to American society.

The new European groups are physically distinguishable on the aggregate from each other and from the Northwestern Europeans, but there is sufficient overlap and variation that such criteria do not operate very adequately. Classifying the noses of 2,836 Jewish men in New York City, Fishberg (1911, p. 79) found that only 14 percent had the aquiline or hooked nose commonly labeled as a "Jewish nose." A pre-World War II study of gestures among Italians (primarily from Naples and Sicily) and Jews (chiefly of Lithuanian and Polish origin) in the ethnic ghettos of New York City found very pronounced and distinctive gesturing patterns for the two sets of groups (Efron and Foley, 1947). But of particular relevance to a comparison with blacks, these bodily movements were not to be found among "assimilated" middle- and upper-class members of these groups. The point is clear-cut, markers or indicators of ethnic origin for the new groups are neither as sharp nor as unavoidable as those for blacks.

Surnames also operate as ethnic markers, often imperfectly, but still with a certain amount of value. But here again this is a cultural characteristic that can be totally eliminated through a name change. Listed below are the stage names of American movie stars along with their original names (from Baltzell, 1966, p. 47). Not only does this list suggest a shift toward Northwestern European surnames (particularly Anglo-Saxon, but with a few French names as well) but it also indicates the possibility of hiding ethnic identity—a possibility that was not open to blacks.

There are a variety of interaction situations in which European ethnic origin is less clearly marked, whereas in all face-to-face situations the vast majority of blacks are marked. The exception, for the latter, are of course those who "pass." But the interesting feature here is that the new groups may unintentionally pass in a variety of situations without making any effort to do so, such as changing their surnames; namely, there are many public instances where determination of ethnic origin among whites is impossible.

In brief, a similar predisposition to discriminate against blacks and the SCE European groups will be more effective against the former in a variety of settings simply because they are more visible. In this respect, ignoring the current thrust toward black pride and a reemphasis on things black, ethnic identity was imposed on blacks. However, for the descendants of the new European groups their identification was more a matter of choice, because, with some effort, it could be changed.

Intermarriage likewise has very different consequences for blacks and for the new European groups. The offspring of black-white matings are

Stage Name	Original Name
Doris Day	Doris Kapplehoff
Lawrence Harvey	Larry Skikne
Tony Curtis	Bernie Schwartz
Karl Malden	Mladen Sekulovich
Marjorie Main	Marie Tomlinson Krebs
Judy Garland	Frances Gumm
Tab Hunter	Arthur Gelien
Casey Adams	Max Showalter
Ginger Rogers	Virginia McMath
Mitzi Gaynor	Mitzi Gerber
Bella Darvi	Balla Wegier
Claudette Colbert	Claudette Chauchoin
Ethel Merman	Ethel Zimmerman
Vic Damone	Vito Farinola
John Ericson	Joseph Meibes
Cyd Charisse	Tula Finklea
Robert Taylor	Spengler Arlington Brough
Dianne Foster	Dianne Laruska
Judy Holliday	Judy Tuvim
Glenn Ford	Gwyllyn Ford
Rita Hayworth	Margarita Carmen Cansino
Aldo Ray	Aldo Da Re
Vince Edwards	Vincent Zoino
Kathryn Grayson	Zalma Hedrick
Donna Reed	Donna Mullenger
Jane Wyman	Sarah Fulks
June Allyson	Ella Geisman
Kirk Douglas	Issur Danielovitch
Danny Kaye	Daniel Kaminsky
Dean Martin	Dino Crocetti
Jerry Lewis	Joseph Levitch

socially defined as black in the United States despite the fact that they
are no closer to one group than the other. Likewise, a black woman who
marries a white man will still be labeled as black. By contrast, ethnic
identity is much more ambiguous for South—Central—Eastern Europeans who intermarry. Women who belong to the new groups will take
the surname of their husband and hence are far less identifiable.
Similarly offspring borne by a woman of new European stock and sired
by a male of old European stock will bear the surname of their father.

   To be sure, a woman of old European origin who marries a South–
Central–Eastern European male may be erroneously identified by her
new surname and likewise their offspring may be arbitrarily classified
under their father's origin if his surname is a clear marker. In general,
however, it is clear that the emphasis on skin color undercuts the
merging of the populations with regard to blacks in a way that does not
operate among the new European groups. There is no question that the
black population of the United States, as a consequence, contains a
substantial contribution from white stocks, particularly the older American groups from Northwestern Europe (see, for example, Herskovits,
1964; Roberts, 1955).

Assimilation

   Although the negative reception accorded the new immigrant groups
from Europe involved a racial ideology, the racial notions underlying the
response of whites toward blacks were both deeper and more pervasive.
There was relatively more of an emphasis on the different cultural
characteristics associated with the new immigrant groups, such as their
ability and desire to assimilate, the absence of skills, and the social
problems generated by their presence. If all of this was taken as evidence
of their biologically inferior nature, nevertheless the emphasis was still
primarily on the new groups' willingness and ability to assimilate into
the mainstream of white society. Without in any way overlooking the
obstacles placed before the new groups and the presence, even today, of
a variety of discriminatory practices, there was a much less powerful
concept of "place" or "station" obstructing the white groups. Thus,
even if some Americans thought in terms of biological inferiority,
individual members of the new immigrant groups or their children could
become more acceptable through de-emphasis of their distinctive
cultural characteristics and avoidance of the strange elements of their
social structure. Indeed, such changes were interpreted as proof that
America was truly the great melting pot and that unlimited rewards
could be obtained by those who knew how to work hard.

Moreover, because the opposition to the new immigrants was based relatively more on their cultural, institutional, and behavioral character- istics, it was also possible for other whites to be persuaded that not all of these distinctive features were in themselves to be so greatly feared. The Catholic Church in America, for example, could and did become a respectable institution; the Jewish mother could and did become part of the folklore in an amused but friendly way; and pizza could become almost a basic staple in the teenager's diet. Almost all of the ethnic groups were able to capitalize on their distinctive cuisine by developing restaurants that would attract other Americans, and, implicitly, in a small way gain recognition and respectability for their culture. But blacks are a glaring exception that is only slowly beginning to change with the new emphasis on, and pride in, soul food.

Blacks in America were generally viewed as a biologically inferior population whose inherent characteristics prevented the performance of certain activities—indeed it was even considered inappropriate for them to try. Observing that a relatively large proportion of successful blacks listed in a Negro directory were light skinned, E. B. Reuter (1918, p. 314) cited this as evidence that even some white blood would improve the abilities and potential of Americans from Africa. Apparently the alterna- tive interpretation, namely that whites responded differentially to blacks in terms of their skin color and nearness to white physical features, was not considered. From this perspective, the "absence" of black culture, as well as the general propensity common to the period for the denigration of African culture and society, was taken as further evidence of the fundamentally inherent causes of black inferiority.

An "etiquette" or set of norms developed among whites about what was considered the "proper" behavior of blacks which defined black efforts to reach equality as inappropriate. The emphasis called for blacks to remain in their station whereas for immigrants it was on their ability to leave their old-world traits and become as much as possible like the older white settlers. Although many blacks sought initially to reach an assimilated position in the same way as did the new European groups, the former's efforts were apt to be interpreted as getting out of their place or were likely to be viewed with mockery. For the new immigrant groups, it was a question of their potential *ability* rather than whether it was *appropriate*. To be sure, even under such circumstances, the recep- tion afforded some of the immigrant groups and their descendants was not entirely warm or without severe difficulty. But the fact remains that the *assimilation* issue was central to the concerns of dominant whites in dealing with the new immigrant groups, whereas for blacks it was a matter of *place* and *appropriateness*.

CONDITIONS OF SETTLEMENT

It is easy to see why many scholars speculate that the imposition of slavery for such a long period must have had a profound impact on blacks as well as the receptivity of whites to them as free men. From a social-psychological perspective, Elkins (1959, pp. 81–139) argues that the institution of slavery had a powerful and harmful influence on Negro personality structure, which undoubtedly exacerbated the difficulties faced in the period after Emancipation. Docility, disinterest in education, acceptance of white control, a sense of subordination and inferiority to whites were the characteristics that white slave owners might encourage or impose on black slaves. If so, the argument runs, these characteristics would not be likely to help blacks make it in the United States after Emancipation, even if whites had been receptive generally to such changes.

Despite the easy temptation to attribute differences between blacks and the new immigrants to the former's history of slavery, these notions should be examined more critically and in terms of their concrete implications for such characteristics as education, family structure, literacy, and the like. Accordingly this issue will be considered in later chapters when specific socioeconomic attributes are examined and compared. However, the differences between the conditions facing blacks after the demise of slavery and the conditions under which the new immigrants arrived are rather glaring.

Settlement Advantages of the Europeans

Immigrants from Europe enjoyed certain advantages over freed slaves at the outset because of differences in the causes leading to their location in the United States. Much of the European migration to the nation, both before and after 1880, was a reflection of economic developments in the United States (Easterlin, 1965, pp. 497–500). The new immigrants arrived under conditions that were harsh, to be sure, but nevertheless their numbers varied with the economic cycles and labor force opportunities for unskilled workers. The importation of slaves into the New World was also motivated by economics, but Emancipation was in no way a simple response to the economic opportunities blacks might enjoy as free men and women. Accordingly, entrance into the labor market as free individuals did not take place when economic opportunities were necessarily at the best—even if we ignore discriminatory practices in the postbellum era. By contrast, the numbers arriving from South–Central–

Eastern Europe responded to yearly or even seasonal variations in labor force needs.

A second advantage, not fully appreciated, stems from the ability of Europeans in the United States to return to their homeland if the difficulties in adjustment were too severe or if the economy turned sour. According to Handlin (1957, p. 203), nearly 4 million immigrants returned to Europe between 1900 and 1930, compared with 16 million who migrated to the United States during this period. Indeed, substantial numbers were more or less sojourners, migrating to the United States only to seek temporary employment, with the intention (not always realized) of returning to Europe.

The escape valve provided by these return movements was particularly important during years when a depressed economy made the job market sluggish in the United States. During the depression year of 1932, more than 100,000 left the nation, with a total of about a half-million for the 1930s (Handlin, 1957, p. 203). Thus not only was there selectivity operating among Europeans arriving in the United States, but there was also an added selectivity among those who chose to remain. This is in sharp contrast with blacks whose ancestors had been brought involuntarily to the United States and who were now native Americans for some generations back, without close ties to their ancient homelands. Only a relatively small number of American Negroes migrated to Liberia, despite the efforts of the American Colonization Society, the proposals of Lincoln during his presidency, and the later campaigns of Marcus Garvey (Franklin, 1956, pp. 234–236, 277, 481).

Another advantage for the new immigrant groups was derived from the ability of their home countries to exert some influence on their treatment in the United States. A number of nations set up bodies to assist and counsel their emigrants. Aside from understandable sympathies for compatriots in distant lands, the emigrants were also of economic importance to European countries because of the substantial sums of money sent back to mates, children, parents, and other kin remaining in the old country. Immigrant remittances from the United States to Europe, amounting to some $275 million around 1910 (Klezl, 1931, p. 405), were of considerable economic importance to a number of European countries.

By contrast, African nations were unable to exert any influence on the treatment of blacks in the United States because almost all parts of the continent were European colonies. The absence of autonomous African nations, coupled with the fact that blacks in the United States were separated by several hundred years from their ancestors, meant that no significant efforts would be made to influence the treatment of blacks in the United States.

Location Within the United States

The new European immigrant groups did not locate in the same parts of the nation where blacks were concentrated. Examining the patterns through 1920, Willcox (1931) observes:

> There is not one state, and has not been for 50 years, in which 10 per cent of the population were of foreign birth and 10 per cent also were of African stock. . . . There are two belts of states, one from Maine to California, in which at least 10 per cent of the population is of foreign birth, the other from Delaware to Texas, in which at least 10 per cent is Negro. The two belts overlap nowhere, but between them is a band from West Virginia to New Mexico, in which neither immigrants nor Negroes constitute 10 per cent of the population. [P. 108]

One observes a consistent decline in the percentage of the black population located in the South between 1870 and the present time (Hamilton, 1964, table 1). But the substantial flow of new European immigrants into the United States between 1880 and 1924 took place at a time when blacks were overwhelmingly concentrated in the South (from about 85 to 90 percent). Compare this with the pattern observed for the European immigrants: Among those arriving during the ten years preceding 1900, only 5 percent were located in the South. Again, according to the 1910 census, only 5 percent of the newcomers between 1900 and 1910 were located in the South. The figure is somewhat higher for the 1910–1920 period (8.5 percent), but is down to even less than 5 percent in 1930 for those migrating to the United States during the preceding decade.

Not only were the two groups located in different parts of the country but they also differed in their rural-urban distributions. The immigrants in the North were an overwhelmingly urban population, whereas only a fourth of the blacks located in the South as late as 1920 were found in urban places (Hamilton, 1964, table 2*b*). The relationship between black and immigrant participation as unskilled and semiskilled laborers in the northern labor force is a matter to be considered in greater detail later, but it is sufficient to note that the two groups differ greatly in the timing of their arrival in the northern and western urban centers. In this regard, notwithstanding the fact that slavery did not end too many years before the influx of new European groups, the former are on the average more recent members of the urban North than are the new European groups.

European Culture

The institutional structure and culture of the United States are basic offshoots of that in Europe, particularly of the British Isles. Regardless of the changes that have occurred in the United States through the centuries since whites first gained a toehold in North America, and notwithstanding the impact of America on the old world, the European heritage in the United States is enormous. One need only list the impact of British legal traditions, the English language, religious institutions, technology, and various forms of social organization to recognize this linkage.

As a consequence, the new immigrant groups enjoyed certain advantages over the descendants of African slaves that were purely a function of their greater similarity to the culture and social organization found among white Americans of older stocks. In classical music, for example, the intra-European variations are far less than the musical differences between Africa and Europe. Thus Paderewski, a Polish pianist and composer, could successfully tour the United States, having his accomplishments evaluated by educated Americans as a contribution to what was labeled as "good music." In the same way, the works of the Polish-born Chopin could be played and appreciated. Indeed, in the case of the classical music tradition, except for Germany and France to a lesser extent, much of the European heritage enjoying prestige in the United States stems from South, Central, and Eastern Europe (see Lieberson and Carter, 1979).

The contributions of blacks to American music, either directly or through their influence on white American musicians and composers, is of course enormous. Indeed, the most distinctive and widespread American musical idiom, jazz, is in its various forms at least substantially the product of black America. Nevertheless, for a long time, the "proper" music—the kind that would be taught in music appreciation classes—was basically the product of Europe and, in no small way, the homelands of the new immigrant groups.

All of this shows that the linkages between the South–Central–Eastern European and the American society created by the earlier Northwestern Europeans were much closer and more readily accepted by the middle and upper classes of white America. Symphony orchestras are basically run by the social and economic elite of their cities. Based on a recent listing of major American symphonic conductors, the birthplaces of 28 were obtained from biographical directories. Sixteen of these, or 57 percent, were foreign born. Not all by any means are from the new European sources (Germany is represented by four; England, France, Sweden, India, and Japan each by one), but still the South–Central–Eastern European countries can claim seven.

This pattern also holds in other arenas where the various SCE European nations are much more closely linked to the United States and Western Europe. A substantial number of American recipients of the Nobel Prize are foreign born, with the South–Central–Eastern Europeans making a significant contribution. Of the 33 Americans receiving the Prize in Physics through 1969, nearly half were foreign born. Germany leads with five winners, but Austria has three, Italy contributes two, and other new sources also contribute one winner each: Hungary, Czechoslovakia, Spain, and Poland. Only three of the 17 Americans winning the Nobel Prize in Chemistry are foreign born, and none of these are from the new sources. However, in physiology and medicine, 18 of the 43 American winners (42 percent) are foreign born. Of these, eight were born in South, Central, or Eastern Europe. The reader should note that this analysis does not include American-born winners of SCE European origin.

Among the 631 members in 1961 of the highly prestigious National Academy of Science, a substantial number (109) were both born and educated outside the nation or were at least foreign born (42) (Weyl, 1966, pp. 30–31). Eastern and Southern Europe contributed 41 of these. (It was not possible to determine the additional number coming from Central European sources separate from Germany.)

The significance of these results for black–new immigrant differences in their experience in the United States is less clear. There is no reason to think that the heritage of Leonardo da Vinci or Michelangelo or the distinction of Enrico Fermi in any way aided Italians in the United States seeking a job in a steel mill or in opening a small store. For readers inclined to emphasize the importance of successful role models, then clearly the South–Central–Eastern Europeans enjoyed certain advantages over blacks insofar as their homelands were more akin to the United States and hence contributed some of the leading intellectual and artistic figures to both Western civilization generally and the United States specifically. Bear in mind that these accomplishments were the product of a very small number of immigrants; the vast majority of migrants from SCE Europe were agricultural workers and unskilled laborers (this discussion is continued in chapter 8). But at least we can agree that these patterns indicate a relationship between the new

Europeans and the dominant white Americans that was much closer than for blacks.

MORTALITY

Racial and ethnic groups may differ in their mortality rates for a variety of reasons, including biological ones. But most likely the predominant source of these differentials in life expectancy is a reflection, directly or indirectly, of socioeconomic conditions. Income, the availability of medical care and its quality, housing conditions, education, occupational hazards, knowledge and interest in proper sanitation, diet, concern with preventive medicine, and the like, are all factors that may be expected to influence mortality. Consideration of the differential rates experienced by the foreign-born and blacks therefore provides a useful general indicator of their relative positions in the United States.

Examination of the mortality experienced by the foreign-born white population and their children in the United States generally indicates higher rates than for the native white segment of the population. However, Negro mortality (in part crudely measured by data for all nonwhites) is for the most part far higher than the rates for the foreign-born whites. Indeed the magnitude of these differences suggests that the immigrant experience was radically different from the blacks'—notwithstanding the fact that immigrants themselves were at a disadvantage when compared with the native white population.

The standardized death rates indicate that native whites have persistently lower mortality than the foreign-born whites in each decade between 1900 and 1950. In turn, the latter have lower mortality than nonwhites (table 2.5). Not only does this pattern maintain itself throughout a half-century of declining mortality for all of the groups but in all cases the gap between the foreign and native whites is much less than between blacks and the foreign whites. In a number of decades, the latter gap is more than twice that between the two white segments of the population. In 1900, for example, the death rates are 20.2, 23.8, and 32.7, respectively for the native white, foreign-born white, and nonwhite males in the registration states. Thus the difference is only 3.6 between the two white groups, whereas it is 8.9 between the foreign-born and blacks. Similarly, the analogous gaps for women in 1900 are 3.9 and 8.8. By 1930, when the difference was only 1.1 between the foreign-born whites (for both men and women) and native whites, the foreign-born enjoyed advantages of 7.6 and 7.9 over nonwhite males and females, respectively.

TABLE 2.5

STANDARDIZED DEATH RATES, BY RACE, NATIVITY, AND SEX, 1900–1950

	Male			Female		
Year	Native white	Foreign-born white	Nonwhite	Native white	Foreign-born white	Nonwhite
1900	20.2	23.8	32.7	18.0	21.9	30.7
1910	18.7	20.3	27.8	15.9	18.6	25.9
1920	15.9	18.7	22.7	14.6	16.7	22.9
1930	14.4	15.5	23.1	11.9	13.0	20.9
1940	13.1	15.3	19.5	9.9	12.5	16.5
1950	11.0	11.7	15.1	7.2	8.6	12.1

SOURCE: White data from Metropolitan Life Insurance Company, 1961, p. 4; nonwhite based on yearly vital statistics.
NOTE: Age-specific rates standardized with age distribution of United States, 1950.

Other data also suggest that mortality among the foreign-born, although higher than that for the native whites, was nevertheless substantially lower than that among blacks even as early as 1900. Table 2.6 provides life-expectancy data for the three groups for both 1901 and 1910. Because of data limitations, it was not possible to compute expectation of life at birth for the foreign-born whites. However, comparisons made at age five are rather revealing. A five-year-old native white boy could expect an average of 55.4 additional years of life, based on the 1901 life table. By contrast, a five-year-old boy born outside the United States, but living in this nation, could expect an average of 2.7 less years of life (52.7 years) than a native white boy. A Negro boy of five could expect only 45.1 years of life on the average, respectively, 7.6 and 10.3 years less than the foreign-born and native white. Again, the gap between blacks and the foreign-born is far greater than the latter's disadvantage from the native whites. Similar results hold at age five for females, as well as for the year 1910. The gap in the average remaining years of life that might be expected on the basis of the 1910 data for five-year-old girls was nearly 10 years between the foreign-born and Negroes, whereas the advantage for native whites over foreign-born white girls was only 2.2 years.

With one minor exception, the advantage of the foreign-born over Negroes is maintained throughout the different age periods shown in table 2.6 for both 1901 and 1910. As one moves up into the older age groups, naturally the magnitude of the gaps is less spectacular because the number of years of life remaining is shortened for all groups. But even at age 21 the foreign-born enjoy an advantage over blacks that is far greater than their handicap when compared with native whites.

An opportunity also exists to compare the mortality experienced by specific South–Central–Eastern European groups with the native white and black segments of the United States population. (Unfortunately, the mortality data analyzed above do not distinguish between the old and new immigrants, and hence probably underestimate the latter's risk of death.) For a variety of different years, data were obtained on infant mortality which are classified by birthplace of the mothers. Infant mortality is extremely important because it was, and remains, a substantial source of death for any population. In addition, infant mortality tends to provide a good indicator of the mortality situation faced by different age segments of the various groups.

Overall, in the United States the mortality rates are considerably lower for the American-born offspring of various new European groups than for blacks. In 1900, the mortality rate for blacks is 297 per thousand live births, compared with 143 among the children of white mothers. The

TABLE 2.6

LIFE EXPECTANCY BY RACE, NATIVITY, SEX, AND AGE, 1901 AND 1910

		Age							
		5		21		45		65	
Race and nativity	Sex	1901	1910	1901	1910	1901	1910	1901	1910
Foreign-born white	Male	52.71	54.24	39.91	40.96	22.40	22.46	10.80	10.58
	Female	54.21	56.30	41.15	42.66	23.40	23.75	11.04	10.93
Black	Male	45.06	44.25	34.52	32.86	20.09	18.85	10.38	9.74
	Female	46.04	46.42	36.31	35.53	21.36	20.43	11.38	10.82
Native white	Male	55.44	55.98	42.50	42.52	25.43	24.74	11.95	11.67
	Female	57.16	58.51	44.23	44.96	26.89	26.51	12.96	12.62

SOURCE: U.S. Bureau of the Census, 1921, tables 13, 15, 16, 18–26.

rates for the children of European-born mothers varies considerably, but are consistently lower than blacks and closer to those for the children of native white mothers. Indeed the infants born to mothers from such new immigrant sources as Hungary, Poland, and Russia had even lower mortality than for all native whites. Of the white groups specified in table 2.7, children of Italian-born mothers had the highest rates, 189, but this was still far closer to the remaining white groups than to the infant-mortality rate for black mothers.

Inspection of the infant-mortality trends is rather instructive. Throughout the period under consideration, despite some exceptions, there is a generally downward thrust in infant mortality for all of the groups under consideration. Moreover, except for 1900, the children born to native white mothers enjoy lower mortality than the offspring of the foreign-born white mothers, and in turn the Negro experience is worst of all (for a possible explanation for the 1900 data, see the notes to table 2.7). For example, in 1917 the rates for the groups in the order mentioned above are 83.2, 103.1, and 148.6. The gap of about 20 between native and foreign-born whites is still less than half of the gap between foreign white and Negro. It is noteworthy that the decline is very rapid for the offspring of foreign-born women such that the gap is very slight in what may admittedly be an unusual year, 1932. Although there is a difference of less than one child per thousand between native and foreign white mothers in 1932, the black infant-mortality rate remains about 32 per thousand greater than either of these populations. The American-born children of Polish immigrant mothers have the highest rates of mortality among the white women specified in table 2.7. In 1917, the Polish rate was both higher than for blacks and higher than it had been in 1900. However, this may be an artifact of some data-reporting problems because "Poland" was an ambiguous concept during World War I. Nevertheless, we observe a fairly consistent decline through the 1920s and early 1930s such that their mortality is more like native whites than blacks.

The data reported in table 2.7 suggest a variety of infant-mortality patterns among the specific European immigrant groups, but always their position was superior to blacks. Some groups, such as the Scandinavians, the British, and the Russians, actually had lower infant-mortality rates than the native white women in all—or virtually all—years. The Russian-born women, with a substantial Jewish component, were of course one of the new ethnic groups. Weber (1962, pp. 350–351) attributes their low rates to observance of the Jewish laws regarding food. Other groups, such as the Italian and Irish, exhibit higher infant-mortality rates than the native whites but still lower than the black rate.

TABLE 2.7

Infant Mortality by Race and Nativity of Mother, 1900–1932

Mother's race or country of birth	Deaths under one year of age (per 1,000 live births)													
	1900	1917	1919	1922	1923	1924	1925	1926	1927	1928	1929	1930	1931	1932
Total	149	94	87	76	77	71	72	73	65	69	68	65	62	58
Native White	142	83	78	68	69	63	65	67	58	62	61	58	56	52
Black[a]	297	149	134	112	120	114	112	112	100	106	102	100	93	84
Austria[b]	NA[f]	124	113											
Hungary	113	124	89	94	91	86	83	86	69	72	72	67	66	58
England, Scotland, and Wales[c]	149	86	73	66	67	61	61	61	56	52	53	49	46	44
Germany[d]	159	98	78	73	71	64	63	66	57	57	56	50	49	43
Ireland	170	100	87	83	77	69	74	73	61	68	61	59	55	51
Italy	189	95	88	82	76	70	70	76	58	68	63	59	58	53
Poland	112	173	124	106	101	92	94	92	77	85	78	73	70	62
Russia[e]	134	85	74	60	56	56	55	54	47	49	48	46	45	42
Scandinavia	114	66	67	59	59	58	56	57	54	51	51	50	49	45

[a] Rate in 1900 includes all "colored"; Negro in other years.
[b] Includes Austrian Poland in 1917 and 1919.
[c] Rate in 1900 is only for England and Wales; rate for Scotland in 1900 is 120.2.
[d] Includes German Poland in 1919.
[e] Includes Russian Poland in 1919.
[f] Not available.

Moreover, by the later 1920s and early 1930s, their mortality experience is not appreciably different from the native whites.

Focusing on New York City, as a way of comparing blacks with European immigrant groups in a setting where both were seeking to improve their living conditions, provides further evidence of a substantial disparity between immigrants and blacks. Applying the age- and sex-specific mortality rates for native whites in registration states to the population of New York in 1920, the standardized death rates per thousand cluster together for the various white segments: 13.1 for native whites of native parentage (third or later generation Americans); 13.8 for the second generation (American-born children with at least one immigrant parent); and 14.5 for the immigrants (first generation). By contrast, the rate for blacks, 25.1, is close to double that for the immigrants. In New York City, whatever liabilities the immigrants may have encountered, and they were substantial, their mortality experience was not very different from the older American population. The black experience, by contrast, was radically different.

These mortality data suggest a great variety of patterns among the different European groups, but they are consistent with respect to one feature. Regardless of how high mortality may have been among the European groups at the outset of this century, each European group's rates were still closer to the native whites' than to the blacks'. To the extent that mortality serves as a general indicator of a variety of handicaps facing different groups, this analysis suggests that the immigrants generally, and South–Central–Eastern Europeans in particular, faced liabilities that were not of the same magnitude as those faced by blacks and, moreover, the liabilities of the former declined far more rapidly.

These differences at the outset in the mortality conditions experienced by blacks and the new immigrants provide a significant quantitative clue to their general positions within the social structure. In the chapters that follow, the impact of these various initial conditions will be considered in some detail for such crucial institutions as the political and legal system, the economy, labor unions, education, and the like.

3

Government: Black Participation and Power

In multiethnic nations throughout the world, government policies have profound implications for the positions occupied by racial and ethnic groups. A politically dominant group (or coalition of groups) may attempt not only to maintain their political power but also to advance group interests in other vital realms such as the economy, education, and social and cultural domains. The subordinate groups, in turn, compete for power and influence in order to employ government as an instrument for improving their positions in these other institutions. In some countries, for example Thailand, the political and economic leaders are members of different ethnic groups, but most commonly groups occupy relatively similar positions in both the economy and the government.

Obviously the federal government, as well as various lesser governmental units, has had important consequences for the new immigrant groups and blacks in the United States during the period under consideration. Not only was slavery the product of political events but also of immigration policies, education, courts and law enforcement, citizenship, military, and taxes. Moreover, government influence has expanded during this century with increasing ramifications for ethnic and racial positions in such domains as employment, housing, social services, welfare, and agriculture. In 1870, the ratio of federal government expenditures to the gross national product was about 0.04; in 1968 the ratio was approximately 0.15 (Lieberson, 1971, p. 576).

Without wishing to judge the merits of current demands from blacks for government programs designed to improve their positions within society, it is important to recognize that a variety of governmental bodies established policies and legislation throughout the period under study which had profound consequences for the various ethnic and racial groups in the United States. More often than not, these have worked to the disadvantage of blacks. Objection to current demands may be fully justified if various political-philosophical assumptions are made, but they are without merit if a pragmatic view is taken of the historical role of government as an influence on race and ethnic relations. As we will see, through much of this period, government policies have not been neutral with regard to the groups under consideration—rather for the most part they have created situations in which blacks have labored under severe disadvantages.

A variety of perspectives are employed in this chapter to examine the linkages between political institutions and the groups under considera-tion, but throughout it is worth keeping in mind that the federal and lesser governments are—and have been—one of the central instruments through which the positions of various race and ethnic groups are maintained or modified in other domains. Beyond this, there is a two-way interaction such that the positions of ethnic and racial groups in nongovernmental domains in turn have ramifications for political power and position.

BASIC SIMILARITIES

Black political efforts have clearly suffered from certain basic disad-vantages that the new immigrant groups did not face, the most impor-tant being the disfranchisement of the vast majority of blacks during most of the period under consideration. But one should take note of several crucial political conditions operating in society for all the groups. Later we will have reason to consider whether the forces were of equal consequence for both South–Central–Eastern Europeans and blacks.

A general prerequisite for political success among both black and new ethnic group candidates is the sizable concentration of compatriots in a voting area. The strength of this prerequisite for political power is difficult to measure in any precise manner because it follows that more officeholders from a particular group will be elected in areas where the group is concentrated because the probability of nomination and elec-tion will be affected by the ethnic or racial composition of the electorate even if only chance factors are operating. However, the operation of ethnic and racial factors in the choices made by voters is very clear. As a consequence, the groups have generally achieved their greatest political power in areas of demographic strength.

Implicit in any discussion of the importance of demographic strength is the notion that blacks and SCE Europeans faced handicaps running for office among voters who were not compatriots simply because of the unfavorable attitudes toward members of these groups held by the population at large. Often blacks and the new European groups vote for ethnic compatriots whenever the opportunity presents itself, but this is more than counterbalanced by an aversion other voters have toward these groups and their candidates. As a general rule, sizable numbers of ethnic compatriots were a necessary prerequisite for those aspiring to political office. The liability that identifiable candidates from a given group face when seeking votes from members of other groups discloses much about the voters and the position of the candidate's group. Full assimilation, in this political context, would mean that there would be no correlation between the ethnic origin of the voters and the candidates they support after differences in social class and the like are taken into account. Indeed, the decline of such linkages is an important indicator of what might be called the process of political assimilation.

The existence of demographic strength, however, has not automatically generated the election of compatriots. Both blacks and the new ethnic groups suffer from "demographic lags" caused by the difficulty of wresting political power away from other groups. Because members of these groups tend to move initially into the older areas of cities, they encounter established political organizations that remain even after the previous residents leave. Often local politicians can maintain their existing power and perpetuate their position even after the ethnic or racial composition of the voters changes. As an intermediary between the area and the larger political system, the ward boss or district leader may continue in power insofar as he is able to deliver the votes. In turn, he can deliver the necessary votes as long as he has favors to dispense from the larger political system. Eventually, the new group is able to break up this delicate balance and establish its own local hegemony, but both blacks and the European groups met resistance from earlier established leaders that could not be overcome immediately after the establishment of demographic strength.

Another cause of this demographic lag, common to the groups under consideration, is the importance of wealth for attainment of political power. Economic progress interacts with political progress such that each tends to help the other (see Ogburn, 1961). Insofar as both blacks and the new immigrant groups were both initially poor and had little education, the financial strength necessary to support a political campaign or influence decision making was slow in coming to these groups.

Moreover, entrance into certain occupations, particularly law, and industries, such as construction, are likely to be pathways into politics and power. Compared with whites of Northwestern European origin, the concentration of the groups under consideration in unskilled and semiskilled jobs also contributed to their demographic lag.

BLACK POLITICAL PARTICIPATION AS VOTERS

An analysis of voter participation requires consideration of blacks separately from European immigrant groups because one of the central issues during this period for the former group was of no significance to the latter; namely, the vast majority of blacks lost the vote at the end of Reconstruction for a substantial length of time. Insofar as a sizable number of blacks were unable to vote during much of this century, efforts to use government as an instrument to advance black interests were badly handicapped. By contrast, not only were immigrants eligible to vote after obtaining U.S. citizenship but their American-born descendants were automatically assured of full political participation.

Thus blacks during most of the period since 1880 have been obliged to pursue political goals that were more or less taken for granted by immigrant groups and their descendants. Whereas blacks have spent much of this period attempting merely to enter the political arena, that is, obtain the right to vote, new ethnic groups could begin to use political participation as an instrument that might aid and support advancement of their interests or, at the very least, would provide an avenue of social mobility for some of their compatriots. White immigrant groups, although faced with disadvantages and obstacles, did not start with the same handicap.

Because about 90 percent of all blacks were living in the South at the turn of the century, and because they could not vote, blacks were more or less wiped out as a political force in the United States. Compared with the antebellum period, when even free Negroes were disfranchised throughout the South and in much of the North and West except for New England (Simpson and Yinger, 1958, pp. 451–452), a certain amount of progress had been made in the South in the years immediately following the Civil War. After the ratification of the Thirteenth Amendment in 1865, which abolished slavery, there were a series of maneuvers on both sides with respect to black voting rights. On the one hand, the "Black Codes" were introduced by various southern states in order to return blacks as much as possible to their pre-Civil War status. In turn, the Fourteenth and Fifteenth Amendments to the Constitution were ratified, designed to prevent states from depriving blacks of their civil liberties, due process, equal protection, and voting rights. Some progress was made in the South during the remainder of the nineteenth century. Between 1870 and 1901, there were 20 black representatives and two black senators elected to the Congress, with as many as seven blacks serving at one period (1876–77). One of the senators occupied Jefferson Davis's old seat from Mississippi.

The restoration of white supremacy in the South began with the so-called Bargain of 1876. The Republicans agreed not to oppose election of Democrats to state office in South Carolina, Louisiana, and Florida, and also withdrew troops from these states. In turn, Democrats agreed to hand Hayes the presidency in his disputed contest against Tilden. By the end of the nineteenth century, a wide variety of procedures were introduced to reduce the black vote in the South. For example, Grandfather clauses, introduced in the 1890s, held that persons could vote only if their grandparents were eligible. Because virtually no blacks had such ancestors, it was clearly an effort directed against blacks, although couched in universalistic terminology.

The net consequence of these and like developments was that immigrants from the new European sources were entering the political arena at a time when the overwhelming majority of blacks in the South had lost their political franchise. In Louisiana, for example, the number of registered voters declined precipitously from 130,000 in 1896 to 5,300 in 1900 to 1,800 in 1916 (Simpson and Yinger, 1958, p. 455). Whereas the various new European groups were able to use an expanding number of voters to gain increasingly sophisticated political goals, blacks were obliged to fight for mere entry into the political system. The estimated number of registered black voters in the South was only 70,000 in the 1920s and 250,000 at about the outbreak of World War II (see table 3.1). Until very recently, blacks in the South were unable to use the vote as a means of influencing the political system and hence to advance their interests.

The grandfather clauses of the 1890s, which were finally held unconstitutional by the Supreme Court in 1915, represent only one of an incredible variety of maneuvers and devices used during much of this century to nullify the potential voting power of blacks in the South. Poll taxes and other legal and nonlegal devices were successfully introduced to keep blacks from voting. Other methods included economic reprisals against blacks seeking to vote, removal of names from registration rolls, and restrictive and arbitrary registration procedures. For example,

TABLE 3.1
Estimated Number of Registered Black Voters in the South

Year	Number
1920s	70,000
1940	250,000
1947	600,000
1952	1,000,000
1956	1,200,000
1960	1,400,000
1964	1,500,000
1968	3,100,000
1969	3,200,000
1970	3,600,000

SOURCES: Simpson and Yinger (1965, p. 307), 1920 through 1960; U.S. Bureau of the Census (1970a, p. 369), 1964 and 1969; New York *Times* (1969, p. 305), 1968; U.S. Bureau of the Census, (1970b, p. 2), 1970.
NOTE: A variety of definitions of the South were used by the sources. Texas excluded from 1964 data.

tests based on the ability of the applicant to read or interpret the Constitution were administered differentially so that blacks would fail whereas whites with the same level of competence would pass. In more recent decades, registration itself was made more difficult, with registrars prepared to close their office doors at the sight of black applicants. Registration procedures have sometimes been prolonged so as to develop long and tedious lines.

A good illustration of these legal maneuvers is provided by the white primary laws in Texas. The first law of this type was passed in 1923, stating that in no event will a Negro be eligible to participate in a Democratic party primary election in Texas. Because nomination to the Democratic ticket in Texas was tantamount to election, this effectively deprived blacks of voting power in the state. The Supreme Court declared this law illegal in 1927. In turn, Texas empowered the executive committee of each political party to decide who could vote. The state's Democratic executive committee decided only whites could vote in the primary, creating an alternative legal device whereby blacks could be barred from political power. In 1932, the Supreme Court, by the narrowest of margins, declared this new device to be unconstitutional. This was followed by a state Democratic convention that declared that only whites could vote. Unlike the previous decision, this was not made by the party's executive committee, but by the entire convention. This ruling was upheld by the Supreme Court as constitutional as long as the state did not pay the expenses of the primary. It was only in 1944 that the Supreme Court finally ruled that primaries had to be open to all.

These are only some of the devices used for minimizing black voting power in the South (for a more detailed review, see United States Commission on Civil Rights, 1968a). It is only in the last few years that blacks in the South have been able to move toward the political power inherent in their substantial numbers in the region. In the 1950s, voter registration movements initiated by black churches and civil rights organizations were successful in increasing the number of black voters (Fisher, 1970, p. 69). Likewise, civil rights acts passed by Congress in 1957, 1960, and 1964 provided some limited assistance to blacks endeavoring to vote in the South, but the Voting Rights Act of 1965 was the most crucial (United States Commission on Civil Rights, 1968a, pp. 10–11). This law provided for direct federal action on behalf of blacks attempting to vote and also suspended the literacy tests that had been used as the principal obstacle to black registration. According to Fisher (1970, pp. 69–70), the number of black voters increased by close to a half-million within a year after passage of the law.

The percentage of eligible blacks and whites registered in 11 southern states before and after the passage of the 1965 Voting Rights Act is shown in table 3.2. Comparisons between columns 1 (Nonwhite) and 2 (White) disclose some substantial increases in these percentages; for example, the percentage of nonwhites (overwhelmingly black in the South) registered in Alabama leaped from 19 to 52 in the course of a few years. Even more spectacular was the shift from 7 to 60 percent of blacks eligible to register in Mississippi. However, one should note that in some states, such as Alabama and Mississippi, there has also been a substantial increase in white registration as well. According to figures gathered by the Voter Education Project, blacks of voting age in the South are still outnumbered by about 5 to 1.

Blacks, however, are becoming an increasingly important segment of the electorate in both the North and South. The number of blacks elected has skyrocketed since the Voting Rights Act of 1965, and one can confidently predict that the numbers will continue to increase as black registration expands and as blacks take advantage of their political potential. There were 4,503 blacks in elected office as of July 1978 (2,733 of them in the South). This compares with totals for the United States of 1,860 blacks in elected office as of March 1971; 1,469 in February 1970; and an estimated 475 in 1967. Nevertheless, this new high for 1978 means that blacks comprise slightly less than 1 percent of all elected officials in the United States. Hence blacks have been, and still are, grossly underrepresented in elected political positions in the nation.

TABLE 3.2
INFLUENCE OF VOTING RIGHTS ACT OF 1965

| | Percentage of voting age population registered in the South | | | |
| | Nonwhite | | White | |
State	Pre-act	Post-act	Pre-act	Post-act
Alabama	19	52	69	90
Arkansas[b,c]	40	63	66	72
Florida[c]	51	64	75	81
Georgia[a]	27	53	63	80
Louisiana	32	59	80	93
Mississippi	7	60	70	92
North Carolina[c]	47	51	97	83
South Carolina	37	51	76	82
Tennessee[c]	70	72	73	81
Texas[c]	n.a.	n.a.	62	53
Virginia[c]	38	56	61	63

SOURCE: U.S. Commission on Civil Rights, 1968a, pp. 12-13.
NOTE: Population data based on 1960 Census. Unless otherwise indicated, pre-Act year is 1964 and post-Act year, 1967.

[a]Pre-Act data for 1962.

[b]Pre-Act data for 1963.

[c]Post-Act data for 1966.

In terms of immigrant-black comparisons, the key point is that a substantial proportion of all blacks in the United States were unable to influence legislation or administrative policies because their potential voting strength was nullified. Indeed, insofar as the electorate was predominantly white and substantially in opposition to blacks, governmental processes in the South were often oriented toward the maintenance of black subordination. As will be seen later, this is a far cry from the situation faced by immigrants and their children.

Outside the South

In many parts of the North, blacks faced a number of obstacles to full participation as voters in the pre-Civil War era (Fleming, 1966, pp. 414–418), but in the period under concern there were no legal difficulties. Massachusetts was one of the few states to elect blacks in the postbellum era, with two men elected to the legislature in 1866. In 1876 the first black was elected to the state legislature in Illinois (Fleming, 1966, p. 424;

Drake and Cayton, 1945, p. 343). But the election of very many black candidates, to say nothing of the acquisition of substantial political power, was slow in coming. One reason was the necessity for the concentration of a large black electorate in northern urban areas before black candidates could be successful—a situation that did not occur in many places until relatively recently. But the factors are far more complex.

Indeed, evidence in the North suggests that voting strength is one route for exercising power in determining political policy, but is by itself insufficient for maximum utilization of the political processes as an instrument for obtaining black ends in other arenas of the social structure. The organization of voters, not only their numbers, is of great importance in influencing government policies. Further, various groups, ranging from labor unions to large corporations, are able to exert additional influences on the political processes. Wealthy contributors to political parties and candidates likewise have additional influence on politics. In these regards, blacks have fared less well than South—Central—Eastern Europeans.

One source of this difficulty stems from a complicated set of linkages between various institutional arenas. In this regard, black disadvantages in some domains have weakened their potential political influences; in turn, a weak political position has operated to create disadvantages for blacks in other institutional domains. For example, black influence in organized labor was limited by the fact that many of the craft unions, in the construction industry for example, have been discriminatory in their membership. As a result, blacks have had very little influence in many unions that themselves attempt to affect local urban politicians. Yet, as a consequence, urban politicians from working-class areas find it very dangerous to take stands contrary to the interests of organized labor.

The construction industry is another example. It appears safe to say that the construction industry is almost always linked to city, county, and state politics in view of the extensive contracts that these bodies may have to offer for the building of highways, schools, institutions, and the like, as well as the need to obtain construction permits and licenses. How do people get into the construction industry as contractors? Very likely most enter as craftsmen who proceed to start businesses of their own. Blacks, as mentioned, are denied entrance to the construction unions and are therefore unlikely to produce many of their numbers as contractors. This means that black politicians—even when they are in a position to influence contracts—may find themselves working with predominately white contractors.

Another way in which these forces interact is suggested by the differential voting patterns among segments of the population. Participation rates tend to go up with education, income, and other facets of socioeconomic status. Because blacks tend to be lower on these dimensions, their frequency of registration or voting is lower than the white aggregate. In this indirect fashion, the consequences of numerical strength are somewhat less than might be expected otherwise.

Demographic Factors

There are also demographic features operating to the disadvantage of black voters in the North. Through most of this period, even in the central cities of northern metropolitan areas, blacks were a relatively small proportion of the population, particularly when compared with the European groups and their descendants. Issues that pitted the interests of blacks against those of whites were likely to work to the disadvantage of blacks if only because of the greater voting strength of whites. Moreover, the clear-cut residential segregation between blacks and whites within cities has been a mixed blessing for black political power. It has meant, of course, the necessary population base for the election of black candidates and political figures. On the other hand, it has meant that many city or state subdistricts are represented by people who are almost entirely immune from any black pressures, because virtually their whole constituency is white. Incidentally, it is through such factors that we gain some insight into politicians who appear to change stances as they move from lesser offices to those encompassing a wider and more diverse electorate. Politicians representing an overwhelmingly white constituency may well take stands that they are prepared to drop when running for an office with a broader electorate that includes more black voters.

A roll call of the leading urban centers is instructive with respect to black–European immigrant differences in demographic strength during 1920. Omitted from consideration are the southern cities where blacks greatly outnumbered the SCE Europeans because the former were disfranchised and such demographic advantages were irrelevant. In Boston, where Italians and Jews faced a monumental task in wresting political power from the Irish establishment, both groups were several times larger in number than blacks in 1920 (table 3.3). Indeed, even in 1940, Jews and Italians still outnumbered blacks by a substantial margin. The story is the same in Buffalo, where Poles and Italians enjoyed enormous demographic advantages over blacks. Even the small number of Jews, 9,700, was still double the number of blacks.

Despite the relatively large number of blacks present in Chicago in

TABLE 3.3

RELATIVE BLACK AND NEW ETHNIC GROUP POPULATION IN NORTHERN AND WESTERN CITIES, 1920 AND 1940 AND SPECIFIC SOUTH–CENTRAL–
EASTERN EUROPEAN GROUPS EXCEEDING BLACK POPULATION (AND NUMBER)

| City | Blacks | | SCE European groups exceeding blacks in year indicated | |
	1920	1940	1920	1940
Boston	16,350	23,679	Italian (77,005); Jewish (60,042)	Italian (91,455); Russian (68,314)
Buffalo	4,511	17,694	Polish (83,344); Italian (34,923); Jewish (9,705)	Polish (90,745); Italian (55,847)
Chicago	109,458	277,731	Polish (318,338); Jewish (159,518); Italian (124,457)	Polish (372,684)
Cincinnati	30,079	55,593	None	None
Cleveland	34,451	84,504	Polish (65,841); Czech (43,997); Magyar (42,134); Italian (35,627)	None
Detroit	40,838	149,119	Polish (128,648)	Polish (169,275)
Indianapolis	34,678	51,142	None	None
Kansas City	30,719	41,574	None	None
Los Angeles	15,579	63,774	Spanish (33,540); Italian (15,691)	None
Milwaukee	2,229	8,821	Polish (70,238); Jewish (11,265); Italian (7,898); Czech (6,745)[a]	Polish (64,655); Austrian (15,546); Russian (15,266); Italian (13,014); Czech (9,200)
Minneapolis	3,927	4,646	Jewish (12,372); Polish (10,689)	Polish (11,217); Russian (11,301); Czech (5,283)
New York	152,467	458,444	Jewish (946,139); Italian (803,048); Russian (221,153); Polish (161,310)	Italian (1,119,169); Russian (928,056)

Newark	16,977	45,760	Italian (63,526); Jewish (39,863); Polish (24,706)	Italian (80,980)
Philadelphia	134,229	250,880	Jewish (143,514); Italian (136,801)	None
Pittsburgh	37,725	62,216	None	None
St. Louis	69,854	108,765	None	None
San Francisco	2,414	4,846	Italian (46,809); Spanish (11,559); Russian (5,871); Jewish (5,598); Greek (3,907); Polish (2,880); Portuguese (2,490)	Italian (57,656); Russian (14,660); Spanish (6,789); Greek (6,428); Austrian (6,296); Polish (5,921)
Seattle	2,894	3,789	Italian (5,526); Russian (3,061)	Italian (7,435); Russian (4,931)

SOURCE: U.S. Bureau of the Census, 1922, 1943b, 1943d.

NOTE: Northwestern European groups are not shown. Data for 1920 are based on mother tongue of foreign stock. Data for 1940 are based on combination of mother tongue and birthplace data (depending on which is larger). In all cases, the European ethnic groups are in varying degrees underestimated.

[a]Greek, Slovak, Slovenian, Serbo-Croat, and Magyar each individually exceed the Milwaukee black population in 1920.

1920, Poles, Jews, and Italians, as well as the Swedish and German groups from Northwestern Europe, enjoyed a demographic edge. Cleveland's Polish, Czech, Hungarian, and Italian components each held a numerical edge over the city's 34,500 blacks in 1920. Of the new groups in Detroit, the Poles were the only group larger in number than the blacks, but the margin enjoyed was in the neighborhood of 3 to 1. Blacks were relatively slow to migrate to Milwaukee; as late as 1940 they amounted to less than 2 percent of the population. In 1920, two years after a Polish-American congressman was elected from Milwaukee, 11 different South—Central—Eastern European groups outnumbered blacks, with the 70,000 Poles being the largest. Similarly, the black component in Minneapolis was very small in 1920, as well as more recently, such that the comparatively small Jewish and Polish settlements were larger—to say nothing of such Northwestern European groups as the Swedes, Norwegians, Germans, and Danes.

In 1920 the largest black settlement in the North was found in New York City. But the 150,000 blacks located in this city have to be contrasted with 950,000 residents reporting Yiddish or Hebrew as their mother tongue; 800,000 with Italian as their mother tongue; 220,000 Russians; a Polish tally of 160,000; as well as the nearly three-quarters of a million who reported German as their mother tongue. Newark, which was later to have a black majority, in 1920 was the settlement of three different South—Central—Eastern European groups who individually exceeded black demographic strength: Italians, Jews, and Poles. The number of blacks in Philadelphia was relatively substantial, but still somewhat less than the Jews and Italians. In Los Angeles, the Russian population was the only SCE European group in 1920 to hold a demographic advantage. But in San Francisco and Seattle, blacks were less than 1 percent of the population and were easily outnumbered by a variety of ethnic groups.

As tempting as it may be to utilize the demographic factor in interpreting the snail's pace of black political gains in the urban North during the better part of this century, clearly much more is operating. If table 3.3 indicates that the demographic factor was a sufficient force influencing black political progress in 1920, the data also show that by 1940 something else was also operating. (In all fairness, it should be noted in that in slightly more than one-half of these northern cities, at least one SCE European group by itself still outnumbered blacks. Moreover, the numerical strength of the new ethnic groups becomes progressively understated because the necessary census sources are restricted to only the immigrant generation and its children. An increasing proportion of each ethnic group's potential numerical strength, assuming no assimilation or disappearance, becomes lost in the data as part of the white population not classified by ethnic origin.)

Despite the fact that by 1940 blacks were larger than any single South–Central–Eastern European group in Cleveland, there was not a black mayor of the city until 1967. In the meantime, Frank Lausche (a Slovenian) and Anthony Celebrezze (an Italian) had served mayoral terms. St. Louis and Philadelphia did not elect black congressmen until 1968 and 1958, respectively. Pittsburgh, as of 1979, had yet to elect one.

Still another demographic feature has operated to the disadvantage of blacks; namely, there is some evidence that white resistance to, and fears of, blacks rises with the percentage of blacks in the community. At some point, when blacks comprise more than half of the population, this is no longer relevant. In settings where blacks are a substantial part of the population, but still a numerical minority, there are grounds to think that opposition may intensify to legislation geared to improving the position of blacks. Wilson (1966, pp. 452–453) observes that the first four states to pass laws barring housing discrimination all had relatively few blacks. These are: Colorado, 2.3 percent; Connecticut, 4.2 percent; Massachusetts, 2.2 percent; Oregon, 1 percent. Under any circumstance, the point remains that black voters in the North did not command the demographic strength to assure a simple majority in favor of their vested interests. Moreover, only with some exceptions in recent years, blacks have not commanded even a demographic majority in any of the central cities. In this respect—although the patterns are changing—South–Central–Eastern Europeans enjoyed greater demographic strength in the North.

Other Obstacles

The problem of political succession was an obstacle to both black and SCE European political power in many northern urban centers. Normally, leaders first arise among each of the subordinate ethnic and racial groups by building a political base within their ethnic group. By organizing an area where substantial numbers of compatriots are located, a leader develops political support that permits dealings with larger political units such as the city or state machine. Most of the groups under consideration did not originally settle in new parts of the city, but located in older areas. Although the older residents in these areas may have moved out, members of the previous ethnic or racial group often maintained control of the existing political machinery. Facing a change-over from one ethnic group to another, the older politicians in the area are able to include the new groups by a process of co-optation. Members of the new group are incorporated within the existing political unit in order to solicit their compatriots' votes. From the perspective of the larger political organization, of which a local leader is a part, discrepancies in ethnic origin between the residential population and the political leaders of an area are relevant only if trouble for the political party develops (for example, through loss of the area's voting support). Often, members of the political party may prefer to deal with ethnic compatriots who are incumbents or leaders of the subareas.

As a consequence, the groups moving into segregated areas of the cities formed the demographic basis for political power, but that power did not come instantaneously with demographic strength. Rather, the earlier ethnic leaders were often able to remain in power long after compatriots had left an area. As long as they were able to incorporate members of the new groups, whether black or some European immigrant population, they were able to deliver the votes and in turn to deliver rewards to their supporters. The Irish in many cities were able in this fashion to hang onto political power long after their demographic base had left an area. This was a problem for Italians, Jews, Poles, and many other of the newer European populations as well as for blacks. But the difficulties facing blacks were even greater. As noted in chapter 2, substantial numbers of blacks did not come to the northern urban areas until after great influx of South−Central−Eastern European immigrant groups. As a consequence, they developed the demographic basis needed to take over their areas' political organizations later. It was not uncommon for areas in which blacks were a substantial majority of the population to remain in the political control of various white groups as well as to have office holders who were white.

The gerrymandering of voting districts in many states created another obstacle for black politicians. Because blacks were not a majority in northern cities until recently, the net consequence was often a reduced voting effectiveness due to the manipulation of district lines that split the black vote into areas where they were less than a majority. Moreover, rural areas were often overrepresented in the legislatures of many states.

Black politicians were often less than militant in the pursuit of black political interests or in doing battle with the established political system. Wilson (1960) has shown that black politicians are under strong constraints to "not rock the boat" when elected as part of a larger political system. Concern with a machine's stability and harmony requires the avoidance of issues that might split the voters currently supporting a political system. Even in the usual case where whites are not in a black politician's constituency, an ability to minimize such issues keeps the party from being cornered into a situation bound to alienate black and/or white voting support. Although elected by blacks, it has not been advantageous for black politicians to antagonize whites when they were part of a larger white-controlled system.

Related to this is the fact that until recently many black leaders, political and otherwise, were themselves the product of a white power structure. Because wealth and power are far more concentrated among whites, it was possible for them to control and determine the rewards that black politicians could obtain. In this sense, it was as if whites rather than the black population created the black leaders—or at least confined the options open to black leaders. Vigorous pursuit of black interests that clashed with the interests and needs of the white majority would clearly be discouraged because the goal of pragmatic politics is always to incorporate as many political blocks as possible under one aegis by minimizing, whenever possible, the conflicts between the various groups. Because the interests of blacks in northern urban centers were in many basic ways at conflict with the interests of other important sources of support to the party, in particular, the white working class, organized labor, and the various immigrant groups, obviously it has been desirable for white politicians to underplay black interests. As a consequence, many black leaders were in a situation where they could ill afford to alienate the dominant—white—community establishment. As will be shown in chapter 5, until recently this has been relatively easy because the South has served as a deflector. Namely, it was possible to focus on the injustices found in the South—a matter important to northern blacks but also not threatening to northern whites.

MAJOR BLACK OFFICEHOLDERS

The slow growth of black political power is illustrated by the election of black congressmen during this century. The term "illustrated" is intentional: One must recognize that political power may be obtained without election and, conversely, office holders may have minimal political power. Certainly, in a complex organization such as the Congress, a small handful of blacks by themselves cannot accomplish too much without gaining entrance into both the informal and formal organization.

The election in 1928 of Oscar DePriest, the first black congressman since George H. White of North Carolina left the House in 1901, illustrates the difficulties of succession as well as the co-optation of blacks by a larger, white-controlled, political system.[1] DePriest had earlier built up a fairly substantial following within the black area of Chicago, serving as the first black member of the city council. In the 1928 primary battle in his district between the incumbent white congressman, Madden, and his black opponent, William Dawson, DePriest supported the former. Dawson, at this point, took a hard racial line in his campaign for black voters. Madden won the primary, but died before the election. DePriest moved in to capture the Republican nomination and become the first black congressman elected from the North. Dawson later became affiliated with the Democratic Party and was elected to Congress from this district in 1942. He shifted his style after gaining office. Wilson (1960) notes that Dawson's emphasis on racial matters and his appeal for support from black voters on the basis of race was muted after Dawson reached his position as a powerful member of the larger Democratic party system in Cook County.

Aside from DePriest's seat, which has been held by blacks since 1929 (a Republican, Arthur Mitchell, between 1934 and 1943; and William Dawson, as a Democrat, from 1943 until his retirement in 1970), it was not until 1945 that another black was elected to Congress, Adam Clayton Powell, Jr. from Harlem. There was a gap then of 16 years between DePriest and Powell. It took another nine years before Charles Diggs, Jr. was elected a congressman by voters in Detroit. The pace quickened, with a congressman elected from Philadelphia in 1958, Los Angeles in 1962, and a second congressman from Detroit in 1964. Before the election of 1970, there were nine black members of the House. Of these, all were from big northern ghettos: St. Louis, Brooklyn, Harlem, Philadelphia, Chicago, Detroit, Los Angeles, and Cleveland. In 1970, three more blacks were elected to the House, representing racially mixed consti-tuencies from Baltimore, Berkeley-Oakland, and Chicago. A special election for a nonvoting congressman from Washington, D.C. added a thirteenth. In 1973, blacks were elected for the first time to fill seats from Atlanta and Houston, and in 1975 a black was elected to the House from Memphis. Nevertheless, the number of black congressmen, 16 at the time of this writing, is far less than proportionate to their numbers in the population.

It is noteworthy that all black members of the House are Democrats. For many years after the Civil War, black political allegiance was very much tied to the Republican Party because of the historical linkage between Emancipation, Lincoln, and Republicans, as well as the fact that the Democratic Party was also the party of southern whites. However, beginning with the Franklin Roosevelt era, there was an important switch to the Democratic Party among blacks, such that in many elections they now form a crucial Democratic bloc in statewide and citywide contests. When Roosevelt first ran for the presidency, his linkage with the Democratic Party, and hence southern whites, as well as the fact that his vice-president was from the South, were liabilities for him to overcome among northern blacks. However, the welfare and other relief plans introduced after his election eventually helped the Democrats break the Republicans' hold. Although performed only with reluctance, Roosevelt's efforts to end discriminatory employment policies were beneficial to the Democrats (Garfinkel, 1959).

However, by the end of the 1970s, few blacks have been able to win statewide offices such as governor or senator. The most notable exception is the now-defeated Edward Brooke, who had been the Republican senator from Massachusetts, having served earlier as the state's attorney general.

CONTEMPORARY DEMOGRAPHIC OBSTACLES

In the past decade or so, major urban centers such as Atlanta, Cleveland, Detroit, Gary, Los Angeles, Newark, and Birmingham have elected black mayors. But the black position remains weaker than what one might expect from the black concentration in these leading cities. This is owing to several disadvantages that black candidates face when seeking votes in city- or statewide elections. First, in most parts of the country white support is required. Second, in such instances where white support is required, it is political suicide for black candidates to take stands that will antagonize the white segment of the electorate. As a consequence, there is merit to the complaint registered by some blacks that blacks who hold state- or citywide offices do not vigorously pursue black ends or are restrained in their willingness to advocate policies that would disturb whites. In one sense, however, this is a demographic tautology. If a "militant" black is defined as one who is prepared to alienate whites, and if alienation of whites is measured by the absence of white voting support, then in most situations it is impossible for these conditions to hold and for a black to be elected. Only where the population forms the bulk of the constituency is it possible for a black candidate to ignore the interests of at least some whites and still stand a chance of election.

In 1967, two blacks were first elected mayors of major northern cities: Carl Stokes in Cleveland and Richard Hatcher in Gary. An analysis of the demographic situation in those and other northern cities in 1967 is revealing. Carl Stokes was elected mayor of Cleveland by 1,644 votes—a plurality of less than 1 percent of the 256,922 votes cast. Not only did Stokes obtain an estimated 96 percent of the black vote, but he also obtained 19 percent of the white vote. In Gary, the election of Hatcher as mayor was based on 95 percent of the black vote as well as 12 percent of the white vote (U.S. Commission on Civil Rights, 1968c, p. 5). Given that Hatcher's margin of victory was 2 percent, and taking into account the fact that there was very little additional voting support from blacks of both cities possible, it is clear that the white vote was of importance. The election of black mayors in both Cleveland and Gary in 1967 was based on exceptionally high proportions of the electorate being black. In 1965, blacks comprised 34 percent of the Cleveland population (up from a total of 16 percent in the course of 15 years), and blacks comprised an estimated 55 percent of Gary's population, although whites slightly outnumbered blacks as registered voters (Hadden, Masotti, and Thies-sen, 1970, pp. 93–94, 112).

Because blacks seeking city- or statewide office need a substantial number of white voters in order to stand a chance, it is difficult to endorse positions that will antagonize white voters. Table 3.4 indicates the percentage of the population nonwhite in each state and region for 1967 (column 2). Observe that these percentages are low in many parts of the nation. Blacks were about 10 percent of the population in the mid-Atlantic region as well as in the more industrialized states of the Midwest, and no more than 6 percent in the New England states. The figures were generally even lower in the western part of the Midwest, the Mountain states, and the Pacific coast. (We should note that these figures overstate black voting power because all nonwhites are included. In Hawaii, Alaska, and several of the Mountain states, the actual proportion of the nonwhite population that is black is rather low. Black demographic strength is also overstated because relatively smaller proportions of blacks are of voting age.) In various parts of the South, of course, their numbers were greater: close to 40 percent of the population in Mississippi, and approximately 25 percent in North Carolina, Georgia, and Alabama.

Table 3.4 indicates the magnitude of white voting support required in order for a black candidate to have been successful in statewide elections. Assuming that an equal proportion of nonwhites and whites vote, and further assuming that 96 percent of all nonwhites vote for the black candidate in a contest between a white and black, then the percentage of white voters needed in order to give the black candidate 51 percent of all votes may be calculated. These figures are shown in column 4 of table 3.4. Even with solid support from black voters, in many states a black candidate would have required close to half of all white votes in order to obtain a minimal victory margin. This is essentially the case throughout New England and from the plains through the Mountain states and on to the Pacific coast. In Massachusetts, for example, former senator Brooke would require virtually half of the white vote (49.6 percent) even under conditions of maximum black-voter support. In the mid-Atlantic and industrialized Midwest states, a black candidate requires about 45 percent or more of the white vote. In the southern states, a black candidate will require from a quarter of the white vote (in Mississippi) to 40 percent or more in states outside the Deep South, such as Delaware, Maryland, West Virginia, Oklahoma, and Texas. It is clear that no statewide contest can be won by a black candidate competing against a white if the former campaigns on a platform that ignores white interests. Of course, no state can be won by a black who is openly opposed by the white electorate, regardless of the black's stand on other issues.

There is an ironic twist to this situation in that the recent legislation facilitating voter registration of blacks in the South occurs at a time when the percentage of black residents in the Deep South has declined (compare columns 1 and 2 of table 3.4). Hypothetically, in 1950—when few blacks were able to vote in these states—it would have taken much less white support for a black candidate to have won a contest. Because of this decline between 1950 and 1967, the minimum percentage of white supporters needed in a number of Deep South states increased: from 14 to 24 in Mississippi, 30 to 34 in Alabama, 31 to 35 in Georgia, 22 to 30 in South Carolina, and 35 to 37 in North Carolina.

Looking at the issue from another perspective, it is possible for a white opponent to ignore the black vote in many states and still be elected if able to obtain only a small majority among the white constituency. This is shown in columns 5 and 6 of table 3.4 which give the minimum percentage of white voters necessary to elect a candidate even if only 4 percent of the black electorate's support is received. In a large number of states, somewhat less than 55 percent of the white vote is required. In the South alienation of the black vote can prove a successful election tactic only if a candidate is able simultaneously to polarize the white popula-tion. In South Carolina and Louisiana, for example, nearly three-fourths of the white vote would be required for a minimal victory, and the percentage required is nearly 80 percent in Mississippi. To be sure, states with the largest percentage of blacks are very likely the ones in which an openly unsympathetic campaign against them will meet with the great-est success among white voters. These issues are more than academic when one considers that the white mayorality candidates in Gary and Cleveland received over 80 percent of their cities' white vote. This analysis suggests that black candidates wishing to run against white candidates in statewide contests can ill afford to antagonize the white electorate. As a consequence, a contest that polarizes whites against

TABLE 3.4
BLACK VOTING LEVERAGE BY REGIONS AND STATES, 1950 AND 1967

| | Percentage nonwhite | | Minimum percentage of white vote needed to elect candidate receiving: | | | |
| | | | 96 percent of nonwhite vote | | 4 percent of nonwhite vote | |
Region and State	1950 (1)	1967 (2)	1950 (3)	1967 (4)	1950 (5)	1967 (6)
New England	1.6	3.3	50.3	49.5	51.8	52.6
Maine	.3	.7	50.9	50.7	51.1	51.3
New Hampshire	.2	.6	50.9	50.7	51.1	51.3
Vermont	.1	.7	51.0	50.7	51.0	51.3
Massachusetts	1.7	3.1	50.2	49.6	51.8	52.5
Rhode Island	1.9	3.0	50.1	49.6	51.9	52.5
Connecticut	2.7	6.0	49.8	48.1	52.3	54.0
Middle Atlantic	6.4	10.4	47.9	45.8	54.2	56.5
New York	6.5	11.4	47.9	45.2	54.3	57.0
New Jersey	6.7	10.6	47.8	45.7	54.4	56.6
Pennsylvania	6.1	8.8	48.1	46.7	54.1	55.5
East North Central	6.1	9.7	48.1	46.2	54.1	56.0
Ohio	6.5	9.0	47.9	46.5	54.3	55.6
Indiana	4.4	6.3	48.9	48.0	53.2	54.2
Illinois	7.6	12.5	47.3	44.6	54.9	57.7
Michigan	7.1	12.3	47.6	44.7	54.6	57.6
Wisconsin	1.2	3.2	50.5	49.5	51.6	52.6
West North Central	3.4	4.6	49.4	48.8	52.7	53.3
Minnesota	1.0	1.7	50.5	50.2	51.5	51.8
Iowa	.8	1.1	50.6	50.5	51.4	51.5
Montana	7.6	9.8	47.3	46.1	54.9	56.1
North Dakota	1.8	2.5	50.2	49.8	51.9	52.2
South Dakota	3.7	4.5	49.3	48.9	52.8	53.2
Nebraska	1.8	2.8	50.2	49.7	51.9	52.4
Kansas	4.0	4.9	49.1	48.7	53.0	53.4
South Atlantic	24.3	21.6	36.6	38.6	66.1	63.9
Delaware	13.9	14.5	43.7	43.4	58.6	59.0
Maryland	16.6	16.6	42.0	42.0	60.4	60.4
Washington, D.C.	35.4	67.2	26.3	0	76.8	*
Virginia	22.2	19.9	38.2	39.8	64.4	62.7
West Virginia	5.7	4.6	48.3	48.8	53.8	53.3
North Carolina	26.6	23.6	34.7	37.1	68.0	65.5
South Carolina	38.9	31.6	22.4	30.2	80.9	72.7
Georgia	30.9	25.9	30.9	35.3	72.0	67.4
Florida	21.8	16.2	38.5	42.3	64.1	60.1

TABLE 3.4 (Continued)

| | Percentage nonwhite | | Minimum percentage of white vote needed to elect candidate receiving: | | | |
| | | | 96 percent of nonwhite vote | | 4 percent of nonwhite vote | |
Region and State	1950 (1)	1967 (2)	1950 (3)	1967 (4)	1950 (5)	1967 (6)
East South Central	23.6	20.5	37.1	39.4	65.5	63.1
Kentucky	6.9	6.9	47.7	47.7	54.5	54.5
Tennessee	16.1	15.3	42.4	42.9	60.0	59.5
Alabama	32.1	27.2	29.7	34.2	73.2	68.6
Mississippi	45.4	37.8	13.6	23.7	90.1	79.6
West South Central	17.2	16.6	41.7	42.0	60.7	60.4
Arkansas	22.4	19.0	38.0	40.4	64.6	62.0
Louisiana	33.0	31.4	28.8	30.4	74.1	72.5
Oklahoma	9.0	9.1	46.5	46.5	55.6	55.7
Texas	12.8	13.0	44.4	44.3	57.9	58.0
Mountain	4.5	5.7	48.9	48.3	53.2	53.8
Montana	3.2	4.1	49.5	49.1	52.6	53.0
Idaho	1.2	1.4	50.5	50.4	51.6	51.7
Wyoming	2.2	2.5	50.0	49.8	52.1	52.2
Colorado	2.1	4.0	50.0	49.1	52.0	53.0
New Mexico	7.5	9.9	47.4	46.1	54.8	56.2
Arizona	12.7	10.0	44.5	46.0	57.8	56.2
Utah	1.7	1.9	50.2	50.1	51.8	51.9
Nevada	6.4	8.5	47.9	46.8	54.2	55.4
Pacific	7.8	10.1	47.2	45.9	55.0	56.3
Washington	2.6	4.1	49.8	49.1	52.3	53.0
Oregon	1.6	2.0	50.3	50.1	51.8	52.0
California	6.3	9.2	48.0	46.4	54.2	55.8
Alaska	27.9	24.4	33.6	36.5	69.2	66.2
Hawaii	77.0	72.6	0	0	*	*

SOURCE: Population data in first two columns are from Metropolitan Life Insurance Company (1969, p. 8).
NOTE: Computations based on the assumptions that nonwhites and whites are equally likely to vote, and that 51 percent of the vote is required for victory. All ages are included.
*Election is impossible with only 4 percent vote from nonwhites.

blacks spells certain disaster for black candidates or white candidates who are strongly sympathetic to black issues. Conversely, a white candidate willing to alienate black voters in a southern state must be certain that the white electorate is polarized to the candidate's side in order to win.

Undoubtedly white aversion to black candidates tends to be least in states where a relatively small proportion of the electorate is black. But even under such circumstances the antagonism of white voters would be sure to spell defeat for black candidates because it could not be compensated for by an equal polarization among black voters. Candidates in southern states who are confident of receiving virtually no support from blacks are obliged to turn race into the central issue for white voters in order to polarize their vote and stand a chance of winning. The potential polarization is easy to see. In the Cleveland mayoralty election, which the black candidate won by a whisker, it should be noted that the white candidate underplayed the race issue (Hadden, Masotti, and Thiessen, 1970).

Analysis of the data in table 3.4 does indicate that even in 1967 blacks enjoyed a powerful position in elections when the race issue was not dominant for the white electorate; for example, when both candidates are white and when nonracial issues are important to the electorate. If we assume that 96 percent of blacks vote for a given white candidate in a two-person contest, then columns 3 and 4 of table 3.4 may be viewed as the minimum percentage of the white vote that a candidate would need in order to get elected. In New York State, for example, a white candidate could be elected if as little as 45.2 percent of the white vote is received if a 96 percent black vote is obtained. In many states, if there is intense competition between the two candidates—and where race does not become the dominant issue—blacks voting en masse can easily determine the victor. In such important presidential states as New York, Illinois, Michigan, Missouri, California, and Florida, a candidate may lose the white vote by a ratio of roughly 45:55 and still win if able to polarize the black electorate. This would hold as well for all statewide contests such as governor or senator.

The issues are very tricky, however. In order for the balance of power to be held by blacks, it is necessary for the white voters to be split on other issues that are not racially based, yet one of the candidates must be considerably more appealing among black voters to generate a substantial black turnout and obtain a solid black voting bloc. There is some evidence to indicate that this was precisely what happened in the South during the 1960 Kennedy-Nixon presidential contest. Apparently, whites viewed the two candidates as fairly similar on the race issue and hence split their votes on other dimensions. On the other hand, blacks saw Kennedy as being more sympathetic, albeit marginally, than Nixon (Middleton, 1962).

Compared with northern states, the demographic situation is more favorable to blacks in the largest cities. Shown in table 3.5 are similar figures for the central cities of some of the largest metropolitan areas. In Washington, D.C., where blacks have a substantial majority, it is clear that a black candidate can easily win with far less than 96 percent support from black voters. Indeed the racial situation in Washington is almost the opposite from that found in northern and western states. Whites would have power only if the two candidates did not polarize the electorate on racial grounds; for example, if both contenders were black. The setting is not entirely analogous because there would be additional leverage for whites in a campaign between two blacks that would not occur for blacks in a situation where two whites were competing. That is, campaigns are very expensive, and white financial support would have an influence, whereas black financial support would not have the same relative significance in settings where blacks were a numerical minority.

TABLE 3.5
BLACK VOTING LEVERAGE BY CITY, 1950 AND 1967

			Minimum percentage of white vote needed to elect candidate receiving:			
	Percentage nonwhite		96 percent of nonwhite vote		4 percent of nonwhite vote	
	1950	1967	1950	1967	1950	1967
City	(1)	(2)	(3)	(4)	(5)	(6)
New York	9.8	18.9	46.1	40.5	56.1	62.0
Los Angeles	10.7	20.5	45.6	39.4	56.6	63.1
Long Beach	2.6	6.0	49.8	48.1	52.3	54.0
Chicago	14.1	29.0	43.6	32.6	58.7	70.2
Philadelphia	18.3	31.3	40.9	30.5	61.5	72.4
Detroit	16.4	40.2	42.2	20.7	60.2	82.6
Boston	5.3	15.2	48.5	42.9	53.6	59.4
San Francisco	10.5	24.2	45.7	36.6	56.5	66.0
Oakland	14.5	32.5	43.4	29.3	59.0	73.6
Washington, D.C.	35.4	67.2	26.3	0	76.8	*
Pittsburgh	12.3	20.4	44.7	39.5	57.6	63.0
St. Louis	18.0	35.7	41.1	26.0	61.3	77.1

SOURCE: Population data in first two columns are from Metropolitan Life Insurance Company (1970, p. 6).
NOTE: Data are for central cities of largest metropolitan areas. Also see note to table 3.4.

Despite the fact that blacks comprise a substantial percentage of the population in these major cities, black candidates for citywide office could not beat a white opponent unless a fair number of votes were received from whites. As a consequence, black candidates would be obliged to court white voters in such cities. Indeed, these candidates would be faced with the need to polarize the black electorate on their behalf without simultaneously polarizing the white electorate to the same degree in their opponent's favor. Because Cleveland's black mayor mustered 19 percent of the white vote in Cleveland in order to win by a bare margin, it is clear that black candidates in many of the northern cities with a smaller black component would require a far more successful campaign among white voters. In Detroit and St. Louis a black candidate would have required, respectively, 21 and 26 percent of the white vote even with 96 percent support from the black electorate. The need for white supporters in other cities would be even greater. In Chicago, Philadelphia, and Oakland, under the voting assumptions made here, it would have been necessary to receive about 30 to 33 percent of the white vote in 1967. In other cities, such as Pittsburgh, New York, Los Angeles, and Boston, an even higher percentage (40) of the white vote would be needed. Conversely, whites who polarize the black vote on behalf of their opponent have to be very certain of obtaining an extraordinary high proportion of the white vote for compensation. In Detroit, to take an extreme case, a candidate who obtains only 4 percent of the black vote could win only if he receives 83 percent of the white voters' support. Clearly, the situation in many of the cities is such as to tend to neutralize the race issue on citywide elections because candidates face substantial losses in either direction. A candidate able to unite the black vote on his behalf can not risk creating an analogous response among whites on behalf of his opponent. On the other hand, a candidate running on an antiblack platform must be sure that this does more than give him a simple majority of white voters; it must generate overwhelming support among whites. In this regard, there are some white voters who will respond negatively to such racially based campaigns—they hold a crucial restraint. Presumably, the proportion of whites who would respond negatively to such campaigns is higher in the North than in the South, and hence such strategies may be less likely in northern cities.

All of the cities shown in table 3.5 experienced a growth in the proportion of nonwhites in their populations during the period between 1950 and 1967 (compare columns 1 and 2). Although blacks do not hold a majority in any of the cities, it is clear that their potential power is mounting. Moreover, in situations where the white vote is split, for example, when two white candidates run or where race is not the dominant issue, then a solid black vote can easily be decisive. From this perspective, column 6 gives the percentage of the white vote that a candidate would need if he was able to obtain bloc support from the black electorate. In New York City, for example, a candidate could lose the white vote by a ratio of 40:60 and still win if he received 96 percent of black voters' support. In Detroit, again to use the extreme, a white candidate could carry an election if he obtained only 20 percent of the white vote but also obtained a 96 percent support level from blacks at the polls. Thus, in a setting where a black candidate faces a substantial handicap among white voters by virtue of his race, it is possible for blacks under certain conditions to exert more influence when both major contenders are white; for example, if whites will split in the manner indicated in column 4 and if blacks vote en masse for one of the candidates.

Because my concern in this study is primarily with previous events, I have not attempted a demographic voting analysis for the current period, although such a project would be interesting, if only for comparative purposes. It is clear, however, that at least until very recently black demographic strength has not allowed black candidates to ignore easily the white voters' interests and concerns. Moreover, the new Europeans had a demographic head start.

TIMING AND POPULATION CHANGES

One important source of black political disadvantage is not directly due to racial factors, but reflects their unfortunate timing with respect to changes that have occurred in society's institutions. By the time the necessary numbers of black voters had been built up in the urban North, machine politics were on their way out.

> The Negro has come of age politically at a time when not only are machines collapsing, but the whole lower-class style of politics—the politics of friendships, trades, patronage, and neighborhood localism— is falling into disrepute. Negroes are expected to climb a political ladder which, as a result of several decades of successful reform efforts, is now missing most of its rungs. For whites, vaulting to the top is easy: television is one way; converting an established business or civic reputation into appointive and elective office is another. But the Negro community lacks the business and civic infrastructure which is necessary to convert private success into public office. Enough money has yet to be earned by enough Negroes to produce a significant precipitate of Negro civic statesmen. [Wilson, 1968, p. 239]

The great wealth required to run campaigns and the decline of machines are in no small way interrelated. Without strong party organizations at the lower levels, it is all the more necessary to use television and other forms of mass media to reach the voters. The sophisticated polling and survey techniques employed in developing campaign strategies are also expensive. Increasingly it is possible for political aspirants to sidestep existing political systems in reaching for important offices (basically, this is what the Kennedy family did). As a consequence, old-fashioned political systems of the sort that used the South—Central—Eastern Europeans, but also provided some returns, are waning. In particular, many are less able to provide the jobs and help that blacks now have the demographic muscle to demand. Make no mistake, city politics is hardly pure, but the machines are generally weaker. Although people of wealth are still able to influence political events, one is tempted to speculate that the poor have even less of an impact than they once did through the earlier forms of political organization.

In another respect, blacks have lagged behind the new European groups. Compared to the latter, blacks were slower in shifting political allegiances to the Democratic Party. This has meant that the new European groups gained an earlier and stronger foothold in the party that has more or less dominated national politics since 1932. Around the turn of the century, both blacks and many of the SCE Europeans were inclined to vote Republican. The new ethnic groups supported the Republicans for a variety of reasons including hostility toward the Irish who were already established in the Democratic Party; pro-immigration policies under Republican presidents; foreign policies pursued by these presidents that exhibited at least some sympathy for concerns of the newcomers with respect to their homelands; and an agricultural orientation among Democrats that held little appeal for the new Europeans piling up in the industrial centers of the North.

Illustrative of this latter point, describing the Democratic candidate for president in 1896, 1900, and 1908, William Jennings Bryan, Lubell (1956) observes:

> His revivalistic oratory might inflame the Bible belt—but in the city he was a repellent, even comic figure. When the "Great Commoner" rose before the 1924 Democratic Convention in New York to oppose denouncing the Ku Klux Klan by name, contending "We can exterminate Ku Kluxism better by recognizing their honesty and teaching them that they are wrong," he was hissed and booed by the galleries.
>
> . . . the traits which made Bryan seem like the voice of pious morality to his Prohibitionist, rural, Protestant following—the liberal use of

Biblical phrases, the resonant Chautauqua tones, the heaven-stomping energy—made him sound like the voice of bigotry to the urban masses. [p. 40]

Although Alfred E. Smith was badly beaten in his 1928 presidential campaign, he successfully served to align the new European groups with the Democratic party, a shift that was to prove of great value to the next Democratic presidential nominee, Franklin Roosevelt.

But the importance of the timing of the SCE Europeans' and blacks' shift to the Democratic party can easily be overemphasized at the expense of recognizing some basic differences. The new European groups were much more closely and deeply intertwined with organized labor, which received a tremendous boost under the Democratic Party in the 1930s. On the other hand, blacks were less deeply linked with the union movement, particularly the craft unions, and therefore the interests of blacks and the new European groups were different. Insofar as the unemployed in both groups suffered during the Depression, they shared common sympathies for the Democratic Party. But insofar as organized labor played an important role in the Democratic Party, the linkage was of greater consequence for the European groups than for the blacks.

ACCEPTABILITY AS A CANDIDATE

Implicit in much of this discussion has been the notion that blacks face a substantial disadvantage because of their race in contests that require white voting support. It is difficult to measure this disadvantage in precise quantitative terms, although race and ethnic origin affects the candidates from all groups. If the necessary data were available, we could cross-tabulate the ethnic and racial origins of voters and the ethnic and racial origins of candidates to determine a set of predispositions. One speculates that voters tend to favor candidates of the same origin, although ethnic and racial groups might differ in the magnitude of self-preference. In addition, one may postulate that candidates of various origins will also differ in their acceptability to voters from other groups. In turn, preferences for various outgroups may vary between voters from different ethnic or racial groups. For example, do Irish voters have a propensity to favor Swedish candidates over candidates of Italian origin, or does the opposite preference hold? Moreover, all of these predispositions will vary from place to place, over time, and also by the nature of the political office. Perhaps the surnames of candidates and other racial-ethnic markers are more influential on voters' preferences in elections for lesser offices where qualifications and issues are less publicized.

Recognizing that many other factors operate in an election, nevertheless it is clear that the racial factor does play a role in influencing a candidate's chance for success. In this regard, it would appear that blacks run under a substantial handicap when seeking votes from a predominantly white constituency. Members of other groups will also face handicaps in analogous fashion. However, the key point—and it is really a matter of conjecture because the necessary data are unavailable—is that candidates from most other groups have less of a liability when seeking support from voters who are not ethnic compatriots.

Politicians among the various South–Central–Eastern European groups, like black politicians, tend to start out in areas where their ethnic constituents form a sizable base of voting support. But, as they move beyond these smaller spatial areas and into bigger voting units where their ethnic support is diluted, obviously variations in acceptability to outgroup voters become more significant. As noted earlier, the relative absence of blacks *elected* on a city-, county-, or statewide basis (except when they are the majority of voters) may well suggest just this sort of handicap. Certainly the relative levels of prejudice against various groups described in chapter 2 are supportive of this inference. But, as inspection of the political situation faced by the new ethnic groups will disclose, there are additional handicaps faced by blacks in the political system.

4

Government: The New
European Groups

The South–Central–Eastern European groups also experienced a considerable lag in attaining the degree of political strength that might be expected on the basis of their numbers. Because a substantial segment of the new European groups are Roman Catholic, inspection of the data on Catholic political participation is informative. However, the reader must recognize that figures include the Irish, a group that has been strikingly visible in some areas of politics, and hence data on Catholics are only suggestive of underrepresentation among the new European groups that are predominantly Catholic.

The *relatively* small number of Roman Catholics appointed or elected to national office until recently strongly suggests that obstacles to their full participation on the national level were not fully eliminated. Through the 1960s there is evidence that Catholic membership in the Senate was approximately half of what might be expected on the basis of their numerical strength in the nation (see table 4.1): In 1969, only 13 of the 100 senators were Catholic. There is crude evidence, from other sources, that Catholic underrepresentation in an earlier period was at least as great (see the Senate data for 1931 in table 4.1). Although biographical materials were insufficient to determine the religion of a full quarter of the Senate, every indication points to a low Catholic figure. Only 13 of the 100 Senators were Roman Catholic in the Ninety-Sixth Congress (1979).

Low Catholic representation in the Senate might be attributed to factors other than a lag in political power; namely, the Senate is designed to represent each state equally, without giving weight to the numbers residing therein. Because Catholics are probably more concentrated than Protestants in the big urban states, their low rate of representation may be due exclusively to this factor. (However, as we will see, this factor does not work for Jews despite the fact they are similarly concentrated.)

The number of Catholics in the House of Representatives is more revealing because each state's representation is roughly proportional to its population size. Throughout the 1960s Catholics were somewhat underrepresented in the House. For example, in 1960 there was a gap of 6 percent (table 4.1). Moreover, although the available data do not go back very far, the gap was even greater in the mid-1950s. By 1979, there were 116 Roman Catholics in the House and they were 27 percent of the membership.

The role of Catholics in the federal judiciary provides further indication that the new ethnic groups have mostly lagged in their full participation in the political system. Although one of the nine Supreme Court positions has more or less been "reserved" for a Catholic, to this author's knowledge the Catholic justices have never been of South−Central−Eastern European origin. (The first and only black Supreme Court Justice, Thurgood Marshall, was appointed in 1967). With respect to lesser federal judicial appointments, which are still important political plums, Lubell (1956, p. 83) notes that the Harding, Coolidge, and Hoover administrations—all Republican—appointed only eight Catholics out of the 207 federal judges named. During the Franklin Roosevelt and Truman administrations, somewhat more than one-fourth of the judicial appointments were given to Catholics. However, Lubell notes that "A glance over the names of the Roosevelt-Truman appointments reveals that the overwhelming bulk of Catholic appointments are Irish. Truman's appointments, however, show a significant quickening of the pace of recognition for non-Irish elements" (p. 83). The historian Jones (1960, p. 237) contends that southern and eastern European immigrants, although growing steadily in number from 1880 onward, "remained for the most part politically backward and leaderless" up to the 1920s.

ITALIANS

Consideration of a specific new group, the Italians, in some ways gives the reader a better appreciation of the political lags experienced by the South−Central−Eastern Europeans groups. Moreover, in examining the

TABLE 4.1

RELIGIOUS COMPOSITION OF CONGRESS, 1931–1969

| | | | | | Percentage distribution | | | | | | |
| Religion | 1931 | 1955 | | 1960 | | 1963 | | 1969 | | Total population, 1957 |
	Senate	House	Senate	House	Senate	House	Senate	House	Senate	
Protestant	73	NA	NA	76	85	77	86	71	85	66
Roman Catholic	3	17	10	21	12	20	11	22	13	26
Jewish	0	NA	NA	2	2	2	2	4	2	3
Other and Not Reported	24	83	90	1	1	1	1	3	0	5

SOURCE: See table 4.2.

reasons for these lags and their dissolution, one uncovers forces that influence blacks as well. Although blacks have operated under some severe handicaps that the new immigrant groups did not encounter, one should also recognize other difficulties in the political system that create similar barriers for both the new European groups and blacks.

It was not until 1950 that the first American of Italian origin was elected to the U.S. Senate, John Pastore of Rhode Island. Only four years earlier he had also been a trail blazer, becoming the first Italian to be elected governor. Pastore's election to governor is in some ways reminiscent of the events that preceded the election of Oscar DePriest as the first black congressman from the North.[1] The Irish, who had dominated Rhode Island state politics for several decades, gave the large Italian population only the minimal rewards necessary for their voting support. J. Howard McGrath had served as governor for several terms, accompanied on the ticket by an Italian lieutenant governor. After the latter resigned to accept a judicial appointment, another Italian was selected for the ticket, John Pastore. The resignation of McGrath in midterm to accept a federal appointment led to Pastore becoming the first Italian governor. It was difficult to prevent him from then running for the governorship. Thus, like the first black congressman from Chicago, a series of unexpected events generated an ethnic shift that would have eventually come, but probably at a later date.

In general one notes a slow and difficult start for Italians in politics that later gradually improves and finally begins to accelerate. The election of the first Italian-American governor was followed in the next 15 years by the election of two additional Italian governors in Rhode Island, two in Massachusetts, and one in both Washington and Ohio (Stone, 1970, p. 123). A former assistant to then Congressman Adam Clayton Powell, Chuck Stone (1970, p. 126) counted 16 Italians by the late 1960s in the House of Representatives. Of these, it is noteworthy that most come from states where a substantial ethnic population base exists.

California	2
Connecticut	2
Florida	1
Illinois	2
Massachusetts	1
New Jersey	3
New York	3
Pennsylvania	2

The recency of this position is clear, however. Lubell (1956, p. 70) counted only eight Italian congressmen in 1948, and this was twice the number of any previous year. Likewise, La Guardia through the 1920s was the only congressman of Italian origin in New York City, despite the enormous population base of the area (Glazer and Moynihan, 1963, pp. 209–210). The first Italian-American federal judge was not appointed until 1936 by President Roosevelt (Lubell, 1956, p. 83); but this came one year before the first black appointment (Stone, 1970, p. 73). It was not until President Kennedy appointed Anthony Celebrezze as Secretary of Health, Education and Welfare that an Italian was named to a cabinet-level position.

Recognition on the lower levels of politics probably comes earlier for most groups because such smaller voting units as wards or state legislative districts are more apt to incorporate overwhelming majorities from a specific ethnic group. Moreover, the lower political levels are often stepping stones to national positions and, therefore, will frequently precede the attainment of more important positions. Comparing the state legislatures of Pennsylvania, New Jersey, New York, Connecticut, Rhode Island, and Massachusetts, Lubell (1956, p. 70) found more than twice as many Italian names in 1951 than in 1936.

Studies of New Haven and New York City, both cities with a substantial Italian population, suggest this time lag is first overcome on the lower political levels. Dahl (1961, p. 44) reports that until 1959 the percentage of New Haven's major and minor elective offices held by Italians was not equivalent to their 31 percent of registered voters. It is noteworthy that the percentage of Italians holding minor office, with one slight exception, increases in each succeeding decade between 1890 and 1959 more rapidly than their percentage in the major New Haven political positions. This gap is specially noteworthy in the earlier decades before and after the turn of the century. Likewise, in New York State an Italian has never been elected governor although they have had nominees for all of the other top state positions (Stone, 1970, p. 122).

SOME GENERALIZATIONS BASED ON THE ITALIAN EXPERIENCE

In considering the processes operating with regard to ethnic political mobility it is important to recognize at the outset the existence of a number of exceptions. Even in the case of Italians, Stone (1970, p. 119) cites such unlikely events as the election of an Italian-American mayor of Mobile, Alabama, in 1894 and the presence of two Italians in the Texas legislature by 1880. Likewise, the first Italian-American members of the House were Anthony Caminetti, elected from California in 1891, and Francis B. Spinola, who served from New York between 1887–1891;

both served before there was a sizable Italian-American voter base. But as a general rule, the factors listed below appear to be particularly important.

Demographic Strength

As noted in the earlier discussion of black lags, there is no immediate or instant correspondence between demographic strength of an ethnic group and their ability to run candidates successfully. Part of this stems from the need for an ethnic or racial group to break into the existing political system of the community. In this regard, Italians faced considerable resistance in many cities from the Irish, who had experienced resistance from Anglo-Saxon Protestants. However, aspirations would be rather limited if politicians restricted their office seeking to those for which members of their group provided a majority of the voters. Instead, the concentration of a substantial number of compatriots, although a numerical minority, may provide the building block for developing a victorious campaign.

La Guardia's successful campaigns for mayor of New York City illustrate these points. The East Harlem area that he first represented in Congress for five terms at the time included an important concentration of Italian voters (Mann. 1965, pp. 29, 131). But his successful campaigns for mayor required support from non-Italian segments of New York City's voters. To be sure, over time, politicians from a given ethnic group may become acceptable candidates to the population at large on the basis of special competence or a unique appeal. But at least in the initial stages, although there are exceptions, the demographic base is crucial. Indeed, there is some evidence to indicate the operation of an analogous process with respect to medical practice: Doctors from various ethnic groups show a propensity to practice in those residential areas of a city where ethnic compatriots provide at least some minimal support (Lieberson, 1958, pp. 544–545).

Socioeconomic Mobility

Linkages between political achievement and various facets of an ethnic group's social and economic mobility are very complicated, involving causal effects in several directions simultaneously. On the one hand, political success may in itself be a form of occupational and economic mobility for the candidates. Of greater significance is the officeholder who is able to influence legislation that is especially beneficial to members of his group or that directly benefits compatriots through contracts, promotions, and appointments. On the other hand, achievement of certain minimal occupational and social levels is often required *prior* to election or appointment. For example, lawyers from an ethnic group have a special impetus to participate in politics as well as a greater acceptability.[2] (A substantial segment of both houses of Congress are lawyers [Ehrenhalt, 1979, p. 7].) Thus variations among groups in their relative number of lawyers will affect their political position. Moreover, political campaigns are often extremely expensive affairs, giving important advantages to populations that are able to draw on wealthy contributors to support their efforts. In brief, a group's success in nonpolitical domains will influence its position in the political arena, and, in turn, political success will tend to advance both a group's interests and specific compatriots in nonpolitical arenas.

How does this work for Italians in the United States? Political developments in Rhode Island leading to the election of John Pastore as the first Italian-American governor and senator provides a number of clues to what Lubell (1956) sums up as "the prime essentials for the political arrival of any minority group—the growth to voting power of its heavy birth rates, plus a rising middle class to provide the necessary leadership and financial support" (p. 79). Although the Italian population in Rhode Island became very large through immigration, their political recognition was minimal for a number of years. The only major appointment made under the Republicans was the naming of an assistant to the attorney general in 1912 at a salary of $1,500 a year. The small Italian middle class had negligible participation in the more desirable city jobs. "In 1910 the Providence Board of Trade could find only one school teacher of Italian descent in Providence's schools, only one policeman, one fireman and two lawyers" (Lubell, 1956, p. 78). Between 1906 and 1924, an average of only one Italian-American per year passed the bar exam in Rhode Island.

However, as the numbers of lawyers increased and as Italian wealth mounted, the stage was set for political attainment. In 1932, an Italian-American first ran for statewide office and preceded John Pastore as lieutenant governor in 1940 and 1942. It is significant that the wealth and economic position of Italians in Rhode Island had increased enormously between the early part of the century and the time when Pastore first ran for governor in 1950.

> In 1910 the Providence Board of Trade valued all the property owned by Italo-Americans in the city of Providence at $5,000,000 with another $4,000,000 in savings. Nearly forty years later, when I visited the Aurora club, the social center of Italo-Americans of wealth, I was given a list of a

score of millionaire members. Included were the heads of four of the
five leading construction companies in the state; the owners of
purportedly the world's largest knife, ring and shoe buckle factories; a
manufacturer of artificial flowers who had parlayed a $200 investment
into a business grossing $700,000 a year. One of Rhode Island's leading
portrait painters told me that about a fifth of all his commissions were
coming from *nouveau-riche* Italo-Americans, where ten years previously
he had none. [Lubell, 1956, p. 78]

Pastore, a Democrat, received a special campaign fund from some of the
wealthy Italians despite the fact that they were Republican.

There are certain "natural" linkages between politics and a variety of
occupational and industrial activities. One of the most fundamental is
money; namely, the costs of political campaigns, whether they be local,
city-, statewide, or national, far exceeds the financial resources of most
individual Americans. As a consequence, particularly with rising campaign costs generated by the usage of television, one has the impression
that exceptionally wealthy individuals, such as the Rockefellers and
Kennedys, enjoy certain inherent advantages. But where individuals
running for office do not have sufficient personal resources, they must
depend on support from other sources. Notwithstanding the contributions that are made on ideological grounds, campaign contributors and
workers often expect returns from their donations of time and money.
Ethnic groups with large numbers of wealthy people or with exceptionally large numbers engaged in activities that have close linkages with
politics, such as lawyers, illicit business operators, the building and
construction trades, and the like, are going to be especially important in
influencing political outcomes and the candidates chosen. The development of a group's position in other domains thus influences their
political position. In turn, this has ramifications for further strength in
those domains that initially generated political power.

The Italians in America are no exception to these generalizations. In
the same fashion as the rise of Italian-American commercial and industrial strength is correlated with their rise to political prominence in
Rhode Island, Dahl (1961, p. 154) observes a correlation between the
growth of Italian political power in New Haven and a rise in the number
of Italian school teachers. Although the mechanisms whereby these two
phenomena are linked are unclear, very likely the results indicate an
increase in the professional and middle-class positions of Italians in New
Haven.

Lopreato (1970), Bell (1966), Glazer and Moynihan (1963), and Whyte
(1943) all suggest linkages between the underworld and politics. Clearly,
many legally sanctioned enterprises depend on political connections and

protection; witness the operation of lobbies on behalf of the oil industry, agricultural groups, the American Medical Association, and the like. However, the illegal operations of the underworld are especially at the mercy of local government practices. And local politicians may often obtain financial support from such sources: There is a linkup between these criminal activities and politics. Lopreato (1970, p. 134) describes

> the splendorous funeral of James (Big Jim) Colosimo, a powerful chief of the underground who was killed in May 1920. His cortege included many prominent politicians. An alderman and a state senator were pallbearers. Standing by, as honorary pallbearers, were eight other aldermen, three judges, several individuals who later became judges, and two congressmen, one of whom later became speaker of the United States House of Representatives.

The attainment of success in underworld activities has provided not only an avenue of economic mobility for Italians, but may from time to time play a role in influencing political attainment. Frank Costello, for example, an Italian-American with underworld ties, provided important financial support for the Democrats in New York City and thereby became a person of considerable influence. According to Bell (1966, p. 180), he "was able to influence the selection of a number of Italian judges. The most notable incident, revealed by a wire tap on Costello's phone, was the 'Thank you, Francisco' call in 1943 by Supreme Court judge nominee Thomas Aurelio, who gave Costello full credit for his nomination."

JEWS

The political position of Jews in the United States only partially fits the general pattern observed for other South-Central-Eastern Euro-pean groups. One reason is that two of the three major Jewish migration waves to the United States came well before 1880. Because the last major wave, from Eastern and Central Europe beginning in the 1880s, was numerically the most important, it is appropriate to include Jews in the discussion of the new European groups. Nevertheless, the analysis is complicated by the fact that many of the early Jewish political figures in the United States were from Germany or at least had come in an earlier period. Compared with Italians or Poles, Jews had a head start because of the relatively larger number of compatriots who had migrated before 1880.

Despite these differences, many of the features of Jews in politics are rather similar to those for Italians and blacks. Jewish members of the House of Representatives come largely from cities where their compatriots are of demographic importance. In 1967 this included single representatives from Chicago, Philadelphia, and Baltimore, six from New York City, four from elsewhere in New York State including the New York City suburbs and one from the New York City suburb of Paterson, New Jersey (Stone, 1970, p. 138). Of the two Jewish senators, one was from New York State and the other from Connecticut, another state with a relatively large Jewish population. Thus Jewish members of Congress, similar to the pattern observed for blacks and other SCE European groups, tend to be elected from areas of demographic strength.

Like other groups, earlier in the century Jews were much more closely aligned with the Republican Party. Among the eleven Jews elected to Congress in the Republican-dominated year of 1920, excluding one socialist, all were Republicans (Fuchs, 1956, p. 63). New York City was then also an important political base, with six of the eleven congressmen elected from that city.

However, in other respects Jews differed from South—Central—Eastern Europeans and blacks. Inspection of Table 4.2 indicates that the number of Jewish members in the House of Representatives does not follow the slow growth pattern of the other groups. By 1918 there were six Jewish members of the House and in 1920 there were eleven. Moreover, from 1920 until relatively recently, the number remained more or less at a plateau, roughly equal to what might be expected on the basis of their proportion of the population. It is not easy to offer a systematic interpretation without going beyond the purposes at hand, however, it appears as if the relatively early entry is to be explained by the German Jews who had preceded the Eastern European wave. The pre-1880 migrations of Jews meant that politically sophisticated, wealthy, and professional segments were available at an earlier date to take advantage of the demographic strength provided by the incoming waves of Eastern European Jews. As will be indicated shortly, Jews of German origin were very prominent among the early Jewish political figures. If this interpretation is correct, then very likely the more or less stable numbers of Jewish congressmen indicated between 1920 and the mid-1960s were due to the fact that the sources of demographic strength were tapped much earlier for Jews than for other groups. Since the mid-1960s the number has jumped. The 23 Jews in the 1979 House amounted to 5 percent of membership and there were seven Jewish senators. This increase is parallel to the Roman Catholic gains in the House except that Jews had a more favorable initial position (see Ehrenhalt, 1979).

TABLE 4.2
NUMBER OF JEWS IN THE HOUSE OF REPRESENTATIVES, 1918—1969

Year	Number
1918	6
1920	11
1926	9
1930	8
1960	10
1963	9
1969	17

SOURCES: Fuchs (1956, pp. 63, 66, 67) for 1918 through 1930; Congressional Quarterly, Inc., 1960, 1963, for 1960 and 1963, respectively; U.S. Bureau of the Census (1970a, p. 360) for 1969.

Regarding appointments to the cabinet and the Supreme Court—thanks at least in part to earlier settlements from Germany and the advantages this offered in terms of wealth, education, and political sophistication—Jews received such appointments earlier than the other groups under consideration. But in this regard, Jews were forerunners of the patterns shown by all of the groups under consideration. Not only were they acutely conscious of such appointments, but so too were the dominant Northwestern Europeans who held the power. Thus the ethnic origin or race of a prospective appointee was, and still is, part of the political calculus in the same way as region, political ideology, and the like.

The first Jew named to a cabinet post was Oscar Straus, appointed secretary of commerce and labor by Theodore Roosevelt in 1906 and later continued in that position by William Howard Taft. A brother of the owners of Macy's department store in New York, Straus's appointment, as well as his earlier political career, was in no small way influenced by ethnic considerations. Straus had been named minister to Turkey in 1887 by President Cleveland as a rebuke to the Austro-Hungarian Empire after the latter had rejected the United States minister because his wife was Jewish (Learsi, 1954, p. 201). Although ostensibly nominated to the cabinet on merit, the appointment was clearly a reflection of Theodore Roosevelt's interest in naming a Jew (Fuchs, 1956, p. 52). It was not until the second Roosevelt appointed Henry Morgenthau, Jr. as secretary of the treasury in 1934 that a Jew again served in a cabinet. Beginning with two appointments under Kennedy, a number have since been appointed by several presidents.

As was the case for the first two cabinet members, the early Supreme

Court appointments were not held by Jews of Eastern European origin. Louis Brandeis was the nephew of an "1848'er" from Louisville who was one of three men who had placed Lincoln's name in nomination for the presidency (Learsi, 1954, p. 93). His nomination to the Supreme Court by Woodrow Wilson in 1916 set off a controversy in the Congress and elsewhere. According to Baltzell (1966, chapter 8), this furor was in no small way linked to an effort by the Old Establishment in the East to maintain their position within the power structure as well as to blatant anti-Jewish feelings of the time. Over considerable objection in the Senate, Brandeis was appointed. His became the "Jewish seat" on the Supreme Court. In 1939 Felix Frankfurter, an Austrian-born Jew, was appointed. In 1962, Arthur Goldberg succeeded Frankfurter, who was followed by Abe Fortas. Since Fortas's resignation, the seat has not been occupied by a Jew. However, between 1916 and 1969, with the exception of the period between 1932 and 1938 when Cardozo (a Sephardic Jew) also served on the Supreme Court, there has been one Jew among the nine justices of the Court.

SOME EXCEPTIONS: ELECTION WITHOUT A DEMOGRAPHIC BASE

One of the most striking features of Jewish political participation in the United States has been the election of candidates to important offices from areas where they had no demographic strength. Although there are examples of this occurring prior to 1880, an examination of the patterns involved will provide valuable clues to the general role of race and ethnic origin in the political system, with implications for black-new immigrant differences. Table 4.3 gives the positions held by Jews in constituencies where substantial demographic strength is absent. The sources of names are drawn largely from Fuchs (1956) and Learsi (1954) with information from other sources. No claim is made that the listing is complete. Moreover, I have not attempted to include what appears to be a growing number of contemporary examples, as Jews move toward greater acceptability as candidates. Two striking features of this table are the election of some Jews relatively early in the nation's history as well as their election from areas with minimal Jewish settlements.

The relative insignificance of the new Jewish wave from Eastern Europe among the officeholders elected in the eighteenth and nineteenth centuries is to be expected, but it is still striking that even when the current century is included there is not one Jew who is clearly identifiable from new sources. Moses Alexander and Simon Bamberger, former

TABLE 4.3
JEWS ELECTED TO MAJOR OFFICES FROM AREAS WITH FEW COMPATRIOTS

Name	Year[a]	Location	Highest office
Lewis Levin	1845	Philadelphia	Representative
David Levy Yulee	1845	Florida	Senator
Judah Benjamin	1852	Louisiana	Senator
Philip Phillips	1853	Mobile	Representative
Henry Phillips	1857	Philadelphia	Representative
Leonard Myers	1863	Philadelphia	Representative
Michael Hahn	1864	Louisiana	Governor
Leopold Morse	1877	Boston	Representative
Benjamin Jonas	1879	Louisiana	Senator
Julius Houseman	1883	Grand Rapids	Representative
Nathan Frank	1886	St. Louis	Representative
Adolph Meyer	1890	New Orleans	Representative
Lucius Littauer	1897	Gloversville (NY)	Representative
Julius Kahn	1898	San Francisco	Representative
Joseph Simon	1898	Oregon	Senator
Isidor Rayner	1904	Maryland	Senator
Simon Guggenheim	1907	Colorado	Senator
Moses Alexander	1915	Idaho	Governor
Simon Bamberger	1917	Utah	Governor
Benjamin Rosenbloom	1921	Wheeling (WV)	Representative
Florence Kahn	1925	San Francisco	Representative
Arthur Seligman	1930	New Mexico	Governor
Julius Meier	1931	Oregon	Governor
Henry Horner	1932	Illinois	Governor
Richard Neuberger	1954	Oregon	Senator

[a]Year first elected or took office.

governors of Idaho (1915–1919) and Utah (1917–1921), respectively, were both German-born. Horner, Meier, and Seligman, respectively, governors of Illinois, Oregon, and New Mexico in the 1930s, were born in their states but were of German-Jewish origin. Likewise, the paternal grandfather of Richard Neuberger, senator from Oregon in the mid-1950s, had come from Germany.

It is difficult to know if this pattern simply reflects the greater dispersion of German Jews as opposed to the later migrants, but it is clear that a different pattern operates for blacks because their average number of generations in the United States is far greater than any of the European groups under consideration. There appears to be strong evidence that the magnitude of anti-Jewish feeling in the the United States had been relatively low compared with the negative feelings directed at blacks. Indeed, anti-Jewish attitudes appear to have increased after the migration of new Europeans began near the turn of the century, particularly in those areas where the newcomers were concentrated in substantial numbers. The exclusion of a prominent Jew from an upper-class resort area in 1870s is cited by Baltzell (1966, p. 119) as an event that gained considerable publicity "because it was something new at that time."

Baltzell goes on to cite other events to support his contention that there had been relatively little anti-Semitism evident until late in the nineteenth century. As late as the 1880s and 1890s, the most socially prominent German-Jewish families of Philadelphia used the same resort areas as their Christian neighbors, but that ended before the turn of the century (p. 120). Bernard Baruch, a financially prominent Jew and member of the Palm Beach Bath and Tennis Club, received a letter asking members not to bring Jews into the club (p. 121). Baltzell goes on to cite various exclusive men's clubs in different cities that shifted from admitting Jews to a policy of exclusion (p. 135 ff.).

Although one could cite other writers who also point to a shift in attitudes toward the latter part of the nineteenth century, there are no quantitative data on the matter for such early periods. There is a danger of using the presumed mildness of anti-Jewish feelings in earlier periods as a circular explanation for the election of a small handful of Jews to political office during that time. If they were elected without benefit of their compatriot's votes, to infer this was a function of little or no prejudice is very tempting and even plausible, but hardly independent proof. Regardless of the causes that will be considered, table 4.3 shows that a number of Jews were elected to important offices during the nineteenth century. These include two different members of the House of Representatives from Philadelphia in the 1840s and 1850s; U.S. senators from Florida in 1845 and from Louisiana in 1852; another representing Louisiana in the House beginning in 1891; a member of the House from St. Louis in the 1880s; the governor of Louisiana in 1864; another senator from Louisiana in the early 1880s; a member of the House from San Francisco beginning in 1898; a member of the House from Gloversville, New York; a senator from Oregon at the turn of the century; another congressman from Philadelphia in the 1860s and 1870s; members of the House from Massachusetts and from Grand Rapids, Michigan, in the 1880s; and a member of the House of Representatives from Mobile, Alabama, in 1853.

Issues

Using a variety of biographical materials to learn more about the Jewish politicians listed in the table, one may guess about the operation of additional forces influencing their political success. First one has the impression that at least several were deeply involved in innovative political ideas—or were at least issue-oriented. In some cases, this meant relatively progressive ideas but the opposite held in other cases. One speculates that politicians in areas without demographic support are more likely to overcome voter antipathy by being sensitive to issues and programs that will capture the new moods of the electorate than are candidates who do not offer any unique, distinguishing ideas or platforms that might generate voter support. In this regard, I believe that black politicians will overcome white antipathy and increasingly run for office in constituencies that are not predominantly black. This will occur not because they abandon a concern for issues that are of particular significance to their compatriots. Some of these issues can be restated to make them appeal to a substantial white segment, or black candidates will incorporate other issues into their campaign that do capture new trends among the electorate.

There are numerous illustrations of issue-oriented politicians among those listed in table 4.3. Simon Bamberger, the first non-Mormon governor of Utah (1917–1921), had been one of the founders of a new political party in the state which opposed the Mormon-controlled Republican Party.[3] Judah Benjamin, the pre-Civil War senator from Louisiana, was a leading advocate of secession; indeed, he later served in Jefferson Davis's Cabinet. Michael Hahn, governor of Louisiana after first serving in the House of Representatives, was also issue-oriented. He was an outspoken opponent of slavery and secession, and ran on the new political platform of the Free Soil Party. Henry Horner was elected governor of Illinois in the early 1930s after first developing a reputation as an innovative judge. Lewis Levin, a member of Congress from Philadelphia in the 1840s, earlier had played a prominent part in the formation of the Native-American Party in that city and also edited and published the Party's newspaper. It was the strong feelings against Roman Catholics and the foreign-born, crystallized in the riots of 1844, that carried the South Carolina native into Congress.

Julius Meier was elected governor of Oregon after the death of his former law partner, the Republican nominee for governor. Because the party refused to name another candidate who would adhere to his colleague's platform, Meier ran as an independent Republican, pledged to cleaning up state government. Indicative of Richard Neuberger's orientation to issues is the fact that he was the first Democratic senator to be elected in Oregon in 40 years. Neuberger had been able to publicize and generate a variety of issues because he had been an important feature writer for a Portland newspaper. Also, in earlier years when he served in the state senate, he was involved in matters pertaining to conservation and other issues that captured statewide attention. Isidor Rayner, senator from Maryland after the turn of the century, had gained national attention as counsel for Admiral W.S. Schley in the Santiago inquiry. In this regard, his position as a leading trial lawyer must have generated considerable publicity.

One research implication suggested by these illustrations is that candidates successful in gaining office in areas without support of ethnic or racial compatriots will tend to be relatively more issue-oriented or otherwise politically distinctive than their rivals. Likewise, compatriots who run in areas of ethnic strength will generally be less likely to have a distinctive approach because there will not be the same handicaps for election.

Occupation and Wealth

One of the problems raised throughout this analysis is the need for an ethnic or racial group to have members who are professionals with wealth and political sophistication. This is striking in the case at hand; occupational data are available for 23 of the 25 Jewish political figures listed in table 4.3. Seventeen of these were lawyers, either exclusively or engaged in additional activities. There are a variety of pathways into politics and, at least for this group, the law had been exceptionally important.

The advantages of wealth are obviously considerable. As noted earlier, political campaigns tend to be very expensive; likewise, important contributors gain considerable influence on political affairs. Crucial to the election of Simon Guggenheim as senator from Colorado in 1907 was the wealth available to this scion of the Guggenheim mining family. Bearing in mind that this took place in the period prior to popular voting for senators, it seems clear that Simon Guggenheim's election by the Colorado state legislature was facilitated by his wealth.

> In 1902, Simon's objective, since he wanted to become senator, was control of the Colorado state election to be held two years later. To achieve this control he must control the State Senate, half of whose members who would be voting for U.S. Senator in 1907 would be elected in 1904; the others would be elected in 1906. Simon and his supporters set out to find men who would "do the right thing at the right time." They were willing to pay expenses for running for the State Senate, and to do anything else necessary to elect these men. [Hoyt, 1967, p. 183]

There is some reason to believe that Jews are relatively important contributors to political parties and hence enjoy a certain amount of leverage as a consequence. In Philadelphia, according to Baltzell (1966, p. 331), most of the largest contributors to the Democratic Party campaign committees in 1960 were Jews and other minorities. Likewise, some Jews in Baltimore were apparently substantial contributors to the Maryland Democratic Party. Among the political figures listed in table 4.3, several were men of considerable wealth. For example, Littauer was a wealthy glove manufacturer in upstate New York, and Julius L. Meier was linked with a major Portland department store as well as being an attorney. Several others were successful merchants and four were industrialists. In terms of the issue at hand, as we have seen, a comparison among the various new European groups and blacks will partially be explained by differentials in wealth.

Visibility

The visibility of blacks relative to the European groups is one of the issues that immediately comes to mind in a discussion of politics or in a variety of other contexts. Members of the European groups are clearly less visible than are blacks, and, hence, even if the electorate had equal antipathy toward both segments of the population, black candidates would run under a greater handicap simply because they would be visible to a greater proportion of the voters.

An inspection of the visibility of Jewish politicians suggests that this factor may operate but that the issue is also more complicated. For the 25 politicians under consideration (see table 4.3), their biographical sketches indicate that ten were active in, or at least members of, Jewish organizations, typically a synagogue or B'nai B'rith. Four were definitely indifferent to their religious background to the point of, in one case, burial in a Catholic cemetery. For the remaining 11, no information was obtained one way or the other. Inferences can not be made about this group because in some cases information simply reflects the brevity of their biographical materials.

Returning to the ten actively affiliated with Jewish organizations, one finds that the vast majority are also members of organizations that incorporate far more than their ethnic community. For example, a number were Masons or belonged to other fraternal organizations. To be sure, membership in a variety of fraternal and social organizations is standard political practice in the United States. Moreover, there is no way of determining whether their affiliations occurred after achievement of political success. However, this situation does suggest that at least some of these political figures may have been fully integrated into the larger communities and, at the same time, at least minimally active as Jews. Compared with blacks, the new European groups have an advantage insofar as they are relatively more able to participate in the larger social system, notwithstanding whatever stigma they may have by virtue of their ethnic origin.

Regional Variation

Table 4.3 indicates some curious spatial patterns for the Jews elected outside of their demographic strongholds. There is a striking concentration in Oregon (two senators and one governor), the Mountain states (governors of Idaho, Utah, New Mexico, and a senator from Colorado), as well as in Louisiana (two senators, a governor, and a member of the House). Likewise, three different Jews were elected to the House of Representatives from Philadelphia during the midnineteenth century. Aside from the very real possibility of chance factors operating, there are two other possible explanations. First, there is considerable variation across the United States in the intensity of anti-Semitism (particularly toward those residing within the ·state), as well as variation in Jewish visibility and the sensitivity of the residents to the issue. In some respects, it may be that the absence of an ethnic "claque" with regard to an election campaign may prove to be more of an advantage than one that vigorously supports their compatriot but does not provide sufficient voting power to insure victory. Following Hawley (1944) and others, there are at least some theoretical reasons to expect that population composition will affect the nature of race and ethnic relations such that increases in a group's proportion of the community will have negative consequences in terms of the response of others. (Possibly the function may be nonmonotonic such that at some point, when the group is a numerical majority, there will be shift in the other direction.) Because we are dealing with states where Jews are a very small numerical minority, it may well be that the gain a candidate obtains in a state where compatriots are perhaps 5 percent of the electorate (and assuming they have a strong propensity to vote for the candidate) is more than outweighed by the loss that is encountered from the remainder of the electorate who have less of a propensity to vote that way. One can only speculate, of course, but it may be that it is better to run in an area where your group amounts to say 1 percent of the voters than in an area where your group is 5 percent of the electorate.

One implication of this analysis is that it may be easier for a black to run for statewide office in cases where his group is an extremely small component of the electorate than in states where blacks are a larger component of the residents, but still not sufficiently large to provide a sizable proportion of the votes needed for election.

POLES

To my knowledge, detailed information about the political activities of other new ethnic groups is not readily available. However, the smattering one encounters appears consistent with the pattern for blacks, Italians, and Jews outlined earlier (recognizing here that the vast majority of major Jewish officeholders do come from areas of demographic strength).

Not until 1918 did the first Polish-American serve in the House of Representatives. He was a Republican lawyer from Milwaukee, a city with a substantial Polish settlement (Swastek, 1952, p. 155). The second Polish-American congressman was elected in 1924 on the Republican platform from Detroit, also an industrial city with a sizable number of Polish residents. A political shift occurred during the Roosevelt era, leading to the election of Polish congressmen on the Democratic ticket.

Despite the candidacy of Edmund S. Muskie for vice-president in 1968, and the success of Polish candidates on the local level, the group's political star has risen relatively slowly. There were nine Polish congressmen in 1967, according to Stone (1970, pp. 143–146), apparently including Muskie's senatorial seat from Maine. There were four Polish-American members of the House from metropolitan Chicago, three from the city and one from the suburbs; two from Wisconsin, including one from Milwaukee; and a congressman from Buffalo, also a city with a sizable Polish electorate; and one from New Jersey. In Connecticut, another state with a large number of Polish residents, the at-large congressional seat has had a Polish incumbent in previous years.

Several of the congressmen have held important committee or subcommittee chairmanships, but their number is not very large. For the most part, Poles have been elected in areas where compatriots are of demographic importance. It was not until the Truman administration that the first Polish-American was appointed to the federal judiciary (Lubell, 1956, p. 84). Likewise, the appointment of John Gronouski as postmaster general in 1963 was the first time a Polish-American was named to a cabinet.

FURTHER GENERALIZATIONS

What does this review of black and South–Central–Eastern European political participation tell us about the pressures and handicaps under which members of these groups operate? The various cases examined here and in chapter 3 suggest several generalizations that appear to include all of the groups under consideration.

Ethnic Composition of the Constituency

The racial and ethnic composition of the electorate is of obvious significance, and thus far appears to be the primary determinant for political success among black candidates and the most frequent factor for the SCE European groups. (The deviation of Jews is more apparent than real. First keep in mind the role of earlier German Jews; second, the list of successful politicians in areas without demographic support covers a long period of time. In most periods, the vast majority of successful officeholders do come from constituencies with substantial ethnic support.)

There is a quantitative issue raised that can not be readily answered, particularly for the new European groups. That is, if each individual member of a given group had the same probability of running for office regardless of the demographic strength of the group in various locations, then clearly a substantial proportion of the group's successful candidates would come from areas of demographic strength. This is simply because there are more members of the group located in the areas of concentration. If, for example, race was totally irrelevant for the selection or election of candidates, there would still be more black officials in Chicago than in Montana simply because the black proportion of the population is so much greater in Chicago. To be sure, it is unlikely that this is a sufficient explanation because it is assumed that an individual's probability of running for office or getting elected does vary with population composition. But given the uneven distribution among the various states and subareas of the nation, the influence of this factor must be considered before the effect of concentration can be isolated.

The Appeal of Various Ethnic and Racial Groups

The relevance of a candidate's race or ethnic origin for the various voter subgroups may vary widely and also over time. For example, a white Catholic running against a black Protestant may enjoy a substantial advantage among white Protestant voters, but not among black voters. However, the advantage a Northwestern European Protestant enjoys with the same set of voters when running against an Eastern European Catholic may be significantly different. The point made earlier in the chapter is that the relative propensities to favor candidates of different origins will vary greatly by both the composition of the voters as well as the combination of candidates. Because voters may know of other issues on which these candidates differ, it is inappropriate to attribute the outcome of any single election as the exclusive product of race and ethnic factors.

Again, a quantitative question is raised that requires data currently not available. Not only may advantages and disadvantages for various race and ethnic combinations of candidates and voters be hypothesized, but these may also change over time. Presumably, the disadvantage faced by a Catholic seeking votes among non-Catholics is less now than it was earlier in the century. The reverse may also be true, as the examination of Jewish officeholders suggested. It is important that the reader recognize that ethnic or racial origin is not to be viewed as a monolithic determinant of an election's outcome, rather it is to be viewed as one of a variety of factors influencing the result of a contest. Depending on the race and ethnic groups involved, as well as the presence of other issues, the magnitude of its importance will undoubtedly vary greatly.

Salience of Race and Ethnic Origin

The race factor particularly distinguishes between blacks and South–Central–Eastern Europeans. Members of specific European ethnic groups are generally far less visible than are blacks. Although members of the different white groups are distinguishable on the aggregate by physical characteristics, the strongest identifiers are surname and self-identification. Hence candidates not closely affiliated with their group or having a name that is not clearly identifiable will likely receive votes from citizens who are unaware of their ethnic membership. In areas of the country where few members of a given group are located, even a candidate with a visible ethnic name may run under less of a handicap because popular awareness of the linkage may be far less.

Under any circumstance, voters who are opposed to black office-holders are going to be far more likely to be aware of the candidate's race than will voters with an analogous propensity to oppose SCE European candidates. It may be that voters with an exceptionally intense distaste for a particular European group will make it their business to learn each candidate's origin, but this would only apply to a small segment of voters. Thus, except for extreme cases, it is reasonable to assume that candidates of new European origin will be less visible than blacks, and hence the handicaps for the latter will be greater even if antipathy toward the groups were distributed identically.

Issues and Elections

Even if a candidate's ethnic or racial origin is widely known and creates a disadvantage, one should not overlook the ability of such a candidate to overcome this obstacle through the introduction of other issues. To be sure, politics in the United States is sometimes bland or so weighted by slogans as to be almost issue-free. Under these circumstances, presumably personal characteristics of the candidates, including race or ethnic origin, will become significant. But often candidates do differ on issues that are of importance to the voters. It would be naive to think that every voter choosing Kennedy over Nixon in their presidential contest was free of antipathy toward a Catholic in the White House. It is more realistic to recognize that many voters believed certain attributes of Kennedy sufficiently compensated for the fact that he was Catholic. In this regard, there is reason to believe that election of some Jewish candidates was a function of their innovative politics such that unique issues were posed which overshadowed the ethnic origin of the candidates.

Access to Politics

Additional extremely important considerations are the different pathways to political position and variations between groups in their access to these pathways. Some start through drudgery at the very bottom of the political system on the precinct level. Others, with eminent and well-publicized roles in realms outside of politics move directly into national or at least statewide political prominence; for example, Ronald Reagan, who moved from movie star to governor of California, and Charles Percy, who shifted from businessman to senator from Illinois. However, despite the presence of several channels, not all are equally good. Moreover, race and ethnic groups differ greatly in their positions relative to these stepping stones. Wealth is obviously no handicap, and differential positions of groups on this dimension will affect their political chances. As a consequence, this feature must be considered in working out the chances affecting each group's political position.

IN CONCLUSION

In some ways, both blacks and the new European groups faced a similar situation. In both cases, major officeholders were not elected unless the group in question had substantial voting strength. Even then, there has been evidence of a "demographic lag" that reflected the influence on politics of other forces such as wealth, a rising middle class, and the like. Superimposed on these inherent liabilities is the legally sanctioned disfranchisement of the vast majority of blacks during most of the period under consideration. In addition to this qualitative difference, blacks differ quantitatively on a variety of the dimensions outlined above. For example, their visibility is greater, they have fewer financial resources, voter antipathy is probably stronger and more widespread, and the number located in such natural political pathways as law, business, and the like, is relatively smaller.

Most important in any comparison between the new Europeans and blacks is the deep chasm between the groups in the issues that they faced. In effect, blacks had to spend much of this century struggling with certain sociopolitical problems that were never an issue for the immigrant groups. John R. Hawkins, an official of the African Methodist Episcopal Church, was asked in 1918 at a meeting in New York City of the Federal Council of Churches, "What does the Negro want or expect?" In looking at the list below of his 14 specific points (Work, 1919, pp. 120–122), consider how few of them would have been relevant to the newest European immigrant. Blacks, however, could not catch up to the new Europeans until these issues were overcome.

1. Universal suffrage
2. Better educational facilities in the South for Negroes
3. The abolition of the so-called "Jim Crow" car system
4. Discontinuance of unjust discriminatory regulations and segregation in the various departments of the government
5. The same military training for colored youths as for white
6. The removal of an imaginary dead line in the recognition of fitness for promotion in military and naval service
7. Removal of peonage system in the South
8. An economic wage scale to be applied to white and colored alike
9. Better housing conditions for the colored employees in industrial plants
10. Better sanitary conditions in certain sections of our cities and towns
11. Reforms in the penal institutions of the South
12. A fair and impartial trial by jury instead of lynching
13. Recognition of the Negro's right and fitness to sit on juries
14. Fair play

5

Legal and Political Issues

The influence of racial and ethnic origin on political careers is a fascinating subject, but the topic's ultimate significance lies in its impact on a group's ability to utilize political institutions as a means for affecting the quality of the group's members' lives. In this regard, a politician's ethnic or racial origin is of considerable importance, but the political issues themselves are of the greatest concern. Likewise, the structure of government is of interest primarily because it has a bearing on laws and policies affecting the relative positions of the groups in other institutional domains, such as schooling, income, occupation, housing, and consumption patterns.

EARLY BLACK POLITICAL ISSUES

Operating with very minimal political power, blacks have been obliged to pursue a variety of political goals that could more or less be ignored by the new European groups. These issues were merely prerequisites for reaching the level of political potential available much earlier to the SCE Europeans.

First and foremost, during almost the entire period under consideration, blacks have been obliged to deal with the very issue of political participation. There is no need at this point to review poll taxes, grandfather clauses, white primaries, and the intimidation of would-be black voters in the South through a variety of devices. Not only did the concentration of blacks in the South, coupled with their political repression, mean the absence of political power based on simple demographic sources of strength, but it also minimized other sources of power and influence that are indirectly affected by the power of the ballot box. Such avenues as wealth, leadership in unions, and corporate positions are also greatly restricted if local, state, and federal legislatures are not merely silent but are actively preventing black development in these areas. Therefore, one can visualize a complex causal network involving government, voting, economic, and social power in which the consequence is a suppressed position among blacks.

According to van der Slik (1969), voting patterns of congressmen on civil rights issues in 1963−1964 are negatively correlated with the percentage of blacks in their congressional districts. This is largely due to the opposition of southern congressmen from districts with a substantial black population. But the net consequence is that even a few years ago blacks were denied this direct demographic source of power.

Although it is difficult to provide solid evidence, very likely the movement of blacks to the North greatly influenced federal policies toward black voting rights in the South. Growing black voting strength in the North, coupled with the concerns of liberal white voters, to an increasing degree meant that politicians aspiring to national office could not overlook the implications of their policies toward the South. It is currently in vogue in some quarters to view liberal whites cynically and with contempt, but in my opinion this is a naive view. Whatever white liberals' attitudes might be with regard to current issues or concerns that affect their immediate bailiwick, it was not very difficult for them to support policies directed toward removing some of the obstacles facing blacks in the South. Although more will be said later when we consider current developments, bear in mind that the crescendo of disillusionment about northern white liberals did not occur until after many of the political and legal restrictions against blacks were eliminated in the South.

Other forces also operated. Not only did blacks develop a middle class that energetically pursued black rights (Ogburn, 1961) through such means as freedom riders, voter registration campaigns, and the like, but some of the newer black organizations in the post-World War II period vigorously, and often with great courage, pressed for voting participation in the South (for example, Waskow, 1967).

Not only was political participation a unique black handicap, but there were a variety of other ways in which immigrants and their children were not subject to the same formal, legally proscribed handicaps. Let it suffice to sum up some of the topics covered by Motley (1966) in her review of the legal status of blacks. In addition to participation in government, there were also numerous Jim Crow laws that affected black usage of a variety of facilities. In the access and use of public transportation facilities, blacks were discriminated against in a manner not faced by the European immigrants. Likewise, freedom of residence was in a number of instances restricted by law. Education in the South during much of this period was segregated by legal devices. In similar fashion, many states, including some in the North, had at one time or another laws that prevented miscegenation. (See Motley [1966, p. 520, note 186] for a list of non-Southern states with such laws.) Discrimination against blacks by unions and private and governmental employers was another obstacle. Finally, blacks had great difficulty obtaining their legal rights from the courts and law enforcement officers.

One should keep in mind that the South–Central–Eastern Europeans were also subject to difficulties in some of these areas. To a unique degree, however, blacks faced legally sanctioned—indeed required—obstacles during much of this period that were, for the most part, not encountered by the European groups. With certain exceptions, the new European groups were subject to the same laws as other whites; whereas for blacks their first obstacle was that the *laws* distinguished them from other segments of the American population.

SOME COMMON PROBLEMS

The new European groups had some special concerns of their own, for example, in foreign affairs affecting their homeland. But a variety of problems were (and are) faced by both blacks and the new immigrant groups in varying degrees. Both groups, suffering from occupational, residential, and social discrimination, shared an interest in supporting legislation and court rulings to combat such handicaps in domains outside the governmental sphere. Issues such as open housing and fair employment practices were of concern to both groups. Likewise, enemies of one group were sometimes enemies of the other. Well-known for its opposition to blacks, the Ku Klux Klan also actively threatened Roman Catholics and Jews.

But in most cases, there were added features that made the issues different for blacks. Aside from disfranchisement and legally supported forms of discrimination against blacks, the new European groups were less severely set off from the remainder of the white working class in the urban North. Because their interests were more closely intertwined with the concerns held by a significant part of the remaining white population, the interests of the South—Central—Eastern Europeans were part of a broader-based movement less closely specified by ethnic origin. During the Great Depression of the 1930s, for example, blacks, South—Central—Eastern Europeans, and other segments of the American population had a strong vested interest in obtaining government aid and support, but blacks were troubled by the handicap of racial discrimination within the governmental programs themselves (Franklin, 1956, p. 523).

There is much to be learned from the varying degrees of difficulty encountered by these groups when facing the same issues. A brief review of lynchings and nativist movements in the United States provides a useful illustration of several important points: First, the new European groups did share some of the same problems as blacks; second, their handicaps were less substantial; third, the immigrant difficulties ended sooner than did the blacks'; fourth, it was necessary for blacks to consume their limited political capital in lengthy efforts simply to reach the same legal status that other Americans enjoyed as a matter of course.

Lynchings

On a variety of occasions, but particularly in connection with labor disputes, various SCE European immigrants met violent deaths. In 1874, Italian immigrants employed as strikebreakers during a Western Pennsylvania coal-mining dispute were killed. During the 1890s there were several outbursts of violence directed against the new European groups: ten striking Slavic and Magyar coal miners were killed and 50 wounded by militia; several immigrants were shot by a sheriff's posse and 138 arrested after an engineer was killed during another strike; and 21 Polish and Hungarian strikers were killed in Pennsylvania during an anthracite strike led by the United Mine Workers Union in 1897 (Higham, 1955, pp. 48, 89—90). A mining town in Southern Illinois, West Frankfort, in 1920 was the scene of mass violence directed against all foreigners, particularly Italians: "Time and again the crowds burst into the Italian district, dragged cowering residents from their homes, clubbed and stoned them, and set fire to their dwellings. The havoc went on for three days, although five hundred state troops were rushed to the scene" (Higham, 1955, p. 264).

As concerns lynching in particular, there are reports of six Italians being lynched during 1895 in Colorado, three in 1896 in a small

Louisiana town, two separate cases of Italians being lynched in the Illinois mining towns during the 1890s, as well as the lynching of eleven Italians in New Orleans in 1891. The Jewish manager of an Atlanta pencil factory was lynched in 1915 after his death sentence for a murder had been commuted by the governor to life imprisonment (Higham, 1955, pp. 90–91, 184–186). The precipitants for the lynchings of the Italians were similar to black lynchings, involving charges against Italians for murder, failure of a jury to convict, and street brawls.

Nevertheless, lynching in the United States was never as serious a problem for immigrants. Over time an increasing proportion of the victims were black. Raper (1970, p. 25) found a marked decrease through the years in the percentage of white lynching victims. During the last decade of the nineteenth century, whites were a third of all persons lynched; by 1930, a year in which 21 persons were documented lynched, only one was white.

This violent treatment of blacks frequently involved at least covert complicity among southern law enforcement agents. As a consequence, considerable efforts were made by black organizations to obtain federal antilynching legislation. The occurrence of more than 70 lynchings during the first year after World War I led the National Association for the Advancement of Colored People (NAACP) to hold a national campaign against lynchings and a fund-raising drive to publicize its program and to defend blacks (Franklin, 1956, p. 478). The NAACP lined up various members of the Congress to support antilynching legislation, and, at their request, such legislation was introduced into the House by L.C. Dyer in 1921. It passed the House but failed in the Senate, despite considerable efforts by the NAACP and others. In turn, blacks attempted to defeat some of the senators who had opposed the Dyer antilynching bill (Franklin, 1956, pp. 478–479, 515). Other efforts to obtain federal legislation against lynchings also failed in 1935 and 1940.

The point of all this is not merely that blacks suffered far more from lynchings than did the European groups, but that black political efforts were directed toward goals and issues that most of the new European groups were not obliged to deal with. Again, the former had to devote their political efforts to issues that would, at best, bring them up to par with the civil liberties enjoyed by the South–Central–Eastern Europeans. The latter, on the other hand, could employ their mounting political power to generate governmental changes that would advance their situation with respect to various "bread and butter" concerns such as unionization and welfare issues. To be sure, there were incidents of violence against these groups, such as the Leo Frank lynching in Georgia or the death sentences in the Sacco-Vanzetti case in the 1920s that created nationwide publicity, but lynching and other forms of violence were increasingly directed mainly against blacks. As a consequence, the elimination of lynching was one of the central concerns of the key pre-World War II organization devoted to advancing black interests, the NAACP. Of course, closely tied to the problem of lynchings were broader objections to differential law enforcement as well as the behavior and attitudes of police and judiciary toward blacks.

Ku Klux Klan and Other Nativist Movements

A brief examination of developments in the Ku Klux Klan, as is the case with lynchings, illustrates that the difficulties blacks faced were also faced by many of the new European groups, albeit less severely. The intimidation of blacks by the Klan is well-known and requires no elaboration here, but perhaps less appreciated is that the Klan was also anti-Catholic and was anti-Jewish. The Klan revived after World War I in response to fears that blacks had moved "out of their place" during the war and in response to nativist antagonism to "foreigners." According to Higham (1955):

> White supremacy remained an important theme even when the Klan spread into the North, but it would be a mistake to regard the Negro issue as the mainspring of its career. Fear of the "New Negro" rapidly declined as he either accepted his old place or moved to northern cities. By mid-1921 the Klan was specializing in attacking white people, and thereafter the great bulk of its disciplinary activities in all parts of the country had to do with whites. [P. 290]

By the time the Klan had reached its high point in 1923, the leading Klan states were in the Midwest—Ohio and Indiana—rather than in the South. In addition, Jews and Catholics were under assault from other nativist organizations during the period under consideration. The American Protective Association, formed in Iowa in 1887, was vigorously anti-Catholic. Its members were required to pledge that they would never vote for a Catholic, never employ one if at all possible, and never strike with Catholics. Another organization, the True Americans, was able to purge Roman Catholics from municipal employment during the 1920s in Birmingham, Alabama. Jews were under severe fire between the two world wars for two rather contradictory charges: On the one hand for being Bolsheviks and otherwise dangerous radicals; and on the other for being part of an international capitalist movement that sought to own and control everything. *The Protocols of the Elders of Zion*, a document falsely claimed to have been written by Jews, received wide circulation in the United States and elsewhere during the 1920s. This document was supposed to reveal a master plan among Jews in the world for financial power, chaos, war, and revolution. Henry Ford sponsored the *Dearborn Independent*, which was rife with anti-Jewish themes. *The Menace*, a decidedly anti-Catholic publication, reached a peak circulation of 1.5 million in 1915 (Higham, 1955, p. 184).

FOREIGN POLICIES

The foreign policies of the United States, particularly as they affected ethnic compatriots overseas, was one political area of considerably greater concern to South–Central–Eastern Europeans than to blacks. Immigration policies were themselves of keen interest, being hotly debated from the turn of the century onward. By and large, the new groups favored minimum restrictions so as to allow the continued flow of compatriots from their European homelands into the nation. The positions held by presidential candidates, aspirants to Congress, and the political parties were examined in this light as the new groups learned to wield their growing voting power. The Republican Party was able to appeal to both industrial employers seeking cheap labor and to the new groups by supporting immigration.

Foreign affairs was one issue that was bound to affect virtually all of the immigrant groups, old and new. Insofar as the United States was involved directly or indirectly in events that had a bearing on the situation faced by ethnic compatriots overseas, it was inevitable that the groups would seek to sway the nation's position. Prior to America's formal entrance into World War I, both old and new European groups attempted to influence American policy in ways that would be compatible with the interests of their homeland. Many Irish- and German-Americans vigorously opposed support of the British. Likewise, Americans of Swedish and Norwegian origin favored neutrality because Russia was on the Allied side (Lubell, 1956, pp. 143–144). Incidentally, during the war itself, Americans of German origin suffered greatly.

In similar fashion, political attitudes toward Franklin Roosevelt and the Democratic Party were affected by developments in Europe leading up to World War II. An analysis of voting patterns in the 1940 presidential election discloses remarkable shifts that can be interpreted in terms of the consequences Roosevelt's pro-British policies had for the ancestral homelands of the various groups of ethnic voters (Lubell, 1956, pp. 140–141). Analyzing the presidential election of 1940, Lubell observes:

Some lingerings of pro-German and anti-British feeling showed up in Swedish and Irish sections. Many Italo-Americans resented Roosevelt's criticism of Mussolini's attack upon France. But in the main the German-Americans were left as the hard isolationist core.

Offsetting their influence was the strength Roosevelt drew from voters of Polish, Norwegian and Jewish extraction because of Hitler's anti-Semitism and his invasion of Poland and Norway. Roosevelt's 1940 vote held up so much better in the cities than in the rural areas partly because the "new" immigrants, drawn so heavily from the Central European countries which Hitler ravaged, were concentrated in the urban centers. [Pp. 144–145]

Currently, Jews tend to respond to U.S. policies toward the Middle East, Poles and other groups from Iron Curtain countries applaud promises to free their ancestral homelands from Russian domination, and blacks have shown increased interest in policies affecting Africa, particularly with respect to the Republic of South Africa. The United States in the past has also been a hothouse for nurturing the activities of ethnic groups engaged in pursuing political changes in the Old World, such as supporting the formation of the Irish Free State, Italian unification, and the creation of an independent Czechoslovakia.

In all of these matters, blacks have been far less involved than the South–Central–Eastern Europeans. Until very recently, the European newcomers identified more closely with their Old World homelands than did blacks with Africa. Not only were the generational ties closer in the sense that many were either foreign-born or only a generation or two removed from the immigrants, a situation not encountered by blacks even in 1880, but the latter could not readily trace their ties to any specific country in Africa. Moreover, aspirations among black intellectuals and the small middle class during much of this period were in a direction that would have been hampered by emphasis on their African origins.

POLITICAL ISSUES AND SOCIAL CHANGE: A PERSPECTIVE

In comparing the political responses of blacks and South–Central–Eastern Europeans, it is useful to consider a distinction among three different types of issues. First, there is the issue of discrimination within and by governmental bodies. Included here are voting restrictions, differential law enforcement, and the variety of laws and judicial decisions by federal and lesser legislatures and courts. Second, there is the issue of governmental activities directed toward eliminating discrimination in other institutions and domains, such as employment, unions, housing, social organizations, and the like. Third, there is the issue of governmental policies involving not simply nondiscrimination in other domains, but specific acts with consequences for the immediate and long-term improvement of conditions faced by an ethnic or racial group; for example, financing black entrepreneurs, the creation of a minimal annual income, and other applications of government resources and pressures on behalf of blacks and ethnics.

As a crude generalization, each of these issues may be viewed as having a certain "natural" chronological sequence during the period under review such as to form stages of political concern. The issue of governmental discrimination comes first, nongovernmental discrimination second, and ameliorative programs last in a sequence of political and ideological developments. It is not difficult to understand why the issues might follow this sequence. Before one can ask the government to do something about discrimination in other social arenas, it is necessary to obtain a satisfactory position within the government itself. Likewise, the elimination of existing discriminatory practices in other institutions would seem to be both more pressing and accessible an issue than pushing for programs designed specifically to improve the situation faced by a race or ethnic group.

Two qualifications are necessary. First, rather obviously this sequence implies a matter of degree and relative emphasis; one should recognize a certain amount of temporal overlap. Likewise, the distinction is not always clear-cut with respect to a given practice or legislative issue. The second point, and this is crucial, is that blacks and new European groups did not enter into each phase at the same time. Thus, blacks have been blocked for a far longer time on the first issue, government itself, than have been the European newcomers. Although the issue is not yet dead for blacks, a very slow improvement occurred earlier in this century, followed by substantial progress only in the most recent decades. By and large, this first issue was of far more severe breadth and magnitude for blacks than for the European groups, albeit the latter also suffered with regard to discretionary matters such as appointments and promotions within government bodies as well as the attainment of political power through elections and other sources of influence.

Once one recognizes that society has been changing during this entire period, then the apparent differences between the demands raised by blacks and the new Europeans can be more fully understood. In effect these groups reached a given stage at different points in time. Because society had changed during the interim, the proposals that each group raises at each stage are different if only because society is different.

Ideological differences between blacks currently and the new immigrants in earlier periods are therefore a product in part of the political lag that blacks faced coupled with the fact that society itself has changed. As a consequence, what appears to be an entirely different set of demands, in point of fact is part of the same general evolutionary process, but arrived at later by blacks.

To what degree is the current set of ideological and political themes within the black community different from earlier developments among the SCE European groups? On the surface, the most prominent feature of the black movement, its multidirectional character, would make this appear unanswerable. There are mass-based groups as well as more elitist or middle-class-oriented segments; there are integrationist and nonintegrationist elements; there are Marxist, socialist, and other revolutionary ingredients taking their inspiration from black Africa, Algeria, Cuba, and Red China; and yet there are others seeking a solution within the existing capitalistic framework. But the most striking changes in the past few decades have been in the thrust away from integration as a panacea, a movement toward mass support, direct action, and a view that a color-blind social structure is no longer satisfactory if its consequences are still unfavorable to blacks. Rustin (1965, pp. 411–412) sums up these changes:

> The civil rights movement is evolving from a protest movement into a full-fledged *social movement*—an evolution calling its very name into question. It is now concerned not merely with removing the barriers to full *opportunity* but with achieving the fact of *equality*. From sit-ins and freedom rides we have gone into rent strikes, boycotts, community organization, and political action. As a consequence of this natural evolution, the Negro today finds himself stymied by obstacles of far greater magnitude than the legal barriers he was attacking before: automation, urban decay, *de facto* school segregation. These are problems which, while conditioned by Jim Crow, do not vanish upon its demise. They are more deeply rooted in our socioeconomic order; they are the result of the total society's failure to meet not only the Negro's needs, but human needs generally.

Is this sort of perspective so unique to blacks? I would argue that in certain fundamental ways it is not different from earlier developments that the European groups supported, such as the movement toward unionization, Social Security legislation, government aid during the Depression, or changes in higher education from an elite institution to one available to a broader segment of the population. Because of the fact that almost to the present day blacks have been compelled to battle with discrimination in and by government, they have been slower to reach the stages where politics becomes a means for advancing their interests in other domains.

Rustin (1965) argues, and I think reasonably so, that it was only in the decade between the 1954 school desegregation decision by the Supreme Court and the 1964 Civil Rights Act that "the legal foundations of racism in America were destroyed" (p. 405). Given the fact that blacks are only now in a position to go beyond the issue of governmental discrimination, the form of their demands will be radically different from earlier periods simply because society has changed so enormously. In particular, the role of the federal and lesser governments has expanded greatly into a variety of domains and consumes an increasing proportion of the economy's total output (Lieberson, 1971). I doubt if a minimum annual income or greater welfare benefits would have been refused in earlier decades by the new European groups, but rather it would have never occurred to anyone to raise such an issue—or perhaps more accurately, such an issue would have been rejected at the time as too radical and as unacceptable.

It is the expanding role of government generally, which can be neither blamed on nor credited to blacks because it reflects a broad, sweeping societal change, that makes permissible a new set of proposals unheralded by other race and ethnic groups. Black demands are really not radically different from the remainder of society's in one sense, but reflect black special interests and needs in a context in which society's political institutions are performing both expanding and novel functions. In an era of farm subsidies and payments for not cultivating the soil, blacks are simply attempting to benefit from the enormous range of new government functions.

Assertions such as the above are difficult to test when not grounded in hard data. However, I find it useful to view a number of differences in immigrant-black political ideology as the joint product of a black political lag in combination with social changes occurring during the interim. Several ideological developments are at least consistent with this viewpoint: The participation and timing of the new immigrant groups and blacks in various radical movements reflect these changes; likewise, developments in education, integration, and attitudes toward white liberals appear to support the thesis presented above.

RADICAL POLITICAL MOVEMENTS

Use of the term "radical" as a label for various ideologies and movements is apt to be misleading in any survey of a fairly long period of time. Much of what was judged to be radical in the 1920s is sufficiently institutionalized and accepted presently as to be almost part of the so-called Establishment. Such is the difficulty in comparing the ideologies held by some black organizations today with those of South–Central–Eastern Europeans in decades past. However, until very recently, challenges to the basic constitutional and economic structure of the United States were far more likely to come from the new European groups than from blacks.

With the Garveyites as the most notable exception, until the last few decades the basic ideology within black organizations has been oriented toward obtaining equal opportunities within the context of the democratic ethos proclaimed in the United States. Whatever the emotional response of some whites might have been to demands for the vote, integration, and the like, the main thrust of the black movement was reformist rather than revolutionary. Indeed, the NAACP's entire strategy for a long time was to use the courts and other political processes to obtain black rights under the Constitution. The growth of the Black Muslims and the rise of Malcom X marked the first numerically important challenge to the assimilation and integration notions pursued by leading black organizations.

The Communist Party made little headway among blacks during its heyday in the United States despite an extensive courtship based on the notion that an overwhelmingly oppressed and disadvantaged population would be receptive to a revolutionary ideology. Such was not the case. Although a black ran as the vice-presidential candidate on the Communist Party ticket in 1932, 1936, and 1940 (Franklin, 1956, p. 516), black membership in the Communist Party was, at its height, no more than proportional to their numbers in the United States. In 1928, there were about 150 to 200 blacks out of a total membership of 14,000; in 1930, there were about 1,000 black members; and in 1940 somewhat less than 3,000. At most, there were never more than about 8,000 blacks in the American Communist Party (based on estimates by Wilson Record reported in Simpson and Yinger, 1965, pp. 192, 319). The Communist Party was relatively early in its attempt to appeal directly to the masses, which included an attack on the black middle class, other black organizations, and black intellectuals. They reversed their strategy around 1935 and began to court these blacks as well as attempt to gain control of other organizations (Meier and Rudwick, 1966, pp. 215–216). Despite the Party's successful efforts to publicize injustices, recruitment was minimal.

Before considering the European immigrant groups' linkages with the Communist Party and other radical movements of the time, the reader should note that it is not my intention to overlook such an important leader as A. Philip Randolph, who played a central role in various movements going back to early in this century when he edited the socialist monthly, *Messenger*. Neither do I want to negate the tremendous impact of W.E.B. DuBois. My point is simply that for the most part the black organizational and ideological thrust through much of the post-World War II era (and even now for many) has been toward securing the rights, privileges, and opportunities available under the Constitution. In this basic sense, blacks were (and many still are) engaged largely in a *reform* movement rather than a *revolutionary* movement. From the perspective of many whites during this century, this movement may have appeared revolutionary in the sense that the various practices opposed by blacks were seen as a fundamental part of the social order—no less sacred than motherhood and apple pie. Nevertheless, the general movement through much of this period has been toward securing the rights and opportunities that are, in theory, available under the existing political-economic system.

The New European Groups

Through much of this century, South—Central—Eastern Europeans were particularly prominent in a variety of radical movements. Indeed, the role of the immigrant in radicalism goes further back than the period under consideration. Of the 17 socialist papers published in the United States in 1876, ten were published in German, three in Bohemian, and one in Swedish. Both the Socialist Labor Party and the anarchist movement of the 1880s included a substantial proportion of German immigrants (Jones, 1960, p. 229). The Haymarket affair in Chicago prior to the turn of the century led to death sentences for six immigrants (five of them were German) as well as one native white, even though the bomb thrower's identity was never discovered (Higham, 1955, p. 54).

Reflecting widespread bombings, bitter and prolonged union-management conflicts, and armchair ideology from anarchists and the like, a "red scare" swept across the United States in the period immediately after World War I. The new European groups were quite prominent; indeed, their alleged radicalism and alien political ideologies were one of the arguments used in the 1920s for shutting off new immigration. Several of the most important strikes involved industries with substantial immigrant employment, for example, textiles and steel (Higham, 1955, pp. 225–226). Efforts were made to deport various immigrants as a means of controlling those engaged in some of these radical movements.

The activities of Attorney General Palmer in handling the red scare involved some striking parallels with those used in the Black Panther raids of the 1960s. His first target was an organization of Russian immigrants, called the Union of Russian Workers.

> On November 7, 1919, the second anniversary of the Bolshevik regime in Russia, Palmer's men descended on Russian meeting places in eleven cities and seized hundreds of members of the organization. Screening for once was swift. Little more than a month later 249 aliens, most of them netted in the November raids, were on a specially chartered transport en route to Finland. From there they traveled overland to Russia through snows and military lines. Some had to leave behind in America their wives and children, at once destitute and ostracized. [Higham, 1955, p. 230]

Early in 1920 this raid was followed with another on the foreign-born members of two communist parties in 33 cities which led to the retention of nearly 3,000 aliens, almost all Eastern Europeans, pending deportation. In general, membership in the American Communist Party during the pre-World War II era included many immigrants from Russia and other Eastern European nations, with a preponderance of Jews (Simpson and Yinger, 1965, p. 229). According to a 1936 *Fortune* magazine article, approximately 3,500 to 4,000 of the 27,000 members of the Party were Jewish (Dinnerstein and Jaher, 1970, p. 246).

In brief, until the post-World War II period, what passed for radicalism in the United States was far more likely to involve SCE Europeans than blacks. The trade union movement, splinter parties, and various small ideological groups were then viewed as radical. And these were the products of white groups, not blacks. The central issues for blacks included getting a chance to participate in the political system, attainment of the remaining full citizenship rights, and being able to get a job. Organizational strength and militancy in dealing with employers was a luxury that few could afford. Indeed, although trade unionism created fear and suspicion among many whites, unions remained largely anti-black until the great industrial unions were created later in the century. One source of conflict after World War I was the employment of blacks as strike breakers during periods of labor-management conflict. Blocked from employment or greatly restricted to the least desirable types of work during normal times, blacks were used by management during periods when the white labor force was troublesome.

VOLUNTARY ASSOCIATIONS AND PUBLIC INSTITUTIONS

For a number of decades, the new European groups were busily engaged in a wide variety of voluntary projects leading to the establishment of their own hospitals, orphanages, old-age homes, social services, and the like. Moreover, they were also eager to maintain their language and other elements of their Old World culture, particularly among their American-born children (Fishman, Nahirny, Hofman, and Hayden, 1966). The contrast with blacks is striking in these areas, but, again, is more readily understood if the general societal changes during this century are taken into account.

The shift in the United States, by no means complete, is toward the expectation that social services formerly provided on a voluntary basis will now be available through governmental bodies and agencies. As a consequence, at a time when there is finally sufficient money in the black community and organizational strength to begin some of these services, they do not develop in the same degree as they had earlier among European groups. At least a substantial part of the difference may be explained as a reflection of the groups' stages of development and societal changes occurring during the interim. In other words, one implication is that new immigrant groups arriving for the first time now would have less of a disposition toward the development of their own ethnic organizations for social services.

With respect to the maintenance of each group's distinctive cultural attributes, the contrast is very striking. As noted earlier, the European groups attempted to provide their offspring with a background in the unique facets of their group and sought to generate pride in their heritage. This was done almost entirely outside public institutions. Parochial school systems developed as well as a variety of ethnic organizations that sought to supplement the American education received during regular school hours. The development of black pride is not basically different from the attitudes that motivated the new European groups in the past decades to create a variety of organizations devoted to maintaining their distinctive cultures. But now the expectation is that the public school systems will provide such an outlet. How do we explain this difference? First, the school systems have changed greatly in many ways during the decades between 1880 and this period of black demands for textbooks, courses, and materials fully appreciative of black contributions. Courses and programs are now offered to meet community needs, regardless of whether they are part of a classical academic program; witness driver education courses in high school. Likewise, schools are less autonomous in the community, their roles are different; graduation from high school is less an accomplishment of great intrinsic merit than a normal expectation. Thus black power to influence such events has finally been reached at a time when the schools are generally more susceptible to local, specialized pressures.

If black pressures on school systems appear novel, it is because they are not entirely parallel to those of the earlier European immigrants. (However, we should not lose sight of the European-language courses offered in schools that reflect more the ethnic composition of an area than "traditional" academic language interests.) But if the pressures are novel, it is just as appropriate to ask why they did not come earlier from the new European immigrant groups as it is to ask why they appear now.

INTEGRATION

The shift in black ideology from an intensive pursuit of integration toward a mixed stand on the topic has to be interpreted as not due solely to the fact that it did not work or that black power requires black isolation. Rather it has to be viewed as a shift from a battle against the legal enforcement of segregation to a position that no longer emphasizes that goal now that legal prohibitions are eliminated and many informal practices are less rigid.

The European immigrant groups were also residentially segregated to a degree that could not be explained in terms of their lower economic position and discrimination (Lieberson, 1963a, pp. 83–91). Indeed, there was a brief period when blacks were slightly less segregated from the native white population than were some of the new European groups. In 1910, for example, Italians were more segregated in all but one of the ten northern industrial belt cities studied by Lieberson (1963a, pp. 128–129). In Philadelphia, the Russians, Roumanians, and Hungarians were also more isolated—indeed, it was not until 1930 that they were less isolated than blacks from the native white population of the city.

The segregation of the new groups, like that for blacks, was a product of both involuntary and voluntary forces. There was a propensity for others to wish to avoid these peoples and also a propensity for members to reside near compatriots. Although it is impossible to weight the relative importance of the voluntary and involuntary aspects (particularly when one considers that the former was at least partially a reflection of the latter), it seems safe to conjecture that residential segregation was more involuntary for blacks and more enforced by legal, semilegal, and organizational elements such as restrictive covenants, real estate boards, government mortgage practices, and the like (see, for example, Mc-Entire, 1960).

As a consequence, the thrust against segregation in housing, to say nothing of schooling, involves the first stage of political development, where governmental bodies and practices are a target, as well as the second stage, when positive policies and laws are expected from the political institutions with regard to practices in other domains. To put it bluntly, it is one thing to be rejected without any right or opportunity to opt for integration, it is another to choose integration (Duncan, 1967). Therefore, what appears to be an inconsistent or at least shifting view toward integration can be interpreted as a manifestation of changing political stages such that its *imposition* or even its *tolerance* by political institutions is a target in earlier political stages, but its existence as a voluntary phenomena is not. Indeed, blacks are in the position of many of the new European immigrant groups in that they are attempting to reach a point where ethnic ghettos or colonies, if they exist, will be there solely because they are wanted by the residents in the area.

NORTHERN WHITE LIBERALS

It is not uncommon for white Southerners, politicians and others as well, to claim that the South has been made the whipping boy for northerners on racial issues. This is not without justification because many of the practices in the South were hardly different from those found in the North—except for the crucial fact that they were enforced by law in the South. For example, witness the resistance to school desegregation in the North despite the absence of legal restrictions. Events during the period at hand provide clues to the recent disillusionment with white northern liberals among at least some segments of black leadership. In this way, we also obtain some clues to the earlier political orientation of blacks in the northern cities.

Until the Supreme Court school desegregation decision in 1954, followed by the civil rights acts, and enforcement of black voting rights in the South, it was possible for an alliance to exist in the North between blacks and white liberals that could overlook or set aside some inherent conflicts that existed between them. With such dramatic events as lynchings, poll taxes, legally enforced Jim Crow policies, and the like, attention could be diverted to issues that did not create any splits within a coalition between white liberals and blacks. It was possible for northern whites to advance the black position by vigorously assaulting the treatment of blacks in the South. These issues posed no danger to the coalition because they had essentially no impact on their northern white constituency. In addition, it was possible for northern black politicians and officeholders, by taking a vigorous stand on these matters, both to prove their concern for compatriots without simultaneously alienating whites operating in the same coalition.

Because of these factors, though attention was not diverted entirely from the extremely difficult conditions faced by blacks in the North, at least it was possible to be actively fighting antiblack policies without being forced to face up to the very difficult issues. Moreover, there were certain shared interests between blacks and South–Central–Eastern Europeans, namely, fair employment practices, discrimination on the basis of ethnic origin or race, and other issues of this sort. Accordingly, some causes could be pursued without splitting black supporters from SCE Europeans and other white segments.

With the decline of legally supported discrimination against blacks in the South, the issues faced in the northern urban industrial centers were less easily concealed or avoided. As a consequence, there has been an increasing inability to hold together a coalition that had proven so successful in the past decades beginning with Franklin Roosevelt. Basically, white liberals of an earlier vintage were important for gaining the first and second stages of political development, but are less likely to be supportive of new procedures and public policies called for in the third stage, namely ameliorative programs that may involve a radical recasting of the social and economic structure of the nation.

Differences in the consequences for voter support when issues are raised on a national plane as opposed to a local level should not be overlooked. In general it is easier to support national legislation or policies that will not alienate a politician's local support base than it is to support policies that have a more direct and immediate bearing on the local scene and hence may alienate a segment of a politician's constituency. The same sort of phenomenon is noted by Wilson (1960) in his discussion of the United Automobile Workers (UAW). Here is a union with a substantial black membershp. The union's sizable number of white members tend to be vigorously opposed to school integration, integrated housing, and the like. As a consequence, the UAW has been more energetic in its political activities on the national plane than in local areas, such as Detroit, where pursuit of certain policies would clearly split its membership.

CONTEMPORARY BLACK LEADERSHIP AND IDEOLOGY

An entire book could be devoted exclusively to the various political leaders and ideologies, past and present, within the black community. Indeed, to sample just a handful, witness such books as those by Broderick and Meier (1965); Carmichael and Hamilton (1967); Essien-Udom (1962); Killian (1968); Lincoln (1961); and Stone (1970). The existence of an almost infinite variety of ideological commitments, ranging from integration to the creation of a separate socialist nation, keep one from recognizing that black ideologies and leadership are influenced in the same way as new European groups. Whatever the developments in the next few years, as in the past, success of various black leaders and ideologies within the black community will be as much the product of the larger white-dominated society as it will be of blacks. As I had occasion to point out in connection with the 1965 race riots,

> the agitation of an effective orator may crystallize the feelings of his listeners after some minor incident, but it is only successful if the groundwork is laid by long-standing, unhealed wounds, which have been neglected. Populations are predisposed to riot, they are not empty vessels which can be filled with venom at the whim of a spell-binder. If false and wild rumors are believed, it is only because there is an element of plausibility or a past history of similar atrocities. [Lieberson, 1966, p. 373]

Black leadership and ideology are a function of white society not simply in the sense that the mass media are controlled by whites and are vital for broad appeal. More basically, one may view any community as consisting at a given time of a variety of ideologies and would-be leaders. The presence of these means nothing in itself, but what is crucial is their ascendancy. In part, the response of the white community determines which ideology and leader will gain an upper hand. Thus if a leader seeks to meet black interests through reform of the existing institutional structure and assumes the good faith of at least some whites, he will need positive responses from the larger system. In other words, there is the need to be able to produce tangible and meaningful evidence that the leader can get things done. Failure means that other leaders and other ideologies become more plausible. In effect, there is a two-way interaction such that the success or failure of a given political philosophy and its execution will determine the future political philosophies and tactics of blacks. At each point, then, the dominant white population holds within it the power not merely to break or make a movement directly, but if the former, then to create indirectly the conditions that will nourish new ideologies and leadership.

BY WAY OF SUMMARY

Blacks are now in a position for the first time to press the government not merely for elimination of discrimination within its own branches or for action to prevent discrimination in other institutions, but also to change the society in ways that will improve black conditions. The nature of these demands may, at first glance, appear radically different from those of the South–Central–Eastern European groups. But one should not lose sight of the fact that the SCE Europeans in earlier decades were promoting ideologies and participating in social and political changes that appeared equally novel to the society.

Part of this difference is due to the fact that in progressing through each stage of political development blacks have been slower than the Europeans. The basic societal institutions had changed by the time blacks entered a stage reached earlier by the new European groups. If the content of the issues raised by blacks currently is different from that raised by the South–Central–Eastern Europeans, in essence this is because society itself is different. Because the latter groups have met their needs in earlier periods with different forms of change—for example, Social Security, job benefits, unionization, growth of public higher education—the expectation should not be that these will provide workable solutions for people decades later who are just beginning to reach out with their political potential.

PART II
Socioeconomic Conditions

6
Education

This part of the volume deals with "bread and butter" issues: education, occupation, and income. Clearly, the general societal forces affecting socioeconomic status have operated less favorably for blacks than for whites. For example, the income and occupational rewards obtained by blacks with a given level of schooling are far less than those reached by whites with comparable years of formal education (see, for example, Siegel, 1965; Blau and Duncan, 1967; Lieberson and Fuguitt, 1967). But more important, there is rather convincing evidence that the various new European groups are presently at no disadvantage when compared with whites of Northwestern European origin. Although the adult members of various white ethnic groups differ from one another in terms of their socioeconomic position in the United States, for the most part these differences are a function of their initial parental positions (Duncan and Duncan, 1968). The intergenerational mobility pattern is more or less identical for the offspring of different white ethnic groups who have comparable parental backgrounds and education. By contrast, Duncan and Duncan (1968, p. 364) find the level of occupational achievement among blacks is much lower than one would expect after taking into account their starting point in the social structure and their formal education qualifications.

The problem posed is very simple: If the new European groups have "made it" to a far greater degree than blacks, what accounts for this differential? If the question is simple, the answer is not. For in exploring the educational, occupational, and income positions of these groups, a wide variety of factors must be considered. It will become readily apparent that the glib and quick "explanations" commonly offered, whether racism or cultural deprivation or what have you, at best are nothing more than oversimplified interpretations of a very complex problem. Widely held interpretations of socioeconomic differences such as the groups' values, kinship structure, nuclear family stability, fertility, and the like will be subjected to a test far more stringent than their "plausibility." Rather, as far as possible, the limited data for the past will be used to determine empirically whether these interpretations are more than merely part of the rhetoric of race relations.

EDUCATION: A CORE FACTOR

From a variety of perspectives, education is a central consideration in any attempt to account for the socioeconomic positions of the groups. On the one hand, educational attainment itself is an important ingredient. For example, Duncan (1961) reports that the educational level achieved by the incumbents of different occupations is one of the two key factors influencing the prestige popularly associated with an occupation. From another perspective, education is a vital determinant of the occupation and income held by members of the labor force. This operates for a variety of reasons. Not only does one's education affect occupational and income life chances, but the education of parents has a bearing on the education and socioeconomic position of the offspring (Blau and Duncan, 1967; Sewell, 1971; Hauser, 1970; Featherman, 1971). The schools serve not only a cultural function, such as preserving and transmitting the past, but also they prepare people for jobs, social classes, and social mobility (Gleason, 1967, p. 23).

Current Situation

In terms of recent levels of educational attainment, the new Europeans are ahead of blacks, although the advantage is decidedly less among younger adults. Based on a survey conducted by the Census Bureau in late 1969, Table 6.1 reports the educational attainment of various major white ethnic groups in the United States as well as blacks. The similarity in educational achievement among younger white adults (25 to 34 years of age) is rather striking. All three of the Northwestern European groups specified—English, German, and Irish—have medians of 12.6 years of schooling. This differs by only one-tenth of a year from

TABLE 6.1
MEDIAN SCHOOL YEARS COMPLETED, 1969

Group	Age	
	25–34	35 & over
Old		
English	12.6	12.2
German	12.6	12.0
Irish	12.6	12.0
New		
Italian	12.5	10.3
Polish	12.7	10.9
Russian	16 +	12.4
Black	12.1	8.2

SOURCES: U.S. Bureau of the Census, 1971, table 13; U.S. Bureau of Labor
Statistics, 1971, table 65.

two of the three new ethnic groups: Italians, 12.5; Poles, 12.7 years. The
Russians, by contrast, have a median of 16+ years of schooling, well in
excess of any of the old European groups. The median educational
attainment of younger adult blacks, 12.1 years, is not too far below the
level reached by most of the white ethnic groups.[1] However, examination of the older adults in each group indicates that the narrowing of the
educational gap is a relatively recent phenomenon. As a consequence,
when adults of all ages are considered, the new Europeans still enjoy a
decided educational advantage over blacks.

The median educational-attainment level for black adults 35 years of
age and older, 8.2, is from 2 to 4 years below the levels reported by
Italians, Poles, and Russians of the same age (Table 6.1). In turn, the first
two of these new groups have lower educational levels than any of the
old European groups. The Russians, a group which presumably includes
a substantial Jewish component, still has a higher median than any of the
old white ethnic groups. Although these results indicate that adults over
35 from three major new European sources enjoy very substantial
educational advantages over blacks, if anything the differences are
understated. Namely, the ethnic categories incorporate persons of
different generations and, therefore, include significant numbers of
foreign-born members of these groups who presumably lower the
medians.

If we compare nonwhite males with second-generation members of
these new European groups, the gaps are even greater. Based on a 1962
survey (United States Bureau of the Census, 1963a), nonwhite males

between 25 and 64 years of age had a mean of 8.2 years of schooling. The levels of schooling are much higher among American-born men of comparable age whose fathers were born in South—Central—Eastern Europe (based on data derived from Duncan and Duncan, 1968, Table 1).[2] Second-generation Polish and Italian men average about 11 years of education, an advantage of close to three years over blacks; second-generation Russians enjoy an advantage of close to five years; and others from SCE Europe have an educational average that is close to 3.5 years greater than blacks. In short, although the relative positions of the new and old Europeans are less clear-cut because of overlaps, the new European groups' levels of education are decidedly ahead of blacks.

As of 1960 there was indication that new Europeans of school age were maintaining their lead over blacks. Table 6.2 gives the percentage enrolled in school by specific ages for blacks, second-generation whites, and whites of third and later generations. The differences between these segments change by the ages under comparison. For the very youngest, children 5 and 6 years old, there are rather substantial differences in the percentage enrolled in school: Blacks are somewhat lower than native whites of native parentage and substantially lower than second-generation whites from both old and new sources. Starting with age 7 and running through age 14, blacks are fairly close to the enrollment rates for the new European groups as well as other native white segments of the population. These are the years when education is close to universal and attendance is required. However, beginning in the midteens, the percentage enrolled in school begins to drop off more rapidly for blacks than for whites of South—Central—Eastern origin (an exception is age 18 if blacks are compared with Southern Europeans). These declines continue into the early-adult ages, with blacks having the lowest enrollment rates except for a slight reversal among those in their early thirties. In short, the black enrollment rates are lower than those groups of either Southern or Central—Eastern European origin.

There are some significant differences among these white groups, particularly in the college-age groups. The percentage enrolled in college or graduate studies is given in table 6.3. In all ages, less blacks are enrolled than are any of the white groups. At age 19, when nearly 10 percent of blacks are enrolled in college, nearly 25 percent of both second-generation Southern Europeans and native whites of native parentage are in college. For second-generation whites of Northwestern and Central—Eastern origin, the figures are, respectively, three and four times those of the black rates.

The results are so consistent as to leave little doubt that black

TABLE 6.2
PERCENTAGE ENROLLED IN SCHOOL, 1960

		Second-generation white			
Age	Native whites of native parentage	Northern or Western European origin	Central or Eastern European origin	Southern European origin	Black
5	44.5	56.9	66.6	59.8	41.8
6	83.8	90.6	92.8	92.8	78.6
7	97.4	97.4	97.4	97.4	95.0
8	98.0	98.2	97.5	97.6	96.2
9	98.1	98.0	97.8	98.3	96.6
10	98.1	97.9	97.5	97.4	96.5
11	98.0	97.7	96.7	97.4	96.3
12	97.8	98.0	98.0	97.3	96.0
13	97.3	97.4	97.3	96.1	94.6
14	95.8	96.1	96.3	95.5	92.0
15	93.5	95.1	94.5	93.1	87.9
16	87.3	90.9	91.0	85.4	80.2
17	76.9	81.6	82.9	72.4	65.9
18	51.0	53.3	59.4	45.2	45.4
19	32.9	39.0	46.4	32.6	28.7
20	23.8	31.4	39.3	23.4	17.3
21	19.0	24.7	30.6	17.6	12.1
22	12.3	16.7	20.2	12.1	8.3
23	9.7	13.1	17.7	8.2	7.0
24	8.1	10.5	14.6	8.1	5.7
25–29	6.1	7.8	8.1	6.1	4.7
30–34	3.1	3.8	3.6	2.7	3.4

SOURCE: U.S. Bureau of the Census, 1964a, table 1.

enrollment rates in 1960 were far behind the new European groups. Indeed, of all the white groups, second-generation whites of Central–Eastern European origin had by far the greatest propensity to attend college. Although Northwestern Europeans exceeded the Southern Europeans, it should be noted that the latter were far ahead of blacks and more or less at about the same level as whites of third or later generation in the United States. To be sure, these tables have certain limitations. Not only are the data cross-sectional, but nothing is indicated about progress, performance, or continuation in school.

TABLE 6.3
PERCENTAGE ENROLLED IN COLLEGE, 1960

| Age | Native whites of native parentage | Second-generation white | | | Black |
		Northern or Western European origin	Central or Eastern European origin	Southern European origin	
17	1.8	4.2	10.3	2.5	1.6
18	20.0	27.4	37.7	19.0	7.4
19	23.9	31.6	40.0	24.0	9.4
20	19.7	26.8	35.3	19.3	8.9
21	15.7	21.1	27.3	13.6	6.5
22	10.0	14.1	18.0	9.6	4.3
23	7.2	11.3	16.2	6.3	3.2
24	5.9	8.6	11.9	5.2	2.3
25–29	4.0	6.1	6.8	4.1	1.9
30–34	1.7	2.5	2.5	1.5	1.1

SOURCE: See table 6.2

Historical Pattern

For a variety of reasons, it is difficult to compare current levels of educational achievement with earlier periods. For one, it is only since the 1940 Census that information was gathered on the years of school completed by the adult population. Second, even when enrollment figures were available for earlier decades, they were not always recorded for specific white ethnic groups. As a consequence, a direct comparison with earlier periods is more difficult than one might otherwise expect. There are, of course, figures on illiteracy going a long way back and we pay attention to these later in the chapter.

There is some indication, however, that blacks were faring comparatively poorer than the second generation, although doing not too badly when compared with the immigrant generation. Using the cross-sectional school attendance data available for specific ages in 1920, one can determine the years of schooling that would be achieved by each group if they maintained their specific rates in each age. The arithmetic mean numbers of years for various male groups are: native whites of native parentage, 10.6; second-generation whites, 10.3; foreign-born whites, 8.9; blacks, 8.2 years. Education among second-generation whites on the average was slightly more than two years greater than among blacks.

The gap between foreign-born children living in the United States and blacks was not so great but still favored the former. Among girls, the average is also highest for native whites of native parentage, 10.7, followed by the second-generation whites, 10.2. In this case the black average of 8.7 is slightly greater than the average of 8.6 for foreign-born white girls. Both blacks and whites of older origin have higher educational averages for females than males. Among the foreign-born whites and second-generation whites, the average length of schooling is longer for males than for females.

Unfortunately, data are not available on the white groups subdivided by European origin, and hence these results are inconclusive. Indeed, examination of these rates for specific cities in 1920 indicates that educational attainment rates for both second- and first-generation whites tend to vary inversely with the percentage of new Europeans living in the city.

An examination of median schooling among various adult-age groups in 1960 provides another way of inferring trends over time. Considering that schooling is both an irreversible status characteristic and is fairly well completed by early-adult ages (particularly in terms of any possible effect on median figures), the schooling reported by the older adult ages in 1960 provides some clue to the relative positions of the groups in earlier periods. Indeed, it would be a perfect indication if there was no differential in outmigration or mortality and if schooling and age are reported accurately.

Table 6.4 gives the cross-tabulation between age and education for males and females among nine specific South–Central–Eastern European groups as well as for blacks. Bear in mind that these data refer to only the second-generation component of each white ethnic group and, further, that blacks living and/or born in the South are not distinguished from their northern compatriots. Without exception, blacks in each age- and sex-specific category have less years of schooling than any of the comparable second-generation white groups. However, the concern here is in making inferences about changes over time through the comparison of specific age groupings.

A highly suggestive pattern unfolds when educational changes by age are examined for each ethnic group. Starting with men who were 65 and over in 1960 (born in 1895 or earlier), one finds that the median black education, 4.2 years, is far below the medians for the new European groups, which range from 7.5 to 8.7. Indeed, the medians among Austrians, Hungarians, Lithuanians, and Russians are at least twice the level for blacks. For the next cohort, those born between 1895 and 1915, the number of years of schooling rises for all the groups, but it is most

TABLE 6.4
MEDIAN SCHOOL YEARS COMPLETED, 1960

Sex and Age	Black	Second-generation white								
		Austria	Poland	Czechoslovakia	Hungary	Yugoslavia	Lithuania	Finland	USSR	Italy
Male:										
25–34	9.8	12.6	12.4	12.4	12.5	12.4	12.8	12.5	13.6	12.2
35–44	8.5	12.2	11.5	11.9	12.0	12.0	12.3	12.2	12.7	11.4
45–64	6.5	9.9	8.9	8.8	9.7	9.1	10.5	8.9	12.0	8.9
65 and over	4.2	8.4	7.5	7.9	8.7	7.7	8.6	7.6	8.6	7.9
Female:										
25–34	10.6	12.5	12.3	12.4	12.4	12.4	12.5	12.5	12.7	12.2
35–44	9.0	12.2	11.3	11.8	12.0	12.1	12.2	12.3	12.4	11.3
45–64	7.4	9.7	8.7	8.8	9.5	8.9	9.9	10.4	11.9	8.7
65 and over	5.2	8.4	7.5	7.9	8.6	8.1	8.5	8.4	8.6	7.9

SOURCES: U.S. Bureau of the Census, 1963b, table 19; 1965, table 12.

rapid for blacks. The jump between 4.2 and 6.5 years, an increase of 2.3 years, is in excess of the increase observed for all but one of the new European groups. Thus the absolute gap between the new Europeans and blacks declined, although the former still enjoyed a substantial edge. However, this pattern is not repeated when persons born in the 1915–1925 decade are compared with their group's preceding cohort. The cohort of black men born during and shortly after the World War I period do not advance as rapidly as most of the second-generation groups. Although the educational medians go up for all of the groups, the substantial rise for blacks of 2.0 years (from 6.5 to 8.5) is smaller than the change in seven out of the nine new European groups. Thus, the educational advantage for the new Europeans is in most cases widened. Among the next cohort, those born in the 1925–1935 decade and thus 25–34 years of age in 1960, the jump of 1.3 years for black men over the 8.5 median in the preceding cohort is larger than the absolute gain for any of the new European groups. Thus, once again, there is the process in which blacks are catching up to the new Europeans, although their levels are still distinctly below that of second-generation members of the new European groups.

The pattern for women is almost identical. In all groups, each cohort's educational level exceeds previous cohorts. Likewise, in all cases, median education for each of the new groups is higher than for blacks of the same age. These changes form an almost identical pattern to that observed for men. The advance of 2.2 years education among black women 45–64 compared with those 65 and over is greater than the gain registered among eight of the nine new European groups. However, the gap widens in the next cohort. In all but one case, women of South–Central–Eastern European origin who were born in the decade beginning with 1915 gain on the preceding cohort of compatriots more than the 1.6-year increase experienced by black women who were born in the same period. In the most extreme instance, the median for Yugoslav women increases from 8.9 to 12.1 years of education, a jump of 3.2 during a period when the increase for black women is only 1.6 years (from 7.4 to 9.0). Again, the pattern is reversed when comparisons are made between the two youngest cohorts. The 1.6-year gain for black women (from medians of 9.0 to 10.6) is greater than that experienced by women from any of the new European groups.

These results are very suggestive. On the one hand, the educational advantage enjoyed by at least the American-born children of the new European groups appears to be one that goes considerably back in time. However, observe that these data do not pertain to the educational situation of the immigrants themselves—a matter considered later in this chapter. All of the groups considered, black and new European, appear to have participated in the general societal process of increasing educational attainment. But most noteworthy is the irregular pattern of their gains. Among the older two generations considered, blacks were gaining more rapidly than were the new Europeans, thus closing the educational advantage enjoyed by the latter. This pattern is also found among the youngest two generations. However, when those born during or right after World War I are compared with the preceding cohort, one observes a period in which the new Europeans were actually widening their advantage over blacks. This peculiar period merits closer examination because it may provide important clues to the forces influencing black and new European education. A more detailed analysis is made in the next chapter, but first it is necessary to place the educational advantage of new European groups in a more general context based on the operation of certain important broad societal forces.

CAUSES

How does one account for the difference between blacks and the new European groups in their educational attainment? No single monolithic factor can be found; their achievement reflects both general educational developments in the United States during a long span of time, some substantial differences between the North and the South, as well as a variety of forces specifically affecting blacks or the new European groups. The differential rewards of education, in terms of occupation and income, also have a bearing because intergenerational shifts in education are influenced by the parental generation's education, occupation, and income. In turning to some of these causes, one must also recognize that their importance is of changing significance during the 100 years since 1880.

LOCATION: NORTH VERSUS SOUTH

Directly or indirectly, one of the central factors accounting for the educational differences is the concentration of the new European groups in the urban centers of the North compared with the concentration of blacks in the South during most of the period. As a result of the fact that the South lags behind the North in economic wealth, and because education is largely financed by local and state revenues, the entire South has been placed at a disadvantage in educational resources. Based on statistics for 1917–1918, Reisner (1922, p. 494) found that the eight states with the lowest amount of taxable wealth per student (below $5,000) were all in the South. Likewise, among the twelve states lowest in their ability to support schools in the mid-1930s, ten were southern (Wilkerson, 1939, p. 48). Because of these economic differences, taxes would have to be considerably higher in the South to provide a level of support equal to that available in some of the northern states. In 1930, for example, Alabama would have had to require a tax rate six times greater than that of California in order to provide as much money per child as the latter state (Bond, 1934, p. 228). Observing that approximately 5 percent of the national income was devoted to education in the 1930 period, Bond goes on to compare expenditures in Mississippi and California. He finds (pp. 228–229) that equalization would have required the former "to devote from 20 to 30 per cent of its total income from all purposes to education, and the other Southern states would have to do the same in but slightly smaller proportion. Not even our most advanced educational systems have found citizens willing to levy such an immense tax upon their resources in the provision of public schools for the children of their communities."

The South lagged behind the remainder of the nation in a variety of important educational developments that worked to the disadvantage of blacks. The provision for free elementary schools occurred much earlier in the North and West, being almost the universal practice in these regions by the time of the Civil War (Reisner, 1922, pp. 398–400). By contrast, at that time, statewide systems of public education were available in almost no parts of the South. Likewise, before 1900 there were relatively few high schools in the South. Wealthier southerners used private schools and academies to prepare their sons for college and private finishing schools for their daughters. Whereas the rapid expansion of high schools in the South did not begin until the first decade of the twentieth century, the provision for public high schools had already spread in the urban North (Good, 1962, pp. 249–250). The development of compulsory school attendance laws and their strict enforcement also occurred considerably later in the South. But as we will see shortly, this was related to some specific racial and ethnic factors.

The educational advantage gained by the new Europeans concentrating in the urban North is illustrated by a comparison of the illiteracy rates among various segments of the white population. Examining the census data for each decade between 1890 and 1920, Willcox (1931, p. 120) reports that second-generation white children have consistently lower illiteracy rates than do whites of older origins (third or later). In 1890, the differences are spectacular, with only 16 percent of the second-generation children 10–14 years old reported as illiterate, compared with fully two-thirds of native whites of native parentage. By 1920, illiteracy had declined enormously, but still only 5 percent of second-generation children were illiterate compared with 11 percent of third- or later-generation white children. The geographical origin of these differences is nicely illustrated in table 6.5. Throughout the Northeast and in the Pacific states there is little or no difference between second- and later-generation whites. In two of the remaining regions, the former have lower rates (presumably reflecting their greater concentration in the urban centers of these regions), and in two regions the native whites of native parentage have lower rates. The sharp differential in the West–South–Central states reflects the sizable numbers of second-generation Mexicans present (Willcox, 1931, pp. 121–122).

The pattern is actually more complex than this, but these results do suggest a general educational advantage to be gained from locating outside the South. Insofar as blacks were heavily concentrated in the South—particularly in the rural areas—and the new Europeans were located in the urban North, blacks were placed at a disadvantage even if the South had been color blind. As we will see, the economic handicap faced by the South was one of the factors contributing to the widespread and intensive educational discrimination against blacks in the South that created an educational obstacle far in excess of what might be expected solely on the basis of regional differences.

TABLE 6.5
PERCENTAGE ILLITERATE AMONG NATIVE WHITE CHILDREN
10–14 YEARS OF AGE, 1920

| | Native whites | |
Region	Native parentage	Foreign parentage
New England	0.3	0.2
Middle Atlantic	0.2	0.2
East-North Central	0.2	0.2
West-North Central	0.3	0.3
South Atlantic	2.1	0.5
East-South Central	2.7	1.2
West-South Central	2.3	13.4
Mountain	0.7	1.1
Pacific	0.2	0.3

SOURCE: Willcox, 1931, table 40, p. 121.

ASSIMILATION AND "PLACE": CONTRASTING IDEOLOGIES OF EDUCATION

Education for the new European groups in the urban North was' approached from an entirely different perspective than was education for blacks in the South. Faced with a substantial flow of immigration from new sources, the educational institutions of the urban North were expected to provide a central mechanism for assimilation. Universal education, which admittedly owed its impetus to earlier forces (Mann, 1968), was to provide the means for teaching the English language, develop loyalty to the new nation through an understanding of its history and opportunities, create the habits of dress, cleanliness, and demeanor that were desired, and generate a literate population that could vote wisely and also contribute productively to the labor force.

By contrast, the provision of education for blacks in the South was made reluctantly and was of relatively poor quality. Preparation for good citizenship was largely irrelevant as blacks were disfranchised and, moreover, the "place" envisioned for blacks in the economic and social structure of the South was hardly compatible with a classical education. Because blacks were to be trained for traditional service and laboring roles (Wilkerson, 1939, pp. 106–108), the concept developed of a "special education" for blacks "that would prepare Negroes for the caste position prescribed for them by white Southerners" (Bullock, 1967, p. 89).

Intelligence and Education

The issue of inherent differences in intelligence between the races is something of a red herring. Not only is it extremely difficult to separate out the environmental from the biological contributions to performance on such tests, but most tasks that people are asked to perform, whether it be at work or in school or in fulfilling traditional familial obligations, do not require the intellectual capacity of a Newton or Einstein. Nevertheless, the notions of racial differences in inherent intelligence are related to the philosophies of education under consideration here. Although it was not uncommon during the period under consideration for whites of Northwestern European origin to view both the new European groups and the freed slaves as intellectually inferior, in general there was a propensity to place blacks as particularly low on the ethnic intelligence scale.

A description of black intelligence, by a northern Civil War general who later founded Hampton Institute, provides a useful way to summarize these widespread misconceptions held after the Civil War.

> [The Negro is] capable of acquiring knowledge to any degree, and, to a certain age, at least, with about the same facility as white children; but lacks power to assimilate and digest it. The Negro matures sooner than the white, but does not have his steady development of mental strength up to advanced years. He is a child of the tropics, and the differentiation of races goes deeper than the skin. [S. C. Armstrong, in Bullock, 1967, p. 76]

As the various types of tests were administered to blacks and whites, a body of social science literature was built up in the twentieth century which tended to interpret lower scores by blacks as a reflection of their inherent abilities rather than as a consequence of environmental conditions (see the review by Viteles, 1928). The scores of southern whites on standardized intelligence tests, lower than those for northern whites, were apt to be interpreted as a reflection of the inferior environment and school conditions in the South. Black–white differences, on the other hand, were interpreted as a function of inherent racial characteristics. (See Thompson [1928] for an excellent criticism and reanalysis of some of these earlier studies.) Thus poor performance by blacks was taken as further justification for the provision for minimal educational facilities rather than as evidence of the harmful consequences stemming from the failure to provide suitable facilities and schools.

Compulsory School Attendance

Legislation requiring school attendance until some minimal age, and its enforcement, provide glaring instances of how black education in the South was approached so differently from the education of the European newcomers in the North. The first compulsory school attendance law was passed in 1852 by Massachusetts, to be sure long before the great flow of South–Central–Eastern Europeans. Moreover, before 1880 some 15 additional northern states had also passed such legislation. Many of these were areas receiving substantial Irish influxes and non-English-speaking immigrants from sources such as Germany. Nevertheless, there is little doubt that the desire to assimilate the new European groups—from whatever source—was an important factor in the passage of such laws in the North. On the other hand, indifference to black education was operating to delay such legislation in the South. Among the 14 states that had not passed compulsory attendance legislation by 1902, except for the marginal case of Missouri, all were southern, border, or southwestern states (based on the listing reported in Thompson, 1920, p. 283).

> There is no doubt that in the Southern States the presence of Negroes in large numbers was a strong deterrent to the enactment of compulsory education laws in those States. It is not due purely to chance that of the 16 States (excluding the District of Columbia) popularly considered Southern, none had enacted such legislation prior to 1893 and only 3 prior to 1905. In the North, where the foreign born constitute a very large proportion of the population, the problem of assimilation has necessitated very rigid requirements, with strict enforcement. [Ross, 1924, p. 39]

Ross (p. 57) later suggests that at least in the 1920s it was the rigid enforcement of these laws that kept the immigrant children in school—given the economic pulls to obtain employment. By contrast, even after the passage of compulsory attendance laws in the South, they were not vigorously enforced for black children—particularly in rural areas. To be sure, many criticisms can be made of the educational programs provided for the immigrants (Thompson, 1920). Indeed, as the reader will see, the evidence is fairly clear that foreign-born children arriving in the United States during the heyday of the new immigration were more or less lost as far as education was concerned. For their American-born children and later generations, however, the urban North was far more successful in providing at least some minimal education than were the institutions of the South in providing educational services for the former slaves and their descendants.

BLACK EDUCATION IN THE SOUTH

Not only were there relatively few public schools in the South prior to the Civil War, but severe restrictions were placed on the education of slaves. With some exceptions, the education of slaves was prohibited by state law and in actual practice. Georgia passed laws in 1770, 1829, and 1853 that prohibited their education; Virginia in 1849; and South Carolina in 1740, 1800, and in 1834. The latter prohibitions also applied to free blacks (for a summary of antebellum conditions, see Bond, 1934, chapter 9). In some places, the education of free blacks was permitted and blacks were successful in establishing their own schools. In other instances, these schools were conducted secretly (DuBois, 1901, p. 21). Among free adult blacks, according to the 1850 Census, fairly sizable proportions were literate, albeit less than among southern whites (Bond, 1934, p. 178). The percentage illiterate ranged from the low 20s in Alabama and South Carolina to 60 percent and higher elsewhere in the South. Assuming that no more than 1 percent of the enslaved black population was literate, Bond (1934, pp. 179—180) estimates that at least 93 percent of all adult blacks were illiterate at the time of the Civil War.

Black education showed promising signs of gaining ground after the Civil War. The Freedmen's Bureau pursued its educational goals with great vigor. By 1870 there were 247,000 students in more than 4,000 schools (Franklin, 1956, pp. 304—305). To be sure, there was substantial opposition to public schools for blacks: economic pressures were applied against blacks; whites opposed mixed schools; and some whites resented payment of taxes for the education of blacks (Bullock, 1967, pp. 41—43, 54—55); but a number of progressive steps toward the establishment of adequate educational facilities occurred. South Carolina's constitutional convention of 1868 established a nonsegregated system of public compulsory education; Alabama and Georgia had one year earlier at least established public schools (saying nothing about either segregation or compulsory attendance); and various other southern states established a public school system which would be available to blacks in their constitutional conventions (Bullock, 1967, pp. 49—51). Of considerable importance in establishing a black educational system were pressures from the federal government as well as the voting strength that blacks enjoyed for a brief period after the Civil War (Bullock, 1967, pp. 58—59).

Most noteworthy, particularly in terms of later developments, there was to be no discrimination in the funding of black and white education. During this period, proposals to divide taxes according to the racial origins of payers (and hence, to reduce sharply funds for blacks) were consistently defeated (Newbold, 1928, p. 211). Expenditures for black and white pupils were identical or, at worst, only slightly different. With blacks comprising 38 percent of North Carolina's public school enrollment in 1873, a third of state support went to their schools (Bullock, 1967, p. 86). School terms were of the same length and teachers received about the same salary. Per capita expenditures for blacks in 1876 were 95 percent of the amount spent per white student in North Carolina. Likewise, the average school term in Alabama for blacks in 1876, 77 days, was four days less than the average for white schools (Bullock, 1967, p. 87). In the period between 1875 and 1890, according to calculations on a per capita basis by Bond (1934, p. 153), for every dollar spent on black children for their teachers' salaries, most commonly from about $1.10 to $1.20 was spent on the teachers of white children. Indeed, per capita expenditures were higher for black teachers in the 1875—1876 and

1878–1879 school years. Although such ratios do indicate an advantage enjoyed by whites, one should bear in mind that by the first decade of the twentieth century, the ratio of black-white per capita expenditures would exceed six-to-one.

For those inclined to interpret the relatively low levels of black educational achievement in terms of values and norms, the evidence for the postbellum period suggests a very different outlook. The number of black children enrolled in southern public schools increased at an impressive rate. Far from indicating apathy toward education, enrollment mounted rapidly: 91,000 in 1866; 150,000 in 1870; 572,000 in 1877; 785,000 in 1880; and slightly more than a million by 1884 (DuBois, 1901, p. 43). Over 60 percent of all black children 5 to 12 years of age were enrolled for school by 1865 (Bullock, 1967, p. 29). The eagerness of blacks in Louisiana is suggested by this account of the Reconstruction period:

> When the collection of the general tax for colored schools was suspended in Louisiana by military order, the consternation of the colored population was intense. Petitions began to pour in. I saw one from the plantations across the river, at least thirty feet in length, representing ten thousand negroes. It was affecting to examine it, and note the names and marks (x) of such a long list of parents, ignorant themselves, but begging that their children might be educated; promising that from beneath their present burdens and out of their extreme poverty, they would pay for it. [Quoted in Dubois, 1901, p. 25]

In some instances, black enrollment rates were actually higher than for whites in the same area; in other cases, although lower, the rates were still impressive evidence of an early eagerness that operated despite a variety of economic and social pressures. In Florida, although blacks were about 30 percent of the population, it was not until 1888 that white school enrollment even exceeded the black number (Bond, 1934, p. 90). In South Carolina's normal school, at one point open to both races, the majority of students were black (Bullock, 1967, p. 56). As late as 1900, the *Atlanta Constitution* reported higher attendance among blacks than whites in some of the overwhelmingly white Piedmont counties in South Carolina. In York and Fairfield counties there were actually more blacks in school than whites; in Spartanburg, with as many as four times as many whites, there were 8,300 whites in school compared with 5,100 blacks (DuBois, 1901, p. 66).

Considering the conditions blacks faced only a few years earlier, their enrollment is impressive even if the white rates were higher. By 1870, 50 percent of the black children were attending school in Arkansas, compared with 63 percent of the whites. In Mississippi, 39 percent of black school-age children were enrolled for school (with a slightly better average daily attendance record than the white pupils), compared with 52 percent of white children. These figures for scattered areas are hardly conclusive, but they raise serious questions about commonly held notions that would ascribe to values and norms much of the immigrant-black difference in educational attainment.

The Beginning of the End

Although many criticisms could be raised, the Reconstruction period was marked by substantial educational progress for blacks through the combined activities of the states, the Freedmen's Bureau, missionaries, and black self-help efforts. A combination of events was soon to send black education reeling at a time when education was expanding rapidly in the United States. The loss of black political power in the South was one of the key factors in this demise and provides an excellent illustration of the complex two-way interaction between a group's political power and its social and economic position.

The rapid increase in white school enrollment between 1880 and 1895 was one of the elements generating this change. Unprecedented demand from whites overwhelmed the existing facilities and the revenues available to support their growing needs. In the brief period of 15 years, between 1880 and 1895, white school enrollment in ten southern states examined by Bond (1934, p. 91) more than doubled, rising from 1 million to 2.2 million. Yet, if anything, state funds available in many southern states were actually declining. Between 1875 and 1880, expenditures declined by 21 percent in nine southern states while enrollment increased 33 percent (Bond, 1934, p. 92). At this time the South sought to meet rapidly mounting demands for education while hindered by a depressed and war-battered economy.

At the same time, black political power in the South was beginning to decline as whites regained their monopoly (see chapter 3). This made the educational funds for black children, initially distributed on a more-or-less nondiscriminatory basis, an increasingly tempting and vulnerable target. This same period was marked by a series of court rulings favorable to segregation as well as the decline of black political power in the South (see, for example, Bullock, 1967, chapter 3). Compatible with these developments was the notion that black educational needs were different from those of whites, and hence an equal distribution of funds for both was not necessary. A special "Negro education" would be developed that would be less expensive, provide less of the standard academic fare, and help train blacks for particular roles that the white South could accept.

The growing white educational needs, the weak economic resources of the South, a decline in black political power, and a basic lack of sympathy among many whites for quality black education was extraordinarily damaging to black education. By 1885, 70 percent of the white children in Mississippi were enrolled in the public school system. Between 1877 and 1885, the average monthly salary of white and black teachers had been identical. After passage of a law permitting differential teaching certificates and allowing for a salary range with each certificate, equality in expenditures for teachers declined at once. With a couple of exceptions, the average salary of black teachers declined each year from 1886 through 1895, whereas white salaries increased for several years. In the 1890s black teachers were earning approximately two-thirds of the average white teacher's salary (Bond, 1934, pp. 94–98). Per capita expenditures for white children in Alabama until 1890 had been only slightly in excess of those for black children. With the passage of legislation giving each county some option in the allocation of funds to the schools of each group, for each dollar spent on black children the discrepancy moved from $1.18 for each white in 1890 to $5.83 per white child in 1909 (Bond, 1934, p. 113).

The Gory Details

In one form or another the funds available for black education in the South have been substantially below those available for whites in the same region. When one considers the added fact that the northern industrial states, where the new European groups and their descendants were concentrated, have resources far in excess of those available even to southern whites, the disparities in educational opportunity between blacks and South–Central–Eastern Europeans are enormous.

Table 6.6 provides detailed comparisons between the educational situation facing blacks and whites in the South during various periods in this century. Because the data are not always consistent over time in either the southern states included or the exact meaning given to a measurement, interpretations of changes over time require caution. In all cases, however, blacks are at a disadvantage.

The average black school term, for example, was only 80 percent as long as whites around 1910 and still no more than 90 percent in the mid-1930s. The educational implications of such a gap, persisting year

TABLE 6.6
Black and White Schooling in the South

Characteristic	Year	Black	White	Black percentage of white
School term (days)[a]	1909–10	101	128	79
	1928–29	144	164	88
	1935–36	146	167	87
Transportation to school (percentage of pupils)[b]	1929–30	0.6	17.4	3
	1944–45	11.0	37.9	29
	1952	31.6	45.5	69
Pupils per teacher[c]	1933–34	43	34	126
	1944–45	36	32	112
	1951–52	26	24	108
Elementary school teachers (percentage with post-high school education)[d] in rural areas	1930–31	77	94	82
	1930–31	64	95	67
Teachers (percentage with four years of college)[e]	1940	29	53	55
(average years of college)	1951–52	3.5	3.8	92
Value of sites, buildings, & equipment (per pupil)[f]	1915	$ 7	$ 30	25
	1935–36	$ 36	$183	20
	1940	$ 34	$162	21
Capital outlays (per pupil)[g]	1940	$ 0.99	$ 4.37	23
	1952	$ 29.58	$ 36.25	82

Annual expenditures				
(per capita state average)[h]	1914–15	$ 4.01	$ 10.82	37
	1929–30	$ 15.86	$ 42.39	37
(per pupil in daily attendance)	1935–36	$ 17.04	$ 49.30	35
	1939–40	$ 18.82	$ 58.69	32
in metropolitan schools	1952	$126.45	$166.32	76
in rural schools	1952	$ 85.10	$138.24	62
Teacher's salaries				
(average monthly)[i]	1909–10	$ 32.67	$ 60.60	54
	1928–29	$ 72.78	$118.01	62
(total in elementary schools)	1935–36	$510	$833	61

[a]Bullock, 1967, p. 177; Wilkerson, 1939, p. 9.

[b]Wilkerson, 1939, p. 19; Simpson and Yinger, 1958, p. 618.

[c]Wilkerson, 1939, p. 21; Simpson and Yinger, 1958, p. 618.

[d]Wilkerson, 1939, p. 22.

[e]Marden and Meyer, 1962, p. 245; Simpson and Yinger, 1958, p. 618.

[f]Bullock, 1967, p. 182; Wilkerson, 1939, p. 30; Marden and Meyer, 1962, p. 245.

[g]Simpson and Yinger, 1958, p. 617.

[h]Bullock, 1967, p. 180; Myrdal, 1944, p. 339; Marden and Meyer, 1962, p. 245; Simpson and Yinger, 1958, p. 616.

[i]Bullock, 1967, p. 181; Myrdal, 1944, p. 319.

after year, is by no means trivial. The gap of 21 days in the mid-1930s is about one school month. This accumulated through the years

> to create a tremendous quantitative handicap for Negro pupils. It means that the average Negro pupil in the South must spend 9.2 years to complete 8 elementary grades with the same amount of schooling afforded for the average white pupil in 8 years. . . . In terms of the number of days pupils actually attend school, the accumulated handicap for the average Negro pupil amounts to almost an additional one-half year. [Wilkerson, 1939, pp. 12–13]

By 1952, black and white school terms were of fairly equal length in the South (Marden and Meyer, 1962, p. 287).

Discrepancies in the educational background of teachers were quite substantial until recently. Inspection of table 6.6 indicates that even in 1940 the percentage of black high school teachers with at least four years of college is only about half that for white teachers. By the early 1950s, these differences had declined substantially in the South. To be sure, the qualifications of black school teachers are in constant interaction with the educational opportunities available to earlier cohorts, the salaries offered to black college graduates, and the criteria used for employment. Although hard data are not available, one encounters a number of earlier accounts of whites being extremely casual in their hiring of teachers for black children.

Blacks were particularly disadvantaged in terms of the diffusion of new educational developments. The lag in the provision of high schools, as well as their inadequacy, is sufficiently important to consider separately. But other new developments were also restricted to whites. As table 6.6 indicates, blacks received an incredibly small proportion of the funds available for bus transportation to schools. This is of particular importance in rural areas where many blacks were located, as well as areas where schools were at considerable distances. In rural North Carolina, for example, where per capita expenditures for white teachers were three times the expenditures for black teachers in 1929–1930, the ratio for transportation funds was 30 to 1 in favor of whites (Bond, 1934, pp. 170–171).

Salaries for teachers of black children were substantially lower than for whites through much of this century, ranging between 54 and 62 percent in the three decades shown in table 6.6. There is good reason to believe that these disparities in salaries are not solely a function of the generally lower levels of preparation among black teachers in that period but also reflect discriminatory payments (see, e.g., Bond, 1934, pp. 93–94). The practice of paying higher salaries to white teachers than to black teachers with the same level of training had declined considerably by the 1950s. In 1952 there was still a yearly difference of $352 on the average in favor of the former, with considerable variation between states. The greatest difference was in Mississippi, $982, whereas black salaries were slightly higher in North Carolina, Oklahoma, Tennessee, and Virginia. These figures reflect higher average training coupled with a greater concentration of black teachers in the better-paying urban areas in these states (Simpson and Yinger, 1958, pp. 617–618).

Other ramifications of the discriminatory educational policies in the southern states include higher pupil–teacher ratios in black schools and sharply discrepant expenditures for buildings and equipment. In all three periods examined, 1915, 1935–1936, and 1940, the value of the physical plant and equipment available to black students was only about 20 to 25 percent of that available per white student (see table 6.6). Likewise, new capital outlays in 1940 were considerably lower for black students. However, this had improved considerably by 1952.

In terms of the overall expenditures for education, up until at least World War II, blacks appear to have received from about one-third to two-fifths of the amount spent for each white student. In the early 1950s this discrepancy had declined, although there was still a substantial disadvantage for blacks in the metropolitan areas and even more for those in the rural South (table 6.6). Thus, whether considered in general or specific terms, the conclusion remains unaltered. Beginning late in the nineteenth century and through most of this century, the resources of the South have not been equitably divided between blacks and whites but have been disporportionately allocated to white schools. Because much of this period has been marked by an extremely high concentration of blacks in the South, their educational advancement has suffered from enormous handicaps. This is particularly the case when comparisons are made with the new European groups and their descendants who were concentrated in the more prosperous urban North.

High Schools

Although public high schools developed in the United States long before the Civil War (see Good, 1962, chapter 8), their spread was relatively slight until the 1870s (Reisner, 1922, p. 454). Around 1890 about 7 percent of the high school-age population was enrolled in public or secondary school, but by 1920 virtually one-third of the population was enrolled, and more than one-half only a decade later. At the outbreak of World War II, close to three-quarters of the population was enrolled (based on rough approximations from statistics reproduced in Good [1962, p. 253]). These rates, at least several decades ago, were incredibly high when compared with European nations (Wilkerson, 1939, p. 35).

An examination of both the spread and quality of black high school education in the South provides a particularly important illustration of the lag experienced by blacks through much of the period under consideration. When one considers that public high school education for whites in the South lagged behind the North to begin with (Good, 1962, pp. 249–250), the results for blacks were disastrous. For example, by 1934 the percentage of southern white high school-aged children enrolled in the public high schools was close to the national average. But for black children in the South, their rate was only a third of the national average (Wilkerson, 1939, p. 37).[3]

In explaining the relatively low participation of southern blacks in secondary education, Wilkerson lists such causal factors as inferior instruction, questionable promotion policies, inaccessibility of schools, and the need of impoverished youngsters to obtain gainful employment rather than remain in school. But the most important factor, argues Wilkerson (1939, pp. 38–39), is the absence of secondary schools available to blacks. The first few decades of this century were character-ized by a very small number of high schools available to blacks. When the DuBois and Dill survey was published in 1911, such major centers as Atlanta, Savannah, and Augusta had no provision for black high school education (p. 127). In the 1915–1916 school year, not only were there only 64 public high schools available for blacks in 18 southern states, but more than half of these were concentrated in four states (Kentucky, West Virginia, Tennessee, and Texas). Only 8,700 blacks were enrolled in public high schools. There were 216 private high schools open to blacks (Myrdal, 1944, p. 950; Payne, 1970, p. 12). Some improvement in the number of available facilities was observed ten years later when there were 801 black schools offering from one to four years of high school work. Total enrollment was 68,606, but the number of fourth-year graduates was only 6,435 (Davis, 1928, p. 130).

Wilkerson observes that "the marked extension of public secondary education which has characterized the Nation during the past half century did not begin significantly to affect Negroes in the Southern States until about 1920" (1939, p. 41). But progress was not altogether satisfactory. In 1930, there were still some 230 southern counties, with populations that were at least 12.5 percent black, that offered no public high schools for members of this group. These counties included 160,000 blacks of high school age. Another 195 counties in the South failed to provide *four*-year high schools, and this affected nearly 200,000 more black children of high school age. Thus, 30 percent of the counties in 15 southern states failed to provide four-year high schools for blacks in 1930 (data reported in Wilkerson, 1939, pp. 40–41). The situation was particularly bad for rural counties. Blacks were about 24 percent of the total rural population in 18 southern states in 1930, but in 1933–1934 only about 7 percent of the rural high schools were available to them and blacks comprised only 4 percent of the rural high school enrollment (Myrdal, 1944, p. 1429). Nevertheless, the number of public high schools available to blacks continued to rise during the pre-World War II period, increasing from 801 in 1925–1926 to 2,305 ten years later (Myrdal, 1944, p. 950).

This survey of the availability of high schools for blacks in the South, dismal as the results may be, actually understates the disadvantages blacks faced in obtaining access to this crucial educational development. DuBois and Dill (1911, p. 129) point out that many of the public high schools early in the century were "high schools" in name only, actually offering little or no work above the grade-school level. "Georgia, for instance, is credited with eleven public high schools for Negroes. As a matter of fact there is not in the whole state a single public high school for Negroes with a four years' course above the eighth grade." According to Bullock (1967, p. 123), as late as 1910 not one of the black high schools was approved for two years of high school-level work. When one considers that there was not yet one eighth grade rural public school available to blacks, the high school situation is hardly surprising. By World War I there were no public standard high schools for blacks aside from a very small number in the large cities and some of the state institutions (Newbold, 1928, p. 213). In 1916, only 47 of the public high schools had four-year courses of study (Brown, 1944, pp. 21–22). Even in 1926–1927 there were only 167 public four-year accredited high schools for blacks and 84 private ones in 16 southern states. Altogether, they had graduated 4,910 students that year. Even this represented a substantial increment, as two years earlier there were but 98 accredited four-year public high schools (based on data reported in Newbold [1928, p. 214]). Even then there was not a single accredited high school for blacks, public or private, in two states with substantial black populations, Alabama and South Carolina. Other important states such as Florida, Georgia, and Mississippi offered, respectively, 2, 6, and 11 accredited four-year high schools. Compared with the immigrant groups in the North, literally generations of blacks were prevented from using education as a stepping stone for upward mobility.

State accreditation of secondary schools for blacks preceded approval by a regional association, the Southern Association of College and

Secondary Schools. If the latter's standards are used, the situation is even worse. Accreditation of black high schools did not begin until 1931 when 20 high schools in Alabama, Florida, Georgia, Kentucky, Mississippi, North Carolina, and Virginia gained approval. Of this small number, 12 were private high schools. As recently as 1942, there were less than 100 approved high schools on the Southern Association's list (72 public and 21 private). There were about 13 times as many approved white high schools as there were those for blacks in 1942 (Brown, 1944, pp. 3–5, 186–187).

Ecological Factors

Much of the situation reported above reflects systematic discrimination against blacks in the allocation of the limited monetary resources available for education in the South. Through a combination of ecological factors, this discrimination was most severe in those parts of the region where blacks were most heavily concentrated. First, the most poverty-stricken areas tend to be those with the largest proportion of black residents. Second, the advantages to whites in diverting funds from blacks increase with the proportion of blacks in the area. Suppose, for example, there is $1.00 per student available in school districts with varying racial composition. Further, suppose that all of the funds are allocated to white schools. In a locale that is 90 per cent white, allocation of all the funds to whites will give each student $1.11. In a district that is 50 per cent white, the same policy will give each white student $2.00. And in a school district consisting of only 10 per cent whites, freezing out blacks will give each white student $10.00. Thus, the immediate net reward to whites for discrimination rises at an increasing rate with the percentage of blacks in the population.[4]

For 11 southern states in 1930, table 6.7 gives the black–white ratio of per capita school expenditures (column 1), an index of economic resources in the state (column 2), and the black percentage of the population (column 3). Using a simple rank-order measure of association, Kendall's tau, the correlation between percentage black and wealth is -.53. This indicates that blacks are indeed relatively more concentrated in the poorer southern states. Moreover, compared to whites in the state, black per capita school expenditures are directly associated with the state's wealth, tau is .53. There is also an extremely high inverse relation between the percentage of blacks in the state and the degree that blacks receive their proportionate share of educational funds, tau is -.78. The partial tau between percentage black and percentage of expenditures received by blacks remains substantially negative even after the

TABLE 6.7
SCHOOL EXPENDITURES FOR BLACKS IN SOUTHERN STATES, 1930

State	Black—white ratio of per capita expenditures	Index of economic resources	Black percentage of population
Alabama	.36	$2133	35.7
Arkansas	.40	2288	25.8
Florida	.31	4142	29.4
Georgia	.28	2266	36.8
Louisiana	.33	3263	36.9
Maryland	.71	6641	16.9
Mississippi	.21	1909	50.2
North Carolina	.48	2641	29.0
Oklahoma	.79	3703	7.2
South Carolina	.22	2149	45.6
Texas	.45	4143	14.7

SOURCE: Bond, 1934, pp. 195, 225, 227.

wealth in each state is taken into account, -.69. This suggests that states that discriminate most against blacks are also the states with the greatest concentrations of this group.

Based on data reported by DuBois (1901, p. 87) for 16 southern states and the District of Columbia in 1899 and 1900, one also finds that the relative equality of funding for black schools compared with white tends to decline with the percentage of blacks in the population (tau between black percentage of the population and the equality in funding is -.66). Perhaps the most dramatic illustration of the increasing inequities blacks face in the heavily black areas is provided by the expenditures for black and white school teachers' salaries cross-tabulated by the black percentage of the county's school population. Because this table was unfortunately buried in the footnotes to Myrdal's monumental volume, it is reproduced here.

Expenditures for black school teachers, with one exception, decline regularly as the percentage of blacks in the county goes up. In counties where blacks are less than 12.5 percent of the population, median expenditures are $8.62; on the other extreme, expenditures are merely $2.12 in counties where blacks are at least three-quarters of the population. The very opposite holds for whites: Per capita expenditures for teachers in white schools mount as the proportion of blacks increases. In counties with the smallest percentage of blacks, the median for teachers is $14.31. This is virtually half of the figure for white teachers in counties that are at least three-fourths black ($28.50). To be sure, expenditures for

TABLE 6.8
POPULATION COMPOSITION AND EXPENDITURES FOR TEACHERS, 1930–1931

	Number of counties	Median expenditures for teachers' salaries in counties with specified proportion of Negroes in the school population, aged 5–19							
Race		0 – 12.4%	12.5– 24.9%	25.0– 37.4%	37.5– 49.9%	50.0– 62.4%	62.5– 74.9%	75.0– 87.4%	87.5– 99.9%
Negro schools	521	$8.62	$5.28	$5.56	$4.46	$3.05	$2.85	$2.12	(only 1
White schools	526	14.31	16.87	21.25	21.25	22.58	26.25	28.50	county)

SOURCE: Myrdal (1944, p. 1271). (Derived from data reported in Bond, 1934, pp. 240-241).

white school teachers are always higher than for black school teachers, but the discrepancy increases sharply in those counties where blacks are a substantial part of the population.

In short, the disfranchisement of blacks meant not only the absence of any direct control over school policies and thus the inequitable distribution of resources in the South, but actually affected blacks most in the very parts of the South where they were numerically most important and hence possessed the greatest potential for political power. Indeed, those areas with the largest proportion of black inhabitants were the areas where whites gained the most from a dual school system.

BLACK COLLEGES AND HIGHER EDUCATION

Higher education is an important avenue of mobility for blacks, particularly *within* the black community, but the magnitude of its impact is not comparable to either the remainder of the population generally or the specific new European groups under consideration. Not only are high school graduation rates substantially lower for blacks, but even black high school graduates who seek the advantages of higher education are severely handicapped. There are, of course, certain general disadvantages that stem from the concentration of blacks in the lower socioeconomic strata and, in turn, the linkages between these characteristics and college attendance. Beyond this, there are some special racially specific handicaps for those black high school graduates who seek the advantages of higher education. On the one hand, the quality of black colleges has suffered from both inadequate financial support and the poor preparation of blacks who had attended substandard high schools and elementary schools. On the other hand, until very recently, there were admission barriers to the less-disadvantaged southern white institutions and many northern institutions. In addition, there were particularly severe obstacles to professional and graduate education. Beyond all of these obstacles, the simple fact is that college education during most of this period had a substantially poorer "payoff" for blacks than new Europeans in terms of occupation and income gained by college graduates.

Through almost the entire period under consideration, black colleges in the South have been the main source of black higher education in the United States. Of the 44,000 college and professional degrees obtained by blacks through 1936, 85 percent were from black colleges (Johnson, 1938, p. 10). These black institutions—more correctly called "predominantly black" as a result of the demise of official segregation—still produced 79 percent of the nation's black graduates a decade ago (Fisher, 1970, p. 19). All of the black land-grant colleges and nearly all of the privately supported institutions are located in the South or in border states.

The forces leading to the establishment of black colleges immediately after the Civil War by church groups and philanthropic organizations provide some clues to their nature and function. Atlanta, Fisk, and Tougaloo universities, as well as Talladega College, were closely linked to the activities of the American Missionary Association in the late 1860s; other church groups were also establishing institutions at the same time (Clift, 1966, p. 367). Howard University owes its origins to the activities of a religious group and the Freedmen's Bureau. By and large this flurry of activity reflected the desperate need for black teachers created by the new educational developments after the Civil War. The Freedmen's Bureau, for example, established normal schools in several southern cities (Bullock, 1967, p. 31). The students attending such institutions at the outset were themselves poorly prepared.[5] When whites regained control of the southern states, graduates of these schools had to meet only the standards that white school boards set for black schools. Because these black institutions of higher learning did not reflect the interests of the white South, ultimately they had to depend on the financial resources available in the black community and from private philanthropy. As a consequence, there was neither white support nor demand for excellence from these institutions.

The interaction between education and political and economic power is demonstrated by the history of land-grant colleges. The Morrill Act of

1862 gave each state public lands to be sold to provide the funds for institutions of higher education:

> The new institutions had to adapt themselves to a society already well supplied with colleges of older types. They had to be different.
>
> One of the early and widely approved ideas was that the colleges were to be inexpensive, for otherwise farmers' and workingmen's children could not afford to attend. It was an "original conception" that the colleges should be free or low-cost schools. . . . The low fees of this new type of public schools, the land-grant colleges, were in harmony with the general trend of the time in public education. [Good, 1962, pp. 306–307]

The original act was clearly intended to benefit groups that were relatively disadvantaged economically. With the demise of slavery, shortly afterward one might have expected such a program to be of great benefit to blacks. However such was not the case. With but a few exceptions, blacks were excluded from the southern land-grant colleges. It was not until the second Morrill Act, passed in 1890 primarily to provide additional financial support for many of the floundering schools, that explicit provision for blacks was made. The law stipulated that states that segregated the races would receive no money unless they provided separate agricultural and mechanical colleges for blacks (Good, 1962, pp. 299–300). This in turn led to the creation of such separate institutions in seventeen southern states.

Ignoring the onus of segregation, the creation of separate colleges in no way meant that they would be adequate to meet the needs of blacks. As state institutions, they were ultimately in the control of whites. As late as 1940, only three of these land-grant college boards had voting black members (Payne, 1970, p. 14). Black land-grant institutions have received far less than their proportionate share of state financial support. In the mid-1930s, among the 17 white and 17 black schools, the latter obtained only 8 percent of the funds received from all sources. When one considers that blacks comprised about 15 percent of the enrollment in southern land-grant colleges, the discrepancy is enormous. For every dollar spent for instruction on white students, only 59 cents was spent for blacks (Wilkerson, 1939, pp. 84–85). More recently, the 1968 enrollment ratio between the predominantly white and predominantly black institutions in 15 states was 5.5 to 1, but state aid for 1969–1970 was in the ratio of 10.4 to 1, and federal aid in 1968 was in the ratio of 8.4 to 1 (Payne, 1970, p. 16). The existence of segregated black institutions permitted the South to remain eligible for federal support but at the same time to conserve the limited wealth of the states for the support of white higher education.

Secondary Education and the Colleges

Drawing on students who had attended inadequate secondary and elementary schools, it is inevitable that black colleges would suffer as well. Of the 8,068 students enrolled in black colleges during the 1898–1899 school year, only 706 (8.8 percent) were college students, whereas 2,969 were enrolled as secondary students (36.8 percent), and 4,393 were taking primary-grade courses (54.4 percent) (DuBois, 1900, p. 16). In 1916 there were only three black colleges (all private) offering standard college programs. As late as 1928, black land-grant colleges had more students enrolled in precollege work than in college studies. Arkansas's black land-grant college (Arkansas A. and M. did not become a four-year college until 1929) and the black land-grant college in Georgia (Fort Valley State) did not graduate its first four-year class until 1941 (Payne, 1970, p. 14).

Given the dismal financial resources available to black colleges as well as the inadequate preparation for college provided by the high schools, the quality of higher education in black colleges was bound to be substandard. It was not until 1930 that two private black colleges were accredited by the Southern Association of Colleges and Secondary Schools (Simpson and Yinger, 1958, p. 647). There was only one black institution in 1933 accredited by the Association of American Universities and seven in 1947–1948. In 1950, about half of the black colleges were neither accredited nor approved by their regional associations (Clift, 1966, p. 384). About one-third of the black colleges and universities in 1960 remained unaccredited (Broom and Glenn, 1965, p. 93).

Until the post-World War II period, except for these black colleges, private and public institutions located in the South were closed to blacks. Preceded by court cases that forced some of the white southern universities to open their graduate and professional schools, undergraduate education is now at least nominally available to blacks in a number of institutions. Arkansas admitted its first black in 1947, and the University of Louisville merged with a black municipal college in 1951. By 1956, only the state universities in South Carolina, Georgia, Florida, and Mississippi had failed to admit any blacks (Franklin, 1956, p. 543). In some cases the resistance was extremely severe. The enrollment of James Meredith at the University of Mississippi led to rioting, the death of two, and the presence of 30,000 troops and 500 marshals in Oxford, Mississippi. Between September 1962 and March 1963, the federal government spent $6 million in connection with Meredith's admission (Simpson and Yinger, 1965, p. 452). The number of blacks at some of these institutions presently is still rather low. But the key point, in terms of the comparison with the new Europeans, is that during most of the period since 1880 the vast majority of blacks lived in an area where they could not take advantage of adequate educational resources.

BLACK HIGHER EDUCATION ELSEWHERE

As for the northern institutions, the situation was also less than sanguine. John Brown Russwurm, who is generally acknowledged to be the first American black to graduate from an American college, took his degree from a northern institution, Bowdoin College, in 1826.[6] However, only 390 blacks had graduated from nonblack colleges by the end of the nineteenth century (DuBois, 1900, pp. 29–30). Virtually a third of these, 128, were graduates of Oberlin College. Other leading institutions were: University of Kansas, 16 black graduates; Bates, 15; Harvard, 11; and 10 each from Yale, University of Michigan, and University of South Carolina.

Altogether, these 390 graduates of northern white institutions (including here the 13 graduates of southern or border-state white institutions) amounted to about 17 percent of the 2,331 blacks completing college by 1900 (based on data reported in DuBois, 1900, p. 42). There is some evidence that northern blacks were more likely to attend college than were their southern compatriots in the latter part of the nineteenth century. Among American-born blacks graduating college between 1880 and 1900, 85 percent were born in the south (derived from Dubois, 1900, p. 42). Using the "colored" population figures from the 1890 Census (which includes groups other than black), the South (including Missouri) was the birthplace of 94.7 percent of the population. Likewise, 90.6 percent of the colored population between the ages of 18 and 20 resided in these states. Thus, there is some crude evidence that blacks from the North were more likely to go to college. However, neither the number of black graduates from northern institutions nor the number of northern-born blacks with college degrees is very impressive.

Sixty-three institutions of higher education in the North were surveyed by the Immigration Commission during 1908–1909. Among the 33,000 students, there were 154 American blacks (based on data in reports of the U.S. Immigration Commission [1911b, volume 1, pp. 157–158]). When one considers that blacks were 3.6 percent of the population in the cities where these schools were located, an enrollment of 0.5 percent black suggests substantial underrepresentation.

Even for more recent periods, the evidence suggests that blacks did not have unhindered access to northern universities. According to Myrdal (1944, p. 633), "Private universities in the North restrict Negroes in rough inverse relation to their excellence. . . . Most of the minor private universities and colleges prohibit or restrict Negroes. Some of these permit the entrance of a few token Negroes, probably to demonstrate a racial liberalism they do not feel." Unfortunately the distinguished private universities were both expensive and used standards that were bound to place many blacks at a disadvantage. A survey of education in Ohio suggests that many of the state's private colleges were refusing to admit blacks well into the 1940s (McGinnis, 1962, pp. 81–82). A survey by Hatcher (1964) of higher education in Indiana disclosed that only 2.9 percent of the total enrollment consisted of blacks, although they comprised 6 percent of the state's high school graduating classes. In fact, there were actually more African students enrolled in colleges in Indiana than American blacks (Clift, 1966, p. 389).

BLACK GRADUATE AND PROFESSIONAL EDUCATION

Obstacles were particularly severe for blacks seeking graduate and professional training after completion of their undergraduate work. Although Howard, Fisk, and Atlanta universities have provided graduate and professional training, all of the black demands could not be met by these institutions. Yet blacks were barred from southern white institutions in their home states. Although willing to provide generally inferior undergraduate facilities in segregated institutions, these states would do nothing for graduate and professional training. Following a Supreme Court decision in 1938 regarding the University of Missouri's refusal to admit a black to its law school, a variety of practices were introduced. Some states provided out-of-state tuition for blacks desiring such opportunities; other states provided separate graduate and professional schools. At that time, "only Maryland and West Virginia moved in the direction of making it possible for Negroes to attend institutions that had heretofore been used exclusively by white residents" (Franklin, 1956, p. 542).

The struggle continued. In 1945, the southern states were considering creation of regional graduate and professional schools for blacks. In

1948, when the Supreme Court ordered Oklahoma to provide some facility for a black applicant to the university's law school, the state's regents created a separate law school within two weeks. Finally, the applicant was able to gain admission to the University of Oklahoma Law School in 1949. The University of Texas Law School was not required to admit blacks until a Supreme Court order in 1950 (Franklin, 1956, pp. 541–543). Thus, during the vast bulk of the period under consideration, the majority of blacks lived where they could not obtain advanced graduate and professional education from their state institutions. With the pressures generated by various Supreme Court decisions, it is significant to note that many southern states established makeshift graduate and professional programs in their existing black undergraduate institutions. There were 18 black institutions in ten southern and border states that provided some sort of graduate or professional work for blacks by 1948. However, it is revealing to note that the *undergraduate* programs in only three of these 18 institutions were approved by the Association of American Universities as adequate to prepare students for graduate work (Simpson and Yinger, 1958, pp. 664–665). The establishment of graduate programs in publicly supported southern institutions, just as in the case of black land-grant colleges in the previous century, was merely a pro forma device to meet outside pressures and with little effort to make these separate institutions of comparable quality.

> Graduate and professional education for Negroes in the South was almost non-existent as late as 1950. No work was offered leading to the doctorate. Two medical schools, Howard University Medical School and Meharry Medical School, supplied four-fifths of all Negro physicians and dentists. Opportunities for legal training and engineering were even more limited. By way of contrast, instruction was available for white students in medicine at thirty-one Southern institutions, in law at thirty-three, and in engineering at thirty-four. [Clift, 1966, p. 384]

Northern institutions have also been restrictive during most of this period, particularly with respect to the professional schools. Only a third of the "nonsegregated" medical schools in the North admitted black students when Simpson and Yinger reviewed the situation in 1958 (pp. 661–662). In 1938, there were 40 blacks enrolled in 17 of the 55 medical schools presumably open to them, and in 1946 there were 85 blacks enrolled in 20 nonsegregated institutions. These figures exclude the black medical schools at Meharry and Howard which were obliged to supply the overwhelming majority of black physicians. According to

Simpson and Yinger (1958, p. 662), dental schools are even more restrictive, and only a small proportion of nursing schools would admit blacks.

IN CONCLUSION

The substantial concentration of blacks in the South during most of the period, coupled with superior educational opportunities available to the new Europeans located in the more affluent North, are by themselves sufficient reasons to generate a substantial disadvantage for blacks in the United States. Even if the educational outcome among the relatively small number of blacks in the North had been identical to the immigrant groups, a vast part of the net differences between the groups' educational attainment would remain.

Table 6.9 indicates the regional distribution in 1900 of blacks, native whites of native parentage, and immigrants from old and new sources. Virtually 90 percent of all blacks in the United States were living in the South-Atlantic or South-Central states; compared with 36 percent of native whites of native parentage, and only 5 percent of either the old or new immigrant groups (columns 1 through 4, respectively). By contrast, only about 10 percent of the nation's blacks were located in the Northeast or Midwest, compared with close to 60 percent of the native whites of

TABLE 6.9

ETHNIC REGIONAL DISTRIBUTION AND CHARACTERISTICS OF THE SCHOOLS, CIRCA 1900

	Percentage in each region, 1900				Length of school year, 1898–1899	Expenditures per pupil, 1898–1899
	Black	Native white of native parentage	Foreign-born			
			Old sources	New sources		
Region	(1)	(2)	(3)	(4)	(5)	(6)
North Atlantic	4	24	41	62	174.0	$20.54
South Atlantic	42	15	2	2	112.6	5.93
South Central	47	21	3	3	103.2	4.67
North Central	6	35	46	26	152.2	14.13
Western	0	5	7	6	148.7	18.98

SOURCE: Reports of the Industrial Commission, 1901, pp. 1, 3.

native parentage and nearly 90 percent of either the new or old immigrant groups.

The educational ramifications of these locational differences are enormous. Just before the turn of the century, the average school year in the South-Central and South-Atlantic states, respectively, 103 and 113 days, compared with 174 days in the Northeastern states (column 5). Likewise, regional differences in expenditures per student ranged from $4.67 and $5.93 in the two southern regions to a high of $20.54 in the Northeast (column 6). These differences are sufficient to produce an enormous gap in the inherent educational opportunities available to the groups under consideration.[7] In 1900, the average school year available to blacks was 113 days compared with 157 days for immigrants from old European sources and 162 days for new immigrants. Thus, the average black school year was only 70 percent as long as that for the new Europeans. Through a period of years this comprises an enormous gap. Indeed, 12 years of schooling at an average of 113 days per year would provide a black child with no more school days than 8.4 years of schooling for new immigrants or their children who averaged 162 school-days per year.

The gap is even greater for expenditures per student, with the black average of $6.47 amounting to slightly more than one-third of the new European average of $17.81. Thus, the locational patterns of the two groups, coupled with massive regional differences in school programs, were sufficient to give the new Europeans an enormous advantage over blacks even if the discriminatory patterns within the South were absent.

But what of education in the North? Can it be said that the two groups were more or less in the same boat? Recognizing that these regional gaps are sufficient to explain a substantial part of the new European—black differences in educational attainment, a comparison between the two groups in the North is by no means unimportant as it provides us with the foundation for understanding the current educational issues faced in the North.

7

Education in the North

In the first chapter I argued that such popularly held concepts as "racism" or "cultural deprivation" should not be used to explain black—new European differences unless they are subjected to an empirical test. In similar fashion, the thoughtful reader might now wonder whether the obstacles found in the South are all there is to an explanation of low black educational attainment. Even without these specific forms of educational discrimination, one can ask, would not black—new European differences in family stability, personality characteristics, cultural heritage, and the like generate a substantial gap in the groups' educational attainment? Granted that familial and other disadvantages may themselves be products of other sources of discrimination, might these disadvantages in turn create a "vicious circle" by severely hampering educational attainment among the children? A historical survey of educational opportunities in the South cannot help provide an answer, as family stability or attitudes toward higher education were hardly relevant in a community without a high school available to blacks.

The educational attainment of northern blacks earlier in this century is, therefore, of great theoretical importance even if most blacks were then residing in the South. Because some of the gross institutional forms of educational discrimination found in the South were largely absent (although not entirely) in the North, a comparison between northern black and South−Central−Eastern European educational attainment under such circumstances is of considerable interest. Moreover, this historical comparison provides an excellent opportunity to determine whether various interpretations of current black−white differences in educational attainment were responsible for the historical development of this gap.

A COMPARISON BETWEEN SECOND GENERATIONS: EUROPEANS AND NORTHERN BLACKS

The groups' actual educational attainment must be measured before various speculations about the possible causes of these differences can be considered seriously. However, such a comparison involves neither all South−Central−Eastern Europeans nor all blacks in the North. Rather, the focus is specifically restricted to the second generation in each European group and a roughly analogous component of the northern black population. The educational attainment of European immigrants (particularly those who migrated as adults or even in their teens) clearly does not reflect conditions experienced in the United States. The educational achievements of the American-born second generation, by contrast, fully reflect their experiences in the United States. Likewise, the southern-born black migrants to the North have educational levels that reflect the opportunity structure found in the South (unless they were small children at the time of migration). "Second-generation" blacks, the northern-born children of southern migrants, have educational levels that reflect their experience in northern institutions.

This generational distinction is generally not drawn between blacks residing in the North. However, if one were justified in viewing southern migrants to the North as an immigrant group, then clearly it would be appropriate to distinguish them from those born in the North. This would be analogous to the distinction between the first and second generations among European immigrants (for example, Italian-born migrants to the United States and their American-born offspring). In both past and present decades, the southern-born proportion of all blacks residing in the North was so high that their inclusion would seriously affect a true determination of educational attainment among blacks exposed to a northern educational system. A comparison between southern- and northern-born components of the northern black population indicates that the former have substantially lower levels of educational attainment. This is more or less to be expected, given the situation in the South described in the preceding chapter. The generational approach is, therefore, of considerable value for analyzing educational attainment and a variety of other characteristics of northern blacks. (For a fuller development of the generational approach to blacks in the North, as well as data on generational differences in their education and the size of the southern-born component in the North, see Lieberson, 1973.)

What follows then is a comparison between South−Central−Eastern European second generations and northern-born blacks of the same age and sex. Native whites of native parentage (persons of at least three generations in the United States) are also included so as to provide a basis of comparison for the various second-generation groups. Ideally, one would like to obtain data on educational attainment among successive cohorts of young adults for as far back as possible, but such data are not available. The Census Bureau did not include a question on formal educational attainment for adults until 1940. However, reports published for 1960 specify education for various adult-age groups in the populations of interest here (U.S. Bureau of the Census, 1963c, Table 3; 1965, Table 12). These data can be used to infer educational attainment among many earlier cohorts. Those who were 65 to 74 years of age in 1960, for example, were born between 1885 and 1895 and reached their early adult years from 1905 to 1915; persons 55 to 64 at the time of the 1960 census were born between 1905 and 1895, and so forth. Thus data for different adult groups in 1960 are used to indicate educational developments in earlier decades among the various second-generation groups.

There are a variety of difficulties involved in such a procedure. Because the results deal with those in a given cohort who have survived until 1960, differentials in migration and mortality will generate a discrepancy of an unknown magnitude between the education received by those in a given cohort and the attainment among those surviving to the census year 1960. Likewise, there is some danger of nativity, educational level, and age being misreported. No full determination of these sources of error is possible, but a reliability test was administered through comparisons between 1940 and 1960 educational responses for the same cohorts. This comparison, described in detail in the Appendix to the chapter, is reassuring as a high degree of consistency in reported education is indicated.

One final limitation before turning to the results. Because the generational approach to northern blacks is relatively novel, the ideal data could not be obtained from published census reports. It is not possible to separate second generation from third and later generations in the North. Moreover, the published materials on educational attainment by region of birth are available for all nonwhites and not separately for blacks. This causes no great difficulty because the overwhelming majority of nonwhites are blacks, particularly as nonwhites born in the West are excluded. The description of educational attainment among the northern black second generation is, therefore, derived from data on nonwhites born in the Northeast and North-Central states.

Second-Generation Whites

For second-generation men of SCE European origin, the attainment of general educational parity with native whites of native parentage (NWNP) does not generally occur until immediately after World War II. It is only among the youngest of the cohorts shown in table 7.1, those born between 1925 and 1935 (and hence reaching adulthood in the ten years following the war), that the new European groups have median educational levels that equal or exceed those among the NWNP men. To be sure, there were some new groups with higher educational levels before then. Among the American-born children of Russian immigrants (presumably a group with a substantial Jewish component), all but the oldest cohort have enjoyed an educational advantage over NWNP males. Indeed, the gap was nearly two years for those born between 1905 and 1915. Likewise, second-generation Lithuanian men exceeded the median levels of educational attainment for earlier white generations in all of the age comparisons in table 7.1.

But basically it is among the cohorts born between 1925 and 1935 that the new European second generation reaches generally favorable levels when compared with the NWNP segment. Italians are the only exception among the nine different new European groups shown, and they are only one-tenth of a year below the NWNP median educational level in this cohort. (New European groups exceeding or equaling the NWNP median for their sex and age cohort are indicated by double or single asterisk, respectively, in tables 7.1 and 7.2)

The pattern is largely repeated among second-generation women (table 7.2). In the 1925–1935 cohort, all but one of the new second-generation groups exceed the median of 12.3 for native whites of native parentage. Women of Italian origin are the only exception, and again the difference is just one-tenth of a year. Among the older cohorts of women, there are cases of second-generation groups exceeding the NWNP educational median—for example, Hungarian women 75 years of age and older in 1960—but these are relatively less common than among men. Among men born between 1885 and 1895, there were three second-generation groups with higher medians than NWNP men, but

TABLE 7.1
MEDIAN EDUCATIONAL ATTAINMENT, SECOND-GENERATION WHITE MEN AND NATIVE WHITES OF NATIVE PARENTAGE, 1960

Cohorts by age in 1960 (and year of birth)	Second-generation whites by origin									Native whites of native parentage
	Austria	Czechoslovakia	Finland	Hungary	Italy	Lithuania	Poland	USSR	Yugoslavia	
25–34 (1925–1935)	12.6**	12.4**	12.5**	12.5**	12.2	12.8**	12.4**	13.6**	12.4**	12.3
35–44 (1915–1925)	12.2**	11.9	12.2**	12.0	11.4	12.3**	11.5	12.7**	12.0	12.1
45–54 (1905–1915)	10.7**	9.2	9.5	10.1	9.0	10.9**	9.2	12.3**	9.5	10.4
55–64 (1895–1905)	8.8	8.4	8.5	8.9**	8.4	8.9***	8.3	10.4**	8.4	8.8
65–74 (1885–1895)	8.4*	8.0	7.6	8.7**	8.0	8.7***	7.6	8.7***	7.7	8.4
75+ (1885 or earlier).	8.2*	7.2	7.0	8.7**	7.4	8.3***	6.9	8.2*	NA	8.2

SOURCE: U.S. Bureau of the Census, 1965, tables 7 and 9.
NA: Not available.
*Group's median equals native white of native parentage.
**Group's median exceeds native white of native parentage.

TABLE 7.2
Median Educational Attainment, Second-Generation White Women and Native Whites of Native Parentage, 1960

Cohorts by age in 1960 (and year of birth)	Second-generation whites by origin									Native whites of native parentage
	Austria	Czechoslovakia	Finland	Hungary	Italy	Lithuania	Poland	USSR	Yugoslavia	
25–34 (1925–1935)	12.6**	12.4**	12.5**	12.4**	12.2	12.5**	12.3*	12.7**	12.4**	12.3
35–44 (1915–1925)	12.2	11.8	12.3	12.0	11.3	12.2*	11.3	12.4**	12.1	12.2
45–54 (1905–1915)	10.7	9.0	11.4	9.9	8.8	10.4	8.8	12.1**	9.2	11.4
55–64 (1895–1905)	8.8	8.4	8.8	8.8	8.3	8.7	8.2	10.1**	8.2	9.4
65–74 (1885–1895)	8.4	8.0	8.3	8.6	7.9	8.5	7.6	8.7*	8.1	8.7
75+ (1885 or earlier)	8.2	7.4	8.0	8.8**	8.1	8.1	7.2	8.3	NA	8.6

SOURCE: See table 7.1.
NA: Not available.
*Group's median equals native white of native parentage.
**Group's median exceeds native white of native parentage.

none of the second-generation groups of women in the same age held a similar advantage over NWNP women.

The patterns differ slightly between the sexes because the ethnic groups under consideration differ in the relative levels attained by men and women. Among blacks and native whites of native parentage, females have higher medians than do males. However, the opposite holds for some of the new European groups, and in other cases the edge women hold over their male compatriots is narrower. In all age categories, for example, Lithuanian second-generation men have higher medians than second-generation women.

Northern-Born Blacks

The median educational levels in all of the northern-born black cohorts are below those attained by the NWNP population of comparable age and sex (compare columns 1 and 2, 4 and 5 of table 7.3). This is in sharp contrast to the new European second-generation groups whose most recent cohorts have equal or higher educational attainment than the NWNP population.

However, the patterns are far more complex than such simple comparisons suggest. In the earlier decades, succeeding cohorts of blacks were in the process of catching up to the white groups, but then suddenly fell back. Looking at successive male cohorts, the NWNPs enjoy an advantage of 1.4 years over the median among northern-born blacks in the oldest cohort, those 75 and over in 1960 (table 7.3, column 3). However, the next cohort of blacks (those 65−74 in 1960) gained a full year in their median compared with a gain of .2 for the NWNP population, thereby reducing the educational gap to .6 years (7.8 versus 8.4). Northern-born blacks were closing the gap rapidly; the difference in median education was only .4 years in the next cohort (those who were 55−64 in 1960). However, the educational distance suddenly widened in the next cohort, those born between 1905 and 1915. Educational attainment increased substantially for black men in this cohort, a gain of .9 years over the median for the previous cohort. But this is contrasted with a gain of 1.6 years among the analogous NWNP age groups. Thus the gap between northern-born blacks and NWNP medians widened again, from .4 among the 55−64 group to 1.1 years among those 45−54 years of age in 1960. This gap of 1.1 years was nearly as large as the 1.4 years reported for the black and NWNP cohorts born some 30 or so years earlier. Because of greater gains among blacks in the younger cohorts, this gap has begun to decline again, it was .7 years among those 25−34 in 1960.

TABLE 7.3

Median Educational Attainment, Northern-Born Blacks and Native Whites of Native Parentage, 1960

Cohorts by age in 1960 (and year of birth)	Men				Women			
	Native whites of native parentage (1)	Northern-born blacks (2)	Difference (3)		Native whites of native parentage (4)	Northern-born blacks (5)	Difference (6)	
25–34 (1925–1935)	12.3	11.6	.7		12.3	12.0	.3	
35–44 (1915–1925)	12.1	11.2	.9		12.2	11.5	.7	
45–54 (1905–1915)	10.4	9.3	1.1		11.4	9.9	1.5	
55–64 (1895–1905)	8.8	8.4	.4		9.4	8.7	.7	
65–74 (1885–1895)	8.4	7.8	.6		8.7	8.2	.5	
75+ (1885 or earlier)	8.2	6.8	1.4		8.6	7.8	.8	

SOURCES: U.S. Bureau of the Census, 1963c, table 3; 1965, table 7.

The pattern is somewhat similar among black and NWNP women. The educational advantage of the latter was .8 years in the oldest cohort, but declined to .5 in the next cohort (table 7.3, column 6). It then widened slightly to .7 among those born between 1895 and 1905. The median educational level in the following cohort of black women jumped 1.2 years, but this was dwarfed by an even larger increase of 2.0 years for the native white of native parentage women. As a consequence, the gap between the black and NWNP medians widened to 1.5 years among those born in the 1905–1915 period. The absolute difference between the two groups was then actually greater than in any of the three earlier cohorts shown in table 7.3. As was the case for men, the gap again started to decline in the younger cohorts and was .3 years among those born between 1925 and 1935.

Changes in the Gap

Not only did northern-born black cohorts come close to reaching the educational attainment of the NWNP population some decades ago, but there are many instances where blacks exceeded the medians attained by some of the second-generation white groups. These advantages are particularly marked among women. In all but the youngest cohort, Polish second-generation women had lower medians than those reached by northern black women (see table 7.4). Likewise, the oldest four cohorts of Czech women have lower educational levels than are found among blacks. Also noteworthy are the four cohorts of Italian women and three Yugoslavian cohorts with lower medians. In short, the educational advantage over northern-born black women was not fully established for all second-generation SCE European groups until recently.

Among males, there are less cases in which northern-born black cohorts had higher educational levels than the second-generation European groups. This reflects the fact noted earlier that black women reach higher educational levels than black men, whereas the opposite is often the case for the second-generation European groups. Nevertheless, three of the four oldest cohorts of second-generation Polish men have lower medians than blacks. In the older male cohorts there are also instances where northern-born blacks exceed or equal the medians among second-generation Czechs, Italians, Yugoslavs, and Finns (table 7.4).

These remarkable fluctuations in the educational distance between northern-born blacks and second-generation white groups, as well as in the NWNP advantage over blacks, call for a more detailed analysis. Several decades ago, blacks enjoyed an educational advantage over

TABLE 7.4
Second-Generation White Groups with Median Education Lower or Equal to Northern-Born Blacks, 1960

Cohorts by age in 1960 (and year of birth)	Males					Females					
	Czecho-slovakia	Finland	Italy	Poland	Yugo-slavia	Czecho-slovakia	Hungary	Italy	Lithuania	Poland	Yugo-slavia
25–34 (1925–1935)											
35–44 (1915–1925)								**		**	
45–54 (1905–1915)	**		**	**		**	*	**		**	**
55–64 (1895–1905)	*		*	**	*	**		**	*	**	**
65–74 (1885–1895)		**		**	**	**		**		**	**
75+ (1885 or earlier)	**				NA	**				**	NA

SOURCE: Based on data shown in tables 7.1, 7.2, and 7.3.

NOTE: The following groups have higher educational medians than Northern-born blacks in all cohort comparisons: Austria, both sexes; Finland, females; Hungary, males; Lithuania, males; USSR, both sexes.

* Second-generation group has same median as Northern-born blacks.

** Second-generation group has lower median than Northern-born blacks.

some of the new second-generation groups and were catching up to others. Likewise, the gap between northern-born blacks and the NWNP population was declining with each succeeding cohort. This is exactly what one might expect for a group starting at the bottom in a fairly open system without discrimination (Lieberson and Fuguitt, 1967)—or at least where the degree of racial discrimination was less severe than the fluidity of the intergenerational mobility structure. Then a sharp setback occurred such that the black advantage over some new European groups disappeared and, more generally, their distance from the white segments increased. What caused this sudden reversal?

The remainder of this chapter and the next one are devoted to the issues raised above: first, considering the influence on these gaps of such widely held factors as family stability, values toward education, residential segregation, and the like; second, accounting for this remarkable reversal such that the distance between northern-born blacks and the new European second-generation groups suddenly widened.

FURTHER DOUBTS ABOUT A CULTURAL INTERPRETATION

These educational results seriously question any interpretation of black—new European educational differences that is based on the assumption that they are the product of initial differences in attitude or orientation toward education. Older cohorts of northern-born blacks were ahead of some second-generation new European groups and were in process of catching up to others. Indeed, for some of the new groups, it is only very recently that their second generations have pulled ahead of northern-born blacks. Such a pattern is hardly consistent with the position that new Europeans were generally more favorably disposed toward education than were blacks. On the other hand, the pattern is consistent with the results reported for the South in the previous chapter. In the postbellum period there was every indication of a massive interest in education among the newly freed slaves.

It is easy enough to describe and appreciate the grand intellectual and artistic heritages of many South—Central—Eastern European groups, but one must be wary of attributing very much to this. Educational developments in Europe at the time of mass migration, as well as the actual characteristics of the immigrants themselves, both indicate that SCE European migrants to the United States enjoyed no educational advantage over blacks migrating from the South at the same time.

Comparisons Between Europe and the South

Mass education in South–Central–Eastern Europe at the turn of the century was far less extensive than in Northwestern Europe. Based on data largely for male army recruits in the 1890s, the median percentage illiterate in eleven Northwestern European nations was 3.7, ranging from 0.1 (in the German Empire and Sweden and Norway) to 17 percent in Ireland. By contrast, the median percentage illiterate among army recruits in nine South–Central–Eastern European nations was 61.7, with the figures ranging from 24 percent in Austria to 89 percent in Roumania (Lieberson, 1963a, p. 71).

The latter nations' rates compare quite unfavorably with native whites of the same age in the United States. Assuming that men in the early twenties are the appropriate age group to compare with army recruits (U.S. Bureau of the Census, 1905, p. 9), their illiteracy rate of 3.8 percent is far below any of the SCE European countries. More to the point are the illiteracy rates among blacks. Of those in the same group living outside of the South, approximately 10 percent were illiterate. This compares quite favorably with even the 24 percent found in Austria. Approximately 39 percent of southern black males in the same age category were illiterate. This is far below the illiteracy rates in Roumania, Serbia, Russia, Portugal, and Spain; it is barely greater than the rates in Italy. Thus the new European groups came from nations where illiteracy was far more widespread than among blacks living in the North, and, indeed, many of the nations had higher illiteracy rates than those found among blacks living in the South.

The Migrants

These educational differences are also reflected in the literacy levels of the new Europeans migrating to the United States in 1900 (table 7.5). Illiteracy among those at least 14 years old ranged from 75 percent (Turkish immigrants) to only 3 percent for those arriving from Bohemia and Moravia. However, the percentage illiterate among blacks in the North of roughly comparable age is 19.7. Thus only six of the 19 groups specified in table 7.5 have illiteracy rates lower than northern blacks. The new Jewish immigrants, a group to be noted later for its high educational aspirations, were slightly more illiterate than northern blacks. Altogether, slightly more than a third of the new immigrants arriving in 1900 were illiterate (34 percent), a rate nearly double that found among northern blacks. Illiteracy among blacks located in the South was considerably higher than among their compatriots in the North and

TABLE 7.5

Illiteracy among South−Central−Eastern European Immigrants (arriving during the year ending June 30, 1900)

Group	Percentage illiterate
Armenian	24
Bohemian & Moravian	3
Bulgarian, Serbian, & Montenegrin	36
Croatian & Slovenian	37
Dalmatian, Bosnian, & Herzegovinian	33
Finnish	3
Greek	17
Hebrew	23
Italian	47
Lithuanian	32
Magyar	17
Polish	32
Portuguese	60
Roumanian	25
Russian	29
Ruthenian	49
Slovak	28
Spanish	5
Turkish	75

SOURCE: Commissioner-General of Immigration, 1900, table 3.

West (51.4 percent among those 15 years of age and older). Hence, although northern blacks enjoyed a substantial advantage over the new Europeans arriving in 1900, this advantage was not shared by their compatriots located in the South.

With the passage of legislation in 1917 requiring a literacy test for admission into the United States as well as the expansion of mass education in Europe, the immigrants arriving after World War I were undoubtedly more literate than their predecessors (see data comparing illiteracy among immigrants in 1910 with 1920 in Lieberson, 1963a, p. 72). Nevertheless, even in 1930, blacks living in the North and West were considerably less illiterate than foreign-born whites (4.6 and 9.9 percent, respectively, for those 10 years of age and older). To be sure, these are not truly comparable figures as the former includes northern-born blacks as well as migrants from the South. On the other hand, the reader should bear in mind that the new European immigrant groups were considerably more illiterate than those from Northwestern European sources. Thus the figure for the total foreign-born undoubtedly understates illiteracy among the South–Central–Eastern European component.

These results, although hardly conclusive, are compatible with the cohort analyses reported earlier. The American-born offspring of new Europeans not only failed to show a stronger propensity toward education than northern blacks early in the period under consideration, but there is also every indication that the immigrants themselves were hardly an educated elite. Accordingly, contrasts between the new European groups and blacks in the North cannot be readily explained in terms of any such "background" factors such as the cultural values or educational norms of the former. The new European immigrant groups came from nations where education was not yet a mass phenomena and, indeed, the actual immigrants to the United States had lower literacy rates (in any language) than did blacks in the North. To be sure, blacks in the North were constantly receiving new influxes of compatriots from the South who had lived in a region where their education was either discouraged or at best minimally tolerated by the dominant white social structure. However, on the whole, it is hard to believe that the later advancements of the new European groups through education reflected any distinctive or particularly strong orientation toward education above and beyond that found among blacks.

One could argue that the new Europeans did have higher educational aspirations than blacks, but early economic hardships inhibited the fruition of such motivations until more recently. There is little to support this alternative interpretation. Research on educational attainment among various ethnic groups by Featherman (1971) casts serious doubts on the ability of achievement motivation or related attributes to account for differences between the groups' educational attainment after various socioeconomic background characteristics are taken into account. Likewise, although educational attainment among European immigrants improved after the introduction of literacy tests (a screening process obviously not operating with respect to black internal migration), it is not likely that this educational upgrading among the immigrants accounts for the reversals in trend noted above. The northern-born black educational position, relative to new European second-generation groups, had already started to weaken by the time a literacy test was enacted in 1917.

Finally, there is additional historical evidence supporting the thesis presented here. Working with data from the 1910 Census, Smith (1972, pp. 309–310) reports that school enrollment among blacks in their late teens exceeded both foreign-born and second-generation white rates in many northern cities. Indeed, in some cases they also exceed the enrollment rates among native whites of native parentage. These enrollment figures clearly indicate that in 1910 blacks in the postcompulsory ages were more likely to be in school than second-generation whites. In the same vein, Nelli (1970, p. 67) reports that Italians around the turn of the century had a very strong propensity to send their children to work as soon as it was possible.

FAMILY STABILITY AND EDUCATIONAL ATTAINMENT

Even if norms and values pertaining directly to education fail to explain the historical pattern, the reader may still wonder whether differences in family structure were responsible for the education gap between the groups. It is widely known that black children are far more likely than whites to be raised in a family in which one of the parents—frequently the father—is absent. (For comparisons between black and white family stability, see Farley, 1970, 1971; and Farley and Hermalin, 1971.) Reflecting both higher illegitimacy rates as well as the greater instability of black families, this subject has been the source of increased debate in the years following publication of the Moynihan Report (Office of Policy Planning and Research, 1965). Both the causes and consequences of incomplete black families are subjects that have received considerable speculation. For some, family instability is interpreted as resulting from a set of discriminatory processes generated by the white-dominated society. For example, Moynihan refers to the fluctuations in black unemployment and their consequences for family instability (Office of Policy Planning and Research, 1965, p. 22). Others have suggested that the greater frequency of incomplete families among blacks is due to normative or cultural differences between components of the American population. One also encounters explanations based on the heritage of slavery, an interpretation that is becoming increasingly doubtful.

The goal here, however, is to deal with the possible consequences of black—new European differences in family structure on differences in educational attainment. No attempt is made to account for the sources of family instability, granted that this is an important research problem, but only to see what light it may shed on the differential levels of educational attainment observed earlier in this chapter. This is no small task. Because various intellectual approaches deal with the family from sharply different perspectives, there is a wide range of reasons offered as to why family instability in itself may have hampered black educational attainment. These include such factors as: the psychological consequences for children raised in incomplete families; the inadequacy of role models for sons when the father is absent; the need for mothers to work and, in turn, their inability to supervise children; the greater chances of juvenile delinquency in broken homes. Two features complicate the task: historical data are less than ideal for dealing with these questions and family instability is related to income and other economic factors that are themselves related to educational attainment. Regarding the latter, as Duncan and Duncan observe, "There is, indeed, a tangled web of relations among economic conditions and family structure" (1969, p. 285). Nevertheless, the questions are clearly important. Did SCE European groups differ from blacks in the frequency of incomplete families? If so, what is the impact of these differences on educational attainment?

Incomplete Families

The available historical data are crude, but they do indicate that the proportion widowed or divorced among women ever married is consistently higher for blacks than among foreign-born white women. Indeed, the latter have dissolution rates that are very similar to those found among second and later generations of white women. Table 7.6 gives the standardized dissolution rates for both 1910 and 1920 among these broad race and nativity categories. Because the age-specific rates among each group of women are applied to the age distribution among NWNP women in each period, differences between the groups' age composition are taken into account. In 1910, the dissolution rate is very similar for the three white components, ranging from .16 among third- or later-generation white women to .17 among foreign-born and second-generation whites. By contrast, the dissolution rate among ever-married black women in the North is .29. Likewise, the standardized figures for 1920 indicate the same clustering for the three generations of white women, but again the dissolution rate is substantially higher for black women (.27 versus .16 and .17 for the whites).

For 1930 it is possible to examine the specific dissolution rates for the new European components of both the first and second generations (not possible for 1910 and 1920). If anything, dissolution rates are even lower for South–Central–Eastern European women than for whites of other origins (table 7.6). Among foreign-born women in the United States from new sources, the standardized dissolution rate was .13 in 1930,

TABLE 7.6
PROPORTION WIDOWED OR DIVORCED AMONG WOMEN EVER MARRIED, 1910–1930

| | | | 1930 | | |
	1910	1920	Old	New	Other
Native white of native parentage	.16	.16			
Native white of foreign or mixed parentage (second generation)	.17	.17	.16	.12	.14
Foreign-born white (first generation)	.17	.16	.16	.13	.16
Black	.29	.27			

SOURCES: U.S. Bureau of the Census, 1913, pp. 517-518; 1922, p. 387; 1933a, pp. 843-844, 1060-1061.
NOTE: Data are for women 15 years of age and older. Direct standardization used for 1910 and 1920, based on each group's age-specific rates and age distribution of ever-married native white of native parentage women. Indirect standardization used for 1930, based on each group's age distribution, actual number of widowed or divorced, and age-specific rates among native white of native parentage women.

compared with .16 among other foreign-born white women. Likewise, the rate of .12 for second-generation women of SCE European origin is below that for second-generation women of Northwestern or other European origin, .16 and .14, respectively. In addition, dissolution among first- and second-generation women of new European origin compares quite favorably with the rate of .15 among third- or later-generation white women in the United States.

Also favorable to the new European groups is their apparent low rate of illegitimacy. The reported illegitimacy rate (measured by the number of illegitimate births per thousand births) for blacks in 1920 was 126; compared with 17 among white women of American birth and 5.2 among foreign-born white women. In turn, immigrant women from SCE European sources had even lower rates than those of Northwestern European birth (Carpenter, 1927, pp. 244–245).

All of these results can be distorted by a wide variety of factors, not the least being intentional or unintentional misreporting such that the unwed mothers report they are widowed or divorced, or women living with a common-law husband report they are married, and the like. Nevertheless, despite the fact that both marital stability and illegitimacy rates are subject to many serious errors and distortions, the reported differences between blacks and new Europeans are so large that one may reasonably conclude that they reflect true differences between the populations.

Working Mothers

Closely linked with family stability is the issue of working mothers. Mothers of school-age children may be obliged to work if no father is present or if the father is unemployed or earns very little. In turn, the argument runs, a decline in the close supervision of children due to the mother's absence will have harmful consequences for the socialization of the child generally and for school performance in particular. Before examining the consequences for children's school performance, let us first consider whether black women were more likely to be working.

Putting together various fragments of information available for earlier periods, there is consistent indication that previously or presently married black women were more often working than were the new Europeans. In 1890, the percentage engaged in gainful occupations is substantially higher for black women than various white components of the ever-married population. By contrast, the differences between first-, second-, and later-generation white women are negligible (table 7.7). Nearly two-thirds of black widows are employed, compared with 21 percent of immigrant widows, 30 percent of second-generation white women, and about one-fourth of native whites of native parentage.

Because interest focuses on those ages where women are especially likely to have school-age children, an examination of these groupings is more important. Again, inspection of table 7.7 indicates that black women in the married, widowed, and divorced categories were far more likely to be working than immigrant or second-generation white women. Among those 35–44, for example, only about 3 percent of married white women were working—compared with one-fifth of married black women. Likewise, the rate for widows among blacks (80 percent) is twice that for first- and second-generation white women (42 and 41 percent, respectively). The substantial differences among divorced women are also in the same direction.

These results are suggestive rather than conclusive. The author was unable to obtain data cross-tabulating work activity by marital status separately for women of South–Central–Eastern European origin. Likewise, the figures refer to the entire United States—a particularly unfortunate situation in terms of the interest in northern blacks. (In general, such gross figures are used here and elsewhere only when it is not possible to obtain the detailed information desired.) Beyond these considerations, the number of each marital component's school-age offspring is unknown. To take an unlikely extreme, for all one knows it could be that none of the black working widows in 1890 had school-age

TABLE 7.7
EMPLOYMENT BY MARITAL STATUS OF WOMEN, 1890

	Percentage engaged in gainful occupations			
Age and nativity	Married	Widowed	Divorced	Single and unknown
10+:				
Native white of native parentage	2	24	43	18
Second-generation white	3	30	48	30
First-generation white	3	21	45	58
Black	23	63	80	42
15–24:				
Native white of native parentage	3	33	40	24
Second-generation white	3	40	45	42
First-generation white	5	51	56	71
Black	24	77	75	55
25–34:				
Native white of native parentage	2	42	48	42
Second-generation white	3	40	53	56
First-generation white	3	54	59	79
Black	23	82	81	78
35–44:				
Native white of native parentage	2	42	48	37
Second-generation white	3	41	48	50
First-generation white	3	42	53	68
Black	22	80	84	79
45–54:				
Native white of native parentage	2	33	40	32
Second-generation white	3	29	38	41
First-generation white	3	28	42	57
Black	21	70	84	77

SOURCES: U.S. Bureau of the Census, 1897, p. cxxix, table 120; 1902, table XLIX.

children, whereas all of the working white widows are of South–Central–Eastern European origin and had enormous families.

For 1910, it is possible to at least focus on the employment patterns among women living outside the South, but the influence of conjugal condition cannot be directly obtained. Using the age-specific employment rates for all women outside of the South as the standard, the results indicate substantially higher employment for black women in the North after age is taken into account. Their rate is .44, compared with

.17, .24, and .22 for third-, second-, and first-generation white women of all origins.

Employment differentials between black and new European women can be most clearly compared with data on large northern cities in 1930 (by this time a substantial segment of the first- and second-generation groups are of South–Central–Eastern European origin). The census provides information on both the percentage of homemakers employed and their location. A homemaker is defined as "that woman member of the family who was responsible for the care of the home and family," with the added proviso that hired housekeepers do not count as homemakers (U.S. Bureau of the Census, 1933b, p. 9). Black home-makers have the highest employment rates in each city examined (compare column 4 with columns, 1, 2, and 3 in table 7.8). In most cases their rates are several times greater than those among either first- or second-generation white women. For example, nearly half of New York City's black homemakers were employed, compared with 10 percent of immigrant homemakers, 14 percent among the second generation, and 18 percent of the NWNP group. As employed black women were at most only slightly more likely to work at home than other groups (compare columns 5 to 8 of table 7.8), this means that they were away from home with a job far more often than the various groups of white homemakers. In short, there is every indication that black women were generally more likely to be employed away from the home than women from the new European groups.[1] In turn, presumably the same differential would hold among those women with school-age children.

Education, Family Stability, and Working Mothers

The key issue remains. It is clear that family instability was far more common among blacks than South–Central–Eastern Europeans. Like-wise, there is every indication that women in the former group were more likely to work. However, it is one matter to show that these group differences existed; it is another to show that black educational levels are lowered because of family instability or because their mothers worked. Attention is now addressed to exactly this question: How much of the difference between black and SCE European school performance might be attributed simply to such differences in family patterns?

Regarding children's *achievement scores* (as contrasted with *formal years of schooling completed*), the evidence consistently indicates that a broken family is of little consequence. Coleman, Campbell, and associates (1966, p. 185) found that black students were far less likely to be residing with their real father or mother (the difference from whites being particularly

TABLE 7.8
EMPLOYMENT OF HOMEMAKERS AND LOCATION OF WORK, LARGE NORTHERN AND WESTERN CITIES, 1930

| | Percentage of homemakers employed | | | | Percentage of employed working at home | | | |
| | Native white of | | Foreign-born white (3) | Black (4) | Native white of | | Foreign-born white (7) | Black (8) |
City	Native parentage (1)	Foreign or mixed parentage (2)			Native parentage (5)	Foreign or mixed parentage (6)		
Boston	19	15	12	42	8	6	13	9
Buffalo	12	10	8	25	8	8	9	9
Chicago	20	15	12	39	5	4	5	8
Cincinnati	15	12	12	39	6	5	4	6
Cleveland	19	15	13	35	6	4	4	7
Detroit	15	12	10	26	7	7	10	13
Kansas City	21	16	10	45	7	8	9	8
Los Angeles	25	23	17	44	5	5	6	6
Milwaukee	17	13	10	26	5	7	7	9
Minneapolis	19	19	12	30	5	6	8	9
Newark	17	13	10	41	8	7	7	4
New York	18	14	10	46	4	3	6	6
Philadelphia	14	12	9	39	5	4	5	4
Pittsburgh	11	9	7	24	9	6	9	7
St. Louis	15	11	9	39	8	8	7	9
San Francisco	28	23	17	43	3	3	5	6
Seattle	22	22	16	33	4	4	6	7

SOURCE: U.S. Bureau of the Census, 1933b, table 14 for each state.

large with respect to father's presence). However, when determining the influence of "structural integrity" (principally the father's presence) on verbal achievement test scores, they find that "contrary to much that has been written, the structural integrity of the home . . . shows very little relation to achievement for Negroes. It does, however, show a strong relation to achievement for the other minority groups" (1966, p. 302.) However, it should be noted that the relative importance of this factor is somewhat greater among blacks in the North than those residing in the South (Coleman, Campbell, and associates, 1966, table 3.221.5, p. 301).

The same general conclusion is supported by Crain and Weisman (1972, pp. 106–107) who also find no relation between home stability and verbal test scores for either men or women. Likewise, Robert Hauser (1973, pp. 60–62) finds very weak correlations between two standard measures of academic achievement and family stability for white students in the Nashville area (Davidson County). Crain and Weisman (1972, p. 108) cite a review of the literature on academic performance by Herzog and Sudia which finds it "unlikely that father absence in itself would show significant relation to poor school achievement, if relevant variables (including type of father absence) were adequately controlled."

Regarding the effect of a broken family on formal educational attainment, the evidence is fairly consistent once the appropriate controls are applied. Crain and Weisman (1972, pp. 106–107) report that family stability is related to educational attainment among women, although not among men. By contrast, Duncan and Duncan (1969) find that the maintenance of an intact family has a fairly substantial effect on educational attainment for male black children. Their analysis, based on the well-known "Occupational Changes in a Generation" (OCG) survey, focuses largely on the influence family stability has for sons' occupational mobility and will be discussed in a later chapter. However, they do observe that black men who lived with both parents "most of the time" have considerably more years of formal schooling than those raised in a family headed by a woman (10.1 versus 8.5 years). Indeed, this difference is greater than that found for white males distinguished by the completeness of their family (Duncan and Duncan, 1969, p. 277).

However, it is another matter to ask how much of the substantial educational gap between the children of intact and broken families can be attributed directly to family stability as opposed to other correlated attributes. Using a path analysis several years earlier, Beverly Duncan (1967, p. 368) obtained a net coefficient of .09 for both races when determining the influence of family stability on educational attainment. Her analysis indicates that family stability is a far less important determinant of educational attainment among black children than their parents' education, and somewhat less important than the influences of either parental occupation or the number of siblings. Indeed, the combined effects of both family stability and parental occupation accounts for only 2 or 3 percent of educational attainment among black children after a variety of other factors are taken into account (Duncan, 1967, p. 370). In this case it would appear that family stability does have an impact on formal educational attainment, but the proportion of variance in educational attainment explained by such factors is not great. In turn, this would suggest that only a small part of the black–new European shifts in education could be explained by the groups' differences in stability. Given the fact that contemporary data are being used to account for early events, it is noteworthy that Duncan's findings about the small net effect of family stability on black education is consistent for several different cohorts. This suggests that these findings may well apply to the earlier periods under consideration. These results indicate that family instability per se is of relatively little consequence for black variation in educational attainment after associated factors are taken into account.[2] Not only is this conclusion supported by Duncan, Featherman, and Duncan (1972, p. 65), but they cite an earlier study that indicates that the net effect of family stability on black educational attainment was even less in older cohorts (p. 64).

The impact of working mothers on their children's educational attainment is less clear. In an early study of black school children in New York City, Blascoer (1915) found a variety of factors working to hamper their school achievement. Of 334 black school children surveyed by Blascoer, only 45 percent lived in families with both parents present (this includes a stepfather or stepmother). There were as many children living with only a mother as with both natural parents. Regarding the issue at hand, she reports that school authorities generally attributed "the large amount of truancy among colored boys and girls to the fact that so many of the colored mothers worked" (1915, p. 18). Moreover, Blascoer claims that "normal home surroundings" were not present among any of the group of truant boys that she studied. "Normal" was defined as "a home in which both parents were living, the father working and the mother remaining at home to care for the children" (p. 135).

Blascoer's survey can be retabulated to show the effect of family stability and working mothers on the chances that children will have problems in school (the latter being based on reports from principals and teachers). There is every indication that the combined forces of stability and a nonworking mother do have an effect on the children. Among the 57 children with fathers present and mothers not working, only 1 was reported in difficulty (table 7.9). This compares with 26 percent among all

TABLE 7.9
Influence of Family Stability and Mother's Employment on Black
Children in School, New York City, 1915

	Percentage of children in difficulty at school	
Employment status of mother	Father present	Father absent
Working at home	24	20
Working away from home	25	29
Not employed	2	—

SOURCE: Blascoer, 1915.
NOTE: No cases reported of children in families with both father absent and mother not employed.

other children, a rather impressive difference despite the small size of the sample. Difficulties in school among the children of working mothers range from 20 percent for those with father absent and mother employed at home to 29 percent for those with mothers working away from home (table 7.9). Thus, the key factor appears to be whether or not the mother works, with relatively small differences related to the presence or absence of a father and whether or not the working mother is able to pursue her job at home. Unfortunately, the sixth cell in table 7.9 is empty because there were apparently no cases in which the mother did not work if the father was absent. (It may be that early in the century children dropped out of school under such circumstances.) Thus the educational consequences for children in incomplete families with mothers at home are not clear from this study.

According to the OCG survey, white women who are heads of households are more likely to work than are black women in the same situation (Duncan and Duncan, 1969, p. 281). In addition, Duncan and Duncan cite 1960 Census data that are compatible with this finding. "Among females who headed a non-farm family which included a child between the ages of six and 17, the proportions employed were 45 per cent for non-whites and 54 per cent for whites" (p. 281). A reexamination of these census data for the North, which is the area of most interest here, indicates an even greater difference; 35 and 55 percent, respectively, of nonwhite and white female heads with a child in these ages are employed. However, the reader should bear in mind that a far larger proportion of black women are in this situation. Incidentally, there is some indication that black males raised in households with female heads have higher occupational attainment if their mothers worked (Duncan and Duncan,

1969, p. 284). Unfortunately, it is not possible to tell whether this means that their educational attainment was also higher.

The Combined Educational Consequences of Family Stability and Employment

The research reviewed above makes it clear that family instability fails to explain much of the educational difference between blacks and South–Central–Eastern Europeans, but less clear is the influence of working mothers. An unusually fine opportunity is provided in the 1960 Census to determine the combined influence of both employment and family stability on the schooling of black and white children. Information on two important facets of school performance is available for white and non-white children specified by age and sex: the percentage enrolled in school and the percentage of those enrolled who are "retarded" (behind the modal grade associated with their age). These school achievement characteristics are available separately for children in families with father and mother present, just one parent present, neither parent present, or not in a family. In addition, each family type is subdivided into whether one or both parents are employed as well as whether there is some adult at home. The information is therefore extremely detailed. For example, one can determine the percentage behind their normal grade among girls 14 to 15 years of age living in one-parent families in which the parent is employed but some other adult family member (e.g., grandparent, older sibling) is present and not in the labor force. The reader should keep in mind that these data are cross-sectional and hence only provide information about the relation between a child's education and the current familial structure and present employment of the adults. Moreover, the data are not restricted to the new European component of the white population but refer to the entire nation.

White children of all ages and in both sexes enjoy an advantage over blacks in both the percentage enrolled in school and the percentage in at least the modal grade associated with their age (table 7.10, columns 3 and 7). These differences are not too great with respect to the enrollment rates, but they are substantial in terms of grade retardation. Nearly 95 percent of white boys 14 to 15 years of age are enrolled in school; an edge of about 4.5 percent over the rate for nonwhite boys in the same age (compare columns 1 and 2). On the other hand, 35.5 percent of enrolled blacks in this age group are behind the modal grade, whereas 15.5 percent of whites are likewise retarded (compare columns 5 and 6). Thus the gap in retardation for boys in this age group is a full 20 percent.

Using a method proposed by Kitagawa (1955), the sources of these racial differences may be analyzed into two separate components. The size of the first component, to be called the "compositional effect," indicates how much of the difference between blacks and whites is due to the fact that their family structure and employment patterns are not the same. If differences between black and white family stability and employment accounted for all of the gap in the enrollment or retardation rates for a given age and sex, then the compositional effect would be 100 percent (in columns 4 and 8, respectively). The second component is a residual one that indicates that part of the gap which cannot be accounted for by the racial differences in family and employment patterns. In other words, this reflects the weighted influence of racial differences in school attendance or retardation rates within each type of family stability—employment situation. The compositional and residual effects sum to 100 percent of the gap shown in columns 3 and 7. If black—white differences in family—employment structure accounted for all of the children's educational differences, then the compositional effect would be 100 percent and the residual effect would be zero. If the former accounted for none of the educational difference between black and white children, the compositional effect would be zero and the residual component would be 100 percent of the racial gap.

Turning first to racial differences in enrollment rates, they are of relatively moderate magnitude until the older ages are reached (Table 7.10, column 3). This is more or less to be expected as school enrollment is mandatory for the younger ages. After the required years of attendance are passed in the late teens, the gap for boys reaches 7 and 8 percent. The racial differences are generally less among girls, and there is a strikingly small difference of 1.5 percent among those 18 to 19 years of age. Inspection of the compositional effect (column 4) indicates that part of the racial difference in enrollment can be accounted for by the differences in the groups' family stability and employment patterns. Generally, these family characteristics account for more of the racial difference among girls than boys. Also, their effect is greater among the older children for whom school attendance is voluntary. From 13 to 37 percent of the racial gap in enrollment among boys (the median is about 25 percent) and from 17 to 100+ percent of the racial gap among girls (the median is about 45 percent) are accounted for by differences in family stability and employment. (The 100+ figure obtained for the oldest group of girls is due to the fact that enrollment rates for blacks in this age are generally higher than for white girls in the same family stability—employment situation based on the average family—employment structure of black and white girls in this age group).

TABLE 7.10

RACIAL DIFFERENCES IN ENROLLMENT AND GRADE RETARDATION, BY FAMILY STABILITY
AND EMPLOYMENT FACTORS, 1960

| | Percentage enrolled | | | Percentage of column 3 due to family factors | Percentage behind modal grade | | | Percentage of column 7 due to family factors |
| | White | Nonwhite | Difference | | White | Nonwhite | Difference | |
Sex and age	(1)	(2)	(3)	(4)	(5)	(6)	(7)	(8)
Males								
5	45.0	41.5	3.5	17				
6	83.9	78.6	5.3	13				
7–9	97.8	95.7	2.1	20	3.4	7.8	4.4	14
10–13	97.7	95.7	2.0	26	10.2	25.0	14.8	11
14–15	94.8	90.3	4.5	29	15.5	35.5	20.0	10
16–17	82.4	74.1	8.3	37	16.0	39.4	23.4	9
18–19	47.4	40.1	7.3	28	22.7	57.3	34.6	16
Females								
5	45.3	44.0	1.3	46				
6	84.2	79.5	4.7	17				
7–9	97.8	96.0	1.8	22	2.5	5.8	3.3	15
10–13	97.8	96.1	1.7	28	6.2	17.1	10.9	10
14–15	94.4	90.1	4.3	44	9.3	24.8	15.5	8
16–17	81.6	73.5	8.1	54	9.7	27.2	17.5	10
18–19	37.9	36.5	1.4	100+*	17.3	46.0	28.7	30

SOURCE: U.S. Bureau of the Census, 1964a, table 3.

* A compositional effect in excess of 100 percent means that black enrollment rates tend to be higher than white rates. If the family composition of blacks and whites were averaged, the black rates would yield a higher enrollment rate.

Looking down column 4 of table 7.10, it is clear that family factors alone will account for a fair part of the racial difference in enrollment, although most of the gap is due to other factors. Among boys, from 13 to 37 percent of the racial differences in enrollment can be explained by black–white differences in their family composition (6 and 16–17 years of age, respectively). Admittedly, the compositional effect is generally larger among girls. To be sure, two-parent families in which the father works and the mother does not are less frequent among blacks than whites. Nevertheless, it would be dangerous to infer that one major reason for lower black enrollment rates is that the "traditional" family structure is less common among blacks. This question will be considered after the components method is applied to the sizable differences in black–white grade retardation.

Unlike school attendance, the racial differences in retardation are quite substantial. Among those enrolled in school, the gap between blacks and whites widens steadily with increasing age. The difference of 4.5 percent among boys 7 to 9 years of age widens to nearly 15 percent in the next age group (10 to 13 years of age), 20 percent in the midteens, nearly 25 percent among those 16 to 17, and a full 30 percent among boys in their late teens (column 7 of table 7.10). The gap between black and white girls in their retardation also widens with increasing age, but it is not as great as that found among boys. Nevertheless the difference is still substantial among girls, increasing from 3 percent among girls 7 to 9 to nearly 30 percent among girls in their late teens.

The combined effects of family stability and employment account for very little of the substantial difference between black and white rates of retardation (see column 8). With the exception of the oldest group of girls, from about 10 to 15 percent of the absolute difference between the races in a given sex and age group can be accounted for by the combined influences of family and employment structure.

The results at this point can be readily summarized. The racial gaps in grade retardation are substantial, but family–employment structure accounts for only a small part of this difference. Family patterns among blacks and whites were probably not a major explanation of black–immigrant differences in school performance. Racial differences in enrollment rates are not substantial in 1960, although they do favor whites. However, a fair part of the racial gap can generally be explained through differences between the groups' family stability–employment patterns.

Great care must be taken before drawing inferences from these results about the specific family patterns causing black–white differences in enrollment rates. It is one thing to find that the groups' family stability—employment patterns account for part of their gap in enrollment. This is different from concluding that the cause necessarily lies in the lower frequency among blacks of two-parent families in which the father is employed and the mother is not. Indeed such an inference would be false. Shown in table 7.11 are the racial differences in enrollment under 11 different combinations of family structure and employment as well as the overall gap. Racial differences in enrollment rates are generally greater for children in two-parent families with only a working father than in most other combinations of stability and employment.

Consider, for example, the enrollment rates among girls 16 to 17 years of age. Among all whites, 81.6 percent are enrolled, compared with 73.5 percent among nonwhites. The difference of 8.1 percent is shown under the first column of table 7.11. Observe that the gap is reduced among girls in two-parent families with just the father working. In this case, the difference is 7.6 percent and again favors whites. In other words, *if all whites and all blacks were in such families, most of the present difference would still remain.* Looking across the row, the gap between blacks and whites is less severe in most other combinations of family stability and employment. Indeed, among those girls living in families where neither of their parents is present, the enrollment rates are considerably higher for blacks than whites (hence the negative value shown). There is only one family situation where the racial gap favors whites more than in the two-parent—father-working combination; this is where one parent is present and is in the labor force with no adult at home (the gap is 9.7 percent).

Generally speaking, table 7.11 indicates that the white advantage over nonwhites in enrollment rates is nearly as great in the traditionally "ideal" combination of two parents and only father working as it is among all families combined. Among the youngest group of boys as well as those 16 to 17 years of age, the gap is actually greater. Because such comparisons involve a severe part—whole methodological problem, inspection of the racial gap within various family—employment combinations is more meaningful. The situation cited above for older girls is rather typical; for most age groups and in both sexes, the racial gap is greater in the ideal family situation than in the vast majority of other stability—employment combinations. The right-hand column of table 7.11 gives the number of other combinations with a higher racial gap. Among males, this ranges from 1 to 3 of the ten other combinations, depending on the particular age; among girls, there are somewhat more combinations with a higher racial gap. But overall, the results clearly

TABLE 7.11
PERCENTAGE ENROLLED IN SCHOOL BY RACE, FAMILY STRUCTURE, AGE, AND SEX, 1960

| Sex, age, and race | Total | Both parents present | | | | | |
| | | | Both parents in labor force | | | | |
		Father in labor force, mother not in labor force	Some family members 20 and over not in labor force	All family members 20 and over in labor force	Mother in labor force, father not in labor force	Neither parent in labor force
Females						
5 years old:						
White	45.3	45.5	43.4	45.6	38.1	35.5
Nonwhite	44.0	44.4	48.2	46.3	36.1	38.0
Difference	1.3	1.1	−4.8	−.7	2.0	−2.5
6 years old:						
White	84.2	84.4	85.4	85.2	84.0	75.4
Nonwhite	79.5	79.8	76.7	80.8	76.3	77.5
Difference	4.7	4.6	8.7	4.4	7.7	−2.1
7—9 years old:						
White	97.8	98.0	98.0	98.3	96.3	95.7
Nonwhite	96.0	96.3	97.1	96.7	96.3	94.9
Difference	1.8	1.7	.9	1.6	−	.8
10—13 years old:						
White	97.8	98.1	98.1	98.2	96.6	95.5
Nonwhite	96.1	96.6	95.6	96.9	95.8	93.8
Difference	1.7	1.5	2.5	1.3	.8	1.7
14—15 years old:						
White	94.4	95.6	96.2	96.5	91.5	90.2
Nonwhite	90.1	91.7	92.1	92.7	91.2	87.9
Difference	4.3	3.9	4.1	3.8	.3	2.3
16—17 years old:						
White	81.6	87.7	87.5	89.3	82.2	76.8
Nonwhite	73.5	80.1	83.4	81.7	77.2	74.6
Difference	8.1	7.6	4.1	7.6	5.0	2.2
18—19 years old:						
White	37.9	42.5	44.1	44.7	35.6	35.0
Nonwhite	36.5	46.3	48.8	45.7	46.1	39.6
Difference	1.4	−3.8	−4.7	−1.0	−10.5	−4.6

SOURCE: U.S. Bureau of the Census, 1964a, table 3.

TABLE 7.11 (Continued)

One parent present			Neither parent present			
Parent in labor force			In a family			
Some family members 20 and over not in labor force	All family members 20 and over in labor force	Parent not in labor force	Some family members 20 and over not in labor force	All family members 20 and over in labor force	Not in a family	Number of family situations with larger black disadvantage than "ideal" family type
46.0	47.3	44.3	34.7	41.4	50.3	
41.1	41.9	48.9	36.6	35.8	47.9	
4.9	5.4	−4.6	−1.9	5.6	2.4	5
80.0	84.8	80.4	74.9	76.8	70.3	
81.1	79.1	82.1	70.5	77.1	72.5	
−1.1	5.7	−1.7	4.4	−.3	−.2	3
96.9	97.8	97.0	95.4	96.0	81.9	
95.1	95.7	95.6	94.2	95.9	90.6	
1.8	2.1	1.4	1.2	.1	−8.7	2
96.5	97.6	97.1	94.4	96.3	80.3	
94.5	96.2	95.1	94.9	95.5	88.8	
2.0	1.4	2.0	−.5	.8	−8.5	4
93.0	94.6	91.5	81.9	70.7	78.7	
88.5	90.1	89.2	86.6	83.2	83.6	
4.5	4.5	2.3	−4.7	−12.5	−4.9	3
78.1	82.5	78.4	49.7	32.9	68.8	
74.5	72.8	73.5	66.6	50.2	67.2	
3.6	9.7	4.9	−16.9	−17.3	1.6	1
38.5	35.7	32.2	23.0	9.3	74.2	
37.1	36.7	37.4	33.8	18.3	57.9	
1.4	−1.0	−5.2	−10.8	−9.0	16.3	4

TABLE 7.11 (Continued)

Sex, age, and race	Total	Both parents present				
			Both parents in labor force			
		Father in labor force, mother not in labor force	Some family members 20 and over not in labor force	All family members 20 and over in labor force	Mother in labor force, father not in labor force	Neither parent in labor force
Males						
5 years old:						
White	45.0	45.2	44.5	45.8	40.1	33.7
Nonwhite	41.5	41.3	43.8	44.1	33.1	34.7
Difference	3.5	3.9	.7	1.7	7.0	−1.0
6 years old:						
White	83.9	84.1	84.6	84.9	77.2	74.0
Nonwhite	78.6	78.8	79.8	81.1	78.3	74.2
Difference	5.3	5.3	4.8	3.8	−1.1	−.2
7–9 years old:						
White	97.8	98.0	97.7	98.2	96.4	95.1
Nonwhite	95.7	96.1	97.1	96.6	94.9	93.4
Difference	2.1	1.9	.6	1.6	1.5	1.7
10–13 years old:						
White	97.7	98.0	97.9	98.1	96.4	95.4
Nonwhite	95.7	96.2	95.8	96.9	95.6	92.3
Difference	2.0	1.8	2.1	1.2	.8	3.1
14–15 years old:						
White	94.8	95.4	95.4	96.3	93.7	88.5
Nonwhite	90.3	91.4	93.1	93.3	88.4	87.9
Difference	4.5	4.0	2.3	3.0	5.3	.6
16–17 years old:						
White	82.4	85.8	87.0	88.1	77.9	71.1
Nonwhite	74.1	77.1	80.7	80.2	73.8	73.0
Difference	8.3	8.7	6.3	7.9	4.1	−1.9
18–19 years old:						
White	47.4	50.7	53.6	55.3	42.8	34.5
Nonwhite	40.1	44.6	57.1	49.3	38.9	42.7
Difference	7.3	6.1	−3.5	6.0	3.9	−8.2

SOURCE: U.S. Bureau of the Census, 1964*a*, table 3.

TABLE 7.11 (Continued)

| One parent present | | | Neither parent present | | | |
| Parent in labor force | | | In a family | | | |
Some family members 20 and over not in labor force	All family members 20 and over in labor force	Parent not in labor force	Some family members 20 and over not in labor force	All family members 20 and over in labor force	Not in a family	Number of family situations with larger black disadvantage than "ideal" family type
38.8	49.9	42.0	36.4	36.3	45.2	
41.2	42.2	46.2	33.7	31.7	45.9	
−2.4	7.7	−4.2	2.7	4.6	−.7	3
85.0	85.9	81.8	77.1	75.2	70.2	
75.6	77.7	79.9	74.2	73.0	76.3	
9.4	8.2	1.9	2.9	2.2	−6.1	2
97.2	97.7	97.0	94.4	96.2	78.6	
95.8	95.5	95.1	93.9	94.9	90.0	
1.4	2.2	1.9	.5	1.3	−11.4	1
97.0	97.5	96.6	94.1	95.4	77.9	
95.5	95.8	95.2	94.1	94.8	86.0	
1.5	1.7	1.4	−	.6	−8.1	2
94.6	94.5	91.3	89.7	88.2	76.9	
89.4	91.1	88.6	88.9	88.3	76.1	
5.2	3.4	2.7	.8	−.1	.8	2
81.4	80.8	71.9	66.8	62.0	43.4	
71.2	75.5	69.4	70.0	68.5	51.1	
10.2	5.3	2.5	−3.2	−6.5	−7.7	1
42.1	44.5	35.6	33.2	21.3	51.2	
38.6	42.1	37.6	35.9	30.1	33.4	
3.5	2.4	−2.0	−2.7	−8.8	17.8	1

indicate that *the less-stable family structure and different employment fre-*
quencies among blacks would not help explain very much of the black—new
European differences in educational performance.

Although not shown, the situation for the racial differences in retardation is even more extreme. The difference in retardation is exceptionally
wide between black and white children in two-parent families where
only the father is employed. Indeed, the gap is greater in these families
than in any other combination of employment and family structure
(there is only one exception, among boys 18 to 19 years of age, and even
here it holds for nine of the remaining ten family combinations).

These results are somewhat surprising and may be easily misunderstood. (After discovering these patterns, for several nights the author
had nightmares of being quoted as advocating the disintegration of the
black family.) On the one hand, it is generally the case that racial gaps
are more severe among children in the traditional family ideal than in the
overwhelming majority of other family situations. However, this does
not mean that the enrollment rates for black children in such families are
lower than those among black children in other family situations. Indeed
the very opposite holds. Among 16 to 17 year old black girls, for
example, the enrollment rate of 80.1 is higher than in all but one of the
ten other family combinations (the exception being 83.4 percent enrolled
among girls in two-parent families where both parents are employed
and there is another adult at home who is not in the labor force). What
happens is that the *relative* differences between the races tend to be
exceptionally large in the ideal family situation. The advantage white
children in such families hold over white children in other family
situations is greater in absolute magnitude than the advantage black
children in the ideal situation have over other black children. In other
words, there is less variation by family types in enrollment rates among
blacks than whites. An increase in the proportion of black children in the
traditional family situation would indeed raise black enrollment rates.
On the other hand, the key point for the issue at hand is that the
black—white enrollment gap is generally quite high between children
who are in such families. Looking again at girls 16 to 17 years of age, the
overall racial difference of 8.1 percent is reduced to only 7.6 percent
among girls from two-parent—father-working families. Except for the
oldest group of girls, this small reduction is the typical case. Hence, if
black and white children were only in such families, nearly all of the
existing difference in their enrollment rates would remain (indeed it
would go up slightly in several age groups of boys). Therefore, it is clear
that the relation between enrollment and family stability—work patterns
are such that the vast bulk of schooling differences cannot be attributed

to the higher rates of family instability among blacks. (Having cleared up the interpretation, the author will probably find himself suffering from an even more horrible nightmare; namely, in which the book is not quoted at all.)

Fertility and Education

Because blacks currently have higher illegitimacy and fertility rates than whites, it is tempting to attribute a fair part of the new European–black differences in educational attainment to these factors. Children in larger families are generally handicapped in terms of their educational prospects. Holding income constant, offspring in large families will be under greater pressure to enter the labor force at an early age in order to contribute to the family's needs. In addition, the financial capacity of parents to support their children's education will decrease with larger families. Beyond this, early parenthood has its own negative consequences for the parents because the presence of offspring pushes the male into the labor force and is likely to truncate the parents' education. In this regard, illegitimacy also creates educational and income disadvantages for the parents (see, for example, Freedman and Coombs, 1966). More generally, of the various family characteristics accounting for racial differences in occupational achievement, Duncan, Featherman, and Duncan (1972, p. 65) find racial differences in family size to be relatively the most significant. However, bear in mind that its absolute importance is not that great.

It is true that blacks have had a higher fertility rate than whites during the post-World War II period. A direct comparison between first- and second-generation European women with the roughly analogous black generations living in the North (those born in the South and North, respectively) indicates that five SCE European groups had lower fertility than the comparable generations of blacks in 1960 (table 7.12). With but one exception, foreign-born Italian women in the oldest category, both northern- and southern-born black women living in the North have more children. Among those in the youngest age grouping, the Russian-born have the highest rate, 1,960 per thousand women, and this is still substantially below that for northern nonwhites of either southern or northern birth (2,487 and 2,234 per thousand, respectively).

Nevertheless, it is erroneous to think that fertility differences between the groups can provide much of an explanation of past educational developments among the groups. Earlier in the century, the new European groups generally had much higher fertility rates than blacks in the North. In 1910, southern-born blacks living in the North had substan-

TABLE 7.12
FERTILITY, 1960

Generation and ethnic group	Number of children ever born per thousand women, by age		
	25—34	35—44	45—54[a]
Foreign-born:			
Poland	1,834	1,920	1,877
Czechoslovakia	1,781	1,849	1,966
Austria	1,548	1,639	1,677
USSR	1,960	1,877	1,729
Italy	1,740	2,177	2,430
Second-generation:			
Poland	1,866	2,091	1,934
Czechoslovakia	1,896	2,131	1,989
Austria	1,819	1,979	1,765
USSR	1,867	2,024	1,746
Italy	1,764	2,010	1,948
Nonwhites living in North:			
Born in South	2,487	2,344	2,301
Born in North	2,234	2,488	2,542

SOURCE: U.S. Bureau of the Census, 1964b, tables 9 and 13.
[a] For nonwhite women 45 years of age and older.

tially lower fertility than foreign-born women from the four South—Central—Eastern European groups for which data are available. For example, there were 488 children born per thousand black women 20—24 years of age, compared with a SCE low of 641 for Russian immigrant women and a SCE high of 1,264 for the Italian group (see table 7.13). With the exception of women in their late teens, the new immigrant women had higher fertility in all age cohorts. The differences are in most cases of a massive nature. The number of children born to immigrant women approaching 30 is essentially twice the number born to black women of southern nativity who reside in the North. Among women 40 to 44 years of age, the rates are still twice as high for those of either Polish or Russian birth than for this black group. Throughout the table, there is every indication that black fertility would, if anything, lead one to expect higher educational attainment.

Fertility rates for first-generation black women in the North remained considerably lower than those for the new European immigrant groups as recently as 1940 (table 7.14). There are a few exceptions for the youngest age cohort, but new European immigrant fertility is still impressively higher than the southern-born black rates. Among women 35

TABLE 7.13

FERTILITY OF SOUTHERN-BORN BLACK WOMEN IN THE NORTH AND IMMIGRANT WOMEN,
1910

| | Number of children ever born per thousand women | | | | |
Age	Poland	Austria—Hungary	USSR	Italy	Black
15—19	77	88	29	188	93
20—24	914	919	641	1,264	488
25—29	2,343	2,115	2,113	2,542	1,096
30—34	3,818	3,189	3,617	3,761	1,647
35—39	5,334	4,394	4,806	5,124	2,285
40—44	6,557	5,147	6,132	5,889	3,023
45—54	7,207	5,802	6,922	5,924	4,027
55—64	7,494	6,048	7,419	5,669	5,037
65—74	7,596	6,334	7,398	5,947	5,815

SOURCE: U.S. Bureau of the Census, 1945, tables 43 and 106.

to 44 years of age, the 1,862 children per 1,000 black women is lower than any of the immigrant groups shown. Jewish women of Polish or Russian origin have about 140 more children per thousand, with other groups higher (the rate for Italian women is close to double that of blacks).

Philip Hauser, observing a similar pattern in Chicago for 1930, has speculated about the reasons for these fertility differentials (1938, pp. 21—24). The propensity toward early marriage among black women helps to account for their higher rates in the youngest ages. But Hauser suggests several factors that tend to reduce their overall fertility rates. Married black women have greater chances of widowhood and are also more likely to work than whites. In addition, Hauser mentions that the greater prevalence of venereal diseases and tuberculosis among blacks raises the level of sterility in the group. Finally, there was probably a greater frequency of self-induced abortions among blacks which led not only to terminating the fetus, but also a permanent condition of sterility when performed crudely.

Clearly there are various technical cautions that the reader should keep in mind. The data presented in the preceding three tables are based on the fertility of women alive at a given census and hence do not take into account differential mortality of mothers (maternal mortality was no trivial factor in earlier decades). The data refer only to children born, not to survivorship. Here, however, higher infant mortality rates among blacks (chapter 2) reduced black dependents more sharply than South—Central—Eastern Europeans. Another factor not considered is the linkage between fertility and the timing of arrival; that is, the age at which

TABLE 7.14
Fertility of Southern-Born Black Women in the North and Immigrant Women, 1940

Number of children ever born per thousand women

Age	Poland			Czechoslovakia	Austria	Hungary	USSR			Italy	Black
	All	Yiddish mother tongue	Other mother tongue				All	Yiddish mother tongue	Other mother tongue		
15–34	1,031	735	1,213	923	951	1,176	1,030	961	1,125	1,388	916
35–44	2,890	2,009	3,096	2,835	2,458	2,365	2,125	2,000	2,290	3,447	1,862
45–54	4,192	2,922	4,366	4,045	3,683	3,305	3,111	2,848	3,451	4,638	2,219
55–64	4,899	3,918	5,084	4,492	4,191	3,837	3,917	3,698	4,208	5,168	2,862
65–74	5,577	5,061	5,689	4,936	4,343	4,169	5,083	4,791	5,500	5,347	3,510

SOURCE: U.S. Bureau of the Census, 1945, tables 40 and 103.

the migrants arrived from Europe (or the South in the case of blacks) is not taken into account as well as their fertility before and after the move. This issue may be important if there is some interaction between age of arrival, pre- and postmigration fertility. But most important, these data do not deal with the average size of family among the groups under consideration. Fertility could be distributed differently among the two groups such that the average number of siblings per black child is greater than among the new European groups even if the latter group has higher total fertility. This could be the case if relatively more black women had no children and hence those with offspring had larger families. Although demographers are inclined to think of groups in terms of their total fertility, this need not be the same as the average size of family experienced by children in each group.

The last issue, being of considerable importance to the fertility question, requires the calculation of a somewhat irregular measure with less than ideal data. For 1930, one can determine the average number of children found in families with at least one child under 21 years of age. For blacks living in the South, the average child lives in a family with a total of 4.7 children; for those living in the North, the average is 3.81. Data limitations prevent decomposition of northern black residents into their region of birth or of white groups into their European origins. This average of 3.81 for northern blacks is below that for all foreign-born whites, 4.00, but is considerably higher than the average for all second-generation whites (3.44). Because the figure for northern black residents includes both northern- and southern-born components, it is reasonable to compare their average of 3.81 with the 3.76 obtained for all foreign white stock (including foreign-born and second-generation whites). The difference is rather small. Moreover, assuming that new Europeans had higher fertility than whites of Northwestern European origin, very likely the figure for the South−Central−Eastern Europeans would be even higher than the 3.81 obtained for blacks living in the North. Thus, even where family size of the children is considered, one can conclude that there is no evidence that the average northern black child was in a larger family than the average new European child.

At this point a straightforward conclusion is appropriate about the influence of various family characteristics on black−new European educational differences in the North. Data limitations notwithstanding, the results consistently indicate that educational differences between blacks and SCE Europeans cannot be explained in terms of their different family structures. There is no question that black−new European family patterns were not the same, but all efforts here have failed to explain educational differences. The gaps between black and white family patterns cannot account for a sizable part of their offsprings' educational gap. If blacks had the same family distribution as whites, only a small part of the existing educational gaps would disappear if all other factors were still operating. Those making contrary claims should be aware that their assertions have no validity unless new empirical evidence is provided.

APPENDIX: RELIABILITY OF THE AGE-SPECIFIC EDUCATION DATA

The analysis of ethnic changes in educational attainment earlier in the chapter is based on data obtained for various age groups in the 1960 Census. As these results include reported education for older populations such as those at least 75 years of age in 1960, it is reasonable to ask whether the patterns obtained are the result of misreporting. The older ages in 1960 may be subject to large-scale overreporting of their educational attainment.

An internal check for the reliability of the educational results is made through a comparison of the 1960 figures with those obtained 20 years earlier for the same cohorts in the 1940 Census. For example, the educational levels reported by second-generation whites 65 to 74 years of age in 1960 can be compared with the levels reported among second-generation whites 45 to 54 years of age in 1940. Differential mortality and migration related to education might lead us to expect some discrepancies between the 20-year periods, but any substantial differences for the same cohort would suggest that the analysis may be based on distorted data and subject to significant errors.

Table 7.15 provides net difference indexes between 1940 and 1950 for specific age groups in the nonwhite and second-generation white populations. (Due to data limitations in 1940, it was not possible to obtain data on either specific second-generation white groups or the northern-born black population.) The widest discrepancies are found among those 25 to 34 in 1940. This is understandable given that some members of the cohort in 1940 had probably not yet completed their education. However, even here the net difference indexes run from only .04 to .07. (A positive index means that the cohort's educational distribution in 1960 is higher than it was in 1940.) In most intracohort comparisons the indexes are even lower, in a few cases actually being slightly negative.

Overall the changes between 1940 and 1960 in the reported educational attainment of a given cohort are rather comparable for nonwhites and

TABLE 7.15

NET DIFFERENCE INDEXES OF EDUCATIONAL ATTAINMENT REPORTED BY SAME COHORT,
1940 AND 1960 CENSUSES

	Age (and census)			
Group and sex	25–34 (1940), 45–54 (1960)	35–44 (1940), 55–64 (1960)	45–54 (1940), 65–74 (1960)	55+ (1940), 75+ (1960)
Nonwhites:				
Male	.07	.01	−.05	−.05
Female	.07	.03	−.01	.01
Second-generation whites:				
Male	.05	.01	.05	−.03
Female	.04	.02	.00	.01

SOURCES: U.S. Bureau of the Census, 1943a, table 18; 1943b, table 26; 1963a,
tables 1 and 2.
NOTE: In order to maximize comparability, data for those 55 and older in 1940 are
adjusted to take into account age distribution of population 75+ in 1960. A slight
discrepancy exists between 1940 and 1960 second-generation data; the former is based
on whites of foreign or mixed parentage whereas 1960 also includes nonwhites in this
generational category.

the second generation. Differences in indexes are at most little more than
.02. For example, a comparison between nonwhite females 55 to 64 in
1960 with the same cohort's educational distribution in 1940 yields a net
difference index of .03; an analogous computation for second-generation
females yields an index of .02. The only exceptions are the results for
males 45 to 54 years of age in 1940 where the indexes are −.05 and .05,
respectively, for nonwhites and second-generation whites. However, in
the same cohort there is virtually no difference for females.

In conclusion, the indexes shown in table 7.15 indicate that the age-
specific educational figures in 1960 are reliable. However, comparisons
with data obtained for the same cohorts when they were 20 years
younger generate rather small discrepancies. With one exception, the
magnitude and direction of these intracohort differences are similar for
both nonwhites and the second generation. The changing patterns of
educational attainment among the groups examined earlier in this
chapter cannot be explained in terms of systematic shifts over time in
their reporting of educational attainment. Clearly the reader should note
that this internal test cannot generate any conclusions about the validity—
as contrasted to reliability—of the educational data.

8

Further Analysis of
Education in the North

INDEXES OF NET DIFFERENCE

Clearly there is no simple explanation for the more rapid educational advances among the new Europeans. As the previous chapter indicated, values and cultural attributes—probably the most commonly held white interpretations for lower black educational attainment in the North—do not provide much of an explanation either directly or indirectly. Because we are dealing with a complicated and subtle set of processes, it is appropriate to examine the problem more closely. A comparison of the changing educational gap between blacks and South–Central–Eastern Europeans is needed which is more precise than that possible through the use of medians. Although the median is a widely used measure of educational attainment, it is nothing more than the exact midpoint of a population arrayed in order of increasing educational attainment and tells nothing about a population's educational distribution above or below that fiftieth percentile. Because two groups with identical medians may differ substantially in their distributions above or below this midpoint, comparisons between groups based solely on the median are very crude and can also be misleading (Wohlstetter and Coleman, 1970).

The measure employed here, the net difference index (ND), is based on each group's distribution in all locations along the educational continuum. If the educational attainment of each member of group A is compared with each member of group B, three sets of A−B pairs would result: those in which A and B have the same educational level; those in which A exceeds B; and pairs in which B exceeds A. By way of illustration, suppose that A and B have the same levels of attainment in 33 percent of the pairings; in 40 percent of the cases A is higher than B; and in 27 percent of the pairs B exceeds A. Subtracting .27 from .40, the ND in this case is .13. (It is necessary to specify the ordering of the subtraction, but the substantive conclusions about the two groups are unaffected). Assuming all possible pairings of As and Bs, the index of .13 means that A's education will exceed B's level 13 percent more often than will B exceed A. If all As exceed all Bs, the index will be ±1.0, depending on the choice of subtrahend and minuend. The value of zero means that the number of pairs in which A exceeds B is equal to the number of pairs in which B exceeds A. Thus an increasing distance in the educational distributions of the two groups is indicated as ND moves from zero toward ±1.0. (For a more detailed discussion of the net difference index, see Lieberson , 1975.)

Northern Blacks Versus Second-Generation Whites

Comparing the oldest and youngest cohorts examined, those 75 and older in 1960 versus those who were 25−34 in that year, it is clear that the new European's educational advantage has improved since the beginning of the period covered. Eight of the nine groups of European men in the oldest cohort had higher educational attainment than northern-born blacks (see the ND indexes in table 8.1); the only exception were the Poles whose ND was zero when compared with black men. These ND indexes were rather substantial for Austrian, Hungarian, Lithuanian, and Russian second-generation groups when compared with blacks, roughly .20 or higher. However, in all but one case the NDs were even higher when northern-born blacks and second-generation Europeans in the 1925−1935 birth cohorts are compared. The only exception is the Hungarians who drop from .38 to .28. But all of the other new groups increase: Finns and Czechs go from .02 each in the oldest cohort to .25 and .24 among the youngest; Poles likewise reach .24, whereas there had been no net difference from blacks in the oldest cohort of men.

The pattern of change is analogous for women, but the starting points are different (bottom panel of table 8.1). In the oldest cohort under consideration, the Czech, Italian, and Polish second generations had somewhat lower educational levels than northern-born black women (NDs are -.05, -.03, and -.09, respectively). In addition, ND is nil

TABLE 8.1

Net Difference Indexes Between Northern-Born Black and Second-Generation White Educational Distributions, 1960

Cohorts by age (and year of birth)	Austria	Czecho-slovakia	Finland	Hungary	Italy	Lithu-ania	Poland	USSR	Yugo-slavia	Change from Preceding Cohort	
										Mean	Median
Males											
25–34 (1925–1935)	.33	.24	.25	.28	.14	.39	.24	.49	.25	.12	.12
35–44 (1915–1925)	.22	.10	.15	.14	.05	.25	.07	.39	.13	.03	.03
45–54 (1905–1915)	.20	.04	.10	.13	.02	.22	.05	.41	.06	.02	.02
55–64 (1895–1905)	.18	.03	.06	.20	.03	.20	.01	.35	.02	.01	.02
65–74 (1885–1895)	.19	.03	−.02	.28	.01	.24	−.03	.27	.00	−.02	.02
75+ (1885 or earlier)	.21	.02	.02	.38	.04	.21	.00	.18	.13[a]		−.03
Females											
25–34 (1925–1935)	.25	.16	.27	.21	.07	.29	.16	.38	.19	.13	.13
35–44 (1915–1925)	.13	.01	.20	.06	−.05	.15	−.04	.29	.06	.05	.06
45–54 (1905–1915)	.09	−.05	.18	.03	−.14	.09	−.10	.30	−.05	.03	.03
55–64 (1895–1905)	.09	−.06	.11	.08	−.14	.06	−.14	.24	−.13	.01	.01
65–74 (1885–1895)	.08	−.09	−.01	.14	−.13	.09	−.15	.16	−.08	−.08	−.06
75+ (1885 or earlier)	.16	−.05	.00	.30	−.03	.08	−.09	.09	.25[a]		

SOURCE: U.S. Bureau of the Census, 1963c, table 3; 1965, table 12.

NOTE: Negative values mean that blacks are higher; positive values mean that the white group is higher.

[a]Based on very small number of cases.

between Finnish and black women; therefore only five of the nine white groups have higher educational attainments than northern-born black women of the same age. However, by the time the youngest cohort is reached, there has been a net gain for seven of the nine white groups relative to black women such that all of the European groups now exceed blacks. It was not until the 1925–1935 cohort that Polish and Italian women passed northern-born black educational levels. Likewise, the four oldest Czech cohorts were less educated than black women and even those 35–44 in 1960 enjoy only a very slim advantage.

Not only is there the question of why blacks fell behind the Europeans, which is by no means trivial, but there are several surprising twists that may help us understand this basic shift.[1] Consider first the relative gains among specific cohorts. First one finds that changes between the oldest and next-oldest cohorts were generally more favorable to blacks when measured by the sensitive net difference index. Northern-born blacks gained on six of the nine European groups of men and seven of the nine sets of second-generation women (compare those 65–74 in 1960 with persons over 75 in that year in table 8.1). In each succeeding wave after that, an increasing number of new European groups gained on blacks, reaching the point such that all nine of the white groups gained on blacks in the shifts between the 1915–1925 and 1925–1935 cohorts.

The last two columns of table 8.1 summarize, respectively, the mean and median changes in ND recorded between succeeding cohorts when the European groups are compared with blacks. In the case of males, one observes a slight negative value in the first change (meaning that blacks gained over the Europeans on the average), and then three additional changes in which there were slightly positive shifts, followed by a massive jump in the European gains (both the mean and median increase in ND being .12). A similar pattern is experienced by the women. Blacks were gaining on the European second generations in the changes between the oldest and next-oldest cohorts—except that the gains are more substantial, the mean and median being -.08 and -.06, respectively. Again the next three comparisons show a mild average upward movement for the Europeans relative to blacks, which in turn is followed by a substantial jump for the most recent period. An adequate and reasonably rigorous understanding of this pattern is not only a fascinating challenge, but itself serves to illustrate how any monolithic explanation is apt to be rather simplistic when confronted with the actual facts. Northern blacks were first advancing slightly more rapidly than second-generation new Europeans, then the relative rates were reversed for several intercohort comparisons, and finally there was a massive upward surge in the gains of Europeans over blacks.

Native Whites of Native Parentage

A comparison restricted to blacks and new Europeans makes it impossible to determine if these shifts in their relative educational gains are due to some unusually rapid increase or decrease by one of the groups rather than exceptional behavior by the other population. Because educational attainment was going up for succeeding cohorts in all of the groups throughout the entire period, the relative magnitude of these gains is really at issue here. Hence it is useful to compare these groups with a third population, native whites of native parentage (NWNP). These are at least third-generation whites in the United States as their parents were both born here and hence their grandparents were either American-born themselves or immigrants to the United States. The European origins of such persons are unknown, but one can be reasonably confident that the older NWNPs in the comparisons are overwhelmingly of Northwestern European origin as relatively few South−Central−Eastern Europeans were in the migration streams before 1880. A distortion does exist in the comparisons over time because the ethnic origins of the NWNP population change with each succeeding age group, but no doubt the vast bulk of the population is of North-western European descent in even the youngest cohort. Hence we have a standard by which to judge the relative velocity of the new European and northern black intercohort changes in educational attainment.

There was a persistent intercohort gain for northern-born blacks compared with the NWNPs. The net educational advantage of the latter over blacks declines in each succeeding wave until the youngest is reached. Among men, for example, ND is .1884 in the oldest cohort, followed by .1678, .1547, .1399, and .1171 before it increases to .1453. Analogous changes are found in comparisons between black and NWNP women (see table 8.2) By contrast, the oldest intercohort comparison for the second generation of nine European groups indicates four shifts in favor of the Europeans and five in which the native whites of native parentage gain (this is the case for both men and women). However, as table 8.2 readily indicates, the European groups gained increasingly with each successive wave not merely over northern-born blacks, as we have seen earlier, but relative to the older white stocks as well. All nine of the European groups gain on the NWNP in the most recent comparison, even though this was a point at which blacks had fallen back relative to the same NWNP group.

These results help clarify the previous comparisons between northern blacks and the new Europeans. Not only were the older cohorts of blacks gaining on the SCE Europeans, but it was also a period when blacks

TABLE 8.2

Net Difference Indexes Between Native Whites of Native Parentage and Northern-Born Blacks and Second-Generation White Educational Distributions, 1960

Cohorts by age (and year of birth)	Black	Austria	Czecho-slovakia	Finland	Hungary	Italy	Lithu-ania	Poland	USSR	Yugo-slavia
Males										
25–34 (1925–1935)	.1453	−.1714	−.0715	−.0943	−.1141	.0158	−.2292	−.0848	−.3416	−.0864
35–44 (1915–1925)	.1171	−.0879	.0296	−.0275	−.0117	.0711	−.1175	.0463	−.2570	−.0028
45–54 (1905–1915)	.1399	−.0611	.1044	.0491	.0114	.1267	−.0774	.0934	−.2705	.0080
55–64 (1895–1905)	.1547	−.0184	.1347	.1081	−.0416	.1391	−.0514	.1511	−.1998	.1442
65–74 (1885–1895)	.1678	−.0140	.1501	.1973	−.1102	.1624	−.0847	.1952	−.1105	.1629
75+ (1885 or earlier)	.1884	−.0123	.1810	.1745	−.2070	.1544	−.0487	.1850	−.0012	.0539
Females										
25–34 (1925–1935)	.1149	−.1188	−.0291	−.1338	−.0852	.0577	−.1633	−.0323	−.2667	−.0545
35–44 (1915–1925)	.1143	−.0017	.1101	−.0760	.0597	.1675	−.0203	.1561	−.1686	.0686
45–54 (1905–1915)	.1587	.0768	.2157	.0090	.1416	.2978	.0745	.2633	−.1237	.2146
55–64 (1895–1905)	.1775	.1047	.2494	.0771	.1039	.3266	.1153	.3193	−.0529	.3073
65–74 (1885–1895)	.1851	.1213	.2927	.1956	.0544	.3246	.0951	.3326	.0350	.2815
75+ (1885 or earlier)	.2269	.0872	.2996	.2297	−.0827	.2063	.1377	.3135	.1343	−.0480

SOURCES: U.S. Bureau of the Census, 1963c, table 3; 1965, tables 7 and 12.

were gaining on the older white stock and when there was little progress for the successive second-generation members of the new white groups relative to the NWNPs. More recently in this century, northern-born blacks continued to gain on the older white stocks, but not as rapidly as did the new European second-generation cohorts—the net effect being a more rapid educational gain for the latter over northern-born blacks as well. This reached a particularly noteworthy shift when those 35–44 in 1960 are compared with the next cohort; the new Europeans gained at an exceptional rate over the NWNPs who, in turn, widened the gap over the northern-born blacks.

The problem, then, is to account for these interrelated events: the massive educational jump among the new Europeans in the cohort born between 1925 and 1935; the sudden reversal in the progress of northern-born blacks relative to native whites of native parentage; the shift in the black position in the North when compared to the new Europeans; and the latter's improvements vis-à-vis NWNPs as well as blacks. We are confronted with the small number of time points and hence will not be able to subject our analysis to some of the elegant procedures for dealing with time series. But it should be possible to achieve a greater understanding of the black–new European educational fluctuations over time in the gap.

CHANGING CHARACTERISTICS OF EUROPEAN MIGRANTS

The dramatic educational advances made by each new wave of second-generation SCE Europeans raises the question of whether the changes are at least partially due to comparable shifts in the background characteristics of the European migrants. We certainly know that the admission policies of the United States became stricter at the same time as the number of immigrants increased radically. The oldest second-generation cohort under study had immigrant parents who had migrated no later than 1885, a time when relatively few South–Central–Eastern Europeans were coming to the United States. Among Italians, for example, at that point the largest number of migrants had been 32,000 in 1882, whereas 25 years later the United States was regularly receiving well over 200,000 immigrants per year from Italy. If the flows increased at a time when the selective processes associated with migration became more demanding, then perhaps a major factor influencing the educational shifts found among the American-born offspring of the immigrants were changes among the new European immigrants.

Timing of the Improvements

During this period new laws were enacted which in varying degrees affected admission to the United States. Ignoring anti-Chinese legislation passed in 1875, the federal government until 1882 did no more than count the immigrants and set minimal living conditions on the ships. In that year, the United States established a modest tax on each new immigrant and prohibited the immigration of convicts, lunatics, idiots, and persons likely to become public charges (Higham, 1955, pp. 43–44). Through the years restrictions were gradually added to European immigration. (The case was far different for Asians, witness the Chinese Exclusion Act of 1882 and the so-called "Gentlemen's Agreement" with Japan.) In 1891, immigration was placed under federal supervision, and paupers, polygamists, and victims of certain diseases were barred; epileptics, prostitutes, professional beggars, anarchists, violent revolutionaries, and assassins were added to the list two years later. In 1907, tuberculars, imbeciles, and those with a record of moral turpitude were also banned. The head tax was also raised several times during this period. In 1917, after advocates had suffered repeated failures for decades, successful passage of a literacy test in any language became a precondition for adult entrance. Health criteria were again widened and the head tax was likewise increased. There were other severe changes in the immigration laws in later years, but they are not central to the topic under consideration. (For a description of the preceding laws as well as later ones, see Jones, 1960, chapter 9.)

The early legislation was of minor consequence; there was no general upgrading in the socioeconomic background characteristics of SCE European migrants to the nation until the 1917 literacy restrictions and the end of World War I. Table 8.3 indicates the illiteracy rates recorded between 1900 and 1920 for selected new European immigrant groups at the time of their arrival. Although there are fluctuations in both directions, for the most part there is little improvement in literacy between 1900 and 1910. Illiteracy drops slightly for some groups—Bohemians, Croats, Italians, Magyars, and Slovaks—but for most groups the 1910 illiteracy rates are higher than those found in 1900. The effect of the new literacy law is dramatically shown by the figures for 1920. Southern Italians have the highest percentage illiterate in 1920, 13.9, but this has to be compared with 1910 when more than half were unable to read or write. The figures are not zero in 1920 despite the literacy test because the law exempted those escaping religious persecution and illiterate members of a family with an acceptable immigrant (Jones, 1960, p. 270).

TABLE 8.3

PERCENTAGE ILLITERATE AMONG SOUTH−CENTRAL−EASTERN EUROPEAN IMMIGRANTS,
1900−1920

Origin	Year of arrival		
	1900	1910	1920
Bohemian and Moravian	3.0	1.1	0.0
Croatian and Slovenian	37.2	33.5	4.7
Dalmatian, Bosnian, and			
Herzegovinian	32.9	39.3	1.8
Greek	17.1	24.0	3.2
Italian (north)	11.5	7.2	1.7
Italian (south)	54.5	51.8	13.9
Jewish	22.2	28.8	6.7
Lithuanian	31.3	50.0	4.2
Magyar	16.6	11.8	0.7
Polish	30.7	35.0	2.6
Roumanian	24.6	36.5	3.2
Russian	27.1	38.1	2.0
Slovak	27.6	21.3	2.9

SOURCES: 1900: U.S. Immigration Commission, 1911a, tables 16 and 18;
Lieberson, 1963a, table 16.
NOTE: Data are for persons 14 years of age and older in 1900 and 1910,
16 and older in 1920.

A detailed year-by-year examination of the illiteracy rates during the
12 years from 1899 through 1910 illustrates rather nicely the absence of
any gradual improvement at that time (table 8.4). For all immigrants
combined, the highest rate of illiteracy occurs in 1907 and the second
highest in 1909. This is not merely due to the changing geographical
origins of migrants during the period. Among Greeks, for example, the
illiteracy rate was lowest among those arriving in 1900 and second lowest
in the preceding year, whereas the highest rate of illiteracy occurred in
1907. A rather similar pattern is found among Jews as well; 19.8 percent
of those migrating in 1899 were illiterate (the lowest figure in the 12-year
span) and the highest illiteracy rates were recorded at the end of the
period, from 1908 through 1910.

The occupations of new European immigrants reported at the time of
their arrival leads to a similar conclusion, but in this case dating back to
1880. Between 1880 and 1895 one finds that the percentage of immigrants
who were either farmers, laborers, or servants was maintained at a very
high level (table 8.5). Except for Poles in 1895 the figures are relatively
steady and are in some cases even higher at the end of the period. (The

TABLE 8.4
FLUCTUATIONS IN ILLITERACY, 1899–1910

Origin	Percentage Illiterate											
	1899	1900	1901	1902	1903	1904	1905	1906	1907	1908	1909	1910
All groups	22.6	23.8	27.6	28.2	24.6	24.0	25.3	27.5	29.4	25.7	28.8	27.5
Greek	22.1	17.1	25.8	29.9	27.7	23.5	22.8	23.5	30.5	28.5	26.0	24.0
Jewish	19.8	22.2	23.3	28.1	26.2	22.7	22.5	26.7	28.6	30.0	28.8	28.8
Slovak	27.4	27.6	30.2	25.5	21.3	27.2	24.2	21.7	21.2	23.4	19.5	21.3

SOURCE: U.S. Immigration Commission, 1911a, tables 16 and 18.
NOTE: Data are for persons 14 years of age and older.

figures through 1895 refer to the migrants' country of last permanent residence or citizenship; whereas the data from 1900 through 1924 refer to the ethnic origin of the persons involved. The two data sets are not comparable in some cases.) Again, between 1900 and 1914 there is no downward thrust in the concentration in these less-skilled positions. There are modest declines for Finns, Jews, Hungarians, and Poles during this span, but fairly sizable increases for Russians and Greeks, with a modest increase also observed for Italians and Croatians. (Incidentally, the relatively low concentration of Jews in these occupations represents an extremely important factor to consider later in dealing with their occupational patterns in the United States.) In the two post-World War I years we see a general decline in the representation of these less-skilled pursuits among the new immigrants when compared with 1914—the only exception being an inexplicable increase among Jews and Croats in 1924.

Implications for the Second Generation

Both the occupational and literacy data indicate the absence before 1917 of an upgrading in the background characteristics of new European immigrants. The improvements shown by several older cohorts of second-generation South–Central–Eastern Europeans clearly cannot be explained by this factor. For example, the second-generation cohort 45–54 years of age in 1960 were all born before the enactment of the literacy test. Hence their gains, as well as those of the older cohorts, cannot be attributed to changes in the characteristics of the immigrant streams. On the other hand, the remarkable gain of the two youngest cohorts could be due at least in part to the upgrading of the immigrants. Those 35–44 in 1960 were largely born in this period (between 1915 and 1925), and the youngest cohort, 25–34, were born in the ten years beginning with 1925. Hence it is plausible that the latter's massive educational jump reflects a set of migratory changes such that their immigrant parents were relatively more educated and enjoyed better jobs than the earlier migrants from SCE Europe. If one assumes that more highly educated parents would have both higher educational aspirations for their offspring and be in a better economic position to support such goals, then this shift in migration could be a major factor accounting for the sudden educational jump among the younger second-generation cohorts.

The employment factor will be considered later; let us first delve further into the evidence relating the upgrading of immigrants to second-generation improvements in educational attainment. A problem

TABLE 8.5
OCCUPATION AT TIME OF ARRIVAL, 1880–1924

Group or Country	Percentage laborers, farmers, or servants									
	1880	1884	1890	1895	1900	1905	1910	1914	1920	1924
Austrian	65	78	85	75			NA			
Croatian and Slovenian		NA	NA		93	94	97	96	59	80
Finnish	93	94	92	90	97	91	92	90	57	66
Greek[a]	75	48	81	68	76	82	94	90	83	67
Hungarian[b]	67	92	91	94	93	92	92	91	53	63
Italian[c]	86	77	89	79	81	83	87	85	70	62
Jewish					23	20	20	22	28	30
Polish	83	81	87	48	94	94	94	92	49	73
Russian	51	67	74	76	76	66	92	94	61	36

SOURCES: U.S. Treasury Department, 1880, table 5; 1884, table 44; 1891, table 38; 1896, table 8; Willcox, 1929, pp. 450–459.

NOTE: Data between 1880 and 1895 refer to country of last permanent residence or citizenship. The percentages are obtained by dividing the sum of farmers, farm laborers, laborers, and servants by the total (excluding occupation not stated and those without occupation because the latter is probably composed largely of women and children). Data between 1900 and 1924 refer to what is called "race or people." The percentages are obtained by dividing the sum of laborers, servants, and agricultural workers by the total (excluding miscellaneous).

NA: Data not available.

[a] N is less than 50 in 1880 and 1884.

[b] Magyars from 1900 onward.

[c] Sicily included in 1884.

with the method used above is that the data do not specify the ages of immigrants at the time of arrival—all that we do know is that the literacy figures refer to those 14 and over in the year indicated. To be sure, the vast bulk of immigrants admitted were not only older than 14, but were concentrated in the ages connected with childbearing. For example, 83 percent of all immigrants between 1899 and 1910 were 14–44 years of age (U.S. Immigration Commission, 1911a, p. 88). However, an alternate approach is to consider how the educational levels vary by age cohorts among the foreign-born. Table 8.6 gives the educational levels of the foreign-born at different ages based on data available for 1960. This is a rough step because we do not know exactly when members of each age group migrated to the United States. For example, the foreign-born 25–34 years of age in 1960 include some who migrated that very year as well as others who had migrated shortly after birth. However, these figures do provide a specific age delineation, go beyond the mere literate–illiterate educational classification provided by the migration statistics, exclude those who left the United States, and take into account immigrant children who were educated in the United States. It seems reasonable to assume that the age-related changes represent at least in part shifts in the educational accomplishments of immigrants over time. Accordingly, these data provide a second imperfect look into the problem at hand.

The educational advances among the older cohorts of native whites of native parentage were steady but not spectacular: a median of 8.2 among men born in 1885 or earlier versus 8.4 for men born between 1885 and 1895. Likewise there was an increment of .4 years between the latter cohort and men born in the next ten years. A much bigger jump occurs in the next two decades, with the median going from 8.8 to 10.4 (for those born between 1905 and 1915) and on to 12.1 (1915–1925) before settling down to a small increment to 12.3 in the next cohort. This pattern is essentially repeated among NWNP women, aside from the fact that they start at a higher initial level.

The ND indexes between different immigrant groups and NWNP men are given in Table 8.6 for four successive cohorts. (Cohorts born after 1915 are irrelevant because their children would almost all be too young in 1960.) The oldest cohort of new European immigrant men are to a large extent less educated than the native whites, with NDs running from .20 to over .50.[2] There are only small changes in the next cohort— indeed the gaps are about as likely to go up slightly as they are to go down. This cohort, born in the ten years beginning with 1885, would have arrived as young adults in the period primarily before the end of World War I and could have started to have children beginning in about

TABLE 8.6

INDEXES OF NET DIFFERENCE BETWEEN EDUCATIONAL LEVELS OF FOREIGN-BORN AND
NATIVE WHITE OF NATIVE PARENTAGE MEN, 1960

Country of birth	Year of Birth			
	1885 or earlier	1885– 1895	1895– 1905	1905– 1915
Austria	.2699	.2643	.0855	−.0509
Poland	.4551	.4711	.2675	.1360
Czechoslovakia	.2555	.2651	.2069	.1038
Hungary	.2159	.2145	.1002	−.0059
Yugoslavia	.4668	.5040	.3906	.2568
Lithuania	.5355	.5063	.1862	−.0797
Finland	.4241	.3858	.2515	.0990
USSR	.3469	.2975	.0829	.0144
Italy	.5114	.5446	.4810	.3878

1905. Hence, the pattern is quite consistent with that obtained earlier with the immigration data. There was no particular advance yet in the educational achievement of the new immigrants coming to the United States, but there was an advance in their American-born children. Those born in the 1905–1915 decade were definitely part of a cohort that gained relative to the NWNP population.

The educational disadvantage among immigrants born in the next two decades declined radically, although for the most part they were still less educated than NWNP men of the same period. Even a cursory comparison between the NDs obtained among the 1905–1915 cohort with the 1885–1895 cohort indicates the massive nature of the changes—for example, from .47 to .14 for Poles, .30 to .01 for Russians, .50 to .26 for Yugoslavs, and .54 to .39 for Italians. These are by no means exceptionally large gains among the SCE groups. The younger two cohorts of immigrant men were largely the fathers of the second-generation cohort born between 1925 and 1935 who reached remarkably high educational levels. Thus this pattern is consistent with the previous data set, on the one hand indicating that the early South–Central–Eastern European second-generation gains did not reflect educational improvements among the immigrants; on the other, the massive gains made later by younger second-generation cohorts did occur after there had been a corresponding educational jump among those migrating to the United States due to tighter admission standards. To be sure, the immigrants were for the most part less educated than native whites of native parentage, but the educational opportunities were less in Europe at that time and hence the immigrants could be quite selective in education without having the same formal attainment (see Lieberson, 1978 for a discussion of ridits and educational level).

It must be noted that it is sometimes necessary here and elsewhere in the study to make assumptions that are not entirely felicitous about the linkage between parent and offspring. This occurs when there are no available data cross-tabulating parent and child. Under such circumstances I have sometimes taken the available information on two sets of people and assumed that they roughly represent the parent–child linkage. For example, if one has data on second-generation Italians who are, say, 20–24, one might compare them with data for foreign-born parents who are, say, 40–54 years of age at the same census. No doubt the immigrant parents of many of the second-generation subjects are included, but it is equally certain that a wide variety of errors occurs because, for example, some parents are dead; others are younger or older than the foreign-born age range included; nonparents are included; some of the foreign-born entered the country long after any of the second generation of a given adult age had been born; the fertility and the social characteristic under study are correlated; and because some of the parents have left the country. Under such circumstances, one would be willing to use this technique only because both of the following conditions exist: The problem is important and no other data are available; one has at least some confidence that these matchings do help answer the question under consideration—if only by giving an idea of the relative shifts for different groups. An excellent criticism of this procedure has been made by Taeuber and Taeuber (1967, pp. 798–808) and the reader would be well advised to consult their work or at least bear in mind the cautions outlined above. With the development of sample tapes from some of the earlier censuses, a step that appears likely as I write this, there will be opportunities to study more systematically some of the conclusions drawn with the techniques employed here. Clearly this match-up procedure is employed where the author believes that the findings are likely to increase our understanding of the processes under consideration.

The Limited Role of Parental Change

Although the rapid educational gains of the second generation are in some way due to the educational upgrading of immigrants to the United States, there must be other factors accounting for the dramatic gains experienced by the new Europeans' American-born children. The second-generation cohorts started to gain on the NWNP's even before the immigrants showed any educational improvements. Moreover, the mobility literature indicates that the new European second-generation educational levels are higher than could be expected on the basis of parental attainment levels and the general societal linkage between parent and offspring. Blau and Duncan (1967, column 5 of table 6.8, pp. 234–235), for example, find that second-generation adult men of all ages from sources other than Northern and Western Europe have educational levels well in excess of that which might be expected on the basis of the occupation and education of their fathers. To be sure, the new Europeans do not have as high a gross level of education as the NWNPs of Northern birth if background differences are not taken into account, but bear in mind that these data refer to all adults and it was only in the younger adult ages that a generally higher level of education was found for virtually all new European second-generation groups.[3]

Somewhat more detailed analyses of the same data set support this general conclusion. Duncan and Duncan (1968, table 2) examine the American-born sons of fathers born in Russia, Poland, Italy, and a residual SCE European category. Compared with all American-born men of nonfarm background (excluding blacks), the second-generation Russians have higher educational scores (1.44 above the grand mean), Poles and Italians are considerably below (-.66 and -.64, respectively), and other South–Central–Eastern Europeans are about the same as all Americans (-.04 below the grand mean). Again, for all four new groups, their educational levels are considerably above that which three family background characteristics (head's education, occupation, and the number of siblings) would lead one to expect. The Italian and Polish second-generation levels are .52 years greater than expected, Russians exceed by 1.48 the level expected on the basis of background characteristics, and other new Europeans are .79 above. It is clear that the new Europeans achieve higher levels of education than can be explained by their parental attainment levels and the general upgrading in education experienced by the society as a whole. Likewise, an examination of educational attainment by detailed age groups indicates that the second-generation men of Eastern and Central European origin in all ages have higher educational levels than all native males to a degree that is in excess of what would be expected on the basis of family background factors (Duncan, 1965b, table 4-1).

One can also take a stab at the question of whether the upgrading in immigrant education helps account for the rapid leap among the new Europeans' younger second-generation cohorts. Working with the data reported by Beverly Duncan in the aforementioned source, one finds that the net deviation of the observed educational level from the level expected on the basis of background characteristics tends to be greatest among the younger cohorts of second-generation Central—Eastern Europeans. Examining the eight specific age groups reported by Duncan (1965b, table 4-1) there is a correlation coefficient of -.66 between the age of the cohorts (with the youngest receiving a one and the oldest an eight). Hence, the specially rapid new European second-generation gains among the younger cohorts are not entirely due to parental upgrading because slightly more than 40 percent of the variance among new European age cohorts in the magnitude of their deviations from the attainment levels expected on the basis of background characteristics is associated with age itself.

In short, the second-generation levels of education are in excess of what might be expected on the basis of parental background and the linkage in the society generally between family background and children's education. The deviations of their observed attainment levels from those expected rise somewhat in this century with succeeding cohorts, indicating that the exceptionally rapid increments for new Europeans found in the younger cohorts are due to more than the upgrading in parental educational levels that occurred after immigration restrictions were enacted. This does not mean that family background was irrelevant, but rather that something else was going on as well that helped to move the new Europeans upward in education. Accordingly, we have to consider both changes in the background factors that normally affect offspring's life chances, such as parental education and occupation, as well as search for some other ethnic-specific factors that may have served to catapult the new European groups' second-generation levels of schooling.

Further evidence exists to support the contention that new European immigrant gains in education among succeeding cohorts do not adequately account for the movement among the second generation. One does not find the kind of linkage between immigrant and second-generation education that would be expected if the sharp increases in the latter's attainment could be adequately explained by changes of a comparable nature in immigrant achievement. For each of the nine SCE European groups, shifts in the proportion illiterate between two adjoining second-generation cohorts (those in 1960 who were 35—44 and 25—34) were compared with the shifts in the illiteracy of their "immigrant mothers." (The latter figure was inferred by applying the illiteracy rates by age for each group of foreign-born women to the age-specific birth rates among foreign-born white women in 1920 and 1930, respectively.) The linkage between intercohort changes in second-generation indexes of educational difference from NWNPs and shifts in the illiteracy of foreign-born mothers is both slight and actually in the opposite direction. The r's for interethnic differences in second-generation educational advances between cohorts and immigrant improvements in education are, respectively, -.32 and -.26 for boys and girls—indicating that groups with the largest relative gains in parental literacy were the groups with smallest intercohort second-generation advances. Given the imperfect measurements available, clearly one would not expect too strong a connection with the measures used even if parental advances completely accounted for the advances of their children, but the absence of *any* linkage in the expected direction between foreign-born educational change and second-generation change would suggest that the parental shifts cannot fully explain why the second-generation new Europeans made such massive educational advances.

CHARACTERISTICS OF BLACK MIGRANTS TO THE NORTH

The characteristics of blacks migrating to the North and West during this period comprise a factor to consider in dealing with new European–black gaps in educational attainment. It is widely assumed that race relations in the North began to deteriorate late in the nineteenth century and early in the twentieth, and that this decline was due not merely to the increasing numbers of blacks who moved to the North but also to their unfavorable qualities in comparison to earlier black residents of the North. If the black movement to the North became less selective of parental qualities that would be favorable to the education of their northern-born offspring, then this shift in migration could be at least partially responsible for the deterioration of the black position relative to SCE Europeans. The position of blacks in the North, relative to the new Europeans, declined earlier in this century not only in the educational domain, but in other areas to be analyzed later. However, although the evidence is not as good as one would want, the deterioration in education does not appear to be due to a decline in the "quality" of blacks migrating to the North and West.

Changes in the ND Indexes

Although blacks fell progressively further behind the new Europeans, the reader will recall that northern blacks did quite nicely relative to native whites of native parentage throughout the period except for the last cohort. Hence this would suggest exceptional performance by the SCE Europeans rather than a deterioration among the northern-born blacks. Table 8.7 summarizes the absolute and relative changes for successive cohorts in the net difference index between northern-born blacks and native whites of native parentage. Regardless of whether absolute or relative changes are considered, the pattern for both sexes generates the same conclusion. Namely, well into the twentieth century northern-born blacks were not merely obtaining more education than the preceding cohorts, but were doing so at a faster clip than the NWNPs and hence reducing the indexes of net difference between the races. Indeed, the sharpest absolute and relative drop occurred between the 1905–1915 and the 1915–1925 cohorts. Thus there is every indication that blacks were doing alright and were successfully narrowing their educational disadvantage with NWNPs.

A closer look at World War I seems to support this conclusion. There are two separate issues. First, did the relative progress of northern-born black children of school age during the World War I period suffer because of the large-scale expansion of the northern black population at that point? Second, given the progress experienced by preceding cohorts of northern-born black children, did the new migrants from the South alter the educational levels of black children born in the North after World War I? The cohort of blacks born in the North between 1895 and 1905 probably comes closest to providing an answer to the first question because these blacks ranged from 5–14 in 1910, 9–18 by 1914, and were 15–24 by 1920. There is some evidence that the progress of this cohort relative to the NWNPs was somewhat slower than that of the preceding cohort (see table 8.7). Among men and women, the absolute and relative drop in the NWNP's advantage was not as large as that experienced in the preceding decade. Bear in mind, however, that the educational gap

TABLE 8.7

CHANGES IN NET DIFFERENCE INDEXES BETWEEN NATIVE WHITES OF NATIVE PARENTAGE
AND NORTHERN-BORN BLACKS, 1960

Cohorts by age (and year of birth)	Change from preceding age cohort			
	Males		Females	
	Absolute	Percentage	Absolute	Percentage
25–34 (1925–1935)	.0282	24	.0006	1
35–44 (1915–1925)	−.0228	−16	−.0444	−28
45–54 (1905–1915)	−.0148	−10	−.0188	−11
55–64 (1895–1905)	−.0131	−8	−.0076	−4
65–74 (1885–1895)	−.0206	−11	−.0418	−18

SOURCE: Based on data reported in table 8.2

between northern-born blacks and native whites did decline during the period, only at a slower rate than that experienced earlier. Moreover, the damage was neither permanent nor irreparable. Black gains increased again during the next two decades so that the shift between the 1915–1925 cohort and the one preceding it is the most favorable change recorded.

In short, there is no evidence to indicate that the movement to the North during World War I—in numbers unheralded up to that time, although dwarfed by later events—was *directly* responsible for a decline in the educational gains of northern-born blacks. Those in the school ages during the World War I period did gain on the NWNPs, albeit at a slower rate than either of the next two cohorts. So it is reasonable to infer that the war did slow down black advances, but they were not aborted or reversed. It may well be that the northern-born black gains slowed down during World War I because of the employment opportunities generated during that period in the North which served to discourage continued schooling (see, for example, Duncan, 1965a). As for the cohort of black children born in the North during the decade beginning with 1915, their educational progress was remarkably strong relative to the NWNP population.

Educational Selectivity Among the Migrants

If this result is somewhat surprising to the reader, it may be due to the widely held assumption that the "quality" of blacks in the North declined with the growth in the black migration northward. To be sure, the nature of black–white relations changed during this century, witness the segregation patterns to be discussed in chapter 9. However, it is one thing to observe these shifts in northern race relations, but a totally different step to infer that they were caused by changes in the characteristics of the migrants as opposed to structural shifts in racial relations in the northern cities. Perhaps contributing to a bias in favor of the first explanation are the differences in imagery generated by the underground railroad or manumitted blacks during the earlier slavery period, as opposed to those generated by blacks enticed to the North by various industrial and railroad recruiters to fill the demands for unskilled labor created in World War I or to serve as strikebreakers. But the data actually available on black migrants to the North indicate a high degree of positive self-selection from those living in the South.

Very little is known in a rigorous quantitative way about the background of migrants from the South earlier in this century and late in the nineteenth because the census did not even ask a question on migration

until 1940. On most attributes, one cannot simply consider the characteristics of blacks in the North because a distinction between northern- and
southern-born blacks was rarely drawn. However, using census survival
ratios, it is possible to describe the educational characteristics of the black
migration to the North for each decade. (The following account is
derived from Lieberson [1978b], which should be consulted for greater
details and qualifications.) Although the 1910–1920 decade was marked
by higher migration rates to the North and West among both literate and
illiterate blacks living in the South, it was particularly the former who
began to move in massive numbers. This pattern was repeated again in
the 1920s, a period in which the movement to the North accelerated.
From 10 to 20 percent of literate young adult blacks living in the South at
the outset of the decade had left for the North during the ensuing ten
years. However, the higher out-migration rates for the better educated
were counterbalanced by the fact that there were so many more
illiterates living in the South. As a consequence, if one compares the
percentage of illiterate black adults in the North in each decade with the
rate expected if there was no in- or out-migration, one finds only minor
differences. In terms of the issue at hand, the general educational level of
blacks in the North was not particularly lowered by the migration
streams from the South compared to what it would have been if there
had been no migration.

Accordingly, one cannot attribute the deterioration of the northern-
black educational position relative to the new Europeans as due to shifts
in the characteristics of black migrants from the South. This conclusion is
also supported by the progressively lower educational gaps found
between the NWNP population and northern blacks until the most
recent comparison. As there was no deterioration in the black educational position in the North through 1930 (data limitations prevented any
inferences about the 1930s), it is unlikely that the remarkable reversal of
black progress relative to native whites of native parentage experienced
by the cohort born between 1925 and 1935 can be attributed to these
background factors.

ECONOMIC POSITION AND OFFSPRINGS' EDUCATION:
A COMPARISON BETWEEN BLACKS AND WHITES

It is clear that the initial new European second-generation gains were
not simply due to improvements in the occupations of their parents at
the time of arrival or in the immigrants' education. Likewise the decline
of the black position relative to the new Europeans was not due to a

deterioration in the educational position of black migrants to the North. Nevertheless, family background characteristics are still extremely important; the later shifts over time in educational position could be due heavily to the improvements in parental position even if something else was going on so that the new European second generations exceed the general societal patterns of intergenerational change and blacks fall below. There is the additional question of whether in these earlier years socioeconomic position among the blacks was as easily transferred to offsprings' educational improvements as it was among the SCE Europeans. We do not know whether the differential gains in education between succeeding black and new European cohorts reflect a constant, increasing, or decreasing role of background factors as opposed to what one may label temporarily as an "ethnic" or "racial effect."

Housing Costs and Education

The necessary economic data are hard to obtain for earlier decades; the Census Bureau did not even ask an income question until 1940. Accordingly, the ideal economic datum, family income, is not available for the groups during the period under study—indeed even the substitute variables can only be used in a limited way. Nevertheless, a study of shifts in housing costs between 1930 and 1940 can be used to examine the effect of economic changes on the education levels achieved by new Europeans and northern blacks. Because the amount families spend on housing is strongly affected by their income, data on the former can be used to infer the income positions of northern blacks and South–Central–Eastern Europeans in both 1930 and 1940 as well as the shifts during that decade. Housing expenditures are affected by other factors as well—for example, family size, location, propensities to own rather than rent, the availability of mortgage money, and the nature of the housing available to each group—but the linkage between income and cost is probably adequate for our purposes.

A gradient clearly exists between housing costs and the educational attainment of both native white and black children. Whether computed by medians or the index of net difference, one finds an upward progression in 1940 between the educational attainment of 15-year-old children and their housing costs (table 8.8). There is a difference of about one year in the median education of the poorest and wealthiest white boys (as measured by the value of their homes), a somewhat smaller gap for white girls, but even larger differences for blacks of either sex. Fifteen-year-old black boys living in homes with rents under $10 (or with an estimated rental of comparable value if owner-occupied), have 8.0

TABLE 8.8

MONTHLY RENTAL VALUE OF HOME AND YEARS OF SCHOOL COMPLETED, BLACKS AND
NATIVE WHITES 15 YEARS OF AGE LIVING IN THE NORTH OR WEST, 1940

	Monthly rental value (in dollars)					
Race and sex	Under 10	10—14	15—19	20—29	30—49	50 and over
	Median years of school					
Black males	8.00	8.23	8.30	8.53	8.80	9.41
Native white males	8.40	8.60	8.74	9.07	9.29	9.45
Black females	8.33	8.56	8.80	9.11	9.19	9.56
Native white females	8.71	9.03	9.16	9.26	9.43	9.57
	Index of net difference with next highest rental group					
Black males	−.0844	−.0108	−.1054	−.1150	−.2864	
Native white males	−.0892	−.0631	−.1070	−.1390	−.1167	
Black females	−.1339	−.0445	−.0941	−.0770	−.2004	
Native white females	−.0933	−.0737	−.0721	−.1297	−.1119	

SOURCE: U.S. Bureau of the Census, 1945b, tables 3 and 4.
NOTE: Monthly rental value of home incorporates the value of owner-occupied homes
estimated in rental terms by the Census Bureau.

years of school completed, whereas the median among those in the
highest rental category is 9.41. Incidentally, the vast bulk of the educational difference between black and native white teenagers of this age is
due to something other than their economic position, at least as tapped
by housing cost. A Kitagawa standardization procedure indicates that
slightly over 70 percent of the average educational difference, by race for
either sex, cannot be explained by differences in housing cost and the
linkage between that factor and educational attainment. Black and white
educational attainment resemble each other only in the highest economic
category.

Cross-Sectional Results

The educational levels reached in 1930 by the second-generation
members of various new European groups can be compared with the
rents and housing values of the foreign-born families of the same origin.
(Because of the way the data are constructed in 1930, one cannot convert
housing values into an equivalent rental value in order to obtain one
housing cost figure for each group as is the case for 1940.) The most
appropriate second-generation cohort for comparison is not entirely
clear; those born in the 1915—1925 decade ranged from 5—14 years of age

in 1930 (possibly a bit too young for their educational progress to be deeply affected by familial economic conditions in 1930). On the other hand, the next-oldest census cohort, ranging from 15–24 in 1930, includes a segment whose education was clearly affected by earlier economic conditions. Thus it seems reasonable to use both of these second-generation groups in the analysis—recognizing again that the parents and children are not specifically linked up. Rather, one makes the assumption that the position of the groups' families with a foreign-born head reflects the relative economic position of the different groups' American-born offspring attending school.

For both age groups, there is a particularly strong linkage between immigrant rental costs and the education attained by the second generation (table 8.9). The connection is not quite as strong for home values, particularly with regard to the educational levels reached by girls, but all in all the attainment of various second-generation groups appears to correlate on a cross-sectional aggregate basis with the economic positions of their parents in 1930. This linkage is not due to ethnic differences in their distribution within regions of the nation and the fact that regions

TABLE 8.9

REGRESSION OF SECOND-GENERATION EDUCATIONAL ATTAINMENT ON 1930 HOUSING COSTS OF NINE SOUTH–CENTRAL–EASTERN EUROPEAN FOREIGN-BORN GROUPS

Variables	Unadjusted figures			Adjusted for regional differences in housing costs		
	r	b	a	r	b	a
Y_1 on X_1:						
Male	−.5418	−.00004	.1980	−.6160	−.3463	.2805
Female	−.1822	−.00001	.1199	−.2696	−.1651	.1854
Y_1 on X_2:						
Male	−.7391	−.0085	.2173	−.7845	−.3242	.2462
Female	−.5535	−.0069	.2425	−.6343	−.2856	.2846
Y_2 on X_1:						
Male	−.6585	−.00006	.3679	−.7190	−.5046	.4737
Female	−.2614	−.00002	.2824	−.3424	−.2558	.3665
Y_2 on X_2:						
Male	−.8269	−.0119	.3661	−.8595	−.4436	.3982
Female	−.6230	−.0095	.4179	−.6963	−.3825	.4672

SOURCES: U.S. Bureau of the Census, 1933c, table 8; and sources cited in table 8.2
NOTE: Y variables are ND indexes for second-generation compared with NWNP, 35–44 years of age (Y_1) and 45–54 years of age (Y_2) in 1960. X variables refer to nonfarm homes of families with foreign-born head in 1930, by median value of owned homes (X_1) and monthly rental of rented homes (X_2).

vary in housing costs. In 1930, for example, the median value of an immigrant's nonfarm home in the mid-Atlantic states was $6,653, compared with $2,537 in the Mountain states; likewise, the median rental was $38 and $19, respectively. However, when standardizing for such regional differences in cost and the ethnic groups' variation between regions in their residential patterns, the correlations between housing cost and children's educational attainment all go up slightly (table 8.9).

Longitudinal Results

These cross-sectional results are interesting, but always the ultimate test requires longitudinal considerations. In this case, do shifts in second-generation educational levels occur because of shifts in immigrant economic positions, as measured here by housing costs? A number of assumptions and adjustments of the sort discussed earlier are again necessary to examine this question, but they are not unreasonable or outlandish. The dependent variable is the shift in educational attainment between the 1905–1915 and the 1915–1925 second-generation cohorts from each of nine different new European sources. These are persons whose crucial educational years would be greatly affected by parental economic changes between 1930 and 1940.[4] These changes are measured against different indicators of immigrant change in economic position between 1930 and 1940: the absolute and relative differences in both rental costs and home values. The economic depression of the 1930s actually lowered housing costs in the period; the median value of nonfarm housing dropped from $4,778 to $2,996 between 1930 and 1940, with rents declining from $27.15 to $21.41 (U.S. Bureau of the Census, 1953a, table S). However, the relative changes between the groups are of concern here. Because regional differences in location are not likely to differ from these groups over ten years, no effort was made to make such an adjustment here. For both male and female second-generation educational attainment, there are linkages between the intercohort shifts and immigrant economic position (table 8.10). A good part of the ethnic differences in the magnitude of their educational gains vis-à-vis native whites of native parentage can be accounted for by one or another measure of immigrant economic shifts. Among boys, as much as 83 percent of the variance between groups' educational attainment is accounted for by these economic variables; among girls, it is lower, but hardly negligible, ranging up to nearly 50 percent.

Educational gains among northern-born blacks between the 1905–1915 and 1915–1925 cohorts can be compared with the amount that

TABLE 8.10

REGRESSION OF CHANGES IN SECOND-GENERATION EDUCATIONAL ATTAINMENT ON CHANGES IN HOUSING COSTS OF NINE SOUTH–CENTRAL–EASTERN EUROPEAN FOREIGN-BORN GROUPS

Independent variable	Unadjusted figures			Predicted change in black ND
	r	b	a	
X_1:				
Male	.6150	.1440	−.3100	−.0462
Female	.6846	.1482	−.3680	−.0965
X_2:				
Male	.9098	.00004	−.1490	−.0907
Female	.6302	.00002	−.1626	−.1335
X_3:				
Male	.4039	.1709	−.2408	−.0151
Female	.4334	.1696	−.2896	−.0656
X_4:				
Male	.6696	.0075	−.0751	−.0266
Female	.6352	.0066	−.1220	−.0793

NOTE: The regression figures in the first three columns refer to the following dependent variable (Y): the ND index for second-generation compared with NWNP, 35–44 years of age minus the index for 45–54 years of age. X_1 is median value of homes (1930 ÷ 1940). X_2 is median value of homes (1930 – 1940). X_3 is median rental values (1930 ÷ 1940). X_4 is median rental values (1930 – 1940). Predicted northern-born black changes in ND as compared with NWNP 35–44 years of age minus ND for 45–54 are based on the regression equation shown and the relevant black changes in housing costs.

might be expected by applying the changes in housing expenditures for blacks living in the North and West to the regression equations obtained when the linkage between education and housing costs was examined among the new European groups. The actual gains of northern-born blacks relative to NWNPs of the same ages are -.0228 and -.0444, respectively, for males and females. (Bear in mind that a negative figure here indicates a black gain in relative position.) These improvements are relatively small for the most part; given the northern black 1930:1940 ratio in median home values, for example, one could expect declines of -.0462 and -.0965 in NDs between northern-born blacks and native whites of native parentage for males and females, respectively, instead of the observed declines of -.0228 and -.0444 (see Table 8.10, last column). Except for the regression of black males on rental values, the general pattern is smaller educational advances for blacks than would be expected on the basis of their economic shifts (as measured by housing costs). We can conclude that black changes in economic position would lead one to expect a narrowing of their educational handicap, and that did occur—although not as rapidly as one would expect based on the new European linkage between housing cost and childrens' educational gains. On the other hand, changes in the relative economic position of these European immigrant groups during the Great Depression appear to be related to the educational shifts experienced by those second-generation members of these groups who were of school age. The relative educational progress of the nine new European groups was very much influenced by the economic progress of their parents.

REGIONAL DIFFERENCES

Regional differences are important in considering educational gains among the new European groups relative to native whites of native parentage. Educational attainment for whites has generally been lower in the South than in other parts of the nation (a matter discussed in chapter 6). Rather small proportions of the new European second-generation groups resided in the South, whereas a sizable segment of the NWNP population was born and raised in that region. Hence, cohort changes in the gap between new Europeans and the NWNP population may simply reflect regional changes in the pace of educational progress. The ideal data, as usual, are not available, but it is hoped that the materials used are adequate for at least a rough answer to the question at hand.

On the one hand, more than a third of the NWNP population 14 years of age or older in 1950 were born in the South (37 percent based on U.S. Bureau of the Census, 1953b, table 3). It is not possible to determine the birthplace of the second-generation Europeans, but the proportion living in the South is uniformly low in 1960, ranging from 4 percent for Finns and Lithuanians to just under 10 percent for Czechs 25 years of age and older.[5] Accordingly, it is clear that regional differences in educational progress would affect the new Europeans differently than the NWNPs. Hence it is highly appropriate to consider whether such regional shifts exist and, if so, whether they correspond to the temporal changes observed between the new Europeans as opposed to the Native Whites of Native Parentage. There are two ways of approaching the problem. First, for 1960, one can compare the educational gap over time between native whites residing in the North with those residing in the South. This is imperfect because current residential data provide only a rough idea of respondents' residence during their school years, and also, the data are affected by selective migration along educational lines. Some of the obstacles can be surmounted by a second procedure using 1950 data that provide information on education for native whites of native parentage by birthplace. In this way southern-born can be compared directly with those born elsewhere. But the most interesting shift, that between the 1915–1925 and 1925–1935 cohorts, cannot be considered with these 1950 data because the latter were only 15–24 years of age at that time and hence hardly through with their education.

Both data sets in table 8.11 seem to indicate a fairly consistent picture: The ND indexes between native whites of southern and nonsouthern birth, as well as those between residents of the two areas, have fluctuated over a relatively narrow range for the different cohorts of men and women. The first two columns of table 8.11 compare the educational levels of native whites of native parentage born in the North and West with those born in the South. For both sexes there is essentially no trend over time in the magnitude of the ND indexes. (A positive index indicates higher educational levels for the northern- and western-born.) The index for the youngest cohort in each case is .01 greater than the index for the oldest age group examined. Minor fluctuations occur, to be sure, but there is no reason to believe that regional gaps in educational attainment widened during this period so as to favor the SCE Europeans who were relatively more concentrated in the North and West than were native whites of native parentage.

TABLE 8.11
REGIONAL DIFFERENCES IN EDUCATIONAL ATTAINMENT

| | Indexes of net difference | | | | |
| | Native whites of native parentage: North or West birth versus southern birth, 1950 | | Native whites: North or West residence versus southern residence, 1960 | | |
Age in 1950	Men	Women	Men	Women	Age in 1960
			.21	.20	25–34
25–34	.27	.25	.23	.20	35–44
35–44	.28	.23	.23	.17	45–54
45–54	.24	.22	.22	.17	55–64
55–64	.24	.23	.23	.18	65–74
65–74	.26	.24	.24	.21	75+
75+	.26	.24			

SOURCES: U.S. Bureau of the Census; 1953b, table 5; 1963c, table 3.

As noted above, the data on birthplace are of little help for the rapid rise between the 1915–1925 and the 1925–1935 cohorts because the latter group was so young in 1950. However, the conclusions drawn above are not altered substantially when 1960 data, based on current residence and for all native whites, are used instead. There is not much of a time trend and, if anything, the ND indexes between regions are slighly lower in the younger cohorts than in the oldest one. In short, the new European second-generation gains in educational attainment are not owing simply to any regional advantage. The intercohort shifts in the gaps between new Europeans and the NWNP cannot be accounted for by this regional factor.

Nevertheless, the regional factor is an extremely important force working to the advantage of the SCE Europeans. It is simply the case that the new Europeans were located almost entirely outside of the South, whereas a sizable proportion of the older white stock population is found in that region. If the wide gaps in educational attainment observed between the southern and nonsouthern components of the NWNPs are in no small way a reflection of regional differences in opportunity structure (or, additionally, the urban–rural distributions within these regions), then the avoidance of the South (or rural areas in these regions) generates a distinct advantage for the new Europeans. Consider, for example, the net difference indexes shown in table 8.12. The first column gives the gaps observed in 1950 between the second generation of all new Europeans and the entire NWNP population. The same new Europeans are compared in the second column as well, but this time with the NWNP population born only in the North or West.

TABLE 8.12

NET DIFFERENCE INDEXES BETWEEN SECOND-GENERATION SOUTH–CENTRAL–EASTERN EUROPEAN MEN AND NATIVE WHITES OF NATIVE PARENTAGE, 1950

Age in 1950	Born anywhere in U.S.	Born in North or West
25–34	.0233	.1321
35–44	.0305	.1464
45–54	.0719	.1714
55–64	.1263	.2191
65–74	.1793	.2779
75+	.1668	.2543

SOURCE: U.S. Bureau of the Census, 1953b, table 5.

NOTE: In order to maximize comparability with the 1960 data sources used, the number with no school years completed was combined with the number completing 1–4 years of elementary school.

(Because the necessary birthplace data for the NWNP population could not be obtained for 1960, observe that table 8.12 refers to 1950. Therefore the youngest cohort shown is not the one that exhibited such an extraordinary educational jump.)

The new Europeans in all periods are about ten points further behind the native white of native parentage population born in the North or West than they are when compared to all NWNPs. Thus, although there is a progressive narrowing of the educational distance between second-generation new Europeans and native whites of native parentage which cannot be explained by shifts in region of residence among either population, clearly the newcomers enjoy a significant advantage because of their locational advantage. This locational advantage is probably due in part to the relatively greater concentration of southern whites in rural areas compared with those located elsewhere and the effect this has on education; but this is a matter we need not pursue here. The key point is that regional factors give the new Europeans an important edge. The new Europeans were initially unable to utilize the enormous advantage in educational opportunity stemming from their concentration in the urban North and West, but this regional advantage did not disappear and they were later able to capitalize on it. Regional differences are therefore an important factor in understanding the new European position over NWNPs, although why and how they were progressively able to take advantage of this locational edge is another matter. Because we are dealing with northern-born blacks, the regional factor is irrelevant for understanding their educational differences from the new Europeans.

RETARDATION: ATTENDANCE VERSUS ATTAINMENT

The census educational measure used in this study pertains to schooling *attained*, as opposed to school years *attended*. If the groups in question differ in their likelihood of being promoted at the end of each school year, then it is possible that these census data mask some underlying differences not in the propensity to go to school, but in the propensity to be minimally successful in school, that is, to at least adequately complete each term. The term "retardation" is often used in this context to refer to children in school who are behind the grade usually associated with their age. The term will be used in that context here and in no way refers to the physiological qualities of the respondents involved.

Two relatively early data sets were uncovered that permit some comparison between the retardation of the new Europeans and blacks in the North: a survey by the Immigration Commission of various northern cities in the 1908–1909 school year; an analysis of selected schools in Chicago during the 1919–1920 year. The Immigration Commission paid considerable attention to education in its report, devoting five volumes to the analysis and covering slightly more than 2 million school children. Only 12 cities, however, received an "intensive investigation" (and then only selected schools in several of these). This is especially tricky for blacks because very likely the schools were singled out for analysis because they were heavily attended by new European groups. Hence the black figures do not necessarily reflect the performance of the majority of blacks in their communities who were attending schools with relatively more of their own group present. (For details on the cities included and the study generally, see U.S. Immigration Commission, 1911*b*, volume 1).

Based on children 8 years of age and older in the school system and defining retardation as a child "who is 2 or more years older than the normal age for his grade" (U.S. Immigration Commission, 1911*b*, volume 1, p. 31), the percentages of retarded children among various racial, birthplace, mother tongue, and origin categories presented in table 8.13 provide some useful comparisons between the groups under consideration. Among the white children of American-born fathers, a relatively small number are retarded in the school performance for their age, 28 percent. This group is largely of Northwestern European origin, for the most part residing in the United States for at least three generations. Children of foreign-born fathers from English-speaking countries fare the same, with 27 percent behind in school. By contrast, the children of foreign-born fathers from non-English-speaking countries do much worse, with 43 percent retarded. Nevertheless, when compared with the 66 percent retardation rate among blacks, it is clear that the children of immigrants from non-English countries are still doing comparatively much better in school. Indeed, as was the case for other phenomena discussed in earlier chapters, their advantage over blacks is still far greater than their lag behind the other white segments of the population.

The children of fathers from the South–Central–Eastern European nations do not have as great an edge over blacks, but it is still considerable, respectively, 50 versus 66 percent. This figure for new Europeans is heavily weighted by Russian Jews, who are relatively low in retardation. Nevertheless, except for Jews born in Poland, who have essentially the same rate as blacks, all of the specific new European groups have better records; the lowest figures are for the Bohemian and Moravian group (35 percent) and the Russian Jews, with the highest

TABLE 8.13
RETARDATION AMONG SCHOOL CHILDREN IN LARGER CITIES, 1908–1909

Child's group	Percentage retarded
American-born father:	
White	28
Black	66
Foreign-born father:	
English-speaking origin	27
Non-English-speaking origin	43
Specific SCE group:	
Bohemian and Moravian	35
Italian (north)	52
Italian (south)	64
Italian (not specified)	55
Jewish (Polish)	67
Jewish (Roumanian)	52
Jewish (Russian)	41
Lithuanian	47
Magyar	57
Polish	58
Portuguese	45
Ruthenian[a]	45
Slovak	55

SOURCE: U.S. Immigration Commission, 1911b, volume 1, table 46.
[a]Based on less than 100 cases.

being for Polish Jews and Southern Italians (64 percent). By and large, the children of fathers born in SCE Europe have lower proportions of backward children in the schools than do blacks.

Other data gathered by the Immigration Commission also seem to indicate that the gap between blacks and the new Europeans is far more sizable than the differences between the latter and the older white stocks. There is an enormous drop in the retardation rates among the generations of new Europeans, but little indication of a similar shift among blacks. Slightly more than one-third of the American-born children of foreign-born men from non-English-speaking countries are retarded, whereas nearly two-thirds are in that condition among their European-born children. Indeed it appears as if foreign-born children coming to the United States are badly handicapped in their educational progress in this nation unless arriving at a very young age. Of those in the school system who were 8 or 9 years of age when they arrived in the

United States, 86 percent are retarded. Undoubtedly these massive differences between the American- and foreign-born offspring of immigrants reflect a variety of factors: changes in the language ability of their parents; exposure to the United States and its culture prior to schooling; relatively greater mastery of English in the preschool years; absence of schooling in Europe; relatively fewer economic strains at home after the parents are settled in the United States; and other factors. But the major point is that the American-born children of immigrants rapidly close the gap with the earlier white groups in terms of their ability to stay in the grade normally reached by children of the same age.

By contrast, there is very little difference among black children between those born in the northern city where they currently attend school and those born elsewhere in the United States. The percentage retarded among children 8 years of age and older is 63 and 72, respectively. Thus the difference is in the direction expected, but there is not the dramatic intergenerational progress analogous to that found among the Europeans.[6]

The Chicago Commission on Race Relations (1922, pp. 256–270) included comparative materials on school performance as part of its study of the conditions leading to the Chicago Riot of 1919. The percentage retarded in schools attended mainly by white Americans of earlier stock (49) is identical to the combined figure for the new groups (based on three schools for each new group: Bohemian, Polish, Italian, and Jewish). By contrast, 74 percent of students attending the predominantly black grade schools are retarded. However, there is considerable variation between schools within each group.

In passing one should note a methodological problem discussed by the commission which could affect the interpretation of these results as well as those reported by the Immigration Commission. The data deal only with children remaining in school at the time of the study, and thus ethnic differences in the propensity to remain in school among those behind in their grades will not be taken into account. In this regard, the Chicago Commission observes that "a partial explanation is to be found in the fact that Negro parents are frequently more interested in keeping their over-age children in school than white parents, especially foreign parents, whose anxiety to have their children leave school as soon as they are old enough to get work-permits is well known" (1922, p. 258).

Another complication in the Chicago study is that many of the black children were from the South. Although no documentation is provided, the commission claims that black children born in the North had no higher retardation rates than the whites (1922, p. 261). However, one should bear in mind that the new European immigrant children also included those who were born overseas. It seems not unreasonable to conclude that *both* data sets seem to indicate that blacks had higher retardation rates than the new Europeans, and, in turn, that the new Europeans had higher rates than the older white groups.

Explanatory Importance

The issue at hand in this comparison between blacks and the new Europeans is not simply whether they differ in their retardation rates, but whether such differences can help account for the pattern in which succeeding cohorts of the former group fall further and further behind the new Europeans. An answer to this question is by no means easy, but a first approximation was attempted by determining in each decade the numbers enrolled in school by nativity, race, sex, and specific age. Blending the rates obtained for each census to estimate the intervening rates, one can then make some estimation of the years of school enrollment as opposed to the years of school completed (with the latter based on the 1960 figures referred to throughout this study). These figures, shown in table 8.14, indicate that shifts in the "efficiency rate" (number of school years completed/number of school years attended) cannot account for the gaps observed in educational attainment.

The efficiency rates are, in all cases, higher for native whites of foreign or mixed parentage (second-generation whites of all origins, old and new) than for nonwhites living in the North.[7] But as the last columns of table 8.14 make clear, the gaps do not progressively widen over time. Indeed, the narrowest gaps are for the youngest age group analyzed here. Hence, although recognizing that blacks did seem less likely to successfully complete their grades, shifts in the attainment gaps over time do not appear to be due to comparable shifts in the efficiency rates.

TABLE 8.14
ESTIMATED SCHOOL EFFICIENCY RATES

Age in 1960	Male		Female		Difference: NWFMP minus nonwhite	
	NWFMP[a]	Nonwhite	NWFMP[a]	Nonwhite	Male	Female
35–44	.9069	.8735	.9080	.9046	.0334	.0034
45–54	.9067	.8322	.9481	.8810	.0745	.0671
55–64	.9181	.8344	.9462	.8719	.0837	.0743
65–74	.9040	.8562	.9418	.9095	.0478	.0323

[a]NWFMP = Native whites of foreign or mixed parentage, i.e., the second-generation.

HARDENING OF ATTITUDES TOWARD BLACKS

Although no evidence has been found to support the contention that the quality of blacks migrating to the North deteriorated (although immigration laws clearly did upgrade the quality of new European migrants), it is still possible that the changing racial composition of the urban North affected the position of blacks in these centers and in turn had some bearing on their educational progress. Unfortunately it is far easier to speculate about such causes than it is to document the operation of such processes with reasonably sound empirical evidence. There are no Gallup Polls to fall back on for these earlier periods, but one can use the patterns of racial and ethnic segregation in these cities during earlier decades as an indicator of whether there was a general deterioration of the black position relative to new Europeans in the urban North (see chap. 9). At this point it is best to confine ourselves to the evidence dealing specifically with changes in educational policy and attitudes toward blacks during this period.

Of course, the situation for blacks was never quite the same for SCE groups. Consider the "Harvard Affair" described by Steinberg (1974, pp. 21 ff). In 1922 Harvard University announced that it was considering a limit on the proportion of Jews at the institution; their numbers had increased from 6 to 20 percent between 1908 and 1922. A storm of protest ensued, leading to considerable controversy and official backpedaling, even though other less blatant practices were instituted to the same net effect. Compare this incident with the black controversy President Lowell of Harvard engaged in one year later. Eager to mix the wealthy and poor students attending the university, residence in freshman dormitories became mandatory for all students—all, that is, except blacks who were banned from these buildings. It is significant not merely that the handful of black students at Harvard were successfully banned, despite protests (Steinberg, 1974, p. 27), but that the threshold was so different for these two groups—in one case acting to isolate the small number of black students from other freshmen (advanced underclassmen were not isolated), whereas in the other there was no such proposal for Jews; rather it was a question of admission policy when the 20 percent figure was reached.

The attitude toward black schooling in the North was initially different than that toward the new Europeans. The concept of separate schools for blacks goes far back in the history of the North. In Detroit, for example, blacks were denied access to public schools until Michigan established separate tax-supported public schools for blacks in 1842 (Katzman, 1975,

p. 23). School segregation was not declared illegal until a state court case in 1867, and whites resisted school integration in Detroit for a number of years after the Civil War (see Katzman, 1975, pp. 50, 84—90 for details). Likewise, New York State allowed separate schools for blacks until 1900 (Ovington, 1911, pp. 18—19). Separate schools were not always introduced with the intent of depriving or harming the black position; Anthony Benezet, a French Quaker who opened the first school for blacks in Philadelphia in 1750, was an advocate of black education, leaving a bequest for their schooling in his will (Wright, 1969, pp. 123—124). This was, of course, during a period in which private education prevailed and the Quakers were vigorously helping to provide black schools; but observe the notion of separate schools was incorporated. It was not until 1881 that an act was passed in Pennsylvania which made the barring of blacks from any school illegal, although it did not abolish the existing separate black schools (Wright, 1969, pp. 124—126). In Boston, black children in the eighteenth century attended public schools with whites, although relatively few took advantage of this opportunity in part because of their treatment in these schools. By the end of the century blacks established their own private schools, and they later requested that a separate school be established by the city of Boston, a request that was not to be fulfilled until 1820 (Daniels, 1914, pp. 22—23, 84). Blacks were later repelled by this situation and in 1855 obtained passage of a Massachusetts law prohibiting racial segregation in the schools. Until World War I blacks were attracted to Boston from the South by the quality of the Boston schools and the opportunity available to their children. Although blacks were less likely to continue their education to high school than were whites, presumably because of economic factors, they were doing well in the system (for details, see Daniels, 1914, pp. 187—190).

Not only was there this unique history of separation, but a deterioration occurred for blacks in the school systems of a number of northern cities at the time of World War I and in the period of extensive migration during the 1920s. An increase in the degree of black isolation in the schools would be expected simply because of the growing numbers of blacks in these cities; likewise, the isolation of new Europeans declined if only because their relative numbers in these cities began to go down. But there is evidence that other factors were operating to isolate blacks; there was a hardening in white attitudes toward black schooling and in white expectations about blacks. In order to avoid racial mixing it was not unusual to enroll or transfer blacks to a school other than the local one (Kennedy, 1930, p. 193). There were separate classrooms in some cities where mixed schools existed. A very fine study of changes in seven cities by Woofter (1928, chapter 10) found that Philadelphia, Indianapolis, Gary, and Dayton had one form or another of racial separation above and beyond that which would have occurred through residential processes alone; New York, Chicago, and Buffalo had no system of separate schools or separate classes within mixed schools. In Chicago, however, around World War I there were instances in which black children were discouraged from enrolling in largely white schools (cited in Kennedy, 1930, p. 194). There were 42 separate public schools for blacks in Pennsylvania according to a 1927 state survey (Kennedy, 1930, pp. 194–195); in communities where it was financially difficult to create separate schools, "Union Rooms" were established in which all black children in the school were placed together regardless of their grade.

The southern-born black children enrolled in the North were specially handicapped because of the poor education received in the South and were often far behind northern standards for their age. This in turn created exceptional discipline problems (Woofter, 1928, pp. 175–176). The Detroit Bureau of Governmental Research in a 1926 publication found sharp differences between northern and southern blacks in their school performance: 5 percent of Michigan-born black children were retarded by grade, whereas more than 21 percent of those from Georgia and North Carolina and 25 percent from Mississippi were retarded (cited in Kennedy, 1930, p. 199). The rise in both black segregation and the size of the southern-born population component meant that the northern-born were increasingly mixed with the disadvantaged southern-born children. There was also a tendency in many cities to exclude blacks from certain courses or programs dealing with commercial activities or skilled trades.

Cleveland provides an example of the subtle and not so subtle ways in which the black situation deteriorated in the North. The Cleveland school system had been integrated from approximately 1840 onward, although there was some resistance until the Civil War (Kusmer, 1976, pp. 16–17). Likewise black teachers were fully integrated into the system, frequently teaching in all-white classes (Kusmer, 1976, pp. 61–62). The situation began to change during World War I when several principals wanted to create segregated classes within their schools. This was only a temporary event, but other changes followed. Two technical high schools in the city had no black students in 1929 and blacks were only 4 percent of the student body at a third one that was actually located in the black area. The school board started artificially to create and maintain school segregation, including the use of busing for such purposes (Kusmer, 1976, pp. 182–184). Some interesting curriculum changes are reported after these racial shifts in enrollment. As the black component of one junior high school increased during the 1920s, foreign languages were dropped, certain industrial courses were increased, and more emphasis was placed on sewing, cooking, manual training, foundry and sheet metal work. Likewise, Central High School, which was serving 61 percent of Cleveland's black high school students by the outset of the Great Depression, gave mathematics to less than half of its tenth-graders, emphasized laundry work in its home economics courses, and dropped Spanish, German, and courses in bookkeeping and stenography.

In short, although there is no exact quantitative way of describing the process and its importance, there is evidence that the position of blacks in northern schools deteriorated during the period under study, whereas there is no comparable indication for the new Europeans. Hence, to some unknown degree, the divergent paths taken by succeeding cohorts in the two groups may reflect these changes in opportunity structure, quality, and—possibly most important of all—the concept and expectation of the role of black and new European education held by the dominant white population generally. As noted at the outset, in the next chapter it will be possible to consider the broader question of whether there was a deterioration in the position of blacks generally in the North such that these school phenomena are merely part of a sweeping societal shift.

REWARDS

There is a relationship between jobs, income, and education such that the employment and income possibilities that exist for the educated members of each group will affect the education achieved by the children. If, because of discrimination or other forces, the occupational and income rewards of a given educational level differ between blacks and new Europeans, then both parental support and children's incentives for achieving such levels may differ, and this in turn would lead to different accomplishments and possibly even a different set of attitudes toward the value and role of education. A crucial issue, then, is the occupational and income rewards attained by different groups with the same levels of education. A fuller look at this issue is postponed until later, but one should briefly note here that the occupational rewards for blacks with a given level of education were less than those obtained by other groups. In turn, this probably had a "feedback" effect on the incentives for education among later black cohorts. Smith (1972, pp. 332–333) claims that a major factor undermining the pursuit of education among blacks was the absence of occupational rewards, a difficulty far greater than any encountered by the European immigrants. He singles out the resistance that occurred during the Great Depression citing the Drake and Cayton study that found that 72 of 90 blacks in one Red Cap local in Chicago were college men and that only blacks with at least a high school diploma were hired for such work. To be sure, there were all sorts of incongruities during the Depression as jobs became so scarce, but it was the case that the material rewards that went with an education were far greater for white groups than for blacks.

I have referred to the situation in many cities where blacks were discouraged from pursuing certain programs in school because such skills would not lead to employment after graduation. A systematic analysis by Edna Kinchion of black high school girls in Pittsburgh gives one a telling quantitative example of this point (her unpublished study is reported in Reid, 1930, pp. 90–91). A high school diploma was not a trivial accomplishment at that time, and might have been viewed as the ticket to some improvement in life for young adults of impoverished backgrounds. Yet more than half of these women were employed to do either general housework (36 percent) or as maids (20 percent). The next most common category, ignoring the 10 percent who did not identify their type of work, was waitress (7 percent), and finally the first white collar position, sheet writer (8 women or 3 percent), which refers to clerks employed in bookmaking and other gambling establishments. (It is unlikely that many self-respecting white girls with a high school diploma at that time would have considered a job working for a bookie.) Overall, high school was not a passport for the more desirable occupations available to the new Europeans. It is not for lack of higher aspirations that these occupations were selected; the Kinchion survey found the most frequently listed occupational ambitions to be stenographer and teacher (in each case 20 percent). As one disgusted black interviewee put it: "The Negro community would be much better off if some employment was provided for our girls after they finish high school that would keep them from working as domestics for rich white folk" (Reid, 1930, p. 90).

In a direct comparison between blacks and various immigrant and second-generation groups in Boston, Thernstrom found that blacks earlier in this century "were receiving substantially more education than European immigrants, and they were to fare far less well in the later occupational competition. In 1910, for example, there were two and a half times as many immigrants as blacks holding white-collar jobs (24 percent versus 10 percent) and four times as many in skilled posts (33 percent versus 8 percent), and the differential was still almost as sharp another two decades later" (Thernstrom, 1973, p. 204). Likewise, Myrdal (1944, p. 303) reports a remarkable ethnic–racial difference in the unemployment rate among young urban males during the middle of the Great Depression. For whites, as you would expect, the unemployment rate declined with education; for example, 56 percent were unemployed among those with minimal education, whereas 18 percent of the college-educated had no job. By contrast, no consistent trend was found between education and unemployment for blacks. In short, at this point one can tentatively conclude that whatever the degree of discrimination faced by new Europeans—and there was a considerable resistance—blacks had even more difficulty converting their educational work into occupational and monetary rewards. But more about this later.

DRAMATIC CHANGES IN THE 1925–1935 COHORT

The sharp jump in education among new Europeans born in the period between 1925 and 1935, as well as the sudden reversal experienced by northern blacks in what had until then been a steady narrowing of their educational gap from the native whites of native parentage, covers a rather interesting period. The education of these children, born either shortly before the Great Depression or during the very worst part of it, was probably greatly affected by World War II and the years immediately following it. It was only around 1940 that the oldest of this cohort approached the age when dropping out of school became an option; for others it was, of course, much later. The youngest in this cohort, for example, were only five years of age in 1940 and the average was about 10. Hence it is rather clear that much of the "action" in differentiating this cohort was destined to take place well into the 1940s and on into the early 1950s. Nevertheless, a consideration of the shifting positions of these ethnic and racial groups might well start with the possible long-term consequences of events that began in the Great Depression. If the violent shifts and fluctuations in the economy during this period affected black and the new European parents differently, then this would have some bearing on the education achieved by this cohort.

Unemployment

By way of overview, the unemployment rate for the civilian labor force in 1930 was 9 percent, having jumped substantially from 3 percent in the preceding year (the rates had been ranging from 2 to 5 percent from 1923 onward). But in 1931 the unemployment rate was 16 percent and moving onward to an extraordinary 25 percent in 1933. Hence, at the very bottom of the cycle, fully a fourth of the civilian labor force was out of work. The rate fluctuated in a downward direction for the rest of the 1930s, but was still rather high in 1940, 15 percent, and then dropped sharply in response to massive needs during World War II (dipping to 1.2 percent in 1944), and moved up to 5 percent by 1950 (U.S. Bureau of the Census, 1975, p. 135). Thus the period covered was marked by massive shifts in unemployment which, if differentially experienced by the groups in question, could have a serious bearing on ability to attend school. Certainly, the ability of parents to continue their children in school beyond the mandatory years would be deeply affected by their own economic circumstances as well as the projected rewards to their children for doing so.

For the United States in 1930 the unemployment rates were actually slightly higher for white men than for blacks (5.4 and 5.1 percent, respectively). This conceals a difference among whites between foreign and native Americans (7.6 and 4.9 percent, respectively) such that the rate for native whites was just a touch lower than for blacks. The narrow gap between blacks and whites is due to regional and agricultural factors. Except for the Mountain states (which are unimportant in terms of the relative numbers involved), in all parts of the North and West black unemployment rates were considerably higher than those for the white segments of the population. In New England, for example, 10.2 percent of black men were unemployed, whereas the rates were 6.3 and 7.3, respectively, for native and foreign-born white men. Among black women it was 6.2 percent, whereas the rate was 3.9 for both segments of white women. As inspection of Table 8.15 indicates, the unemployment rates were generally lower for all of the groups in the South, but particularly for blacks. Their rates for the most part were lower than those among white men, and in the East−South−Central states black women also had specially low rates. Because blacks were still concentrated in the South in 1930 (76 percent of black gainful workers in the United States), the lower unemployment rates of that region have a great impact on the national comparisons. Even in the South, the black advantage is due to their especially high concentration in agriculture and, in turn, the exceptionally low unemployment rates among those employed in that industry. Probably even marginal activity in agricultural work did not register as unemployment in 1930. Among black gainful workers in the South, 52 and 35 percent, respectively, of men and women were in agriculture—the comparable figures for southern whites were 40 and 16 percent. The class A unemployment rate for white men in agriculture was one-tenth of one percentage point greater than

TABLE 8.15
Unemployment Rates, 1930

Location	Men White All	Men White Native	Men White Foreign-born	Men Black	Women White All	Women White Native	Women White Foreign-born	Women Black
United States	5.4	4.9	7.6	5.1	3.4	3.4	3.6	3.7
North and West:								
New England	6.6	6.3	7.3	10.2	3.9	3.9	3.9	6.2
Middle Atlantic	6.7	6.3	7.8	11.4	3.7	3.7	3.6	6.0
East-North Central	6.8	6.1	9.3	14.3	3.6	3.6	3.4	8.7
West-North Central	3.5	3.4	4.5	8.7	2.6	2.6	2.3	6.4
Mountain	5.0	4.9	5.7	5.7	3.3	3.3	3.0	5.0
Pacific	6.6	6.4	7.3	9.2	4.5	4.6	4.1	7.1
South:								
South Atlantic	3.1	3.0	4.4	3.3	2.4	2.4	3.5	3.4
East-South Central	2.4	2.4	2.8	2.1	2.3	2.3	1.8	1.5
West-South Central	3.6	3.7	2.9	3.4	2.8	2.8	1.5	3.1

SOURCE: U.S. Bureau of the Census, 1932, pp. 232-234.
NOTE: Class A unemployment as a percentage of gainful workers.

for black men, and the white female rate was actually about three-tenths of one percentage point lower than the rate among black women. The unemployment rates in the nonagricultural industries of the South were about 1 percent higher for blacks than whites in each sex. (The above figures are computed from data reported in the U.S. Bureau of the Census [1931, tables 24, 33, 35, 37].)

All of this suggests that the local labor market greatly affects the unemployment rates for each group—witness the consequences above of shifting from national to regional data. It is just as well to draw this conclusion as the only workable data for 1950 are for metropolitan areas (nine of them, all in the North and West). Accordingly, for each of four periods, the relative positions of the groups will be examined in·these nine major urban centers. (Specific racial and ethnic data are available for four different periods: the census taken in April 1930; a special census taken in January 1931; and the regular censuses of 1940 and 1950.)

Certain technical problems should be noted before turning to the analysis. First, immigrant data are available in three of the four periods for all foreign-born men and do not permit separation of the South—Central—Eastern Europeans from others. Second, it is not possible to limit even roughly the analysis of the foreign-born to ages that are most likely to represent the parents of the relevant 1925–1935 second-generation cohort. This is also the case for blacks. Finally, unemployment is notoriously difficult to conceptualize or to measure adequately. Accordingly, there are a number of shortcomings and shifts in the census definitions used in each period. The 1930 and 1931 data are roughly comparable (type A unemployment data are used for both periods, defined as "Persons out of a job, able to work, and looking for a job"). The only difficulty is that the 1931 survey did not gather data on those who were working; hence it is necessary to use the 1930 figures on gainful workers for both periods. There is no comparability between either of those years and the data employed in 1940 (see U.S. Bureau of the Census, 1944), but there is a reasonably high degree of comparability between the 1940 and 1950 delineations of unemployment.

In most of the metropolitan areas in 1930, the lowest unemployment rates for men were among the native whites and the lowest rates for women were most often found among the immigrants (table 8.16). Without exception, the highest rates among women in each city were found among blacks; and only in San Francisco and Los Angeles were black men employed more often than immigrants.

A radical change occurred by January of 1931—less than a year after the April 1930 census. Of course, the rates were sharply higher by then. Unemployment for native white men, which had ranged from 7 to

TABLE 8.16

Metropolitan Unemployment Rates, 1930–1950

City	1930 Male Native white	1930 Male Foreign-born white	1930 Male Black	1930 Female Native white	1930 Female Foreign-born white	1930 Female Black	1931 Male Native white	1931 Male Foreign-born white	1931 Male Black	1931 Female Native white	1931 Female Foreign-born white	1931 Female Black
Boston	8.7	8.9	9.5	4.2	4.2	7.4	22.6	21.7	22.0	15.3	10.1	23.6
Chicago	9.8	11.8	13.1	5.5	4.3	9.8	23.4	24.6	40.3	16.9	12.0	55.4
Cleveland	10.6	12.5	20.8	4.7	4.0	11.0	24.6	27.5	47.5	14.8	11.3	49.6
Detroit	10.4	12.4	21.8	5.7	4.6	14.5	24.4	24.3	51.3	16.2	10.5	68.9
Los Angeles	8.0	8.9	8.5	5.5	5.5	7.1	18.4	12.6	28.6	12.8	7.5	36.6
New York City	8.1	9.0	10.1	5.0	4.5	6.4	17.7	19.5	25.1	14.2	10.9	26.6
Philadelphia	8.3	8.3	13.4	5.6	4.9	6.8	23.6	21.8	39.5	18.6	11.8	36.9
Pittsburgh	8.4	7.8	12.0	3.3	2.5	6.7	22.7	20.2	36.7	14.2	6.9	41.0
San Francisco	6.8	8.8	7.4	3.9	3.3	5.1	15.1	11.8	14.0	9.1	6.6	18.8

City	1940 Male Native white	1940 Male Foreign-born white	1940 Male Black	1940 Female Native white	1940 Female Foreign-born white	1940 Female Black	1950 Male Native white	1950 Male Foreign-born white	1950 Male Black	1950 Female Native white	1950 Female Foreign-born white	1950 Female Black
Boston	12.1	9.6	15.0	11.4	6.1	11.1	6.6	5.7	10.2	3.9	3.5	6.3
Chicago	10.5	9.4	17.1	9.6	5.5	22.4	3.4	3.7	10.9	3.0	3.3	12.4
Cleveland	10.3	11.2	16.5	10.6	6.2	20.5	3.7	4.3	11.4	3.3	3.4	9.8
Detroit	9.7	8.6	16.0	11.7	7.1	18.6	5.7	5.0	11.4	5.2	4.3	12.5
Los Angeles	10.6	12.0	17.7	10.2	8.9	16.4	6.6	8.6	12.2	7.2	8.1	10.8
New York City	14.3	13.0	20.3	14.4	9.4	16.1	5.9	6.7	11.5	4.5	5.1	8.0
Philadelphia	13.6	11.3	29.9	14.3	7.4	21.3	5.2	4.4	12.9	3.4	3.0	9.1
Pittsburgh	15.3	12.1	25.4	15.3	7.7	25.2	6.3	4.9	13.2	4.7	3.3	11.1
San Francisco	8.8	9.3	11.8	9.5	7.9	14.6	6.7	7.8	16.1	6.6	6.9	17.2

SOURCES: 1930: Class A unemployed from U.S. Bureau of the Census, 1931, table 8 of each state section; gainful workers in 1930 from U.S. Bureau of the Census, 1932, pp. 370–373. 1931: U.S. Bureau of the Census, 1932, pp. 370–373. 1940: U.S. Bureau of the Census, 1943c, table 50 of each state volume. 1950: U.S. Bureau of the Census, 1952, tables 35 and 36 of each state volume; U.S. Bureau of the Census, 1954, table 11.

NOTE: The data for 1930 and 1931 are based on class A unemployed. New York City excludes Staten Island and Queens. Gainful workers in 1930 used as denominator in computing 1931 rates. Data in 1940 refer to Metropolitan Districts. Data in 1950 refer to Standard Metropolitan Areas. Data are for nonwhites in 1950, blacks in other periods.

11 percent in these nine centers in April 1930, now ran from 15 to 25 percent, with an average native white unemployment rate of more than 20 percent in these cities. Blacks and immigrant men experienced sharply higher unemployment rates as well. But the striking fact is that the immigrants fared far better than either native whites or blacks of the same sex. This is true whether one considers the relative or absolute changes between the two years. For example, the unemployment rates in 1930 had been lower among native white men than the foreign-born in all but two cities, Pittsburgh and Philadelphia (in the latter they were identical). One year later, the ratio of native white to foreign-born white unemployment rates had increased in all nine cities—indeed, in five of them the unemployment rates for native white men were higher than for the immigrants (compare columns 1 and 2 in table 8.17). A similar pattern of change is found among women. Native whites more often had higher unemployment rates than the immigrants even in 1930, but again the ratios in all nine cities increased in 1931 and hence were more unfavorable to native whites (compare columns 5 and 6, table 8.17).

For the most part, these *relative* shifts in unemployment were also accompanied by greater *absolute* increases for the native whites compared with the foreign-born (see columns 17 and 18 for males and 20 and 21 for women, table 8.17). The native white unemployment increases were much greater than those experienced by immigrant women and generally somewhat greater among the native white men when compared with immigrants. All of this suggests that the immigrants were badly hit by the worsening depression, but not quite as badly as the native whites in these cities. Indeed, the former clearly improved in their position relative to native whites.

The immigrant–black comparison is of greatest interest. Unemployment among black men had been higher in all but the two western cities in 1930 and in all cases among women (table 8.16). The relative gap by 1931 had widened for men in every city except Boston (table 8.17, columns 9 and 10), with unemployment now higher for blacks in all nine cities (table 8.16). The relative gaps had also widened among women in all cities, in some places the increases were rather spectacular (table 8.17, columns 13 and 14). This is because the unemployment increases among black women were nothing short of incredible in a number of cities; for example, two-thirds of all black women in Detroit were unemployed in 1931, compared with 16 and 10.5 percent, respectively, among native and immigrant white women (Table 8.16). The unemployment rate for black women was about 50 percent in such major centers as Chicago and Cleveland, with it ranging between 36 and 40 percent in Los Angeles, Philadelphia, and Pittsburgh.

It is not merely that the *relative* increases in unemployment were greater for blacks; the *absolute* increases were also far larger for blacks than immigrant whites except for Boston. There are a number of cities where the increases for black men were 12 or 15 percentage points greater than those experienced by the immigrants (table 8.17, column 19 versus 18). The gaps were even greater than that in Detroit and Los Angeles. Given the extraordinarily high unemployment rates in 1931 among black women, it is not surprising that their absolute increases in unemployment between 1930 and 1931 were considerably greater than those observed among immigrant women. Increases in the unemployment rate for black women ranged from about 40 to 55 percentage points in Detroit, Chicago, and Cleveland, whereas for immigrant women they ranged from 6 to 8 points (table 8.17, column 22 versus 21).

Unemployment declined considerably by 1940 from the highs observed in the early 1930s, but nevertheless the rates were still substantial. A comparison between 1931 and 1940 is not ideal: The data are based on metropolitan districts in the latter year and hence include suburbs and adjacent urban centers; the minimum age in the coverage was raised from 10 to 14; and, most important, the definition of unemployment changed drastically.[8] The most meaningful comparison between 1940 and 1931 is probably made by an examination of the relative positions within each period rather than by consideration of the absolute shifts. Little need be said about women in the labor force; in all cities, the ratio of black to immigrant unemployment rates declined in 1940 from the extraordinary peaks found in 1931. However, the immigrant women still had far lower unemployment rates than those found among either native white or black women and the ratios were still higher in 1940 than they had been in 1930 in eight of the cities. Hence, the recovery of black women between 1931 and 1940, although more rapid than that experienced by immigrants, still did not return them to their 1930 position (table 8.17, columns 5–7, 13–15).

The pattern is somewhat different among men. The shifts between 1930 and 1931 had been favorable, relatively speaking, to immigrants compared to other whites. This is the case in 1940 as well; the ratio of native white to immigrant unemployment rates had increased in seven of the nine areas, indicating that the immigrants were relatively better off in 1940 than in 1931 when compared with native whites (table 8.17, columns 1–3). As for blacks, in six of the nine centers the unemployment gaps worsened for them in comparison with changes experienced by the immigrants—the exceptions being Cleveland, Detroit, and Los Angeles (columns 9–11). Overall, for both men and women, the immigrants did relatively better than blacks during the depression. In all but

TABLE 8.17

RATIOS OF NATIVE WHITE AND BLACK UNEMPLOYMENT RATES TO FOREIGN-BORN RATES, 1930–1950, AND ABSOLUTE CHANGES, 1930–1931

| | Native white ÷ foreign-born white | | | | | | | | Black ÷ foreign-born white | | | | | | | |
| | Male | | | | Female | | | | Male | | | | Female | | | |
City	1930 (1)	1931 (2)	1940 (3)	1950 (4)	1930 (5)	1931 (6)	1940 (7)	1950 (8)	1930 (9)	1931 (10)	1940 (11)	1950 (12)	1930 (13)	1931 (14)	1940 (15)	1950 (16)
Boston	.98	1.04	1.26	1.16	1.00	1.51	1.87	1.11	1.07	1.01	1.56	1.79	1.76	2.34	1.82	1.80
Chicago	.83	.95	1.12	.92	1.28	1.41	1.75	.91	1.11	1.64	1.82	2.95	2.28	4.62	4.07	3.76
Cleveland	.85	.89	.92	.86	1.18	1.31	1.71	.97	1.66	1.73	1.47	2.65	2.75	4.39	3.31	2.88
Detroit	.84	1.00	1.13	1.14	1.24	1.54	1.65	1.21	1.76	2.11	1.86	2.28	3.15	6.56	2.62	2.91
Los Angeles	.90	1.46	.88	.77	1.00	1.71	1.15	.89	.96	2.27	1.48	1.42	1.29	4.88	1.84	1.33
New York	.90	.91	1.10	.88	1.11	1.30	1.53	.88	1.12	1.29	1.56	1.72	1.42	2.44	1.71	1.57
Philadelphia	1.00	1.08	1.20	1.18	1.14	1.58	1.93	1.13	1.61	1.81	2.65	2.93	1.39	3.13	2.88	3.03
Pittsburgh	1.08	1.12	1.26	1.29	1.32	2.06	1.99	1.42	1.54	1.82	2.10	2.69	2.68	5.94	3.27	3.36
San Francisco	.77	1.28	.95	.86	1.18	1.38	1.20	.96	.84	1.19	1.27	2.06	1.55	2.85	1.85	2.49

Unemployment rate increases between 1930 and 1931

	Male			Female		
City	Native white (17)	Foreign-born white (18)	Black (19)	Native white (20)	Foreign-born white (21)	Black (22)
Boston	13.9	12.8	12.5	11.1	5.9	16.2
Chicago	13.6	12.8	27.2	11.4	7.7	45.6
Cleveland	14.0	15.0	26.7	10.1	7.3	38.6
Detroit	14.0	11.9	29.5	10.5	5.9	54.4
Los Angeles	10.4	3.7	20.1	7.3	2.0	29.5
New York	9.6	10.5	15.0	9.2	6.4	20.2
Philadelphia	15.3	13.5	26.1	13.0	6.9	30.1
Pittsburgh	14.3	12.4	24.7	10.9	4.4	34.3
San Francisco	8.3	3.0	6.6	5.2	3.3	13.7

NOTE: Table 8.16 for sources and definitions.

one center, immigrants had more favorable ratios in 1940 than in 1930. Indeed, by 1940 immigrant women had substantially lower unemployment rates than even native white women, and among men the foreign-born living in Boston, Chicago, Detroit, New York, Philadelphia, and Pittsburgh had lower unemployment rates than did the native whites.

The second-generation cohort under study was between 15 and 24 years of age in 1950, with a midpoint of 20. Hence it is reasonable still to consider whether the unemployment patterns among immigrants in that year might have any bearing on the spectacular developments in that cohort. Indeed, this is probably an especially important period as the cohort is almost entirely at a point where school attendance is optional rather than mandatory. Bear in mind that there were some shifts in the definition and measurement of unemployment in 1950 as well as changes in the metropolitan delineations. The immigrants did not fare as well as the native whites between 1940 and 1950. A sharp decline occurred in the native white–immigrant unemployment ratios among women, but there were also declines for men in seven of the nine cities (table 8.17, columns 3 and 4, 7 and 8). The pattern of change was somewhat different for black-immigrant comparisons among women; in five cities the ratio went down but in four places it actually went up—meaning that the position of black women deteriorated even more during the decade relative to immigrant white women. Under any circumstance, in all but one city the relative position of black women was still worse in 1950 than it had been in 1930 (columns 13–16). Between 1940 and 1950 the position of black men relative to immigrants actually deteriorated in nearly all of the places (table 8.17, columns 11 and 12).

Summarizing Developments Between 1930 and 1950

A summary of developments during this period, when the midpoint of the cohort moved from kindergarten to college age, is complicated for immigrant–native white comparisons, but is clearer for immigrant–black shifts. Hence the latter will be left for dessert. The problem with immigrant–native white comparisons during this period is that different conclusions are drawn for men and women. For the former, despite the drop off between 1940 and 1950 in the advantage held by immigrants, it was still a period in which they gained on native whites. In 1930, immigrant unemployment rates were lower than the native white figures in only one city, whereas this was the case in four places in 1950. More important, in seven of the nine urban centers the net change in the ratios during the 20-year span was favorable to the foreign-born. To be sure, this understates some of the dynamics of the changes because, if anything, the advantages held by immigrants were even greater in the middle of this period. For women, however, there was an overall decline in the position of immigrants relative to native whites. In 1930, the unemployment rate for native white women was as high or higher in all nine cities; the gap in these rates moved up earlier in the period, but by 1950 had fallen off to the point that in seven of the centers they were lower than those found in 1930. The situation for immigrant–native white comparisons is therefore very complicated. Among men there was a set of fluctuations which did generally work to the favor of the immigrants, but the opposite holds for women. It is difficult to evaluate these contradictory trends, although one is inclined to give more weight to the male experience because they were in those years far more likely to be in the labor force and hence serve as a major source of income for whites. One can conclude that there is some indication of labor market changes which may have helped accelerate the education of the second generation from South–Central–Eastern Europe relative to NWNPs, but in all fairness the evidence is not terribly strong.

A clearer picture emerges regarding black–immigrant comparisons during this period. The unemployment of black men worsened relative to the immigrants in every city and the same was the case for women in all but one city. One has to compare the absolute values in Table 8.16 to gain some appreciation of the massive nature of the shift. To take a modest example, in Boston the unemployment rates for blacks and immigrant men had been fairly similar in 1930, 9.5 and 8.9, respectively. In 1950, unemployment was slightly higher for blacks, 10.2 percent, whereas the rate for immigrants was now 5.7. In Chicago, blacks shifted from 13.1 to 10.9 during the 20 years, whereas the foreign-born changed from 11.8 to 3.7. In Los Angeles, New York, and San Francisco, the rates were not too different between immigrants and blacks in 1930, but moved in the opposite direction during the 20-year span.

In short, there are certain changes in employment during this period which roughly correspond to the educational developments under consideration. The second-generation cohort starting and largely completing school during this span had an increase in educational attainment over the preceding cohort which was far more rapid than that experienced by native whites of native parentage. The latter, in turn, widened its advantage over blacks. In the case of the economic variable being considered here, we also find a substantial deterioration in the unemployment situation of blacks as opposed to either of these white groups during the same time span.[9] This may explain the surprising turn with respect to the education ND between northern-born blacks and native whites of native parentage. Likewise, there are dramatic gains in the employment situation of immigrants as against blacks during this period which suggest a line of explanation for the change in their educational positions as well. (In passing, one should also note that the current issue of black unemployment is not a problem that is particularly novel to the present time. In nothern cities black rates were much higher than were those among whites prior to the increased automation of menial industrial work. Moreover, the low unemployment rates in the South very likely represented nothing but hidden underemployment due to southern blacks eking out a bare living in farming.)

It is, of course, another question as to why the immigrant experience during the Great Depression—bad though it may have been—was not as severe as that experienced by native whites and blacks in the same cities. Moreover, it is not possible with these data to determine whether there were changes in unemployment before 1930 in the same direction and magnitude as those found in the 1930–1950 period. However, these and earlier cautions notwithstanding, the data suggest that the remarkable educational shifts observed for the 1925–1935 birth cohorts of blacks and new Europeans occurred during a period in which the groups experienced radically different changes in their unemployment rates in the North.

CONCLUSIONS

Why was the educational progress of new Europeans so rapid during this century when compared with the changes experienced by either northern-born blacks or whites of Northwestern European origin? The greater concentration of new Europeans in the urban centers of the North and West is, in no small way, a major source of their advantage over other whites because a sizable segment of Northwestern European whites in the United States are located in the South and in rural areas—a situational factor that works to their offsprings' disadvantage. Thus if the new Europeans are compared with older stocks born only in the North or West, the results are not particularly favorable to the former. Nevertheless, as this regional advantage existed for a long time, it is not entirely clear at this point what finally led to its manifestation. Of this, more later.

The new Europeans enjoyed certain advantages over the northern-born blacks, but this geographical factor was not one of them. Blacks leaving the South were also highly concentrated in the great urban centers of the North and West, the very places where the new Europeans were achieving such spectacular gains. There are a number of other factors accounting for these differences. For one, the migration processes were radically different for these groups and worked to the advantage of the new Europeans. The movement of blacks from South to North after the end of slavery was largely an uncontrolled movement, notwithstanding the attempts made from time to time in the South to restrict the exodus of blacks. On the other hand, during the same period, the federal government changed its role from nearly a passive existence to one of increasing control over the movement of immigrants into the nation. As a consequence, the new Europeans were upgraded not merely through developments in their homeland, but through the increasingly stringent standards of admission to the nation. The upgrading of succeeding waves of immigrant parents in turn appears to be linked to some of the educational progress made by the relevant cohorts of American-born offspring. It is not that blacks moving to the North were deteriorating in quality during this period, indeed there is strong evidence to the contrary such that efforts to explain their weakening position in these terms are unjustified. But there was not the same kind of screening process operating as for the new Europeans. This is hardly the whole story, although the initiation of literacy requirements may have played a particularly important role in the massive upgrading experienced by the youngest cohort considered here. There is more to the matter because the correlation between shifts in educational attainment for successive waves of parents and children is rather weak at some points. Earlier second-generation new Europeans had begun to make educational progress at a more rapid rate than blacks even without a concomitant change in the immigrant waves.

The World War I period per se can be ruled out as a *direct* factor influencing the relative gains experienced by these groups. At most, there was a slight slowdown during World War I in the educational progress exhibited by succeeding waves of northern-born blacks relative to the progress of native whites of native parentage. Also of no importance are changes in the success rates of blacks and new Europeans attending school; these do not appear to be related to shifts in their levels of educational attainment. In other words, ethnic—racial differences in the propensity of educators to promote students, or temporal shifts in these promotion rates, are unrelated to changes in the groups' educational attainment.

Economic forces appear to be a powerful factor. Gains in parental economic position are strongly linked to the relative progress of new Europeans and northern blacks. The spectacular discrepancy between the youngest cohort of new Europeans and northern-born blacks is associated with equally sizable differences in employment experienced by their parents during the period beginning with the Great Depression and running through the early post-World War II period.

In chapter 9 it will be possible to consider whether the deterioration of blacks relative to new Europeans was part of a general lessening of the black position in the urban North, perhaps as a function of their growing numbers at a time when migration from Europe was restricted. Likewise, a fuller consideration will be made of a feedback process such that the educational levels achieved by these groups were affected by the relative encouragement received by new European and black children for remaining in school (primarily through the potential economic rewards). The provisional evidence gathered at this point would suggest that both the deterioration and feedback factors operated to widen the educational gaps between the groups. Whereas education was seen as a major instrument for assimilating these new European groups who were so radically different, policies toward blacks shifted over time as their presence in many cities increased. The different educational opportunities offered to blacks were accompanied by informal as well as legal steps taken to isolate them from whites in the schools. Similarly, there is clear evidence that economic rewards were not the same for blacks and new Europeans with similar educational credentials. To be sure, there is no denying that SCE Europeans were discriminated against in these domains; rather it is a question of relative degree when compared with blacks. One would expect such gaps to have a dual influence on the education sought by these groups: Not only was there less incentive or reward for schooling among the next wave of black children in the North, but their parents had fewer monetary resources than they otherwise would have had to maintain their offspring in school for a longer period.

Finally, although the preceding chapter considered whether cultural and normative differences might be responsible for some of these educational changes, it is best to review quickly the reasons for thinking that they were unlikely to be important causal factors. Bear in mind, however, that shifts may have occurred since then as the groups' cultural and normative values respond to the realities. But there is no indication that blacks were initially any less interested in education, or less willing to sacrifice to achieve it, than were the other groups on the average. The reader will recall, for example, that black educational gains in the early cohorts were as large or larger than those experienced by the average new European group.

9

Residential Segregation

Because spatial isolation is a powerful indicator of a group's general position within a community, changes in the magnitude and direction of black and South—Central—Eastern European residential segregation should help determine whether there was a deterioration in the position of blacks in the North relative to the new Europeans from late in the last century through the early decades of the twentieth.[1] Obviously shifts in spatial isolation will have an impact on the educational issues discussed in the preceding chapter, for example, the composition of schools attended by the groups. Indeed, more generally, segregation influences a wide variety of social phenomena such as intermarriage, linguistic assimilation, and even the maintenance of a group's distinctive occupational composition. (These and other factors have been considered for the period of interest in Lieberson, 1963a, chapters 5 and 6.) But the main concern here is not with the consequences of segregation, rather it is with using spatial isolation as an index of the relative positions held by blacks and SCE residents of the urban North through the years.

THE MEASUREMENT OF SEGREGATION

No single segregation measure is "correct" for all purposes: the choice for use depends on the specific research goals involved. (For a review of many of these measures that is still of considerable value, see Taeuber and

Taeuber, 1965, appendix A.) The index employed here is a modified form of P^*, a measure described by Bell (1954) in his restatement of the Shevky—Williams index of isolation. Because this measure is less known than the more widely encountered index of dissimilarity and because several new wrinkles are developed here, a brief exposition of the pros and cons of the measure may be of value not only to readers wishing to have a clear understanding of the results, but also to those stewing over the choice of a measure for their own research.

For some research purposes, the similarity between groups in their spatial distribution among the subunits of a city is all that one wishes to know. For such purposes, the index of dissimilarity (D) has certain very clear advantages that have been discussed elsewhere in considerable detail (Taeuber and Taeuber, 1965). The index value is unaffected by the relative numbers of the groups involved (except for problems of sampling errors) and its interpretation is both convenient and easily understood. The latter feature is irrelevant here because P^* is also easily interpreted and understood. The first quality is a double-edged sword. As I have noted elsewhere, it is often important to take into account the actual numbers of the groups involved because "the effect of a given index of dissimilarity on other social phenomena will be influenced by the relative numbers of the groups involved. The implications of the same index value in two cities, one with a small percentage Negro and the other with a large percentage, will be very different. The likelihood of interaction with whites will be much less in the latter community" (Lieberson, 1969, p. 859).

Consider, for example, columns 1 and 2 of table 9.1 which provide a hypothetical population distribution of blacks and whites in the subareas of a city in which there are no other groups. The index of dissimilarity obtained from these two columns, 56, is unaffected by the total numbers of blacks and whites in the entire city, B and W, respectively. Thus if each number in column 2 were divided by 10 so as to make B=W=100, the D index would remain at 56. The index of dissimilarity by itself is inadequate for some research because D is insensitive to the actual interaction potential between the groups, a factor that is affected by the relative numbers as well as the pattern of spatial segregation. One would have to combine the index of dissimilarity with some measure of population composition.

By contrast, the P^* index combines the ethnic—racial composition of the city with differences in the group's spatial distributions to yield an index value that has a very clear and useful meaning. Unlike D, there is a set of different P^* indexes because, as we shall see, the degree of isolation is not symmetrical for each group when paired together. Let the subscripts preceding and following P^* indicate, respectively, the group from whom and to whom the interaction is directed. Thus, for a randomly selected member of group X in a city, $_xP_y^*$ gives the probability that someone else selected from the same residential subarea will be a member of group Y. Only in the exceptional case where the number of X and Y in the city is identical will $_xP_y^* = {_yP_x^*}$. $_xP_x^*$ refers to the isolation experienced by members of group X in the city, that is, for a member of group X randomly selected in the city, $_xP_x^*$ gives the probability that someone else chosen from the same residential area will also be a member of group X. In other words, it weights the proportion X is of the population in each subarea by the number of Xs residing in each of these subareas (Farley and Taeuber, 1968, p. 956). Likewise, $_yP_y^*$ refers to the average isolation experienced by members of group Y in the city, and $_yP_{non-y}^*$ refers to the proportion of non-Ys living in the average subarea in which Ys reside. (These procedures are an extension and elaboration of the initial P^* measure described in Bell which applied to what is labeled here as the isolation of a group, $_iP_i^*$.)

In its most general form, the equation for the index is:

$$_xP_y^* = \sum_{i=1}^{n}\left(\frac{x_i}{X}\right)\left(\frac{y_i}{t_i}\right),$$

where X is the total number of members of group X in the city, x_i is the number of group X in a given subarea, y_i is the number of group Y in the subarea, and t_i is the total population of the subarea. (It is possible for y_i to refer to group X when the simple isolation of the group is being measured.)

The computation of P^* is quite simple and an illustration will help the reader gain a conceptual understanding as well. Suppose one wishes to know about the probability of blacks interacting with blacks. One determines the total population in each subarea, t_i (table 9.1, column 3), and then divides the number of blacks in each subarea, b_i, by this total (column 4). The resulting black proportions in each subarea are then weighted by the proportion of all blacks in the city who live in each subarea, b_i/B. Thus using the data in table 9.1, the P^* index for blacks interacting with fellow blacks is:

$$_bP_b^* = \sum_{i=1}^{n}\left(\frac{b_i}{B}\right)\left(\frac{b_i}{t_i}\right) = \left(\frac{30}{100}\right)\left(\frac{30}{400}\right) + \left(\frac{10}{100}\right)\left(\frac{10}{300}\right) + \left(\frac{0}{100}\right)\left(\frac{0}{300}\right)$$

$$+ \left(\frac{60}{100}\right)\left(\frac{60}{100}\right) = .3858.$$

TABLE 9.1
COMPUTATION OF P^* INDEX

Subareas	Number			Black proportion of subarea total
	Blacks	Whites	Total	
A	30	370	400	.075
B	10	290	300	.033
C	0	300	300	0
D	60	40	100	.600
Sum	100	1,000	1,100	

This means that the average black in the city lives in an area where .3858 of the residents are black. This figure can be readily compared with the value that would occur if there was no segregation in the city and if there were no random fluctuations from area to area. This is simply the proportion blacks are of the total city population; in this case, $B/T = 100/1,100 = .0909$. The difference, $.3858 - .0909 = .2949$, is the excess proportion encountered by the average black compared to the value expected if the black component in each subarea was the same as the black proportion of the entire city population.[2]

Assuming there are only two groups in the city, whites and blacks, the average proportion of whites (w) encountered by blacks in their residential areas is simply 1 minus the proportion of blacks encountered by blacks. Thus $_bP_w^* = 1 - {_bP_b^*} = 1 - .3858 = .6142$. Because whites comprise .9091 of the city population (1,000/1,100), the difference between $_bP_w^*$ and the proportion that would occur in the absence of segregation is $.6142 - .9091 = -.2949$—the same value as obtained above except in the opposite direction. This figure gives the decrease in contact with whites for blacks compared to what would occur in the absence of any segregation.

An important quality of P^* is that the results are asymmetrical for the groups, that is, $_bP_w^* \neq {_wP_b^*}, {_bP_b^*} \neq {_wP_w^*}$. Hence, if we saw above that the average black in the city lives in a residential area where .6142 of the residents are white, this does not mean that the probability for a randomly selected white having contact with blacks is also .6142. In point of fact, except for the rare case when the two groups have exactly the same number of residents in the city, it is certain that the other index will be different. In the present case, one would weight the black proportion in each subarea population (table 9.1, column 4) by the number of whites (column 2) rather than the number of blacks (column 1) if the goal is the proportion of blacks living in the average white's subarea ($_wP_b^* = .06132$). (For those oriented to demographic standardization methods, these differences are analogous to the effect of using different population weights for a given set of rates.) P* therefore has another strong advantage for any segregation research that seeks to measure the actual magnitude of isolation between the groups; it takes into account the fact that the probability of a given member of group X interacting with a Y is not the same as the probability of a given member of group Y interacting with an X.[3] We shall make good use of this inequality.

In the course of this generalization of P*, an exact equation was developed for determining $_wP_b^*$ if $_bP_w^*$ is known:

$$_wP_b^* = (_bP_w^*)(B/W) \,.$$

From this equation, which can be used to derive either index from the other as long as the relative size of B and W are known for the city, it follows that a change in one P* of a given magnitude has a different effect on the other index, the difference being a function of the ratio between W and B. Thus, if $_w\Delta_b$ represents a change in $_wP_b^*$, it follows that the change in the $_bP_w^*$ index, $_b\Delta_w$, will be a function of B/W as such:

$$_b\Delta_w = \frac{_w\Delta_b}{\dfrac{B}{W}} \,.$$

This is extremely important because it means that the greater the difference between two groups in their total numbers in the city, the greater will be the differential consequence of a change in segregation. More about this shortly.

Finally, given a group's isolation index, a conversion exists for determining the other group's isolation in the simple case where only two groups are present.[4]

$$_bP_b^* = 1 - \left[\left(\frac{W}{B} \right) \left(1 - {}_wP_w^* \right) \right] \,.$$

There are, of course, a number of other technical issues in the computation of segregation indexes—for example, the spatial grid used, the number of spatial units, and the like—but these have been carefully considered elsewhere and there is no point rehashing the discussion at this point (see Taeuber and Taeuber, 1965; Lieberson, 1963a). Particularly important here is the necessity for the period under study to rely largely on ward units that both vary greatly in number between cities and, in some cases, over time within the same city.

BLACK SEGREGATION, 1890–1930

Black isolation was rather slight in 1890 among the 17 leading cities of the North and West (listed in table 9.4). The mean $_bP_b^*$ was .0665, indicating that the average black lived in a ward where well over 90 percent of the population was not black $(1 - .0665)$. (To be sure the degree of isolation would have shown up greater than that if smaller subarea data were available for the cities.) Although black isolation increased slightly between 1890 and 1900 and again in the next decade (see table 9.2, column 1), in five or six of the cities there were actual declines in the $_bP_b^*$ from the preceding decades (columns 2 and 3). But the next two decades were marked by massive increases in the isolation of blacks from others in these cities, with $_bP_b^*$ going from .0971 in 1910 to .1676 in 1920 and then on to .2991 in 1930. The level of black isolation increased in virtually all cities during these decades (columns 2 and 3).

Ignoring the causes, the numbers in the first column of table 9.2 summarize an important and fundamental shift in the position of blacks in the North—they were far more isolated than they had ever been before. Black isolation in the average major urban center of the North in 1930 was about 4.5 times greater than it had been in 1890. Indeed, $_bP_b^*$ had tripled in the 20 years since 1910. Whatever the cause, this was bound to have important consequences for blacks in the North. Such a massive jump meant that blacks would be increasingly isolated on all other factors that are related to residence, for example, schools, community participation, local organizations, and local government services such as police, sanitation, and the like.

Naturally one would like to know why segregation increased for blacks. Because a group's isolation is affected by the racial composition of a city as well as the group's spatial distribution, the most reasonable starting point is the increase in the black proportion of the population in these centers. In 1890, blacks were about 3 percent of the population on the average in these large cities. (Black isolation in that year was somewhat more than double the level that would occur if $_bP_b^*$ was solely a function of population composition and the races were evenly distributed throughout the city.) In the ensuing decade, the black proportion increased in most of the centers (table 9.2, columns 5–7), with the average reaching .0331 in 1900. The isolation of blacks also went up somewhat during that period, as was noted earlier. The changes between 1900 and 1910 indicate that something more was going on to raise black segregation than merely compositional changes. There was essentially no change in the mean black proportion of the population—indeed the black component actually

TABLE 9.2

BLACK AND WHITE SEGREGATION, 1890–1930 (17 LEADING NONSOUTHERN CITIES)

Year	Mean $_bP^*_b$	Number of cities in which $_bP^*_b$ since previous decade:		Mean black proportion of population	Number of cities in which proportion since previous decade:			Mean $_wP^*_w$
		Increased	Decreased		Increasd	Decreased	No change	
1890	.0665			.0296				.9718
1900	.0783	12	5	.0331	12	5	0	.9688
1910	.0971	11	6	.0333	7	9	1	.9698
1920	.1676	17	0	.0458	16	1	0	.9615
1930	.2991	16	1	.0647	16	1	0	.9541

NOTE: For list of 17 leading cities, see table 9.4

went down in more than half of the cities (table 9.2, columns 5–7)—but $_bP_b^*$ nevertheless increased from .0783 to .0971. (The average black proportion was unchanged during this period because the increases in the number of blacks were accompanied by massive increases in the number of whites in these centers—this was a high point for the migration of SCE Europeans.) This would suggest that black isolation was going up even when the proportion did not. Likewise, increases in the black proportion in the next two decades do not appear to be of the magnitude that would generate the changes in P* described earlier.

A more formal examination of this is provided through the regression of each city's $_bP_b^*$ on the black proportion of the population in each period. The results, shown in figure 9.1, indicate a sizable increase in black segregation beginning in 1910, net of the influence due to population composition. There was very little increase between 1890 and 1900, but this was followed by successively greater increases in the ensuing decades. Particularly noteworthy are increments in the Y intercept, indicating greater isolation for blacks per se, regardless of their composition in the city.

Table 9.3 shows a true upward movement in segregation during the period even when the X variable for a given decade is compared with the range found for the preceding period. (Because the black proportion of the city population tends to move upward over time, it is necessary to compare the regressions with the same range for the independent variable.) Between 1900 and 1910, there is a sizable increase in the regression coefficient, indicating a rapid rise in black isolation. A similar pattern is found when 1920 is compared with all cities in 1910—except here the race effect per se is greater, witness the jump in a (the Y intercept) as well as in the regression coefficient. Between 1920 and 1930 there is likewise a shift in both coefficients.

In short, black segregation in the urban North increased from 1900 onward not only because their proportion of the population grew, but also because the same composition led to more isolation than it had during earlier decades. Insofar as residential segregation not only has consequences for a group's position but can also serve more generally as an indicator of the group's general position within the community, these figures indicate that the position of blacks began to deteriorate sharply at the outset of this century.

SOUTH–CENTRAL–EASTERN EUROPEAN SEGREGATION

How does the magnitude of new European segregation compare with blacks'? The earliest year with SCE segregation data available for a large

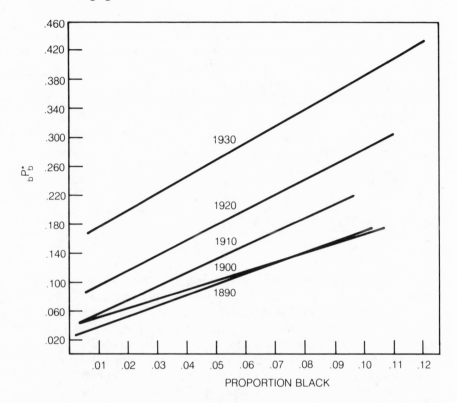

Fig. 9.1
Regression of Black Isolation Indexes on Proportion Black,
17 Leading Nonsouthern Cities, 1890–1930

NOTE: The cities used for computation are: Boston, Buffalo, Chicago, Cincinnati, Cleveland, Detroit, Indianapolis, Kansas City, Los Angeles, Milwaukee, Minneapolis, Newark, New York City, Philadelphia, Pittsburgh, St. Louis, and San Francisco

number of cities is 1910. All 17 of the cities used earlier in the black analysis have data permitting segregation measurements for the Austrians and Russians, all but one for Italians, 15 report data on Hungarians, and the relevant data are available for Greeks and Roumanians in 10 and 9 cities, respectively. The number was too small to merit inclusion of groups such as the Finns and Portuguese, and data for other new groups were not available.

Unfortunately, there are some sticky technical matters to resolve before comparing the segregation of these groups with black isolation. The Census Bureau reported the necessary spatial data only for the foreign-born component of each SCE group. By comparison, the segregation

TABLE 9.3
REGRESSION OF $_bP_b^*$ ON THE BLACK PROPORTION
OF THE POPULATION (17 LEADING NONSOUTHERN CITIES)

Year	r	b	a
1900	.81	1.2621	.0365
1910	.87	1.8393	.0373
1910	.88	1.8887	.0343
1920	.69	2.4384	.0618
1920	.67	2.0846	.0722
1930	.63	3.3280	.1127

NOTE: First year shown in a pair includes all 17 cities; second row is for those cities
10 years later with a black proportion of the population falling within the range existing
in the first decade of the pair.

figures for blacks are not restricted to just the southern-born but include all members of the group. If only the immigrant generation is measured, this will underestimate the segregation of the new European groups because the American-born component will be counted as "others" and thus will generate a lower index for the group than would occur if we knew that these nonimmigrants were in fact ethnic compatriots (in many cases, simply their American-born offspring still living at home). This is no problem if all one wishes to do is tap the segregation of the foreign-born, and often that is all that one can do. Obviously, it is less than ideal here because we want to find out if blacks were more or less segregated than the Europeans.

Solving this problem requires certain assumptions that are quite reasonable, but are almost certain to be less than 100 percent correct. The Census Bureau did publish second-generation ethnic data by wards in three cities in 1910: New York, Philadelphia, and Chicago. In each of these cities second-generation figures were available for only four of the new European groups (Austrians, Hungarians, Italians, and Russians). One can compare the segregation of the foreign-born alone with the P* indexes obtained when the second generations are included in order to generate a procedure whereby P* for the combined two generations can be estimated from the data available in the other cities for just the first generation. As one might predict, the correlation between P* for just the foreign-born and P* for the combined generations is rather high (r is .9846). This is to be expected if only because of the part—whole nature of the relationship as well as the inclusion of American-born members of the households.[5] The regression equation, $Y = -.0014 + 1.5205X$, where Y is the estimated P* for the two generations combined and X is the P* observed for the foreign-born, can be used to estimate the isolation of the two combined generations in 1910. Nothing can be done with the third and later generations of each new European group. This is probably not too great a problem for 1910 because for the most part the groups had only begun to come in sizable numbers to the United States in the preceding 30 years, and it is therefore reasonable to assume that a rather small proportion of the new Europeans were of the third or later generations.

Figure 9.2 compares the isolation of six SCE groups with that observed for blacks in 1910. Italians were far more segregated than blacks when their proportion of the city's population is taken into account and the same holds for Russians in nearly all cities. Further, there is relatively little difference between Hungarians and blacks in their P* values. Austrians are considerably less segregated than blacks, when population composition is taken into account. As for Greeks and Roumanians, the interpretation of their differences from blacks is tricky because the white groups' proportion of the population in most cities is so much less than the black figure found in any of the places. Indeed, comparing the range of black and Greek proportions, there are only three cases in which they overlap, and likewise only five in which the Roumanian proportion of the population is at least as large as the black level. A more appropriate step is to apply the Greek and Roumanian regressions of segregation on composition to the limited number of cities in which the black proportion of the population is small enough to be covered by these equations. In two of the three cities, the actual black segregation index was less than would have been predicted by the two-generation Greek pattern; in three of five cases, the black isolation was greater than expected on the basis of the Roumanian pattern. Overall, there are four cases in which blacks were less segregated and four in which they were more segregated than would have been expected from the Greek and Roumanian linkages between P* and population composition.

In summary, although black segregation in 1910 had increased over the preceding decade, their isolation was not as great as that experienced by several of the new European groups after taking the influence of composition into account. Blacks were substantially less isolated than Italians and also Russian Jews (in cities where the latter were at least 2.4 percent of the population); also $_bP_b^*$ was only slightly higher than the analogous index of Hungarian isolation. Greek and Roumanian comparisons are tricky, and the best one can conclude is that no clear difference

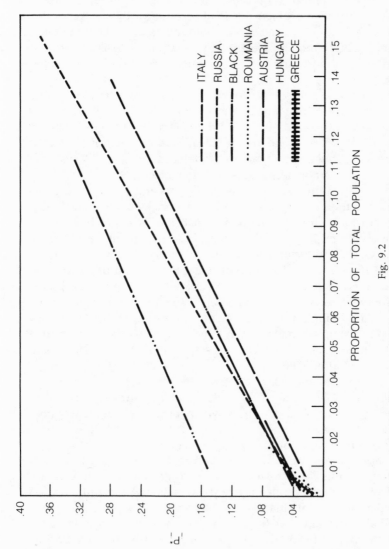

PROPORTION OF TOTAL POPULATION

Fig. 9.2

Regression of Two-Generation SCE Groups and Blacks on Their Proportion of the Population, 17 Leading Nonsouthern Cities, 1910

NOTE: For list of cities see note to Figure 9.1.

is revealed between these groups and blacks when the latter are considered in cities where they too are an extremely small proportion of the residents.

Turning to the actual magnitude of black and ethnic segregation, as opposed to the analysis of segregation net of population composition, blacks were far less isolated than a number of the new European groups in many of the leading urban centers. The number of SCE European groups with P* indexes varied from 4 to 6 in each city; yet at least one of these white groups was more segregated than blacks in all but Cincinnati, Indianapolis, and Kansas City (see table 9.4).[6] Blacks were less segregated than Russians (assumed to be largely Jewish in most cities) in all but three cities, less segregated than Austrians in 9 out of 17 places, and less segregated than Italians in 10 out of 16 centers. In some cities these differences in segregation were massive—although the reader should recognize that the higher white isolation reflected compositional factors as well as a propensity to be more isolated even with composition held constant.

In each of the ten cities in which the black proportion of the population falls within the white range on the compositional variable, an additional way of comparing black–SCE segregation is possible. Namely, the SCE regression of segregation on composition is determined and then applied to the black compositional figure. The actual level of black segregation in six of these cities was less than expected on the basis of the white regression, and in four places blacks were more isolated than one would expect on the basis of white patterns.[7] Hence, on this basis too there are grounds for viewing blacks in 1910 as not an unusually segregated group when compared to the new European groups. This holds even without taking composition into account. The average isolation index for Russians (based on the two generations) in 1910 is higher than blacks, .1500 versus .0971, but is even higher for the foreign-born Russians alone (see table 9.5). This is the case even more strongly for Italians: The average black P* index is .1021 in the 16 cities for which Italian data are available, whereas the Italian immigrants alone have an index of .1336, and it is .2047 for the two generations combined. Greeks, Hungarians, and Roumanians are all considerably less isolated than are blacks (although, as the earlier analysis indicates, this is due to their smaller numbers), with the Austrian P* indexes averaging only slightly less than blacks.

The higher levels of segregation among many of the new European groups are not due to statistical errors in the estimation procedures used for the second generation. Even among the first generation alone, Italians and Russians are more isolated. Moreover, black isolation is

TABLE 9.4
BLACK AND NEW EUROPEAN ISOLATION, 1910

City	Black	Austrian	Greek	Hungarian	Italian	Roumanian	Russian	Number of white–black comparisons in which blacks are:	
								More segregated	Less segregated
Boston	.1134	.0104	.0198	NA	.4453	NA	.2803	2	2
Buffalo	.0572	.0962	NA	.0627	.3870	NA	.1022	0	4
Chicago	.1512	.2530	.0103	.0317	.2105	.0133	.2004	3	3
Cincinnati	.1317	.0104	NA	.0883	.0328	.0057	.0889	5	0
Cleveland	.0788	.2088	NA	.1851	.2283	.0066	.1986	1	4
Detroit	.0676	.1286	NA	.1015	.0963	NA	.1270	0	4
Indianapolis	.1845	.0361	.0068	.0350	.0171	NA	.0455	5	0
Kansas City	.2168	.0031	.0457	.0020	.1314	NA	.0443	5	0
Los Angeles	.0381	.0156	NA	.0049	.0226	NA	.0408	3	1
Milwaukee	.0193	.0747	.0279	.0699	.5617	NA	.0931	0	5
Minneapolis	.0167	.1176	NA	.0285	NA	.0285	.0814	0	4
Newark	.0538	.0998	NA	.0454	.2357	.0186	.2236	2	3
New York City	.0665	.1681	.0065	.0600	.2450	.0436	.3401	3	3
Philadelphia	.1566	.0398	.0039	.0837	.2613	.0136	.2656	4	2
Pittsburgh	.1200	.1080	.0249	.0249	.1071	.0358	.2008	5	1
St. Louis	.1718	.0595	.0312	.0883	.0734	.0119	.1941	5	1
San Francisco	.0067	.0179	.0337	NA	.2201	NA	.0232	0	4

NOTE: White groups are for two generations.
NA: Data for the group are not available for this city.

TABLE 9.5
NEW EUROPEAN RESIDENTIAL SEGREGATION, FOREIGN-BORN AND TWO GENERATIONS,
COMPARED WITH BLACKS, 1910

| Group | Arithmetic mean indexes of isolation | | |
	Foreign-born	Two generations	Black comparison[a]
Austrian	.0559	.0852	.0971
Greek	.0148	.0211	.1207
Hungarian	.0421	.0608	.1020
Italian	.1336	.2047	.1021
Roumanian	.0139	.0197	.1052
Russian	.1014	.1500	.0971

[a]The mean $_bP_b^*$ is for those cities in which indexes are available for the SCE group specified and therefore varies slightly from group to group.

lower in the three cities with two-generational data available. The black isolation index was .0665 in New York in 1910, whereas the indexes for Russian Jews, Italians, and Austrians were .340, .245, and .168, respectively. In Philadelphia, the black index was .157, whereas it was about .26 for both Italians and Russians. Austrians, Italians, and Russians also had higher indexes in Chicago than did blacks. Hence, even if the analysis is restricted to the three cities in which new European second-generation data are available, the broader conclusions remain unaltered.[8] Finally, restricting the analysis to just the similarity of the spatial patterns, an earlier study (Lieberson, 1963a, pp. 126–132) showed that the indexes of dissimilarity for blacks in 1910 in many cases were lower than those for a number of the new European groups even though only the foreign-born generation was included.

SHIFTS IN THE RELATIVE POSITION OF BLACKS AND NEW EUROPEANS

The new European groups in 1910 were in many instances more isolated than blacks, both because their numbers were far greater than the black numbers in some cities and because there were greater indexes for many of the white groups even when matched up with blacks numerically. This raises the natural question of whether the new European indexes were as high or higher than the blacks before 1910 and whether the new Europeans experienced increases in succeeding decades as did blacks. Unfortunately, there are limited data available for the new European groups before 1910 in published sources.

Early Evidence

The data available for New York City (combined with Brooklyn) in 1890 and for Boston in both 1880 and 1890 all indicate that blacks were then relatively less isolated than were the new European groups. Four SCE groups in New York ranged from 0.5 to 3.8 percent of the population in 1890, with isolation indexes ranging between .08 and .10 for the Hungarians and Bohemians, respectively, to a rather massive .345 for the Russian and Polish populations, combined and .22 for the Italian group.[9] The black segregation index of only .057 was lower than any of these groups even though the number of blacks exceeded those of the Hungarian and Bohemian groups (see table 9.6). It is therefore obvious that blacks were far less isolated in New York in 1890 than would be expected on the basis of the new European pattern. A formal test indicates that a $_bP_b^*$ index of .16 would be expected for blacks, rather than

TABLE 9.6
EARLY SEGREGATION INDEXES, 1880 AND 1890

New York City (includes Brooklyn)			Boston		
Group	Index of isolation	Proportion of population	Group	Index of isolation	Proportion of population
1890			*1880*		
Russia and Poland	.3447	.0378	Austria	.0014	.0006
Hungary	.0796	.0070	Poland	.0065	.0012
Bohemia	.1041	.0054	Russia	.0033	.0010
Italy	.2208	.0288	Italy	.0323	.0035
Black	.0572	.0158	Portugal	.0205	.0016
			Black	.0752	.0162
			1890		
			Hungary	.0021	.0005
			Bohemia	.0057	.0005
			Italy	.1370	.0145
			Black	.1037	.0192

SOURCES: U.S. Census Office, 1883; Billings, 1894, 1895.

about .06 if the regression equation of segregation on composition for the four new European groups is applied to them.[10] These figures for New York in 1890 cannot be compared with changes in later decades because a different set of spatial units was employed (see sources to table 9.6); indeed, the black index here is different from that reported earlier for New York in 1890 when ward data were used. However, whether the comparisons are in absolute terms or with population composition taken into account, one can clearly conclude that blacks in 1890 in New York were less isolated than the new European groups who were beginning to arrive.

For Boston in 1890, there are residential data available for the small number of Hungarians and Bohemians in the city as well as the 6,500 Italians and 8,600 "colored" (presumably virtually all being black). As fine a grid as possible was used, including the subdivision of wards available in several cases (again it is not possible to compare these figures with the previously reported ward data for 1890). The pattern again shows that blacks were less segregated than Italians (.1037 versus .1370), even if the latter were a smaller component of the population. Regressing the three new European groups' segregation on their proportion of the population leads one to expect a higher black segregation index than was actually found (.18 versus .10).

Black segregation can be compared in 1880 with the indexes for five different new immigrant groups in Boston. Sizable immigration had not really started yet and blacks were therefore much larger in number (see table 9.6). In this case, the regression approach is the only reasonable basis for making any comparisons—and even then it is necessary to assume that the regression equation is relevant to the outlying value of the black proportion of the population. Hence the analysis must be made with caution. Among the five immigrant groups specified in table 9.6, there is a fairly close linkage between their level of segregation and their proportion of the total population ($r^2 = .90$). Applying this regression to the black proportion of Boston's population, in 1880 one would expect a black isolation index of .17, well over double the actual value found for the group at that time.

The 1890 analysis for New York and Boston, as well as the 1880 data for the latter city, all indicate consistently that blacks were not unusually isolated when compared with the patterns found among the new European groups in these centers. This conclusion holds in 1890 not only when group size is taken into account, but also for the raw isolation indexes. Therefore, the black—new European differences found in 1910 seem to hold up for limited comparisons in earlier years as well.

Later Evidence

Was the growing isolation of blacks during the earlier decades of this century a distinctive process or did the segregation of the SCE groups likewise increase during the decades following 1900? This is an extremely important question because it deals with whether blacks and new Europeans shared a common shift in position. There are no two-generation data for any of the cities in 1920 to help create estimates as was done in 1910, but it is easy enough to examine shifts in immigrant segregation during the decade. To an overwhelming degree, the SCE groups and blacks moved in the opposite direction. In all 17 cities, Austrian isolation was lower in 1920, as was the case in the vast majority of comparisons for Roumanians (declined in seven out of nine places); Hungarians (12 out of 15); Italians (12 out of 16); and Russians (12 out of 17). In the Greek case, there was an increase in five of the ten cities during the decade. The average segregation index among all six of the immigrant groups declined between 1910 and 1920 (table 9.7, columns 1 and 2), a shift clearly opposite to that occurring among blacks. Moreover, these declines for some groups exist despite the fact that the immigrant proportion of the total city population had increased between 1910 and 1920 (see columns 3 and 4 of table 9.7 for Roumanians, Greeks, and Italians).

A direct comparison, which takes the changing population composition into account, is provided through the regressions given in table 9.7 and the lines shown in figure 9.3. In the case of Italian immigrants, in all but one city (Buffalo), they are less segregated in 1920 than would have been predicted on the basis of the linkage between segregation and population composition abstracted in the 1910 regression. Although the magnitude of the declines is less striking, in all instances the Austrians and Greeks are less segregated in 1920 than the 1910 pattern would lead one to expect, and there are relatively few exceptions for the Hungarians and Roumanians. Russians are the only exception to this general pattern, with immigrant isolation in 1920 often being higher than expected on the basis of the 1910 pattern.[11] This is also exhibited in the two regression lines that cross.

It is a bit premature to conclude that the new Europeans and blacks were moving in opposite directions as far as segregation goes. This is because it is possible only to measure segregation of the foreign-born component of each of the white ethnic groups whereas the isolation of all blacks is determined. It would be more appropriate if the spatial isolation of all blacks and all members of each white group were compared, or, on the other hand, if the immigrant generation of whites was com-

TABLE 9.7

CHANGES IN FOREIGN-BORN SEGREGATION, 1910–1920

| Birthplace | Arithmetic means for the foreign-born | | | | Regression of isolation on composition | | | | | |
| | Isolation indexes | | Proportion of the population | | 1910 | | | 1920 | | |
	1910	1920	1910	1920	r	b	a	r	b	a
Austria	.0559	.0154	.0247	.0094	.9336	2.0482	.0054	.9705	1.7675	-.0012
Greece	.0148	.0119	.0023	.0031	.6087	3.9495	.0058	.7990	2.2993	.0046
Hungary	.0421	.0302	.0132	.0089	.8083	1.9138	.0168	.7259	2.3038	.0098
Italy	.1336	.0928	.0252	.0276	.3582	1.8434	.0872	.6982	1.8655	.0413
Roumania	.0139	.0104	.0028	.0033	.8647	4.0924	.0024	.7431	2.0794	.0036
Russia	.1014	.0708	.0373	.0277	.9357	2.4065	.0116	.9056	1.7373	.0228

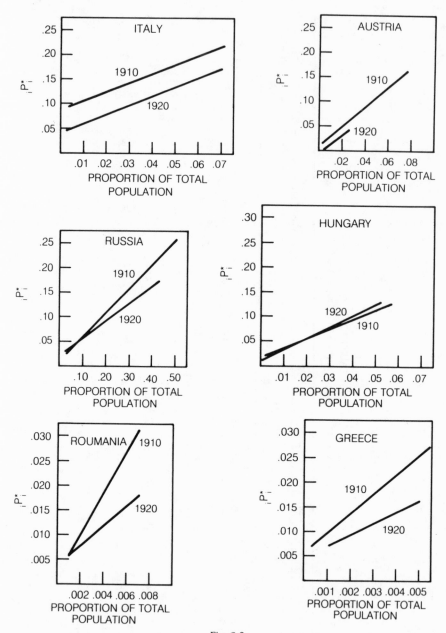

Fig. 9.3
Regression of SCE Foreign-Born on Their Proportion of the Population,
17 Leading Nonsouthern Cities, 1910–1920

NOTE: For list of cities see note to Figure 9.1.

pared with the southern-born black migrants. As matters now stand, the second and later generations are absent from the white group analyses and may understate ethnic segregation. Fortunately, it is possible to estimate the combined two-generation level of segregation in both 1910 and 1920 with a single method that appears to be fairly accurate. Let us assume that the second generation of a given group has the same spatial distribution as the first generation in a given city for a given period; i.e., the index of dissimilarity between generations is zero. If this were to be the case, then:

$$P^*_{a_1 + a_2} = \left(P^*_{a_1}\right)\left(1 + \frac{a_2}{a_1}\right),$$

where $P^*_{a_1 + a_2}$ is the combined isolation of the first and second generations of a given ethnic group; $P^*_{a_1}$ is the isolation of the first generation; and a_1 and a_2 are the respective numbers of first- and second- generation members of the ethnic group living in the city. If, for example, the first generation has an isolation index of .05, and if there are 2,000 and 1,000 members of the second and first generation of the group living in the city, then in accordance with the above formula, the combined segregation of the two generations would be:

$$\left(.05\right)\left(1 + \frac{2,000}{1,000}\right) = .15.$$

The formula shown above was inferred on the basis of various data sets and found to provide an exact measure of the combined two-generation segregation index if the first and second generations have identical proportional distributions throughout the city's subareas. In practice, obviously the index of dissimilarity between the generations will not be zero; the question is how different they are. In other words, does this assumption generate significantly misleading conclusions? There is strong evidence that it does not. The reader will recall the four SCE groups in each of three cities for which combined two-generation segregation indexes could be computed in 1910 because the relevant data were available. By using just the first generation P*s and applying the above equation, the appropriateness of the assumptions can be tested by comparing the 12 estimated two-generation indexes with the actual ones. Listed in table 9.8 are the actual 1910 two-generation indexes for each group in each city along with the two-generation indexes estimated by the formula solely on the basis of the immigrant group indexes coupled with the ratio of the number of second- to first-generation members of the group in the city. The reader will observe how close the

TABLE 9.8

ACTUAL INDEXES OF TWO-GENERATION RESIDENTIAL SEGREGATION AND ESTIMATES
BASED ON LIMITED DATA, 1910

	Two-generation isolation indexes	
City and group	Actual	Estimated
Chicago:		
Austrian	.2530	.2534
Hungarian	.0317	.0320
Italian	.2105	.2212
Russian	.2004	.2137
New York:		
Austrian	.1681	.1779
Hungarian	.0600	.0610
Italian	.2450	.2516
Russian	.3401	.3661
Philadelphia:		
Austrian	.0398	.0423
Hungarian	.0837	.0953
Italian	.2613	.2574
Russian	.2656	.2769

estimated indexes are to the actual ones. The correlation between them
is .9977, but more important the intercept is nearly zero and the slope
almost unity. (If the estimated index was identical to the actual one—or
if the assumptions were exactly met—these are the values of the
intercept and regression coefficient that would result.) The intercept is
−.0002 and the regression coefficient of the actual indexes on the
estimated ones is .9612. This means that the combined two generations
are slightly less isolated in most instances than was predicted under the
assumptions of the model used. The deviations are in this direction
because, as one might expect, the second generation is generally somewhat less segregated than the first generation.

In point of fact, there is independent evidence indicating that the
immigrant and the American-born offspring were not very segregated
from each other earlier in this century. The indexes of dissimilarity between first and second generations in Chicago in 1930 are relatively low,
averaging about 11 for the old groups and about 8 for the new Europeans
(Duncan and Lieberson, 1959, table 1, column 5). The second-generation
new European groups in each of ten cities in 1930 were not that much
less segregated from the native whites of native parentage than were the
immigrants (Lieberson, 1963a, table 13, columns 6 and 7). The reason for

this is relatively simple. In earlier decades a substantial part of the second-generation component of each new European immigrant group was relatively young and hence living at home with their foreign-born parents. On the average, among the second generation of 19 new European groups in the United States in 1930, 85 percent were 24 years of age or younger, with the figure ranging from 70 percent for the Austrians to 97 percent for the Greeks. The average Northwestern European group, having been in the United States in sizable numbers for a longer period, had only 35 percent of the second generation who were 24 or younger (computed from U.S. Bureau of the Census, 1933a, p. 806). Unfortunately comparable data are not available for 1920 or 1910, but it is virtually certain that the proportion of SCE second generation in the younger ages would have been even greater then. At any rate, there is good reason for viewing this procedure as a valid way of determining whether the new Europeans also experienced increasing segregation during this period. (In applying this technique to 1920 data it was necessary also to employ this procedure to recompute the 1910 two-generation estimates so as to have comparable data. This leads to slightly different 1910 estimates than were employed earlier.)

In the vast majority of cases, there was a sizable decline in SCE segregation between 1910 and 1920. Among Austrians, for example, the 1920 regression line abstracts the lower segregation experienced by that group when proportion of the population is taken into account (figure 9.4). Although not shown, in addition the actual scatter of the 1920 points are all below the 1910 line. This is essentially the case for Roumanians, Russians, Greeks, and Italians—except that in a few instances there are cities in 1920 which exceed the 1910 regression line. But overall the pattern of decline is found for these groups as well as for Hungarians. Although the latter's 1920 regression is barely lower than the 1910 line, Hungarians are less segregated in 1920 for the overwhelming bulk of the cities.

In short, there is every indication that the spatial isolation of new Europeans and blacks was indeed moving in opposite directions earlier in this century. Late in the last century and very early in this one blacks were actually less segregated than were some of the SCE migrant groups, but conditions were completely reversed by 1920. These results are not an artifact of the measure used here; indeed they are quite consistent with results obtained using the index of dissimilarity (Lieberson, 1963a, chapter 4). Insofar as segregation reflects a general state of the group, we can infer that the black position in the North began to deteriorate early in this century, at about the time when the new European groups began to improve. It is impossible to pin these shifts to an exact date, but we now know that the black position—as measured by segregation—began to

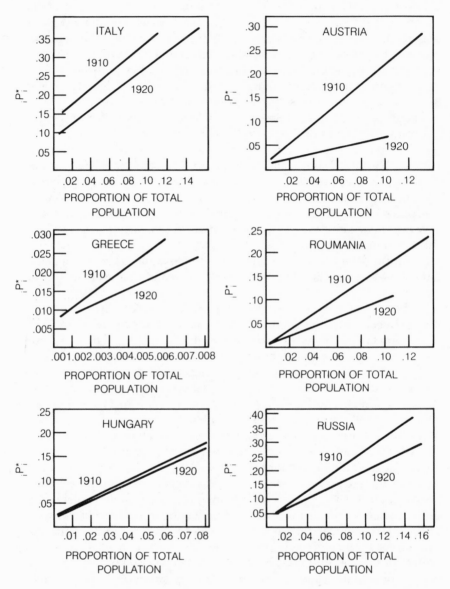

Fig. 9.4
Regression of Two-Generation SCE Groups on Their Proportion of the Population,
17 Leading Nonsouthern Cities, 1910–1920

NOTE: For list of cities see note to Figure 9.1.

deteriorate between 1900 and 1910, in other words before the World War I decade. The relevant data for comparing the new European groups during this decade are not available, but we at least know that a decline was witnessed between 1910 and 1920 in their segregation and that as late as 1910 many of the new European groups were more segregated than blacks.

NEW QUESTIONS

The task at hand is basically finished as the initial question about shifts in positions of the groups has been answered. However, one's curiosity is naturally aroused by two central questions. First, why were the new European groups more segregated than blacks late in the nineteenth century? Indeed, as recently as 1910, the new European groups on the average were somewhat more segregated than blacks. The second main question refers to the shifts experienced during this century. In particular, why did black segregation go up and why did the SCE groups go down? It would be foolhardy to attempt a detailed explanation here because such a task would call for a separate book. But the conditions that apply to new European–black comparisons are obviously of great interest here and are worth touching on.

There were several forces contributing to the initially lower black segregation indexes. Blacks were particularly likely to be employed as servants in white homes and were often housed with the whites in servant quarters. Although black districts existed, such a pattern helped to scatter blacks through at least the middle- and upper-class white areas of the city. Another factor pertains to the nature of black and new European settlement in these northern cities. Blacks living in these cities late in the nineteenth and early in the twentieth centuries were wise in the ways of the urban North. Because migration from the South was not important yet, a strikingly large segment of the northern blacks had been born and raised in the North—a pattern that was to change later (see, for example, Kusmer, 1976, p. 161; Spear, 1967, pp. 138–146). Moreover, the absence of sizable black migration meant that blacks were not the same threat to whites that their absolute numbers and rates of change were later to create. A black living nearby did not in the eyes of the whites signify an approaching onslaught of black hordes moving into the area.

By contrast, the SCE Europeans were indeed new to the United States; there were few predecessors to help them get established and cope with the alien ways. There was much to be said for living with compatriots who shared a common non-English language, distinctive cultural styles, religions different from the churches established by the earlier groups, and a common homeland. The new Europeans were to grow in numbers and were certainly more of a threat to dominant white groups than were blacks. A new SCE European neighbor could indeed represent just the tip of a massive iceberg of newcomers ready to move in *en masse*. It was also the case that the new Europeans were probably more different and stranger than were blacks in a wide variety of cultural and stylistic forms. In recent years it has been the vogue for blacks to emphasize their distinctiveness and blackness, but bear in mind that late in the nineteenth century and through much of this century blacks were "assimilationist" in outlook, seeking to avoid and de-emphasize the appearance of any distinctive black qualities and were oriented toward an emphasis on their commonality with whites of Northwestern European origin. This was also a period when massive numbers of some of the new European groups obtained employment in various factories, largely as unskilled workers. Accordingly, with transportation not well developed, great concentrations of the groups developed in the areas around their places of employment. Black employment was then more scattered and less likely to be in factories; hence this factor operated less to concentrate their residences.

The later reversal in the relative segregation of blacks and new Europeans is due in part to shifts in these earlier conditions. The immigration of SCE groups declined sharply during World War I and, except for a few years after peace, never did reach its earlier levels. The new groups were becoming veterans of life in the United States—not only was a growing component of American-birth, but even the average immigrant segment had a long residence in the United States because there were relatively few new additions. The opposite was the case for blacks, whose numbers mounted rapidly and posed more of a threat to the dominant whites than did the SCE groups. The southern-born rural component was also growing much more rapidly than the northern-born segment. As blacks filled industrial niches and the servant role declined, there was less of a spatial dispersion due to the latter factor. Although it is clear that urban transportation reached a new high point in ease and minimal cost, I doubt if this was a serious factor in explaining the different shifts for blacks and the new Europeans because one would have expected it to operate the same for both segments.

Further, one may speculate that new European segregation had relatively more of a voluntary component in it compared with black isolation. To be sure, it is difficult to distinguish between voluntary and involuntary segregation, to say nothing of measuring it, because it is often hard to know whether choice of one's own group for neighbors is a response to real or anticipated trouble with outsiders, and hence whether such "voluntary choices" are themselves the products of outside forces. Both factors exist, the difficulty is in dealing with a kind of murky middle ground which is the product of neither purely restrictive discriminatory practices nor some massive ingroup passion that overpowers any other housing market considerations. However, I suspect that the new Europeans were pulled together initially more by choice than were blacks and that they were later prepared and willing to move into less densely concentrated ethnic enclaves. This did not mean the absence of compatriots, but more of a mixture. Indeed, success in America meant getting away from the Old World ethnic ghettos initially established as a means of adaptation.

The reader should bear in mind that the above interpretation is highly speculative, called into play by the somewhat surprising patterns found earlier in the chapter. However, I have gathered at least some data on a number of these factors which suggest that further attention to the problem will be of value.

SERVANTS AND SEGREGATION

Early in this century, a sizable segment of black men and women in the North were employed by whites as servants or domestics in one form or another (see chapter 10). A large number of these lived with their employers; in his classic survey of Philadelphia at the turn of the century, DuBois (1967, p. 454) found that one-half of the women and one-fourth of the males employed in the seventh ward lived in their employer's homes. Obviously such a pattern would tend to lower the segregation of blacks because a significant number would be scattered in predominantly white areas. It is this factor that helps explain the lower black–white segregation indexes observed in earlier decades in the South as well as the upward shifts as black domestic employment later declined (see, for example, the discussion of Charleston, South Carolina, in Taeuber and Taeuber [1965, pp. 45–49]). As long as a sizable number of blacks were employed as servants in the North, this would reduce the segregation measures between the races because many would be residing in close proximity to whites rather than in a solid black ghetto area. With the decline in such servant activities as a source of black employment, one would expect a one-time shift in black segregation due to this factor.

This is precisely what happened. The proportion of blacks employed as servants declined in almost all 17 cities under consideration during each decade between 1890 and 1920. And in each of these decades there is a modest negative correlation between the magnitude of these declines in the proportion of blacks employed as servants and increases in the city's segregation.[12] The high point in this effect is between 1900 and 1910, with r = −.44, which means that nearly 20 percent of the variance between cities in their changes in segregation during that decade can be accounted for by the changing proportion of blacks working as servants. This is largely a one-shot phenomenon. The correlation drops to −.26 in the next decade, meaning that about 6.5 percent of the changes in 1910−1920 segregation can be explained by shifts in servant employment; likewise the correlation is −.27 for the period between 1890 and 1900. Of special interest here: the proportion of blacks employed as servants actually went up in all 17 cities between 1920 and 1930, but changes in segregation and changes in such employment actually had a positive linkage during that span, r = .37. The reasons for this employment change will be considered in a later chapter, but the point to be recognized here is that employment as servants helped dampen black segregation in the early decades of the century and its decline was a factor leading to the later increase in segregation.[13]

TIMING OF ARRIVAL

It is almost a sociological cliché to observe that blacks began to move to the North in sizable numbers after migration from South−Central−Eastern Europe declined. Is this temporal difference partially responsible for the temporal shifts in segregation? If one assumes that the southern-born migrants among blacks and the European-born immigrants among the SCE groups differ from later generations (respectively, northern-born blacks and American-born SCE whites) in ways that affect their position in the communities, then this may have an important bearing on the timing of the groups' shifts in segregation.

First consider blacks. Only 32 to 34 percent of blacks living in the North and West between 1870 and 1890 were of southern birth. This figure increased steadily after these dates in response to the massive waves of migration: 39 percent in 1900, 42 in 1910, a giant leap to 52 percent in 1920, and another jump to 58 percent in 1930. There was a dropoff during the 1930s and a small rise during the 1940s, which were followed by declines in recent years (Lieberson, 1973, p. 552). Between 1880 and 1930, the southern-born proportion of the black population living in the North came close to doubling. This is in striking contrast to the new Europeans whose immigrant component was steadily declining during much of this period.

Although there was a small rise among the new European groups between 1900 and 1910 (table 9.9), from then on a steady decline is observed in the first-generation component for most of these groups. Among Poles, for example, little more than half were foreign-born even in 1900. Although this figure increased slightly in the next ten years, it then declined steadily so that the foreign-born comprised only one-third of the first two generations of Poles in the nation in 1940. As a more careful inspection of table 9.9 will disclose, the figures for Poles are not exceptional; for example, the decline in the foreign-born component among Russians is quite comparable, and other groups have even sharper drops, witness for example Greeks and Italians.

The decline in European migration to the United States also meant that the immigrants in the country had a progressively longer average length of residence because there were relatively few greenhorns arriving. By 1930 well over half of the immigrants from most new European sources had been living in the country for at least 20 years (table 9.10). Thus, not only were immigrants of declining importance for the SCE ethnic groups, but the immigrant component itself increasingly consisted of persons experienced in the life of the urban North.

TABLE 9.9
Foreign-Born Percentage of Two-Generations, 1900–1940

Birthplace	Year				
	1900	1910	1920	1930	1940
Poland	54	56	47	38	34
Austria	52	54	41[a]	39	38
Hungary	64	70	53[a]	46	44
Russia	63	60	48	43	40
Finland	NA	60	50	44	41
Roumania	NA	71	61	50	47
Greece	NA	91	77	57	50
Italy	66	64	48	39	35
Spain	NA	60	61	53	44
Portugal	NA	51	49	42	35

[a]Prewar boundaries.
NA: Data not available in 1900.

TABLE 9.10
LENGTH OF RESIDENCE IN THE UNITED STATES, 1930

Immigrant group	Percentage living in U.S. at least 20 years
Austria	64.8
Czechoslovakia	67.3
Finland	66.9
Greece	37.1
Hungary	61.1
Italy	54.2
Lithuania	65.5
Poland	58.2
Roumania	58.0
Russia	61.3
Yugoslavia	53.7

SOURCE: U.S. Bureau of the Census, 1933a, chapter 9, table 2.

Relevance to Segregation

There are several indications that the birthplace of blacks does indeed affect their segregation. In an earlier study I found that increases in the northern- and southern-born components of a city's black population between 1940 and 1960 have different effects on black segregation. The partial regression coefficients suggest increasing segregation due to gains in the latter component and decreases due to gains in the northern-born segment. Moreover, the variance in intercity shifts in segregation explained by gains in the total black population is considerably less than what can be accounted for when the birthplace distinction is applied (Lieberson, 1973, pp. 556–557). Again, in considering here changes in black segregation between 1900 and 1930, one finds that shifts in the northern- and southern-born components appear to have rather different consequences. The partial regression coefficients based on 15 of the 17 cities (relevant birthplace data were not available for Minneapolis and San Francisco) are: $b_{YX_1 \cdot X_2} = -.0034$; $b_{YX_2 \cdot X_1} = 3.0461$, where Y is black segregation in 1930 minus black segregation in 1900; X_1 is the northern-born proportion of the black population in 1930 minus the analogous proportion in 1900; X_2 is the southern-born proportion of the black population in 1930 minus the analogous proportion in 1900. As was the case for the more recent period, only a small part of all the variance between cities in the changes in black segregation can be accounted for by these crude measures (in this case, 18 percent), but again there is some indication with these ecological correlations that a generational effect was operating.

Immigrant length of residence also affects segregation of the foreign-born in a manner consistent with the notions advanced here about differences between blacks and the new Europeans. Those old and new European immigrant groups in each of ten cities with a large component of recent arrivals tend to be more segregated even after socioeconomic factors are taken into account (Lieberson, 1963a, pp. 44–73). A more demanding test is performed here: Intercity differences in each group's P^* indexes in 1920 are regressed on the length of residence of the group in each city, net of the population composition effect. The results vary between groups, but segregation of Greeks, Hungarians, and Russians does appear to vary between cities in a way that reflects the length of the group's residence in the United States; cities with relatively high segregation (relative to what would be expected on the basis of population composition) are also cities in which a smaller proportion of the immigrants have been in the United States for at least 20 years.[14] On the other hand, Roumanians and Italians have essentially no correlation between intercity differences in the length of residence of the foreign-born and their segregation.[15]

In terms of the question at hand, both black and new European segregation patterns appear to be similarly influenced by generational factors. Ecological correlations suggest that southern-born blacks were more isolated than northern-born blacks. Likewise, there is some indication that length of residence in the United States influences the white ethnic group segregation levels in American cities. (No linkage was found between generation and segregation for the new Europeans, but I believe that its empirical absence here is due to the early period under consideration, a period in which a huge part of the second generation was still children or young adults and hence likely to still be living with their foreign-born parents.) Because the southern-born component of the black population was increasing and the immigrant SCE component was declining, this common factor would tend to generate different segregation trends for the groups under comparison here.

EARLY SETTLEMENT PATTERNS

The SCE ethnic groups were for the most part numerically insignificant in the United States until late in the nineteenth century. Relatively speaking, blacks were more important and had established some position in the larger northern centers at an earlier period. Consider, for example, the number of immigrants from various SCE European sources and blacks living in various cities in 1890, shortly after the new waves had begun. With the exception of New York, the premier port of debarkation for international migrants, and Milwaukee, there are very few instances in which the new groups were as large in number as were blacks. Data limitations prevent inclusion of the second generation, but it is unlikely that they would have been very significant in number yet. Greeks provide the most extreme comparison; there is no city with even 500 immigrants from that source in 1890—clearly they are dwarfed by blacks. Likewise, there are only two cities in which the number of Austrian immigrants exceeds the number of blacks: New York and Milwaukee. In most instances, the differences are quite sizable. In similar fashion, there are more Hungarians than blacks in only one city: Cleveland; Italians exceed blacks only in Buffalo and New York; and Russians exceed blacks only in New York and Milwaukee. Looking across the columns of table 9.11, one is struck by the massive differences in the numbers of blacks and new Europeans living in these cities. The 8,000 blacks residing in Pittsburgh in 1890 amounted to 3.3 percent of the city's population, yet this is about 3.5 times the number of Russians in the city, and an even greater gap exists compared with the 2,000 Italians, 1,200 Austrians, 800 Hungarians, and the handful of Greeks. Even a quick look at table 9.11 will disclose many cities in which blacks far exceed the new Europeans.

PREJUDICE AND THE INCREASE IN BLACK SEGREGATION: AN ALTERNATIVE INTERPRETATION

The outbursts and physical violence directed at blacks early in this century by whites threatened with encroachment, coupled with the increases in the indexes of residential dissimilarity between the races, have led others to conclude that there were basic attitudinal changes toward blacks (see, for example, Spear, 1967, p. 23; and the mounting concern about black crime in Thompson, 1926; Boie, 1928). It is a particularly tempting and widely held view that white attitudes were transformed by black increases associated with the World War I era and later. A different interpretation is possible, one which is not necessarily a substitute for the "deterioration" theory, but rather adds a simple but radically different factor that appears to be overlooked. Namely, the increasingly violent resistance to blacks as well as their mounting segregation may well reflect in part the same underlying disposition toward blacks as existed earlier, but merely with a new set of appropriate responses generated by the much larger proportion of blacks found in these cities. To be sure, supporting the deterioration thesis is the fact that black isolation increased from 1900 through 1930 even when black composition is held constant (figure 9.1). However, one distinct advantage of the Bell-type measure is that it allows for an asymmetrical look at segregation, recognizing that the average isolation from whites experienced by blacks in a city is not the same as the average isolation from blacks experienced by the average white.

Suppose one assumes that whites are essentially uninterested in the degree to which the average black has contacts with either blacks or whites, but they are concerned with the frequency of contact that the whites themselves have with whites and blacks (earlier in this chapter it was shown that these are not the same events). In addition, assume that at the end of the last century and well into this one whites dominated the situation in these cities, to a large degree determining the residential conditions faced by blacks. Moreover, let us assume that the average white wishes to live in an area where the overwhelming majority of residents are also white. All of these assumptions seem extremely reasonable. Consider their ramifications for black isolation by bearing in mind that relatively minor shifts in the ratio of blacks to whites in a community can lead to massive changes in black isolation if the isolation of whites is to remain unchanged. This is implied by the equations developed earlier and will be applied shortly.

The average $_w P_w^*$ index found in the 17 leading northern cities in 1890 is .9718 (table 9.12, column 1). For the average city, this means that the typical white lived in an area where 97.18 percent of the residents were white. These indexes ranged from highs in excess of .99 (Milwaukee, Minneapolis, San Francisco, and Buffalo) to a low of .8994 for Kansas City. If one assumes that the propensity to be isolated from blacks is distributed roughly the same way among whites in each of these cities, but that the ease of doing so varies inversely with the black proportion of the population, then the strong inverse linkage between the two factors makes sense. The black proportion of the population in Kansas City, for example, was higher than in any other of the 17 places (.1032), whereas it was less than .01 in Buffalo, Minneapolis, Milwaukee, and San Francisco.

Overall the average level of white isolation declined slightly in 40 years, with $_w P_w^*$ moving from .9718 in 1890 to .9541 in 1930. (See the summary figures for columns 1 through 5 in table 9.12.) Thus, although black segregation increased massively during this span, it was not sufficient to make up for the growth in their proportion of the population,

TABLE 9.11

NUMBER OF BLACKS AND SCE EUROPEAN IMMIGRANTS, 1890–1910

City	1890						1900						
	Black	Austria	Greece	Hungary	Italy	Russia	Black	Austria	Greece	Hungary	Italy	Rou-mania	Russia
Boston	8,590	391	29	188	4,718	4,305	11,591	1,115	281	330	13,738	68	14,995
Buffalo	1,169	1,036	6	80	1,832	610	1,698	776	46	215	5,669	4	1,199
Chicago	14,852	6,043	245	1,818	5,685	7,683	30,150	11,815	1,493	4,946	16,008	287	24,178
Cincinnati	11,684	389	19	120	738	978	14,482	654	53	208	917	4	1,976
Cleveland	3,035	2,533	12	3,210	635	1,482	5,988	4,630	42	9,558	3,065	39	3,607
Detroit	3,454	658	4	112	338	669	4,111	471	18	91	905	11	1,332
Indianapolis	9,154	66	3	56	112	140	15,931	255	29	138	282	8	338
Kansas City	13,895	282	3	141	611	543	17,567	375	16	118	1,034	20	941
Los Angeles	3,190	162	6	19	447	73	2,131	316	20	60	763	10	233
Milwaukee	467	928	17	197	137	548	862	1,616	26	381	726	35	1,135
Minneapolis	1,354	571	8	269	140	994	1,548	1,133	55	581	222	417	1,929
Newark	4,271	941	2	430	2,921	1,295	6,694	4,074	37	1,325	8,537	205	5,511
New York City	25,674	27,193	263	1,222	39,951	48,790	60,666	71,427	1,309	31,516	145,433	10,499	155,201
Philadelphia	40,374	2,003	31	1,354	6,799	7,879	62,613	5,154	176	2,785	17,830	1,036	28,951
Pittsburgh	7,957	1,196	12	794	1,899	2,279	17,040	3,553	70	2,124	5,709	141	4,107
St. Louis	27,066	1,586	8	253	1,295	1,538	35,516	2,563	38	561	2,227	80	4,785
San Francisco	28,301	1,263	113	167	5,212	1,064	1,654	1,841	199	315	7,508	51	1,511

1910

City	Black	Austria	Greece	Hungary	Italy	Rou-mania	Russia
Boston	13,564	2,413	1,497	426	31,380	373	49,753
Buffalo	1,773	9,284	220	2,442	11,399	106	11,349
Chicago	44,103	132,059	6,564	28,938	45,169	3,344	121,786
Cincinnati	19,639	1,638	180	6,344	2,245	454	4,999
Cleveland	8,448	42,059	275	31,503	10,836	761	25,477
Detroit	5,741	14,160	584	5,935	5,724	313	18,644
Indianapolis	21,876	1,227	249	852	658	132	1,251
Kansas City	23,566	570	758	332	2,579	155	3,403
Los Angeles	7,599	2,510	361	819	3,802	297	4,758
Milwaukee	980	11,553	1,104	5,571	3,374	267	11,992
Minneapolis	2,592	6,075	463	1,176	653	1,412	5,654
Newark	9,475	12,963	297	6,029	20,493	1,160	21,912
New York City	91,709	190,237	8,038	76,625	340,765	33,584	484,189
Philadelphia	84,459	19,859	589	12,495	45,308	4,413	90,696
Pittsburgh	25,623	21,400	773	6,576	14,120	1,521	26,391
St. Louis	43,960	11,171	1,312	8,758	7,594	1,055	15,480
San Francisco	1,642	4,641	2,274	1,247	16,918	583	4,640

NOTE: Data for Roumanian immigrants not available in 1890. Data are for colored in 1890, blacks in 1900 and 1910. This shift is of minor consequence because "colored" is largely black in most cities, but probably accounts for the massive drop between 1890 and 1900 in San Francisco and the lesser drop in Los Angeles (due to Asians being listed as colored in 1890).

TABLE 9.12

Indexes of White Isolation, Changes in Black Isolation, and Changes Necessary for $_wP^*_w$ to Remain Stable, 1890–1930

City	$_wP^*_w$					Increase in $_bP^*_b$ between:							
						1890–1900		1900–1910		1910–1920		1920–1930	
	1890 (1)	1900 (2)	1910 (3)	1920 (4)	1930 (5)	Needed (6)	Actual (7)	Needed (8)	Actual (9)	Needed (10)	Actual (11)	Needed (12)	Actual (13)
Boston	.9831	.9803	.9817	.9811	.9783	.1116	-.0207	-.0197	.0492	.0655	.0386	.1455	.0403
Buffalo	.9929	.9959	.9961	.9919	.9817	-.4827	.0338	.0403	.0128	.5085	.0452	.5625	.1396
Chicago	.9880	.9839	.9826	.9739	.9780	.2530	.0235	.1106	.0467	.4366	.2302	.2675	.3227
Cincinnati	.9630	.9582	.9504	.9408	.9343	.1094	.0067	.1667	.0307	.2557	.1365	.2320	.1767
Cleveland	.9890	.9853	.9860	.9656	.9575	.2592	.0280	-.0400	.0041	.6111	.1598	.3647	.2708
Detroit	.9841	.9864	.9884	.9635	.9430	-.1512	.0080	-.1553	.0044	.6611	.0790	.4128	.1648
Indianapolis	.9216	.9118	.9161	.9049	.8984	.0726	-.0221	-.0076	-.0340	.1387	.0485	.0742	.0270
Kansas City	.8994	.8957	.9180	.9202	.9270	.0361	.0054	-.1274	-.0853	-.0016	.0196	.0156	.0794
Los Angeles	.9753	.9795	.9765	.9744	.9759	-.2014	-.0013	-.1276	.0065	.1150	.0396	.1326	.1784
Milwaukee	.9979	.9971	.9974	.9954	.9891	.2879	.0102	-.1369	-.0051	.4416	.0217	.6070	.1226
Minneapolis	.9921	.9925	.9916	.9898	.9912	-.0479	-.0002	.1090	.0006	.1762	.0037	-.1563	-.0040
Newark	.9777	.9736	.9735	.9603	.9257	.1621	.0143	.0012	-.0008	.3248	.0160	.5177	.1584
New York City	.9851	.9830	.9817	.9778	.9712	.1334	.0142	.0825	.0174	.2765	.1378	.3476	.2134
Philadelphia	.9655	.9576	.9514	.9372	.9078	.2033	.0469	.1006	-.0072	.2308	.0512	.2968	.0648
Pittsburgh	.9688	.9509	.9557	.9428	.9346	.3600	.0389	-.0963	-.0003	.2332	.0452	.1944	.1028
St. Louis	.9437	.9425	.9435	.9300	.9314	.0350	.0169	.0320	.0461	.2590	.1226	.1605	.1711
San Francisco	.9939	.9952	.9961	.9953	.9942	-.2780	-.0026	-.2367	-.0040	.1674	.0033	.1981	.0068
Arithmetic mean	.9718	.9688	.9698	.9615	.9541	.0507	.0118	-.0076	.0188	.2882	.0705	.2572	.1315

NOTE: Needed change refers to the increase in $_bP^*_b$ that must occur if $_wP^*_w$ is to remain unchanged from its initial value during the ten years specified. This is based on the changes in racial composition during the period. A negative value means that the black proportion declined and a drop in $_bP^*_b$ of the amount specified could occur without lowering $_wP^*_w$. For computational ease, it is arbitrarily assumed that all nonblacks are white. This is overwhelmingly the case in virtually all of the cities.

and hence the average white was somewhat less isolated in 1930 than in 1890. If one views a white desire to have minimal contact with blacks as the driving force of residential segregation, then the increases in $_bP_b^*$ observed during this period may be viewed not simply as the product of an increased antipathy toward blacks but as the outcome of an effort among whites to retain their minimum contact with blacks during a time when the increasing black proportion of the city population made this increasingly difficult. Indeed, the $_wP_w^*$s actually declined slightly.

A key factor in all of this is the changing black proportion of the city's population and the consequences such changes have for shifts in $_bP_b^*$. In Pittsburgh, for example, the average white isolation was .9688 in 1890, and the isolation index for blacks was .0814. Given that the black proportion of the city's population increased from .0328 in 1890 to .0529 in 1900, one may ask what would the black isolation index have to be for white isolation to remain at .9688? If $_wP_w^*$ is to remain at .9688 and given that $W/B = .9471/.0529$, substituting in the equation below and solving for $_bP_b^*$,

$$_bP_b^* = 1 - \left[\left(\frac{W}{B} \right) \left(1 - {_wP_w^*} \right) \right] = .4414.$$

This represents a massive shift from the .0814 observed ten years earlier and indicates how a small increase in the black proportion of the population can, under some circumstances, require an enormous jump in $_bP_b^*$ if the dominant whites are to maintain $_wP_w^*$ at a constant level. Actually $_bP_b^*$ increased to only .1203 in 1900, with the white isolation index declining from .9688 to .9509. Clearly black isolation may rise while at the same time a decrease in white isolation occurs due to shifts in population composition that are not entirely compensated. An increase in black isolation need not solely reflect a shift in white attitudes toward blacks, but in part may be reflection of whites attempting to maintain the same level of isolation from blacks as they had earlier.

Columns 6 through 13 of table 9.12 compare the actual black segregation changes with those needed during each decade if the city's index of white isolation is to remain unchanged during the same period after taking black compositional change into account during the span. Between 1890 and 1900, the average city needed an increase of .0507 in black isolation (column 6). This is because the black proportions were increasing only modestly in most places during this span—indeed, in a number of places the black proportion declined and hence produced negative changes, which means that black isolation could have gone down the amount specified and $_wP_w^*$ would have remained unaltered. As modest as these changes may be, the actual black shift averaged only .0118 (column 7).

The 1900–1910 span is quite interesting; although blacks increased in absolute number, their proportion of the population declined because of the massive new European immigration occurring in many centers. The average change in black segregation necessary for white isolation in 1910 to remain unchanged from 1900 was actually slightly negative, meaning that black isolation could have declined somewhat in many places (column 8). The actual changes were, on the average, slightly upward, .0188. During the next two decades, thanks to rising black migration northward and declining European flows, the black proportion of the population increased sharply in many places and it would have taken massive increases in black isolation (columns 10 and 12) if white ingroup contact were to remain unaffected during the decade. In fact, black isolation did go up sharply during these years, but the key point is that it was generally not as sizable as the rises needed (compare columns 10 with 11, and 12 with 13). As a consequence, in the typical northern city, white isolation from blacks went down slightly even though black isolation from whites at the same time increased. For example, the average black isolation index increased .1315 in the 1920s, a rather large jump in such a short span. Nevertheless, the average increase in black isolation needed during that span if the white isolation in these cities was to remain at their 1920 levels was .2572. Hence, from this perspective, we can see black isolation as increasing but at less than the rate necessary to maintain white avoidance of blacks in their residences. Milwaukee provides a nice example of this with $_bP_b^*$ increasing from .0410 to .1636 between 1920 and 1930. Considering that the black proportion of the city's population increased from .0048 to only .0129, surely the reader must feel confident that here is evidence of an increasing level of isolation of blacks not due merely to population composition but reflecting a change in attitudes. In point of fact, white isolation was extremely high in Milwaukee in 1920 (.9954) and would have required $_bP_b^*$ to increase to .6070 during the decade for $_wP_w^*$ to have remained unaltered.[16]

CONCLUSIONS

The basic concern of this chapter stems from an assumption that residential segregation can serve as an indicator of general shifts in the positions of the groups. Late in the nineteenth century and as recently as 1910, blacks were less segregated than were a number of the new European groups. The SCE Europeans had enormous incentives for self-segregation, being so totally alien to the culture and ways of life in the United States and with only a minimal number of predecessors available to help them. By contrast, blacks in these cities were largely of northern birth and hence experienced in the ways of Chicago, New York, Philadelphia, and so on. Moreover, they were still small enough in number to pose little threat to the dominant whites, who, incidentally, were probably more acquainted with blacks than the strange newcomers.

There was no change in black isolation between 1890 and 1900, net of population composition, but the isolation of blacks began progressively to widen during the succeeding decades. Some of the new European groups were more segregated than blacks in 1910 and others were less isolated. Between 1910 and 1920, new European isolation went down net of composition, whereas black trends were strongly in the opposite direction. Accordingly, one can safely conclude that there were sharply different shifts in the positions of these populations during the period of concern.

A complete explanation of the shifts in segregation has not been attempted, but some of the factors commonly offered to account for these changes have been found to be less than convincing. In particular, the rise in black isolation is probably not simply explained by a rise in antiblack sentiment. Although such changes cannot be ruled out— indeed they are suggested by the shifts in the regression of black segregation on composition—there is also evidence to support the presence of a very different force; namely, increasing black isolation occurred simply because whites in each city were attempting to maintain the degree of isolation from blacks that existed before the new flows from the South started. Because the growing black population in each city made the maintenance of such isolation from blacks more difficult, the net consequence was greater segregation of blacks. Indeed, even with the increasing segregation of blacks, white isolation from blacks declined slightly. Thus, although black isolation went up massively earlier in this century, white isolation from blacks did not increase. In addition to altering white attitudes toward blacks, very likely the grow-ing waves of blacks in the urban North brought out incipient behavioral predispositions toward blacks that were unnecessary earlier when there were so few blacks in these cities. It is unlikely that changing transporta-tion patterns in the cities can account for much of the increase in black isolation because during the same period white ethnic groups were shifting in the opposite direction. I have attempted to suggest ways in which forces affecting segregation were moving in opposite directions for blacks and the new European groups, but the key point, the central conclusion, is the general shift in group positions suggested by the decline in new European isolation and the increase in black segregation.

10

Earning a Living: 1900

A substantial part of present-day occupational and income differences between whites (including the new Europeans) and blacks is due to one form or another of discrimination against the latter (Ashenfelter and Taussig, 1971; Featherman and Hauser, 1978, pp. 352–353). It is safe to say that equality between the groups in their jobs and incomes would go a long way toward eliminating other gaps that are found between these populations. Elegant statistical techniques are not needed to document the massive differences that existed between new Europeans and blacks by the end of World War II. In 1950, blacks with any earnings had a median income of $951, compared with incomes well in excess of $2,000 for the five new European groups with two-generation data available in that census (see table 10.1). The net difference indexes run around −.50 when these groups are compared with blacks in terms of income. Even when only blacks living outside of the South are compared with these new European groups, the income differences are massive, running from −.26 to −.37. Striking too are the occupational gaps. Among male nonfarm workers, 2.9 percent of blacks were professionals in 1950. By comparison, the white figures range from 5 percent for Italians to more than 6 percent for Poles and Czechs, nearly 10 percent for Austrians, and more than 13 percent for Russians. Likewise, about 30 percent of blacks not working on farms were employed as laborers, whereas the SCE figures were no more than one-third as high. Again, these gaps are still massive when new Europeans are compared with blacks living outside of the South (table 10.1).

TABLE 10.1
INCOME AND OCCUPATIONAL COMPARISONS, BLACKS AND NEW EUROPEAN GROUPS
(TWO-GENERATIONS), 1950

| Group | Median income | Index of net difference in income versus: | | Percentage among nonfarm workers who are: | |
		All Blacks	Blacks residing in North	Professionals	Laborers
Polish	$2419	−.51	−.30	6.3	8.3
Czechoslovakian	2339	−.47	−.26	6.5	9.0
Austrian	2440	−.50	−.30	9.7	6.4
Russian	2717	−.55	−.37	13.5	3.0
Italian	2295	−.49	−.27	5.0	11.2
Black	951	−	−	2.9	30.6
Only residing in North	1628	−	−	2.8	24.6

SOURCES: U.S. Bureau of the Census: 1953c, table 9; 1954, table 20.

The concern in this chapter and the next is not with the glaring and massive economic differences in recent decades, but with finding out more about conditions earlier in this century which led to the present situation. What were the new European−black occupational gaps? What was the role of labor unions in this situation? Were the new European immigrants more skilled than the blacks who migrated from the South? How important were educational differences between the groups? In accordance with the ladder theory of mobility, did the movement of blacks to the North raise the position of the new Europeans already there? In an effort to understand the forces that led to the current set of economic conditions, these and related issues will be considered with the limited data available for earlier periods. To be sure, the occupational composition of blacks at the turn of the century has been considered before (see Meeker and Kau [1977] and the literature cited therein), and some work has been done on the European immigrant groups— particularly based on the Immigration Commission studies (a classic being Hourwich [1912]; a more recent example involving the controversy between Higgs [1971] and McGouldrick and Tannen [1977] to be discussed in the next chapter)—as well as the analysis of the 1900 ethnic occupational data by Hutchinson (1956, chapter 8). However, to my knowledge there has been no systematic comparison between blacks and the new Europeans, nor has there been a detailed analysis of the specific occupations held by blacks in 1900.

Because the census data on the occupations of new Europeans and blacks in northern cities in 1900 are extraordinarily detailed, one can determine just how different the positions of these groups were only a few decades after large-scale European immigration had commenced. However, one cannot blithely compare occupational compositions without first developing theoretical notions about how the occupational outcome for racial and ethnic groups in each community is affected by broad societal forces. Not only is it necessary to know what to look for, it is not entirely clear how to compare these groups without such a consideration.

A MODEL OF OCCUPATIONAL COMPOSITION

Let us start with certain simple assumptions about ethnic and racial groups, the cities in which they live, and the linkage with population composition.

1. *The occupational composition of a community is essentially independent of the ethnic-racial composition of the population.* The economic activities of a city are largely independent of its ethnic composition, but are a function of geography, raw materials, other natural resources, political factors, historical forces, markets, and other nonethnic factors. Associations between ethnic and occupational-industrial composition of communities are due to the groups pursuing certain jobs, for example, Slavs and the steel industry, rather than the steel industry moving to areas where many Slavs reside. There are, of course, some exceptions to this, such as when labor cost is the primary determinant of an industry's location or when groups with distinctive skills and interests set up certain trades where they are located or even provide specially important markets. As an example, a number of cities in which Germans settled in large numbers became major beer-producing centers, and the special meat slaughtering requirements for kosher beef affected the location of meat packers in the East (Lieberson, 1963a, p. 160). However, the linkage between the garment industry in New York and Jews is not such a case because, for example, the men's clothing industry had existed well before Eastern European Jews migrated to New York in sizable numbers and there were important locational factors giving New York City an advantage in women's clothing in addition to the presence of a skilled work force (Rischin, 1962, pp. 61-65). In general, then, although racial and ethnic groups have certain distinctive dispositions toward certain jobs and away from others (see assumption 5 below), this will at most only modestly shift the economic activities in the community.

2. *Groups differ in their "objective" qualifications for various occupational activities.* Racial and ethnic groups on the aggregate may vary considerably in their education, knowledge, skills, background, personality

characteristics, work orientation, ability to speak English, ambition, and the like—all factors that affect their qualifications for various jobs and their chances for promotion. To be sure, the presence of such objective differences need not explain very much of the actual gaps between the groups in their occupational attainment. In other words, these gaps are not necessarily an indicator of such objective differences (a point that assumption 3 makes clear). Nevertheless, the existence of such differences at the initial stages in contact means there is every reason to expect *some* occupational differences between the groups even if all employment factors were totally unaffected by ethnic origin and race. To be sure, such objective factors may operate but still account for only a small portion of the observed differences in occupational pursuits.

3. *Group membership directly affects occupational opportunity.* Employers, co-workers, customers, and the like may have preferences or dispositions for one group or another. These dispositions can range from modest to extreme levels of intensity. They vary by the occupational role involved; for example, the ethnic origin of a parish priest or physician may be more relevant (Lieberson, 1958) than the origin of someone who delivers mail or picks up garbage. Also such preferences may vary between groups in their intensity, although as a general rule the preference for compatriots is strongest of all, and there will certainly be a rank order of desirability among outsiders such that not all outside groups are equal. (See my discussion of the analogous situation in politics in chapter 3.) Further, the intensity of these preferences may change over time. In short, there is some form or another of prejudice operating to affect group opportunities in the work world—but the magnitude of these prejudices as well as their actual consequences for employment will vary between jobs and over time. Bear in mind that these dispositions are not the only forces affecting employment opportunities, witness assumption 2 above. Further, because each group differs in its set of prejudices, it follows that increases in self-employment, ability to employ others, the economic demands that a group can generate for its own members, and various other changes within the group can affect this factor over time without any change in the dispositions of others.

4. *Occupations differ in their desirability.* Clearly jobs differ in income, security, nonmaterial rewards, dangers, prestige, working conditions, capital requirements, opportunities for advancement, and the like. There is reason to believe that these factors may shift over time.

5. *Groups differ initially in their dispositions toward certain jobs.* Groups may differ in the importance they attach on the aggregate to the various features of each job, for example, long-term future potential versus current income; risk versus security, and the like. This was particularly apt

to be the case for groups early in their settlement in the nation when many were considering an eventual return to the old country and so were specially interested in immediate rewards rather than long-term considerations. In a similar fashion, the situation would operate for blacks migrating to the North seeking only temporary employment and planning to return to the South. Moreover, although groups tend to rank jobs similarly with respect to prestige and desirability, there are some differences in dispositions toward various kinds of work in the Old World and these are carried over here initially. A number of decades ago Glick (1942) observed that assimilation in some respects involves a shift in the way work is evaluated. This will help to explain some of the remarkable early differences between the groups in the way they oriented themselves to certain jobs.

Consequences

It follows from these assumptions that the operation of prejudices will create a discriminatory system if the groups favored by attitudes of employers, current employees, and markets are not disqualified on other factors such as their skills, disposition, and the like. Under such circumstances, a rank order of jobs for a given group will be generated. If group X enjoys a favorable situation among employers, then members of the group will tend to pile up as much as they can in the more promising jobs, leaving the least attractive ones (as that group defines attractiveness) for the non-X population. If within the non-X population there are further subdivisions by race or ethnic origin in terms of desirability, such that Y is preferred over other non-X groups, then in turn the Ys will tend to get first crack at the jobs that Xs either do not desire or are unable to qualify for. One may move on and on down the path until all groups have attained their positions. If there are more potential workers than jobs, those at the bottom of the order will have exceptionally high rates of unemployment. Clearly, this pecking order does not mean that all of the very best jobs are filled by Xs and that all of the worst are filled by non-Xs, but rather refers to some aggregate structure that would result. This, then is rather compatible with various queuing theories developed in connection with racial differences in income and employment (Thurow, 1969, chapter 4; 1975; Hodge, 1973). Another necessary assumption is that employers are relatively homogeneous in their ethnic preference ranking.

It follows from these assumptions also that dominance will tend to perpetuate further dominance. This is because the dominant group—almost by definition—is likely to be employers, key co-workers, and form a specially important market, and their offspring will also be most suited and in the best position to obtain the most desirable jobs because their parents can invest more in their training. Because this is not the only force operating to determine offsprings' positions, there can be modifications if prejudice eases up and a noncaste system is operating (see Lieberson and Fuguitt, 1967) or if there are changes in population composition, labor force needs, or other forces.

An extremely important implication of the queuing generated by these assumptions is that the occupational composition of a given ethnic or racial group will vary between communities in accordance with the group's proportion of the population and in accordance with the racial-ethnic composition of the city. If the most favored group is 10 percent of the population, then it can tend to pile up in the most desirable 10 percent of the jobs. But if the most favored group is 20 percent of the labor force and all other forces are the same, then the group will concentrate in the top 20 percent of the occupational opportunities. Accordingly, the best jobs open to the second-ranked group (the Ys) will be at the ninetieth percentile in the first city but at the eightieth percentile of desirability in the latter place.

If the group at the bottom of the ethnic-racial hierarchy amounts to Q percent of the population, then it will find the Q least-desirable positions available (assuming employment opportunities are available for all). If Q is large, then the group will have opportunities higher on the occupational hierarchy because the more highly ranked groups are not pushing as far down; if Q is a small percentage of the population, then there will be room for them at the very bottom only because non-Q will compete successfully for the other jobs because non-Q would be such a large proportion of the population. Incidentally, one can understand why shifts in unemployment would be most radical for the group at the bottom of the queue because such a group would tend to be pushed out of jobs when a wave of unemployment hits. On the other hand, at times when there is a labor shortage, this group would find new job opportunities because the non-Qs could not fill all of the "traditional" employment opportunities. Obviously, this is oversimplified in the sense that all sorts of assumptions are made about qualifications, and it is unlikely that most systems would be either so precise or so discriminatory such that all of the most desired jobs would go to the X group without exception. Among other factors, as a group gets larger it is likely to develop certain internal strengths that will support some occupational activities even if outsiders are totally against their holding the position. Hence, if the black population base is large enough, there will be support for black doctors, black clergy, and so on, even if they remain totally unacceptable to others. Likewise, there will develop certain entrepreneurial possibilities and other employment shifts will occur. At any rate, this is most compatible with Hodge (1973), who for somewhat different reasons theorized that the unemployment differential would decline with increases in the disadvantaged group's proportion of the population.

One would expect certain linkages to occur between the population composition of a city and the jobs that are held by the different groups. This is because both the jobs and the groups are hierarchical. Insofar as the queuing effect operates (and obviously it is not the only factor), the group at the bottom of the ethnic-racial ranking can only go upward occupationally when there are fewer of the other groups around. For the group at the top of the hierarchy, their average job ranking will tend to go downward only because of competition from compatriots; hence, it will be lower when they are a larger proportion of the population. On the other hand, groups in the middle are affected by whether their non-compatriots are of higher or lower positions in the ethnic hierarchy. The procedure used here, in which the group's proportion of the population is the key independent variable, is adequate for intermediate groups insofar as the relative numbers of noncompatriots above and below the group are roughly constant in each city. (If the ethnic hierarchy is adequately determined in this chapter, then in future work it would be more appropriate to consider intermediate groups also in terms of the proportion who are above and below them in each city.) At any rate, artificial changes in the composition of a city would not alter a group's position particularly—except insofar as a stronger within-group market is created for compatriots. Rather, the association with composition reflects the opportunity pulls of different communities which are due to shifts in labor force needs and the groups available to fill expansions in demand. Basically, this is the story of World War I when the new Europeans were not available at a time when American industry was booming. This meant unheralded opportunities for blacks in the urban North.

Some Examples

The 1900 Census, which reports rather detailed occupational data for a number of relevant groups in each of 78 large cities (12 of which are southern), provides some nice examples of the consequences of these propositions about composition. Figure 10.1 links the black proportion of each city's male work force with the black proportion of men employed as servants or waiters. In all of the cities there are relatively more black servants and waiters than there are black workers. (The solid

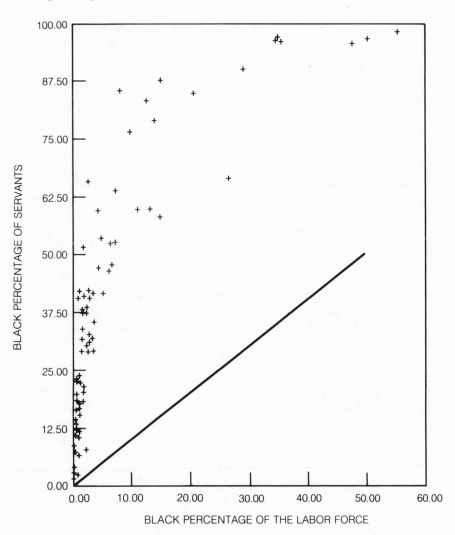

Fig. 10.1
Black Percentage of Servants by Labor Force

line of equality indicates the situation where the proportion of blacks in the occupation and the proportion of blacks in the work force are identical.) Observe that there is a very sharp and rapid rise in the black proportion of all servants and waiters; for example, blacks are 25 percent of all servants when they are only about 1 percent of the male work force; they are 50 percent of the servants when they are 6 percent of the work force.[1] Later increases are much smaller, although nearly all of the servants are black (98 percent or so) in cities with the largest percentage of the population black.[2]

Whereas the servant occupation appears to be one left to blacks even when they are a very small proportion of the population (such that whites occupy nearly all occupational positions), virtually no blacks were employed as carpenters in cities where 8.5 percent or less of the male workers were black (figure 10.2). The increase is slight after that, but then begins to rise at an increasing rate such that the black proportion of carpenters exceeds the line of equality in some of the cities with a sizable black proportion of the work force. This appears to be a job that is reasonably desirable for groups ahead of blacks on the queue. Hence blacks attain minimal representation in carpentry when the white population is a fairly sizable proportion of the population. But opportunities do open up for blacks when at some demographic point the relative number of whites is small enough that they can concentrate on even more desirable positions. Then the opportunity to be a carpenter opens up rapidly as the percentage of blacks increases.

Occupations vary in the point at which unity is crossed for blacks. This is due not only to the queuing effect but also to a variety of other forces such as skills, the ability of blacks to create their own market, and the like. However, one assumes that the point of equality in most cases largely reflects the interaction between queuing and composition. Consider the "banking, brokers, and bank officials" category. There were virtually no blacks so employed even in cities where about half of the male work force was black (see figure 10.3). The highest black proportion of the banking category among any of the 78 cities was about 2 percent, and this was in a city where blacks were about 50 percent of the work force. Presumably this occupation is very attractive to white men and so they did not give this pursuit up even when the demographic composition of the city meant relatively less competition from other whites. This was also an occupation in which black economic power was so weak that the relative size of the black population had virtually no impact on their ability to obtain jobs in this field.

There are, of course, more complicated situations. In the case of clergy, for example, blacks create their own segregated market and hence whites cannot fill up all of the niches regardless of the attraction such a professional position might have held for them. This creates the dualism indicated by the graph in figure 10.4. The black proportion of the clergy in most cities slightly exceeds their proportion of the work force. There is nothing here to suggest a queuing effect such that one group replaces the other in these functions.

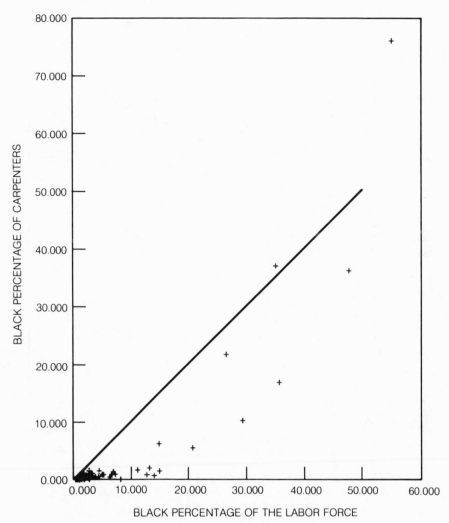

Fig. 10.2
Black Percentage of Carpenters by Labor Force

BLACK AND NEW EUROPEAN QUEUES: A COMPARISON

How important were these occupational queues in 1900, and, more-over, how different were blacks from new European groups in their positions in these queues? Was the advantageous position that the SCE groups presently hold evident during the early period of contact in the

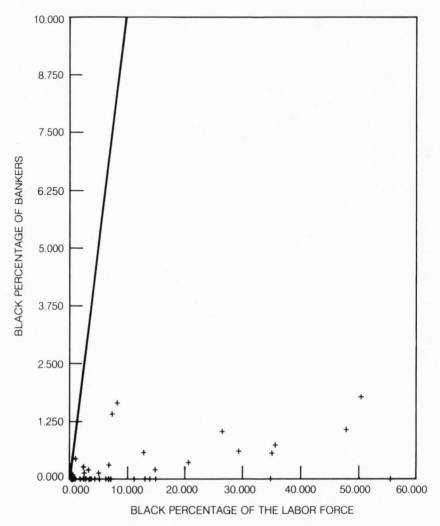

Fig. 10.3
Black Percentage of Bankers by Labor Force

urban North? (At this point, only the 66 northern cities will be considered in the analysis.) For each occupation, one ought to be able to state the point at which the group's percentage in the job first equals or exceeds the group's percentage in the population. But this is not possible because blacks in 1900 as well as the SCE groups are at most only small proportions of the population in the urban North. As a consequence, for

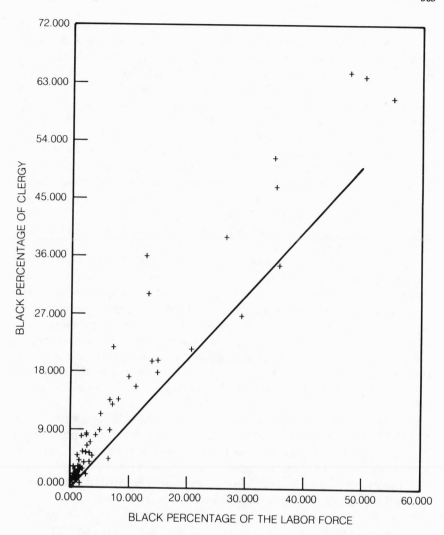

Fig. 10.4
Black Percentage of Clergy by Labor Force

a large number of jobs the equality point is not seen with the data available over the range covered. Projecting the computed regression line out beyond the observed values is not entirely satisfactory because there is good reason to believe that when the group does begin to participate in the occupation, it does so in a nonlinear fashion (see figure 10.2). Consider for example black carpenters and joiners in the North (figure 10.5). One observes only a very slight increase in the black proportion in this occupation as their proportion of the population goes up (the regression slope is .12646), and projecting beyond the data one would conclude that about 13 percent of all carpenters would be black even when blacks made up the entire population of the city![3] Hence, although a linear approach is perfectly adequate for the narrow compositional band covered in the North, its appropriateness for extrapolation is rather doubtful in many cases.

For every occupation and group, a regression like that shown in figure 10.5 was computed across all of the northern cities to determine the linkage between each group's proportion of the city's male work force and its employment in the job. With these regressions one can calculate the group's proportion of a given occupation when the group amounts to a specified segment of the population. As inspection of table 10.2 indicates, the range for the four South–Central–Eastern European groups—Austro-Hungarians, Italians, Poles, and Russians—makes it reasonable to compare them with blacks in the urban North in 1900 when each is 5 percent of the population. Such a comparison is meaningful if one assumes that the point of unity for a given group in an occupation is correlated with the point it has reached when its proportion of the city's male work force is .05. Although difficulties exist, clearly the procedure allows a reasonable and systematic comparison between the four new European groups and blacks in terms of their relative similarities in their occupational composition net of the demographic effect.[4]

The .05 value for X is not possible for native whites of native parentage (NWNP) males because their proportion of the city population ranges from .11 in Milwaukee to .76 in Reading. This is no problem for comparisons with two old European groups, Germans and Irish, or with blacks (see their ranges in table 10.2), all of whom can be compared satisfactorily when their proportion of the city population is .12. As a result, this level would not be appropriate for each of the new European groups. Accordingly, their data were combined and a separate regression so computed because the SCE combined proportion ranged from .01 to .20 in these cities. In this way comparisons are directly possible between the new European groups and native whites of native parentage. A more thorough consideration of the technical issues involved is given in the Appendix to this chapter.

Professional Occupations

There is indication of a very steep queue among the groups with respect to the professional occupations. Native white of native parentage

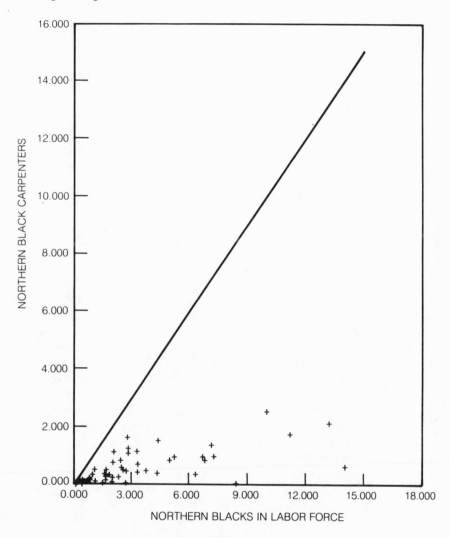

Fig. 10.5
Northern Black Carpenters by Labor Force

males hold 35 percent of all professional positions when they amount to 12 percent of the population in a city. All of the other groups in the study are not only well below this level but are less than the 12 percent parity; Germans and Irish are each about 8 percent of the professionals, blacks are just a shade under 6 percent, and the SCE are lowest with 3.8 percent. It is noteworthy that the Irish and German groups, although occupying an intermediate position, are closer in their professional

TABLE 10.2
RANGE IN PROPORTION OF MALE WORKERS IN 66 NON-SOUTHERN CITIES, 1900

	Range	
Group	Low	High
Austro-Hungarian	.0005	.1354
Black	.0008	.1404
German	.0045	.5595
Irish	.0260	.4054
Italian	.0002	.0828
Native white of native parentage	.1124	.7622
Polish	.0005	.1119
Russian	.0012	.0656
SCE[a]	.0079	.2019

SOURCE: Based on analysis of data reported in U.S. Bureau of the Census, 1904.
    [a]Based on combined data for Austro-Hungarian, Italian, Polish and Russian.

levels to blacks and the new Europeans than to the older whites in the nation. The NWNP dominance is almost without exception, as they occupy the highest rank for all but the musician-music teacher category, where they are a close second to blacks (for details, see table 10.3). Germans rank second or third in ten of the occupations, and the Irish occupy one or the other of these ranks in 12 cases. The new Europeans and blacks clearly bring up the rear among the professional occupations. Most of the professional occupations require far more education than these groups had at that time. Hence, this is not that much of a test of the queuing notion as one would expect a small proportion of both groups to be in most professional pursuits.

Regarding differences between blacks and the new Europeans, it is difficult to determine their relative order on the queue—or indeed if one exists at the bottom. On the one hand, black men have both a higher overall proportion in professional activities than the SCE and a higher average proportion in the 14 jobs specified, but blacks are in last place in nine professional categories whereas the new Europeans are last in only three (Table 10.3). Blacks enjoy second place ranks in three professions, however: clergy (21 percent when blacks are 12 percent of the population), musicians and music teachers (18 percent), and teachers or professors (15 percent). As a result of these three activities, blacks have a higher overall professional level than the new Europeans. In many of the other activities there are small differences of 1 or 2 percentage points favoring the latter; these include the job categories of architects, dentists, electricians, engineers, journalists, lawyers, the literary and scientific

TABLE 10.3
PROFESSIONAL OCCUPATIONS HELD BY MALES IN NON-SOUTHERN CITIES, 1900 (WHEN
GROUPS ARE 12 PERCENT OF THE WORK FORCE)

Occupation	Percentage of the occupation				
	Black	German	Irish	NWNP	SCE
All professional	5.9	8.3	8.0	35.2	3.8
Actors, professional showmen	9.1	5.9	12.4	30.6	2.7
Architects, designers, draftsmen	.005	11.3	4.4	31.3	2.5
Artists and teachers of art	3.5	14.0	4.6	19.9	8.8
Clergymen	20.8	9.5	10.7	25.6	8.3
Dentists	1.4	5.7	4.7	39.5	1.9
Electricians	0.5	8.8	8.7	27.8	1.5
Engineers and surveyors	0.5	5.8	5.6	49.6	1.1
Journalists	1.2	5.6	8.5	37.8	3.3
Lawyers	1.7	4.6	9.3	49.2	2.1
Literary and scientific persons	1.2	11.5	5.3	30.9	3.4
Musicians and teachers of music	17.9	18.1	3.9	16.0	13.3
Government officials	1.6	6.9	14.5	27.5	2.1
Physicians, surgeons	3.6	6.6	6.7	40.5	3.6
Teachers, professors	14.5	7.9	7.3	32.9	9.8
Rank	Number of occupations				
1	0	1	0	13	0
2	3	6	5	0	0
3	1	4	7	1	1
4	1	3	0	0	10
5	9	0	2	0	3
Average percentage in detailed occupations	5.5	8.7	7.6	32.8	4.6

SOURCE: See table 10.2

professions, and government officials (see details in table 10.3). In
another category, medicine, the gap is virtually nil between the groups.

In short, although blacks presently differ sharply from the new
Europeans in their concentration in professional activities, in 1900 there
was no clear indication that such a gap was forthcoming. Blacks had a
higher proportion in professional activities than did the new Europeans—although that was due to a concentration in a small number of
activities. Among most of the others, the new Europeans had a slight
edge. Overall, one can conclude that both groups were at the bottom of

the professional ladder in the North with no clear or substantial over-riding difference between them.

Domestic and Personal Services

Many of the service occupations are probably among the less-rewarding jobs available, as a quick glance at the pursuits listed in table 10.4 will show. And so, if occupational choice was purely a function of a queue, one would expect the dominant groups to avoid these pursuits unless the dominants were such a massive part of the labor force that all of the more attractive alternatives were also held by compatriots. On the other hand, such jobs would be relatively available to those groups at the very bottom of the employment hierarchy. Not only is there a queue indicated by the aggregate data, but it is one in which there is a sharp difference between blacks and new Europeans. Native whites of native parentage participate least in this category, holding 9 percent of the jobs when they are 12 percent of the population; Germans are very close to this figure, 11 percent; and Irish are intermediate at 16 percent.[5] The SCE Europeans and blacks are most concentrated in these activities, but there is no ambiguity about who belongs where in the ranking: Blacks are an incredibly high 34 percent of all those employed in such occupations, whereas the SCE group holds 21 percent of such jobs when they are 12 percent of the population.

Inspection of the detailed occupations within the domestic and personal service rubric indicates that the rank ordering is far more com-plicated than in the professions. To be sure, the average proportion in the 12 occupations is clearly highest for blacks (see table 10.4), but it is actually lowest for the SCE Europeans in most instances, with the other groups occupying intermediate positions. Some of the occupations fit neatly into a queue expectation. For example, blacks are most concen-trated in barbering (27 percent), the new Europeans are second (23 per-cent), and the NWNPs are a distant last (only 4.5 percent). In similar fashion, the concentration in laborers not otherwise specified fits into this pattern (blacks and new Europeans are first and second with massive concentrations, 33 and 26.5 percent, respectively) and NWNPs are last with 5 percent. In similar fashion, but from the other end of the queue, blacks and SCE Europeans are the least concentrated of the groups in the military, hotel and boarding, and watchman–policeman–fireman categories, with NWNPs most concentrated in the first two jobs and exceeded only by the Irish in the latter category.

On the other hand, there are a number of jobs which make no sense from purely a queuing perspective (assuming that the NWNPs are

TABLE 10.4

DOMESTIC AND PERSONAL SERVICE OCCUPATIONS HELD BY MALES IN NON-SOUTHERN
CITIES, 1900 (WHEN GROUPS ARE 12 PERCENT OF THE WORK FORCE)

Occupation	Percentage of the occupation				
	Black	German	Irish	NWNP	SCE
All domestic and personal	33.6	10.8	16.0	9.2	20.5
Barbers and hairdressers	26.8	20.6	5.2	4.5	23.2
Bartenders	4.1	19.1	21.1	5.5	7.0
Hotel and boarding house keepers	5.1	15.3	14.0	20.1	3.6
Janitors, sextons	53.7	8.8	11.3	14.1	5.7
Laborers not specified	33.3	9.7	18.4	5.3	26.5
Launderers	10.2	4.3	4.7	13.6	2.3
Nurses	9.6	7.4	13.4	24.3	2.0
Restaurant and saloon keepers	6.5	25.2	16.7	6.7	12.3
Servants and waiters	74.3	7.6	8.9	13.9	4.1
Soldiers, sailors, and marines	9.6	11.8	12.6	18.1	4.9
Stewards	33.7	9.8	13.8	16.9	2.1
Watchmen, policemen, and firemen	5.0	9.9	25.5	13.2	2.2
Rank	Number of occupations				
1	5	1	2	4	0
2	1	2	3	4	2
3	1	3	6	0	2
4	3	6	1	2	0
5	2	0	0	2	8
Average percentage in detailed occupations	22.7	12.5	13.8	13.0	8.0

SOURCE: See table 10.2

understood to be first in 1900). In some cases, this may reflect distinctive
cultural features. For example, in the case of restaurant and saloon
keepers or bartenders, the odd hierarchy is probably due to differential
attitudes toward alcohol found in 1900. Blacks and NWNPs are similar in
being relatively underrepresented in such pursuits, differing from each
other by less than 0.5 percent in the former and little more than 1 percent
in the latter. By contrast Germans and Irish are especially active in these
pursuits. There are other jobs in which, again, blacks and the SCE
occupy opposite ends of the continuum with NWNPs much closer to
blacks. Blacks occupy first place as janitors, servants and waiters, and
stewards with extraordinarily high rates of concentration (54, 74, and

34 percent, respectively) when they are 12 percent of the population. The NWNPs are distinctively below this level, but still they securely occupy second place with 14 percent as either servants and waiters or janitors and with 17 percent as stewards. By contrast, the SCE are lowest of all the groups, ranging from 2 to 6 percent in such occupations. In these instances, clearly blacks and the new European groups were not in the same situation. The odd order may be due, I speculate, to the Engligh-language situation such that either blacks or English-speaking whites were far more acceptable to employers than were strange foreigners. This would apply to situations involving servants, waiters handling and presenting food, stewards, and janitors and sextons with access to either one's home or place of worship. Another possibility for the NWNP rate is that there was no servant tradition among many of the SCE groups such that it might be viewed as a suitable calling. This is a matter meriting further investigation as it seems to be such an anomalous result, but the key conclusion for our purposes is that a number of the domestic service jobs do not exhibit a queue whatsoever. There are some sharp gaps between blacks and the new Europeans among other service jobs as well—launderers and male nurses—where the black proportion is considerably higher than the new European level and where the NWNPs have the highest participation of all.

Notwithstanding these exceptions, the overall black—SCE European patterns are consistent thus far with a queuing process. Blacks and the new Europeans are highly concentrated in domestic and service occupations, activities that are generally considered less desirable. But there are some sharp differences between the two groups in this domain even in 1900. First, blacks have a much higher concentration overall in the category. Second, there are a large number of jobs in which the gaps between SCE Europeans and blacks are exceptionally wide. This shows up not only in the rankings summed up in Table 10.4, but also in the fact that there is essentially no correlation between the groups' concentration in each of the 12 domestic and service occupations (r is .12). By contrast, there is a correlation of .81 between black and new European concentration in the 14 professional occupations. To be sure, if the native whites of native parentage generally occupy the top position within the queue, then there are some very odd results right off the bat because they should normally be expected to be either the most-concentrated or least-concentrated group with each occupation (depending on the job's desirability). But here there are several situations in which blacks are most concentrated and the NWNPs are second-most concentrated or where NWNPs occupy first place and blacks occupy second place. I believe this points to the operation of more than a queue in the placing of jobs—a pattern that occurs for some of the other detailed occupations as well.

Trade and Transportation

The overall pattern in trade and transportation is quite comparable to that for professionals. Native whites are first among all the groups, 23.5 percent, the Irish and Germans hold second and third place, respectively (both below the parity of 12 percent), and blacks and new Europeans bring up the rear with almost identical positions (7 percent of the jobs when they are 12 percent of the population). Not only is there general evidence of a hierarchy, but the old European groups are closer to the black and SCE level than to the NWNP concentration—just as was the case for professionals.

Among a large number of occupations there is a very orderly queue. For example, NWNPs are very important as bankers and brokers, 47 percent; the Irish and Germans occupy a distant second and third place, 8 and 7 percent, respectively, with both blacks (0.5) and the SCE (1.8) very low. This pattern is found in nine other occupations as well: bookkeepers, agents, commercial travelers, livery men, salesmen, street railwaymen, both linemen and operators in telephone-telegraph, and foremen-overseers in trade or transportation (table 10.5). Blacks are last, the South–Central–Eastern European groups not much ahead of them, native whites are most important, and the Irish are second and the Germans third (with the German/Irish order sometimes reversed).

There are two important exceptions to this general pattern, both involving retail activities. In the case of merchants and dealers, blacks are last at 1.7 percent and NWNPs are highest at 16.5 percent, but the SCE and German groups trail closely (16.1 and 15.4 percent, respectively). The similarity between SCE and NWNPs is due to the Jewish segment of the new immigrants. At the 5 percent level of composition, Russians (largely Jewish) hold 12 percent of the jobs in the merchants-dealers category. However, the gap between SCE groups and blacks is due to more than this factor; blacks at the 5 percent composition level are a minuscule 0.7 percent of the merchants in northern cities, whereas Italians are slightly in excess of parity, and Poles and Austro-Hungarians are still considerably ahead of blacks even though they are below parity (see table 10.6). In the case of hucksters and peddlers, the SCE groups are separated from blacks in the same pattern as found in some of the service occupations. NWNPs and blacks are both sharply underrepresented as hucksters and peddlers, 4 and 5 percent, respectively, at the 12 percent population level (see table 10.5), whereas the new Europeans

TABLE 10.5
TRADE AND TRANSPORTATION OCCUPATIONS HELD BY MALES IN NON-SOUTHERN CITIES, 1900 (WHEN GROUPS ARE 12 PERCENT OF THE WORK FORCE)

Occupation	Percentage of the occupation				
	Black	German	Irish	NWNP	SCE
All trade and transportation	7.1	9.8	11.5	23.5	7.4
Agents	0.9	8.4	9.0	28.3	3.9
Bankers, brokers, and bank officials	0.5	7.1	8.3	47.5	1.8
Boatmen and sailors	38.4	6.6	12.7	19.9	2.6
Bookkeepers, clerks, and stenographers	1.0	8.6	10.0	33.6	2.4
Commercial travelers	0.2	8.2	6.9	35.9	4.2
Draymen, hackmen, and teamsters	21.4	10.3	14.7	13.0	3.7
Foremen and overseers	0.8	7.9	19.4	26.4	2.2
Hostlers	49.3	6.3	15.6	13.4	2.3
Hucksters and peddlers	4.8	8.9	5.5	4.0	49.7
Livery stable keepers	3.3	8.1	16.6	22.3	3.3
Merchants, dealers, and peddlers	1.7	15.4	8.0	16.5	16.1
Messengers, packers, and porters	35.2	9.7	11.3	14.7	4.9
Newspaper carriers and newsboys	8.6	10.5	6.9	8.9	17.3
Salesmen	0.7	11.4	8.9	23.9	5.3
Steam railroad employees	4.5	6.6	20.0	23.2	8.7
Street railway employees	1.6	6.8	15.2	22.9	2.1
Telegraph and telephone linemen	0.8	6.0	21.4	21.8	0.9
Telegraph and telephone operators	0.1	5.5	15.7	38.5	1.8
Undertakers	9.9	9.6	15.3	10.1	4.7
Rank	Number of occupations				
1	4	0	1	12	2
2	0	4	11	3	1
3	1	9	5	3	1
4	3	6	1	0	9
5	11	0	1	1	6
Average percentage in detailed occupations	9.7	8.5	12.7	22.4	7.3

SOURCE: See table 10.2

are heavily engaged in these activities, amounting to 50 percent of all incumbents when they are 12 percent of male workers. However, here all four of the new European groups are above parity at the 5 percent level—indeed at that point they exceed the concentration achieved by either blacks or NWNPs when at 12 percent of the population. Jews, as table 10.6 shows, again rank incredibly high, 43 percent of the hucksters and peddlers when they are 5 percent of the population, but Italians, Poles, and Austro-Hungarians all exceed equity too, although far less spectacularly. There are a few other occupations in which blacks are closer to the NWNPs than they are to the SCE Europeans, messengers— packers—porters, sailors, and draymen (table 10.5). In these three cases, blacks were specially concentrated and new Europeans disproportionately absent from such work.

Overall, NWNPs enjoy a significant edge over the remaining four groups in the trade and transportation occupations, with blacks and new Europeans both strongly underrepresented and differing very little from one another in most occupations. Both were excluded from white-collar jobs to an almost equal degree. Among male bookkeepers, clerks, and stenographers, for example, the SCE representation at the .12 population level was barely higher than the black concentration, .024 versus .010. At the 5 percent level of population, the black figure was only minutely smaller than the Polish and Italian figure and not that much smaller than either the Russian or Austro-Hungarian figures (table 10.6).[6] But there are some significant exceptions in trade which portend important developments for the new Europeans that are not shared by blacks.

Manufacturing and Mechanical Pursuits

It is in the manufacturing and mechanical pursuits that we find a truly sharp divergence from the overall patterns observed thus far. Blacks are at the bottom, filling 5.6 percent of such jobs when they are 12 percent of the work force. In this case, next to last place is occupied not by the new Europeans but by native whites, who are barely more concentrated than blacks (6.6 percent). The remaining three groups are clustered relatively close together. Germans are most concentrated with 14.8 percent, the SCE Europeans are second with 12.2 percent, and the Irish are slightly below parity, 11.3 percent. This pattern checks out at the 5 percent population level as well, with 2.1 percent of blacks in these pursuits, Germans at 6.6 percent, the Irish at 4.7 percent, and three of the specific new groups slightly in excess of parity (Austro-Hungarians, 6.0; Poles, 5.5; and Russians, 6.4), and Italians are somewhat below (3.8).

TABLE 10.6

TRADE AND TRANSPORTATION OCCUPATIONS HELD BY MALES IN NON-SOUTHERN CITIES, 1900 (WHEN GROUPS ARE 5 PERCENT OF THE WORK FORCE)

Occupation	Percentage of the occupation				
	Black	Austro-Hung.	Italian	Polish	Russian
All trade and transportation	3.1	2.3	2.4	1.9	5.4
Agents	0.5	1.6	0.5	1.0	4.2
Bankers, brokers, and bank officials	0.2	0.8	0.5	0.3	1.3
Boatmen and sailors	14.5	0.8	1.1	0.4	1.1
Bookkeepers, clerks, and stenographers	0.6	1.3	0.6	0.6	1.6
Commercial travelers	0.1	2.1	0.1	1.0	3.3
Draymen, hackmen, and teamsters	9.5	1.6	1.5	1.8	1.3
Foremen and overseers	0.5	0.9	0.9	0.7	0.7
Hostlers	21.8	1.3	0.6	1.0	0.5
Hucksters and peddlers	2.0	7.4	11.6	11.3	43.4
Livery stable keepers	1.5	1.2	1.3	1.0	1.9
Merchants, dealers, and peddlers	0.7	4.4	5.6	3.4	12.0
Messengers, packers, and porters	16.1	2.4	1.9	1.5	3.2
Newspaper carriers and newsboys	5.7	4.3	6.0	1.3	15.6
Salesmen	0.3	2.1	1.0	1.6	5.0
Steam railroad employees	1.7	3.2	5.2	2.9	0.8
Street railway employees	0.6	0.6	0.8	1.0	0.6
Telegraph and telephone linemen	0.4	0.5	0.5	0.2	0.3
Telegraph and telephone operators	0.1	0.9	0.8	0.3	0.5
Undertakers	3.6	2.5	2.3	2.4	1.0
Average percentage in detailed occupations	4.23	2.1	2.3	1.8	5.2

SOURCE: See table 10.2.

Blacks are in last place in 50 of the 63 detailed occupations listed within this category and are in first or second place in only five occupations (table 10.7). The Germans are the dominant group even in the detailed occupations, holding either first or second place in virtually every case. The new Europeans are clearly in second place, well ahead of blacks but distinctly behind Americans of German origin. They are the most concentrated group in ten occupations, occupy second place in 19, are in third place in ten, are fourth in 22, and are the least concentrated of the groups in only two occupations.

This pattern, in which blacks and NWNPs are so close, is not as anomalous as one might first think. If these are intermediate-level jobs, then they may for the most part not be terribly attractive to the NWNPs but still be highly appealing to some of the other groups. Hence NWNPs are less than proportionately concentrated in them by choice, whereas blacks are also not in these pursuits because there are other groups (the new Europeans included) ahead of them on the employment queue.

Although the new European groups have similar concentrations in some of the specific manufacturing jobs, in other cases they differ widely from each other in a manner that probably reflects the skills brought from their homelands. (This can occur for some minority of a group even if the vast majority are unskilled.) Inspection of table 10.8 discloses a number of jobs in which all of the SCE groups were underrepresented; for example, they range from 1 to 2.4 percent of the printers and from 0.7 to 1.8 percent of the plumbers. But on the other hand, at the same .05 compositional level, Italians and Poles are 21 and 12 percent, respectively, of the brick and tile makers, whereas both Russians and Austro-Hungarians were below unity (1.6 and 3.8 percent, respectively). Italians were likewise exceptionally high in other stone-related occupations. At the 5 percent level they are 14 percent of marble and stone cutters; 9 percent of masons; 10 percent of miners and quarrymen. With one exception, the other three new European groups were all below parity. There are many other cases of ethnic specialization shown in table 10.8. Italians amounted to 15 percent of confectioners; Russians and Austro-Hungarians were 33 and 18 percent, respectively, of tailors (a job that was disproportionately also held by Poles and Italians, albeit in less impressive numbers). Russians and Austro-Hungarians were estimated to be 13 and 9 percent, respectively, of tobacco workers in the urban North (in 1900 this meant largely cigar makers); the former were 10 percent of clock and watch makers (this may well have been a pathway to entry into the jewelry business) and Austro-Hungarians were 10 percent of saw and planing mill employees. Russians were a full 49 percent of all shirt, collar, and cuff makers. All four new European groups exceeded equity as boot and shoe makers, but they varied greatly: Poles, 5.5 percent; Austro-Hungarians, 9 percent; Russians, 13 percent; and Italians, 25 percent. Russian men were 42 percent of the hat and cap makers. Poles and Austro-Hungarians were 11 and 8 percent, respectively, of iron and steel workers; the former were also 14 percent of leather curriers and tanners.

TABLE 10.7
MANUFACTURING AND MECHANICAL OCCUPATIONS HELD BY MALES IN NON-SOUTHERN
CITIES, 1900 (WHEN GROUPS ARE 12 PERCENT OF THE WORK FORCE)

Occupation	Percentage of the occupation				
	Black	German	Irish	NWNP	SCE
All manufacturing and mechanical	5.6	14.8	11.3	6.6	12.2
Bakers	1.1	37.9	6.0	7.8	12.0
Blacksmiths	2.5	14.3	16.9	9.4	7.6
Bleachery and dye work operatives	2.8	14.2	11.4	6.1	10.8
Bookbinders	0.5	19.8	8.3	8.0	6.2
Boot and shoe makers and repairers	3.2	22.9	8.8	5.5	32.5
Bottlers and soda water makers, etc.	1.2	36.2	7.0	2.9	10.2
Brassworkers	2.0	15.1	13.9	12.3	6.7
Brewers and malsters	1.4	71.7	3.3	2.1	5.5
Brickmakers and potters	21.1	10.5	9.3	5.5	20.3
Broom and brush makers	2.3	16.9	12.9	6.5	6.5
Butchers	2.6	32.8	7.4	10.3	11.5
Butter and cheese makers	3.1	11.3	11.1	6.9	7.9
Cabinet makers	0.4	34.4	2.4	4.1	10.2
Carpenters and joiners	1.7	12.2	7.0	12.1	4.9
Clock and watch makers and repairmen	1.2	18.8	3.5	11.3	12.0
Confectioners	2.0	20.9	6.1	8.3	16.0
Coopers	1.4	22.6	11.8	0.4	7.9
Cotton mill operatives	0.1	8.0	11.0	0	16.7
Electroplaters	0.2	17.5	9.0	11.3	6.9
Engineers and firemen (not locomotive)	8.0	9.6	16.7	15.5	2.3
Engravers	0.4	21.9	6.0	15.2	3.4
Fishermen and oystermen	4.9	6.2	6.3	8.6	8.8
Furniture manufacturing employees	0.6	19.3	5.9	9.1	15.6
Gas work employees	6.7	6.4	35.7	7.5	7.3
Glassworkers	1.0	19.2	13.1	10.7	6.9
Gold and silver workers	1.0	19.6	4.1	3.2	7.6
Harness and trunk makers	0.2	21.9	7.1	8.5	11.3
Hat and cap makers	0.3	13.6	7.1	0.5	43.8
Hosiery and knitting mill operatives	0	19.0	18.2	1.7	14.7
Iron and steel workers	6.3	12.4	16.8	4.4	14.0
Leather curriers and tanners	4.7	18.3	12.6	5.9	17.6
Machinists	0.6	14.1	11.0	15.0	3.8
Manufacturers and officials	1.9	11.8	8.9	26.7	5.3
Marble and stone cutters	3.9	12.1	17.3	4.0	15.3
Masons (brick and stone)	25.5	11.8	17.4	3.7	10.9
Meat, fish, fruit canners, and packers	16.5	15.0	15.3	3.9	19.4
Millers	2.4	13.4	11.0	11.3	6.5

TABLE 10.7 (Continued)

Occupation	Percentage of the occupation				
	Black	German	Irish	NWNP	SCE
Miners and quarrymen	23.5	5.9	14.5	13.4	14.1
Model and pattern makers	0.1	12.9	6.3	11.9	2.1
Painters, glaziers, and					
varnishers	2.2	12.3	8.5	14.5	5.1
Paper and pulp mill					
operators	9.6	10.5	9.5	8.2	14.0
Paper hangers	7.0	8.0	8.4	18.8	10.0
Photographers	2.4	9.2	4.5	19.1	5.9
Piano and organ makers	1.5	24.8	4.8	11.7	7.6
Plasterers	15.1	8.4	21.0	0.6	6.5
Plumbers and gas steam					
fitters	2.2	11.5	24.0	9.8	2.7
Printers, lithographers,					
and pressmen	2.0	12.2	10.5	14.1	3.9
Roofers and slaters	8.4	16.0	20.5	12.0	2.8
Rubber factory operatives	1.7	11.7	10.0	14.8	9.6
Saw and planing mill					
employees	10.2	12.8	10.6	4.5	15.0
Shirt, collar, and cuff makers	0.2	8.1	6.0	9.1	36.9
Steam boiler makers	0.2	11.5	28.5	5.0	4.5
Stove, furnace, and					
grate makers	0.7	14.8	12.6	1.1	7.1
Tailors	1.5	25.1	5.9	1.6	40.8
Textile mill operatives	2.8	16.1	8.9	5.7	10.5
Tinplate and tinware makers	0.8	18.5	11.6	6.7	8.9
Tobacco and cigar factory					
operatives	2.9	31.5	6.3	7.2	17.6
Tool and cutlery makers	0.02	16.1	8.0	9.8	7.1
Upholsterers	1.8	22.5	8.8	10.4	6.9
Wheelwrights	0	26.1	8.3	9.9	8.2
Wire workers	2.9	13.4	11.3	8.7	16.6
Wood box makers	0.6	25.7	7.5	3.6	11.7
Woolen mill operatives	0.5	13.9	16.3	1.8	11.4
Rank	Number of occupations				
1	3	33	10	7	10
2	2	17	12	13	19
3	1	8	28	16	10
4	7	3	13	18	22
5	50	2	0	9	2
Average percentage in					
detailed occupations	3.8	17.5	10.8	8.3	11.3

SOURCE: See table 10.2.

TABLE 10.8

MANUFACTURING AND MECHANICAL OCCUPATIONS HELD BY MALES IN NON-SOUTHERN
CITIES, 1900 (WHEN GROUPS ARE 5 PERCENT OF THE WORK FORCE)

Occupation	Percentage of the occupation				
	Black	Austro-Hung.	Italian	Polish	Russian
All manufacturing and mechanical	2.1	6.0	3.8	5.5	6.4
Bakers	0.5	6.8	5.2	3.5	3.7
Blacksmiths	1.1	3.9	1.8	4.0	2.7
Bleachery and dye work operatives	1.2	5.6	6.2	3.2	3.8
Bookbinders	0.3	3.7	1.9	0.8	4.6
Boot and shoe makers and repairers	1.4	9.1	24.6	5.5	12.7
Bottlers and soda water makers, etc.	0.6	4.3	2.4	2.2	9.4
Brassworkers	0.7	5.1	1.8	4.8	1.7
Brewers and malsters	0.4	4.1	0.5	3.9	0.2
Brick makers and potters	8.3	3.8	20.7	12.0	1.6
Broom and brush makers	1.0	1.6	1.7	3.0	5.8
Butchers	1.0	6.0	1.7	4.4	7.3
Butter and cheese makers	1.2	4.4	1.9	5.7	5.0
Cabinet makers	0.3	10.4	2.0	3.2	3.1
Carpenters and joiners	0.8	2.7	1.8	1.7	2.8
Clock and watch makers and repairmen	0.4	4.5	1.7	3.0	9.9
Confectioners	1.0	2.9	14.6	1.9	5.8
Coopers	0.8	6.1	2.3	1.9	1.4
Cotton mill operatives	0.1	0	14.2	6.9	0.3
Electroplaters	0.3	5.5	1.9	2.1	2.0
Engineers and firemen (not locomotive)	3.3	1.5	0.7	0.8	0.6
Engravers	0.2	2.6	0.6	0.5	1.6
Fishermen and oystermen	2.4	0.9	6.2	6.6	0.7
Furniture manufacturing employees	0.4	6.8	7.1	8.4	4.5
Gas work employees	2.9	3.6	1.0	4.6	0.8
Glassworkers	0.5	1.8	4.2	3.8	1.6
Gold and silver workers	0.5	3.8	1.8	0.9	5.0
Harness and trunk makers	0.1	5.6	1.7	3.7	8.1
Hat and cap makers	0.1	9.5	2.3	5.3	42.2
Hosiery and knitting mill operatives	0	4.8	0.5	4.4	11.1
Iron and steel workers	0.2	8.1	2.8	11.1	2.1
Leather curriers and tanners	1.8	9.3	1.3	14.0	3.4
Machinists	0.3	2.7	0.8	1.5	1.1
Manufacturers and officials	0.7	2.2	1.2	1.2	5.5
Marble and stone cutters	1.6	2.4	13.7	1.5	0.1
Masons (brick and stone)	10.1	3.2	9.4	2.7	0.7
Meat, fish, fruit canners, and packers	5.6	14.1	4.3	13.9	2.9

TABLE 10.8 (Continued)

Occupation	Percentage of the occupation				
	Black	Austro-Hung.	Italian	Polish	Russian
Millers	1.2	3.1	2.3	3.4	2.4
Miners and quarrymen	8.5	3.1	9.7	6.7	2.0
Model and pattern makers	0.048	1.2	0.8	0.5	0.6
Painters, glaziers, and varnishers	1.0	2.3	1.3	2.3	5.4
Paper and pulp mill operators	3.6	3.6	6.5	17.1	2.0
Paper hangers	4.1	3.0	1.3	1.1	16.9
Photographers	1.2	3.3	2.2	0.8	5.4
Piano and organ makers	0.6	6.7	4.0	3.1	0.9
Plasterers	7.1	1.4	4.6	4.3	0.6
Plumbers and gas steam fitters	0.9	1.5	0.7	1.1	1.8
Printers, lithographers, and pressmen	0.8	2.4	1.0	1.3	2.0
Roofers and slaters	3.1	2.5	0.5	1.3	1.6
Rubber factory operatives	0.9	2.7	4.5	7.3	2.3
Saw and planing mill employees	3.8	10.3	1.1	9.5	1.2
Shirt, collar, and cuff makers	0.1	9.2	2.0	1.3	48.8
Steam boiler makers	0.1	2.8	0.6	2.3	0.8
Stove, furnace, and grate makers	1.0	3.3	4.5	4.6	2.4
Tailors	0.9	17.7	8.6	8.9	32.7
Textile mill operatives	1.1	4.0	3.4	7.3	4.0
Tinplate and tinware makers	0.4	4.2	1.5	3.6	6.3
Tobacco and cigar factory operatives	1.2	8.6	1.9	4.8	13.3
Tool and cutlery makers	0.1	5.0	3.0	1.3	1.6
Upholsterers	1.4	2.9	0.8	1.5	6.5
Wheelwrights	0.1	6.0	1.4	8.6	1.5
Wire workers	1.2	8.2	4.6	6.3	3.1
Wood box makers	0.7	6.8	1.7	6.1	2.2
Woolen mill operatives	0.2	9.4	4.4	5.0	3.1

SOURCE: See table 10.2.

An Overview

In terms of the broad occupational categories, there are some very significant similarities between blacks in the North and South—Central—Eastern Europeans in 1900, similarities that are also compatible with queue theory. Blacks and the new Europeans both have small proportions employed as professionals and in trade and transport (in both instances NWNPs occupied first place). In domestic and personal service work, NWNPs were most underrepresented and blacks and new Europeans most concentrated—albeit the black figure was substantially higher than the SCE level of overall concentration. In addition, there was a fairly close correspondence between blacks and the new Europeans in their relative level of concentration among the specific jobs within some of these broad categories.

Additionally, there was something else going on. At the very least, there were sharp differences between blacks and new Europeans in some specific occupations, for example, clergy and teachers in the professional category. But beyond this, blacks and new Europeans differed sharply with respect to the manufacturing and mechanical world. The new Europeans were at about par overall in this arena, although both blacks and NWNPs were strongly underrepresented. Specific new European groups varied widely in their degree of concentration in many of these jobs in a way that I believe reflected skills brought here and other interethnic differences in disposition. In summary, there were many similarities between new Europeans and blacks in the urban North in 1900, but there were already a number of significant differences between them in their occupational pursuits. Some of these are consistent with a queuing perspective in which blacks rank lower than do the SCE white groups, but in other instances there were forces operating that a simple queue cannot explain.

A NORTH–SOUTH COMPARISON

To what degree did the occupational pattern of blacks in the North represent nothing more than a continuation of their patterns in the urban South in 1900? If a queue existed in the South which generally relegated the least desirable jobs to blacks, then perhaps the same set of forces was operating in the North. On the other hand, perhaps the position of blacks in the urban North was affected by the presence of groups that were numerically unimportant in most cities below the Mason-Dixon line. Because composition affects the occupational patterns, a direct comparison between the regions is difficult because the black proportion in southern cities was far higher than in the North. Another difficulty occurs because the data in 1900 are available for only 12 southern cities (Atlanta, Baltimore, Charleston, Louisville, Memphis, Nashville, New Orleans, Richmond, San Antonio, Savannah, Wilmington, and Washington). For those occupations in which at least eight of these cities had relevant data, the black proportion of men in the occupation was regressed on the black proportion of the population (analogous to the computations described earlier for northern cities). The regression equation thereby obtained was used to estimate the black proportion in the occupation when blacks were 34 percent of the population in a city (a point about midway in the range for the 12 southern centers). Despite the small Ns, in many cases a fairly strong relationship was observed between the two variables (see Appendix).

Are blacks in the North and South concentrated in the same occupations? This is the key question. Because whites in the South are a smaller portion of the work force and therefore do not have to accept certain work that must be taken in the North, the point of equity is not an entirely relevant issue under queue theory. Blacks in the South should be above equity in some occupations for which they are disproportionately low in the North. On the other hand, the queuing proposition would lead one to expect that if blacks were above their equity point in the North, then they should certainly be above the 34 percent equity point in the South as well because there would be even less white competition in the latter area.

In terms of the broad set of five occupational categories, the northern pattern has an important deviation from the southern experience, although the latter is generally followed (table 10.9). In only one of the categories in the North do blacks exceed equity: domestic and personal services (when blacks are 12 percent of the male work force, black men hold 34 percent of these jobs). This exists in the South as well, where blacks hold about 64 percent of such jobs when they are 34 percent of the population. Blacks, who are slightly below equity in northern agricultural jobs, are considerably above equity in the South. This is a shift that could easily be expected under queue theory. The rank position of blacks in each occupational category is generally similar in the two regions. (Because of the almost certain nonlinear functions that operate across the broad population range represented in North–South comparisons, and because of the absence of compositional overlap between the regions, it is not appropriate to compare the respective regression slopes.) There is a striking deviation between the regions with respect to manufacturing and mechanical jobs. Although blacks were underrepresented in this category in the South, 26 percent of such workers when 34 percent of the work force, this is still closer to equity than in either the professional or trade categories (13 and 22 percent, respectively). In the North, by contrast, the manufacturing category has proportionately fewer blacks than trade and transportation or even the professional occupations (table 10.9). The relative void in manufacturing and craft jobs noted

TABLE 10.9
OCCUPATIONS OF BLACKS IN NORTHERN AND SOUTHERN CITIES

Occupation	South (at 34 percent of population)		Nonsouth (at 12 percent of population)	
	Percentage of occupation	Rank	Percentage of occupation	Rank
Agricultural pursuits	43.8	4	11.4	4
Professional services	13.2	1	5.9	2
Domestic and personal services	64.2	5	33.6	5
Trade and transportation	21.9	2	7.1	3
Manufacturing and mechanical pursuits	25.7	3	5.6	1

SOURCE: See table 10.2.

earlier for blacks in the North is all the more a puzzle because it represents something distinctive about their northern experience and would not have been anticipated from their patterns in the South.[7]

Detailed Analysis

In all but the manufacturing area, the relative position of blacks in the detailed occupations within each broad category is remarkably consistent between the two regions. Among the eight professional occupations for which comparisons are possible, the rank order correlation (Kendall's tau) is .86, indicating that their positions within the professional occupations in the South are to a high degree found in the North (table 10.10). At most, the professional occupations are no more than one rank apart in their relative positions in the two regions. The only important deviation is that blacks in the North exceeded equity as musicians and as teachers, whereas they did not in the South—a deviation from what would be expected if the queue was the only factor operating to determine occupation and the queuing order was identical in the regions. The teaching deviation may well reflect regional differences in the educational opportunity structure in 1900 and hence is probably not too serious a concern.

The relative position of northern and southern blacks among specific domestic and personal service occupations is also highly correlated, tau is .90. All four of the specified occupations in this category in which blacks are above unity in the North—barber, janitor, laborer, and servant—are all above unity in the South as well (table 10.10). Likewise, there is considerable continuity between South and North in the rank order among 12 trade and transportation occupations, tau is .85. Of the three positions in which northern blacks exceed 12 percent, two are well in excess of the analogous point in the southern regressions (blacks are 70 percent of draymen and 81 percent of hostlers), and the third position, boatmen, also exceeds the equity point.[8] Thus the trade occupations also fit into a consistent pattern in which the relative occupational participation of blacks in the North is closely linked to their roles in the South.

It is among the 21 manufacturing jobs that the North displays the greatest deviation from the southern pattern. The rank order correlation is only .40 between the southern and northern ranks among these jobs. To be sure, the only jobs in which blacks exceed equity in the North, masons and plasterers, are also exceeded in the southern equation. By contrast, boot and shoe makers and repairers, saw mill workers, and coopers were relatively important jobs for blacks in the South but are far below equity in the North. This is to be expected if occupational choice were purely a queue; as the black proportion mounts, there should be an increasing number of jobs in which blacks exceed equity because whites need no longer compete for them as their proportion of the work force declines. But the low rank order correlation between North and South in this area supports the observation made in DuBois's classic turn-of-the-century study that blacks in the North did not participate as readily as in the South in their craft occupations (1967, pp. 126–131). I assume that North–South differences between blacks in the manufacturing and mechanical jobs reflected the greater competition blacks received in the North from the new European groups—at least this was the domain in which black–new European differences were so sharp.

Adjusting for the fact that blacks were a smaller proportion of the population in northern cities and therefore some whites were obliged to go further down the occupational hierarchy than in the South, the jobs available to blacks in the North were the very same ones in which blacks in the South were most concentrated; with few exceptions, those jobs unavailable to blacks in the South were also kept from blacks in the North. On the other hand, as we have seen, there were jobs available to blacks in the South that they did not hold in the North. The North may have differed from the South several decades earlier with respect to their attitudes toward slavery and, of course, in the sides that they took in the Civil War; but when it came to employment, in 1900 the two patterns were very similar.

TABLE 10.10

Occupation	South (at 34 percent of population)		Nonsouth (at 12 percent of population)	
	Percentage of occupation	Rank	Percentage of occupation	Rank
Professional				
Clergy	42.8	8	20.8	8
Electricians	2.8	2	0.5	2
Engineers and surveyors	1.2	1	0.5	1
Lawyers	3.7	3	1.7	4
Musicians and teachers of music	23.8	6	17.9	7
Government officials	4.5	4	1.6	3
Physicians	7.3	5	3.6	5
Teachers	27.1	7	14.5	6
Tau = .86				
Domestic and personal services				
Barbers and hairdressers	59.3	4	26.8	4
Bartenders	17.4	2	4.1	1
Janitors	74.0	6	53.7	6
Laborers, not specified	69.0	5	33.3	5
Launderers	25.3	3	10.2	3
Servants	88.7	7	74.3	7
Watchmen, policemen, firemen	7.6	1	5.0	2
Tau = .90				
Trade and transportation				
Bankers, brokers, and bank officials	0.6	2	0.5	3
Agents	5.4	6	0.9	6
Boatmen and sailors	38.1	10	38.4	11
Commercial travelers	1.1	3	0.2	2
Draymen, hackmen, and teamsters	70.2	11	21.4	10
Foremen and overseers	7.9	7	0.8	5
Hostlers	80.6	12	49.3	12
Hucksters and peddlers	33.2	9	4.8	9
Salesmen	2.6	4	0.7	4
Steam railroad employees	28.0	8	4.5	8
Street railway employees	4.9	5	1.6	7
Telegraph and telephone operators	0.4	1	0.1	1
Tau = .85				

TABLE 10.10 (Continued)

Occupation	South (at 34 percent of population)		Nonsouth (at 12 percent of population)	
	Percentage of occupation	Rank	Percentage of occupation	Rank
Manufacturing and mechanical pursuits				
Marble and stone cutters	15.3	8	3.9	16
Masons (brick and stone)	52.5	20	25.5	21
Plasterers	60.3	21	15.1	20
Plumbers and gas steam fitters	9.5	5	2.2	12
Bakers	20.7	11	1.1	4
Printers, lithographers, and pressmen	4.9	3	2.0	11
Blacksmiths	29.8	16	2.5	13
Boot and shoe makers and repairers	37.6	17	3.2	15
Butchers	24.2	12	2.6	14
Saw and planing mill employees	49.3	19	10.2	19
Cabinet makers	8.8	4	0.4	1
Carpenters and joiners	27.9	15	1.7	7
Confectioners	20.3	10	2.0	10
Coopers	40.2	18	1.4	5
Tailors	19.9	9	1.5	6
Tinplate and tinware makers	11.4	6	0.8	3
Engineers and firemen (not locomotive)	27.0	14	8.0	18
Upholsterers	25.4	13	1.8	8
Iron and steel workers	15.2	7	6.3	17
Machinists	3.4	2	0.6	2
Manufacturers and officials	2.6	1	1.9	9
Tau = .40				

SOURCE: See table 10.2.

APPENDIX

The basic data used for most of the analysis in this chapter are provided here along with a brief discussion of some issues not covered earlier. There are several difficulties with the data that the reader should recognize. Obviously the census delineation of occupations in 1900 as well as its determination of work status are different from present usage. Moreover, the ethnic delineations are somewhat different from what we are accustomed to in recent decades because they are based here on the birthplace of the subject's parents (favoring the foreign-born parent if one parent is American-born). Because the American-born offspring of immigrant parents and the immigrant parents themselves would normally be indistinguishable under this procedure, first and second generations are pooled with the available data. This has no impact on either the black or NWNP data, nor is it a serious issue for the occupational groups—other than that the generation effect is not taken into account.

There is some danger that a tautological approach to queuing may be used, to wit, the assumption is made that the NWNPs enjoy the most desirable occupations because they occupy the highest position on the queue. It would be better if the more desirable jobs could be measured independently, say through income or some other criteria. Although such data are available on the aggregate, I could not come up with an attractive and suitable set for use with these occupational figures. Accordingly, one should recognize that a risk does exist that the jobs are being tautologically defined as desirable or undesirable, depending on NWNP participation. However, given the patterns exhibited in specific jobs, for example, the NWNP concentration in the professions, it is unlikely that this is a serious risk.

In examining the data presented in table 10.11, the reader will recognize that the Ns vary between occupations. This is because not all occupations were listed for each city (not necessarily due to the absence of such employment, but rather to the relatively small Ns involved). The census was not always consistent from city to city in the fineness of its occupational delineations. It was therefore necessary occasionally to combine occupations reported separately in some cities. The agricultural occupations were left out of the analysis in the North because they seemed irrelevant to the urban issues and probably, for the most part, reflect nonurban activities occurring within the cities' boundaries. At any rate, the necessary data are provided (table 10.11) for these activities as well (see pocket).

The reader will immediately see that the correlation coefficients vary considerably between occupations. I have not taken these too seriously because there is an arithmetic bias in the direction of a positive linkage between a group's proportion of the work force and its proportion in a given occupation. This is because the range of possible occupational values is affected by composition. Second, my primary concern has been with providing an estimate of the point at which equity is first reached.

Although scatter diagrams have been carefully considered, all of the regression equations are based on a linear model. This is because in many instances there was not that much nonlinearity within either the North or the South when they were considered separately (as in table 10.11), although there was for the entire national set of cities. But equally critical is the fact that a nonlinear fit would have meant that a few outliers would have greatly altered the general model used and this seemed undesirable enough with a linear procedure, let alone with curve fitting. Also the reader should observe that no attempt was made to adjust for missing cities or to deal with interactions between the groups present. Likewise, no attempt is made to deal with variation between cities in the work force demands.

11

Occupational Trends Earlier in this Century

The existence of broad occupational similarities between SCE Europeans and blacks in 1900, notwithstanding some significant differences already showing up in manufacturing and craft employment, is one of the main findings in the preceding chapter. For example, both groups were underrepresented in the professions as well as in trade and transportation; both were disproportionately concentrated in services. Even in the cases where they did differ, neither group was necessarily enjoying very favorable economic positions. Yet we know that the SCE groups have made enormous progress during this century such that the "ethnic effect" among white groups is relatively small by one criterion (Featherman and Hauser, 1978, pp. 475–479), and in another sense some of the new European groups now exceed the national average (Greeley, 1977). When did these occupational changes occur in the century? Were they due mainly to recent shifts or did they occur in a steady fashion or was the greatest shift earlier in the century? Why did they occur? This chapter deals with some parts of this rather complicated story.

OCCUPATIONAL CHANGES

In order to measure occupational changes among blacks and new Europeans, I resort to a technique used earlier for analyzing educational trends, namely, cross-tabulating different birth cohorts by their occupational composition in 1960. This is a stickier application because occupation is a changing characteristic whereas educational attainment is essentially fixed after the early adult years. In discussing the 1960 occupational composition of men born between 1905 and 1915 there is no assurance that they held the same jobs ten years earlier—let alone when they were the same age as some of the younger cohorts. The life cycle, cohort, and period effects are all compounded in more complicated ways than one would like. Hence, in addition to all of the reservations discussed in chapter 6, the occupational analysis does not benefit from the basic irreversibility found in the case of educational attainment. Nevertheless this procedure provides an unusually interesting way of dating key turns and shifts in the occupational fortunes of blacks and white groups.

Initially focusing on the professional occupations, consider the proportion of men in each cohort so employed. Professional occupations are specially useful because they are generally high in the prestige hierarchy and because they are probably less affected by either unemployment or changes in the life cycle than are other pursuits. One can therefore be reasonably confident that the vast bulk of comparisons reflects true cohort differences or similarities rather than merely life cycle changes. In order to match the results as closely as possible, I compare northern-born blacks living in the North in 1960 (based on Census Public Use Sample tapes employed in an earlier study by Lieberson and Wilkinson [1976]) with the published data in 1960 on various new European second generations as well as native whites of native parentage.

The most striking feature for all five new European groups is a massive jump between the 1915–1925 and the 1925–1935 cohorts in the concentration in professional jobs. The Russians (largely Jewish) were heavily concentrated in professional occupations before then, but even in their case a 50 percent jump occurs (table 11.1).[1] Poles in professional occupations doubled during this period, from .11 to .20; Austrians climbed from .15 to .23; Czechs increased from .11 to .19; and Italians also went up by more than 50 percent, from .09 to .15. This climb was not due solely to a general increase in professional employment; the analogous change for native whites of native parentage was much smaller, from .14 to .17.

By contrast, except for Jews, gains in the professional proportion for these new European groups and NWNPs were relatively slight between the 1895—1905 cohort and the next one.[2] There was somewhat more of a change between the 1905–1915 and the 1915–1925 cohorts, but still it was dwarfed by the massive shift in favor of the new Europeans that

TABLE 11.1

PROPORTION OF MALE NONFARM LABOR FORCE EMPLOYED AS PROFESSIONALS, SECOND-
GENERATION NEW EUROPEAN GROUPS, NORTHERN-BORN BLACKS, AND NATIVE WHITES
OF NATIVE PARENTAGE, 1960

	Age in 1960			
Country of origin	25—34	35—44	45—54	55—64
Austria	.23	.15	.13	.11
Czechoslovakia	.19	.11	.08	.08
Italy	.15	.09	.07	.07
Poland	.20	.11	.08	.08
Russia	.31	.20	.18	.15
Blacks (northern-born)	.08	.06	.05	.03
NWNP	.17	.14	.10	.10

SOURCE: U.S. Bureau of the Census, 1965.

occurred for those born between 1925 and 1935. These are, of course, the very same second-generation new European cohorts that experienced such a sharp upgrading in education.

It is illuminating to compare this pattern with that for northern-born blacks. Their proportion in professional occupations in the oldest cohort, .03, was below that for the new European groups, .07 and upward.[3] But the northern black level of progress was not inconsiderable in the first few cohort comparisons. Their increase to 5 percent professional in the 1905—1915 cohort exceeds in absolute amount that recorded for all but the Russian group and exceeds even them in terms of the relative gain. The pattern is less clear in the next contrast, between those 35—44 in 1960 and those 45—54. Blacks born in the North and living there gained less in an absolute sense than any of the groups, but in relative terms their rate of gain exceeded four of the five new European groups and was essentially the same as that for NWNPs. However, in the most recent period, by the criteria of either absolute or relative gain, blacks were well below the increments experienced by the SCE or NWNP populations.

There is a striking parallel between the relative rates of black—SCE European occupational change and the educational shifts discussed earlier. The sharpest new European gain was in the 1925—1935 cohort, the one that entered the job world for the most part after World War II. As was the case for education, there were earlier indications that blacks were reducing the professions gap, but then a radical set of shifts occured such that the new Europeans advanced rapidly relative to both blacks and the NWNPs. In the youngest cohort, all but second-generation Italians exceed the NWNP proportion in the professions.[4]

The question naturally arises of whether these professional changes correspond simply to those experienced educationally or whether more complex processes were operating. A simple standardization procedure provides an answer. For each age, the proportion of all white males in the United States in 1960 employed as professionals is determined in accordance with their level of education. As one might expect, these proportions vary greatly by the amount of schooling. For example, among men 25 to 34 with four or more years of college, 55 percent are employed as professionals, whereas the figure is 21 percent for those with one to three years of college. Applying the relevant age- and education-specific rates to the educational distribution for each cohort of new Europeans and northern blacks, it was possible to determine the "expected" number of professionals. The ratios of actual to expected number of professionals are shown in table 11.2. A ratio above 1.0 means that the group's proportion in the professions is greater than would be expected on the basis of its educational levels and, of course, less than unity means the opposite.

It is clear that the recent increase is largely due to changes in the groups' educational levels; among all of the new European groups in all age periods these figures tend to hover around unity. There is a small rise in all five cases between the 1915–1925 and the youngest cohort, but the increase is too small to explain the massive rise in professionals. The rise that had begun with the 1915–1925 cohort was due exclusively to increases in education because, when compared with the preceding decade, it occurred even though the A/E ratios declined for all five groups. A contrast with northern-born blacks is illuminating (although

TABLE 11.2

RATIO OF ACTUAL TO EXPECTED PROPORTION OF MALE NONFARM LABOR FORCE EMPLOYED AS PROFESSIONALS, 1960

Country of origin	Age in 1960			
	25–34	35–44	45–54	55–64
Austria	1.09	1.03	1.11	1.19
Czechoslovakia	1.14	1.09	1.12	1.25
Italy	1.10	1.02	1.11	1.23
Poland	1.12	1.04	1.08	1.13
Russia	1.05	.99	1.07	1.16
Black (northern-born)	.61	.64	.60	.41

NOTE: Expected proportion in professions derived by applying the white male cross-tabulation between education and occupation in 1960 to the educational distribution for these groups. Actual proportions in professions are given in table 11.1

the reader should remember that their figures are based on a relatively small sample). The ratio in all periods is substantially below unity, indicating that blacks hold far fewer professional jobs in each cohort than would have been expected on the basis of their levels of education. This is radically different than the pattern for the new European groups. Thus, there is a strong indication of some discriminatory functions operating to hold blacks back occupationally in a way that did not operate for the new Europeans. Black gains in education had less of an impact on their occupational structure than did new European gains in schooling because, in effect, a sizable part of the black increment was lost in the job market—at least as measured by their professional activities.

Overall Changes

There are important changes for these cohorts in other occupational pursuits as well. The index of dissimilarity provides a general and quick summary of the gaps between the groups in their overall occupational patterns. The index is less than ideal because it does not order the occupations and hence one cannot determine whether one group holds more or less desirable jobs than another—it merely summarizes the differences that exist (Johnson, 1973).[5] There are several striking features to the patterns shown in table 11.3. First, the occupational distributions of the new European second generations are far closer than are northern-born blacks to the NWNP pattern. For example, among four of the new European groups aged 55–64, their indexes range between .08 and .09 whereas the black–NWNP index is .38. This is also the case in the youngest age cohort as well. (Second-generation Russian Jews do have a high index, but this is due largely to their greater representation in professional occupations, managers and proprietors, and sales, with smaller representation than NWNPs in blue collar and service activities.)

Particularly interesting are the shifts between the cohorts of each group. Blacks were shifting quite rapidly in the older cohorts; their index of .09 between the oldest two cohorts is in excess of that experienced by any of the other groups. Blacks also had the highest index of change in the next intercohort comparison, .08 (see table 11.4). This was due largely to a massive shift out of the service occupations, which declined from 29 percent of the employment in 1960 for the 1895–1905 cohort to 15 percent of the 1915–1925 cohort. However, in the youngest two cohorts the black index of change is smallest of any of the groups, .05 as opposed to indexes ranging from .07 (Italians) to .12 and .13 (Poles and NWNPs, respectively). The overall level of change between the oldest

TABLE 11.3

OCCUPATIONAL DISSIMILARITY BETWEEN SECOND-GENERATION NEW EUROPEAN GROUPS,
NORTHERN-BORN BLACKS, AND NATIVE WHITES OF NATIVE PARENTAGE (MALES), 1960

	Age in 1960			
Comparison	25—34	35—44	45—54	55—64
NWNP versus:				
Austrian	.11	.03	.06	.08
Czechoslovakian	.07	.11	.12	.09
Italian	.05	.08	.08	.08
Polish	.04	.09	.09	.09
Russian	.30	.25	.30	.32
BLACK versus:				
Austrian	.40	.44	.38	.41
Czechoslovakian	.32	.29	.30	.32
Italian	.30	.28	.30	.30
Polish	.35	.28	.31	.30
Russian	.53	.50	.54	.58
BLACK versus:				
NWNP	.33	.36	.38	.38

and youngest cohorts specified is quite high for blacks, .17, when compared to all but the Russian group. But it is striking how small their post-World War II cohort change was.

This pattern is consistent with the earlier observation about professional occupations; blacks were different from the new Europeans at the outset, but their progress was not unfavorable until one reaches the

TABLE 11.4

INTRACOHORT INDEXES OF OCCUPATIONAL DISSIMILARITY, MALES, 1960

	Intracohort comparison			
	25—34 vs.	35—44 vs.	45—54 vs.	25—34 vs.
Group	35—44	45—54	55—64	55—64
NWNP	.13	.04	.05	.14
Black	.05	.08	.09	.17
Austrian	.10	.04	.07	.13
Czechoslovakian	.10	.04	.07	.12
Italian	.07	.03	.04	.09
Polish	.12	.04	.05	.14
Russian	.11	.06	.07	.18

1925–1935 cohort. For that age group, whose career development took place at the end of World War II (they ranged between 10 and 20 years of age in 1945), there was an incredible shift in a favorable direction in new European second-generation employment patterns. This shift far exceeded that experienced by northern-born blacks.

OCCUPATIONAL CHANGES AMONG IMMIGRANTS AND BLACKS IN SEMISKILLED WORK

There is evidence that important changes were occurring among the foreign-born in lower-level occupations long before this post-World War II period. These improvements were probably a necessary precondition to the later transformation of the second generation into professionals and highly educated persons. A group does not normally go from one extreme to the other in either the occupational or educational structure, but rather experiences a series of modest improvements. A large number of blue-collar tasks in many factories do not require highly skilled craftsmen but are performed by totally unskilled laborers or by semiskilled operatives. Earlier in this century the censuses often distinguished between these two types of work in specific industries. As a result one can determine the number of laborers in the automobile factories of Detroit as well as the number in semiskilled positions. As best as I can tell, the 1910, 1920, and 1930 censuses were rather vague about the basis on which the distinction was drawn. The only exception was an occasional reference to semiskilled workers operating machines. The classification advanced by Edwards for arranging occupations, although done in connection with the 1940 Census, probably conveys the basic difference:

> Those manual pursuits—usually routine—are considered semiskilled for the pursuance of which only a short period or no period of preliminary training usually is necessary, and which in their pursuance usually call for the exercise of only a moderate degree of judgment or of manual dexterity, and which usually call for the expenditure of only a moderate degree of muscular force.
>
> Unskilled occupations are considered to include those manual pursuits—usually routine—for the pursuance of which no special training, judgment, or manual dexterity usually is necessary, and in which the workers usually supply mainly muscular force for the performance of coarse, heavy work, or for the performance of services—usually personal. [Edwards, 1943, p. 176]

In short, semiskilled labor was less physical and demanded somewhat more judgment.

The unskilled and semiskilled parts of the blue-collar world were an area in the urban North where both black migrants from the South and the new European immigrants could seek a foothold as initial skills were probably not a major factor (see the Appendix to this chapter for a discussion of the educational differences between semiskilled and unskilled men in 1940). Is there any indication of sharp differences between these groups?

1920

The ratio of unskilled to semiskilled workers (to be referred to simply as the "ratio" and as the "concentration in unskilled work") was computed for each specific industry in the larger northern cities in 1920. Because a minimum of 50 men was required for computing a ratio, the number of possible comparisons between different groups varied because there were many cases when less than 50 blacks were employed in either category in an industry. There is a very clear general pattern; in 135 out of 152 comparisons between blacks and immigrants within specific industries of specific cities (it was not possible to distinguish between white immigrant groups), the ratio of unskilled to semiskilled was higher for blacks. In turn, in 262 out of the 270 possible comparisons, the foreign-born were more concentrated within the unskilled jobs than were second-generation whites. There is no clear hierarchy between second-generation whites and the NWNPs, with the former slightly more concentrated in unskilled work than the latter, 143 as opposed to 122 cases. The last finding is consistent with the notion that by the second generation a considerable decline existed in the disadvantage experienced by the white groups. However, it may also reflect the jobs held by rural older white groups who were migrating to the cities.

If a substantial gap existed between blacks and the white European immigrant groups in northern factories in 1920 with respect to positions for which no true craft or skill was involved, the question is raised as to why this occurred. Two strong possibilities exist, and they are not mutually exclusive. One is that these gaps reflect a simple queuing process such that employers found the immigrants more desirable than blacks and hence were inclined to favor the former for semiskilled work and relegate blacks to laboring jobs. A second is that the immigrants in 1920 on the average had been in the North longer than blacks as immigration from Europe had declined during World War I whereas blacks migrated in sizable numbers during this period. Hence the new Europeans had more experience in factories and therefore more opportunity to move from unskilled to semiskilled jobs. In sum, the black–white immigrant differences may have been due to differences in their timing of arrival in the North and so at least partially to their positions on a color-blind ladder rather than a discriminatory queue.

A 1910 Comparison

One way of dealing with this question is to examine the position of blacks and immigrants in 1910, a period when the Europeans were coming in massive numbers and before the black movement to the North had accelerated. Is there any indication at that time of higher unskilled proportions among blacks relative to immigrants? Had their relative positions changed during the 1910s in a fashion comparable to the shift in migration streams? In only a small number of cases can specific industry and city data be compared ten years earlier. This is because in many industries there were less than the 50 blacks necessary to compute a ratio. The automobile industry in Detroit provides a nice example of this. In 1920, there were more than 4,500 blacks among the 60,000 unskilled and semiskilled workers in the city's automobile factories; by contrast, in 1910, there had been only 25 blacks among the 10,000 with such jobs. This is a shame because it would have been interesting to compare the ratios in 1910 with those for 1920 when the black ratio was 4.8, far worse than the immigrant figure of 1.4.

Among the ten cases in the North and three for the South in which interdecade comparisons are possible (shown in table 11.5), the black ratio increased during the decade in all but one instance. In other words, blacks were relatively more semiskilled in 1910 than in 1920 when compared with white immigrants. Not only did the latter have a higher unskilled ratio than blacks in the stockyards of Chicago in 1910, as well as in 1920, but their ratio was higher than the black figure among those working in the blast furnaces of Columbus and Pittsburgh, the car and railroad shops of St. Louis, and the tinware factories of Baltimore. This suggests that at least an important part of the weaker black position found later in the century was due to differences in their timing of migration and hence entry into the northern labor market rather than purely a function of a discriminatory employment queue, although that factor is not ruled out. In 1910 one finds the white immigrants enjoying a relatively less advantageous position when compared with blacks in the same industry and city. This suggests not discrimination but that the

TABLE 11.5
Relative Frequency of Semiskilled and Unskilled Employment among Foreign-Born White and Black Men, 1910–1920

City and industry	Ratio of laborers to semiskilled				FBW:black ratio	
	1910		1920		1910	1920
	FBW	Black	FBW	Black		
Baltimore						
Tinware and enamelware factories	2.359	2.217	3.071	4.100	1.064	.749
Birmingham						
Blast furnaces and rolling mills	3.017	6.034	4.081	11.024	.500	.370
Chicago						
Slaughtering and packing	7.817	1.360	1.364	.833	5.748	1.637
Columbus						
Glass factories	1.648	2.647	.435	2.171	.623	.200
Blast furnaces and rolling mills	16.957	11.353	6.173	7.802	1.494	.791
Louisville						
Cigar and tobacco factories	.293	.530	.542	1.116	.553	.486
New York City						
Ship and boat building	.429	2.739	.637	.743	.157	.857
Philadelphia						
Blast furnaces and rolling mills	1.696	7.212	2.411	5.370	.235	.449
Ship and boat building	2.000	5.889	.811	3.725	.340	.218
Pittsburgh						
Blast furnaces and rolling mills	10.195	9.941	10.699	19.247	1.026	.556
St. Louis						
Blast furnaces and rolling mills	3.105	6.538	2.432	9.387	.475	.259
Car and railroad shops	5.433	3.107	1.463	2.402	1.749	.609
Cigar and tobacco factories	.121	2.443	.118	3.328	.050	.035

SOURCE: U.S. Bureau of the Census, 1914, 1923.

sizable northward migration of blacks during the World War I period coupled with the decline of European immigration led to the immigrants being the more experienced industrial population by 1920.

Developments in 1930

During the 1920s immigration from Europe declined and the black movement from the South increased considerably. Accordingly, the ladder effect would predict an increasing advantage for immigrants and further deterioration of the black position during the decade. In 73 percent of the 78 interdecade comparisons possible between 1920 and 1930, the position of the foreign-born whites improved relative to blacks. This was not due to any slackening of black advances because at the same time they improved in 67 percent of the comparisons with native whites in their relative concentration in unskilled jobs. As one would therefore expect given these facts, the foreign-born generally gained on the native whites—in 91 percent of the 78 comparisons (in 1930 it was not possible to subdivide the native white group). For whatever the reason, the fact remains that immigrants were making progress in the factories at a more rapid rate than blacks earlier in this century, although the latter's position relative to immigrants was not all that bad in 1910.[6]

In brief, foreign-born whites in the blue-collar world were upgraded relative to the positions occupied by blacks in the same industries and cities. It is not clear how many of these changes were due to a ladder effect (reflecting the fact that immigration from Europe declined sharply whereas the movement of blacks from the South accelerated) as opposed to employer preference for SCE whites over blacks. The ladder effect would occur because the new Europeans were becoming a more experienced population and so might be expected to work their way up from unskilled to semiskilled jobs over time, whereas massive numbers of new, inexperienced blacks were arriving during this period. Employer preference for SCE whites over blacks would mean the operation of a queue affected by changing composition in the labor force of the factories. If the SCE proportion of the work force declined and the black proportion increased and if a hierarchy operated, then a similar shift would also be expected in the relative numbers of semiskilled and unskilled workers. I suspect that both forces were operating to widen the occupational gap between the groups. Regardless of the reason, a key point is that there was a distinct upgrading in the position of white immigrants relative to blacks in the factories of the North with respect to jobs for which the large numbers of unskilled in both groups were potential competitors. In later decades, as we have seen, there was a sharp upgrading in the position of the second generation, at least with respect to entrance into professional occupations.

There is evidence that supports the ladder assumption, namely length of residence in the nation is linked positively to economic position. This is reported by Higgs (1971), who overdid the matter by concluding that there was no discrimination against new European immigrants earlier in this century after timing of arrival, skills, literacy, and the like were taken into account. (A more elegant analysis by McGouldrick and Tannen [1977] has modified such conclusions about the absence of discrimination). The census does not provide the necessary cross-tabulations for the periods of interest, but data reported by the United States Immigration Commission (1911c, tables 11 and 30) for industrial workers from each of 33 foreign-born white groups seem to indicate that about half of the variance between the groups in income is accounted for by differences in their median years of residence in the United States ($r = .70$). Although there is a tendency for the two subsets of groups, new and old, to have separate clusters on the scatter diagram such that the new are more recent migrants and have lower incomes, the moderate correlations obtained within each class indicate that there is something operating here independent of any old–new effect. Thus length of residence influences income separately among the old and new groups (the r within the new category is .51 and within the old category it is .43).

LABOR UNIONS

No consideration of shifts in the relative positions of blacks and new Europeans is possible without at least some analysis of the role of labor unions. But there is another reason for being interested in this topic: an examination of labor unions also gives one a feel for the general institutional forces affecting new European and black job opportunities earlier in this century. Blacks were largely excluded from labor unions until the industrial movement spearheaded by the CIO in the 1930s. (At this point I rely on the review of the trade union movement from the Civil War to 1910 by Bloch [1969, chapter 5] who provides a clear indication of the resistance to black participation and membership.) Such a resistance served to enhance the bargaining power of the unions, and this effect was particularly pronounced on the local level rather than at the national level (Bloch, 1969, pp. 79–80). The exclusion of blacks can be traced back a long way; for example, the caulkers in Boston (1724), the shipwrights, carpenters, and typographers in New York (respectively in 1802, 1806, and 1817). Again the formation of national labor unions in the mid-nineteenth century was marked by the use of one method or another to exclude blacks. None of the 32 unions in the 1860s accepted blacks (Bloch, 1969, p. 81).

During the era of the National Labor Congress between 1866 and 1878, the national organization was often sympathetic to black membership, but the specific locals kept blacks out. The Knights of Labor initially were also receptive to black membership. According to one estimate cited by Bloch (1969, pp. 88–89), at one time there were more than 400 all-black locals and a total black membership (including mixed locals) of more than 90,000. But the Knights of Labor declined around 1886 and were succeeded by the American Federation of Labor (AFL). Although espousing the desire for black membership on the national level, in effect the trade unions and locals kept blacks out for many decades or, at best, allowed them only to belong to separate black locals that were ultimately controlled by whites. A brief survey of racial policies in both the AFL and in independent unions in the 1920s and 1930s indicates massive discrimination against blacks (Bloch, 1969, pp. 104–105, 110–111). In the earlier period, the only unions even nominally giving blacks equal status were the International Ladies Garment Workers Union; the International Association of Longshoremen; the Motion Picture Projectionists Union; the Journeymen Tailors' Union of America; and the Brotherhood of Painters, Decorators and Paper Hangers of America. Bear in mind that in some cases practices were left to local jurisdiction so that locals may have barred black membership despite national acceptance. Of the remaining unions surveyed, large numbers either placed blacks in segregated or auxiliary status (including the American Federation of Teachers, the United Textile Workers, the Brotherhood of Carpenters and Joiners of America); or excluded blacks by "tacit consent" (such as in the Machinists, Electrical Workers, Sheet Metal Workers, and Journeymen Plumbers unions); or simply excluded blacks in their constitution (the case for a large number of transportation and communication unions listed by Bloch). Not much had changed by the end of the 1930s in either the AFL or the independent unions (Bloch, 1969, pp. 110–111).

The disposition of labor unions toward South–Central–Eastern Europeans is not as easily determined. But this uncertainty is itself part of the answer. For example, unlike the situation for blacks, to my knowledge there were no unions that officially excluded the new Europeans or relegated them to second-class membership or a segregated position. To be sure, there was considerable antipathy toward these people. Early in the century union leaders often found that native

American workers or Northwestern European immigrants had a strong desire to disassociate themselves from these new people either at work or in their union membership (Brody, 1965, pp. 42–43). The new Europeans were opposed because they were seen as cheap labor competition (Higham, 1955, p. 45; Taft, 1964, pp. 305–307). Organized labor attempted to block and discourage immigration and also supported various laws designed to restrict competition, in some cases directed at immigrants generally rather than those from the new sources.

> Under the spur of widespread unemployment the United States House of Representatives passed a bill in 1886 prohibiting the employment on public works of any alien who had not declared his intention to become a citizen. The Senate failed to act on the proposal, but some of the states proceeded to adopt regulations to the same effect. In 1889, Illinois, Wyoming, and Idaho banned nondeclarant aliens from both state and municipal projects. [Higham, 1955, p. 46]

At the tail end of the century, some unions began to exclude aliens from membership if they had not declared their intention to become citizens. New York State and Pennsylvania in the mid-1890s excluded all non-citizens from public works jobs. A few years later, in 1897, Pennsylvania required a special state tax on the wages of alien workers and introduced residence and language requirements for certification as a miner (Higham, 1955, p. 72). Likewise Arizona passed a law in the 1890s, supported by the miners, requiring that in places employing more than five people at least 80 percent of the workers be American citizens (Higham, 1955, p. 183).

There is certainly evidence that in some cases opposition was directed toward specific SCE European groups. According to the labor historian, Henry Pelling, the building trades discriminated against Jewish craftsmen, limiting them to less desirable work (1960, p. 212). Organized labor early in this century began to distinguish between old and new sources of immigration and hoped to reduce the latter's competition (Higham, 1955, p. 112). Not only were the new European groups largely unskilled at a time when the union movement was oriented toward craftsmen, but also there was some definite prejudice against these groups even on the part of the labor leaders (Jones, 1960, pp. 222–223). Similarly, according to Lopreato (1970, p. 96), Italian immigrants were initially not welcomed by labor unions.

Nevertheless, the dispositions toward the new European groups were not the same as those held toward blacks. There is both descriptive evidence in support of this contention as well as some indirect empirical support.

An Empirical Comparison

The detailed occupational data for 1900, analyzed in the preceding chapter, were helpful in that they showed that the new Europeans did have greater employment in all sorts of manufacturing jobs, a category that also includes the crafts. However, here we are concerned with progress over time during this century and the role that unions played. Accordingly, I considered the detailed data for occupation by nativity for 1950 reported in Hutchinson (1956, table A-2a). With these special tabulations it is possible to compare the second generation of the new and old European groups with blacks (the latter in the U.S. Bureau of the Census, 1956, table 3). One would prefer detailed union membership data by ethnic origin, but that is not possible. Accordingly, in looking at the different craftsman participation rates, one has to bear in mind that some or all of these occupants may not belong to unions. Such ethnic-specific data were not available for an earlier period.

The second-generation white groups of Northwestern European origin on the average have a larger segment of their nonfarm experienced civilian labor force employed as craftsmen than does the average new European second generation, 25.3 percent versus 20.6 percent. However, both compare quite favorably with the 10.1 percent of blacks employed as craftsmen or the 16.3 percent of the second-generation Mexicans.[7] This is not entirely helpful because a low figure could reflect a group's concentration in other positions that may be even more rewarding. For example, second-generation Russians barely exceed the black level, but no doubt for radically different reasons, namely their concentration in even more attractive activities. Accordingly, it is helpful to compare the relative numbers of craftsmen to semiskilled operatives. Of the two subsets of blue-collar work, on the aggregate one would expect the craft jobs to be more desirable. How do the groups compare in their relative frequency within such forms of employment? A very sharp difference is found. All ten of the Northwestern European groups have ratios in excess of unity (meaning there are more craftsmen than operatives); all 11 of the new European second-generation groups have ratios below unity (table 11.6). The mean new European ratio, .80, although substantially below the Northwestern ratio of 1.39, is still far above the black ratio of .38. The new European figure is roughly midway between the black and old European ratios of craftsmen to operatives, albeit somewhat closer to the former.

It is helpful to compare these groups in terms of their concentration in specific craft occupations. In only a handful does the average new European group exceed Northwestern Europeans in their percentage of

TABLE 11.6
RELATIVE EMPLOYMENT OF MEN IN CRAFT AND SEMISKILLED OCCUPATIONS, 1960

Group	Percentage craftsmen, foremen, and kindred	Ratio of craftsmen to semiskilled
NWNP	23.0	.97
Blacks	10.1	.38
Second-generation white groups:		
Northwestern Europe	25.3	1.39
Denmark	27.8	1.58
England and Wales	24.0	1.32
France	24.4	1.30
Germany	27.2	1.38
Ireland	20.0	1.16
Netherlands	27.0	1.17
Norway	25.7	1.54
Scotland	23.2	1.33
Sweden	26.6	1.60
Switzerland	27.0	1.52
South—Central—Eastern Europe	20.6	.80
Austria	21.1	.85
Czechoslovakia	26.5	.88
Finland	25.4	.89
Greece	13.3	.64
Hungary	23.5	.85
Italy	21.5	.74
Lithuania	21.9	.77
Poland	22.9	.70
Roumania	13.3	.89
Russia	11.9	.86
Yugoslavia	25.2	.76
Mexico	16.3	.55

SOURCE: Hutchinson, 1956, table A-2a.
NOTE: Only nonfarm workers included for computation of percentages.

the nonfarm labor force in such employment. The exceptions are rather interesting. About 0.2 percent of the average new European group is employed as tailors or furriers, which is about 2.5 times greater than the comparable figure for old European groups (table 11.7). Likewise, the ratio favors the new with respect to bakers, construction machine operators, toolmakers, and miscellaneous metal workers. The very opposite occurs for many of the traditional construction crafts. The average for new Europeans in carpentering is 50 percent of that for the old groups, about two-thirds in the case of electricians and masons, 60 percent for painters, and 70 percent for plumbers. Overall, the new Europeans and blacks are well behind second-generation whites from the Northwestern European sources,.the latter's percentage is exceeded in only five of the 17 specified occupations by the SCE and in only three occupations by blacks (masons, miscellaneous building, and tailors).

The position of the new Europeans is distinctly more favorable than that of blacks—and that is really the key issue. In only three of the 17 occupations do blacks exceed the average new European second-generation group in the percentage of the nonfarm work force employed in the job. These are: masons, 0.68 versus 0.37; miscellaneous building, 0.84 versus 0.43; and a minuscule black advantage among painters, 0.85 versus 0.84. A regression analysis for these 17 occupations shows an enormous difference between blacks and new Europeans with respect to craft occupations. Regressing the average new European percentage of nonfarm labor force in each occupation (X_1) on the comparable percentage for the average Northwestern European group (X_2), one finds a close linkage, r is .9335, with $r^2 = .87$. This is not a terribly odd finding because crafts that occupy a relatively large segment of one group's labor force might well be expected to be relatively important to another group as well. The regression is the key here, $X_1 = .1567 + .7082X_2$; the mean new European percentage in most of these occupations is lower than what would be expected if they held the same position as the second generation from earlier European sources. However, the distinctive position of blacks (X_3) is indicated not only by the even lower regression coefficient, but by the rather low correlation found between their relative percentages in each craft occupation and that for new (r = .5260, $r^2 = .28$) or old European groups (r = .5824, $r^2 = .34$) The regression of blacks on the old European proportions in each occupation, $X_3 = .2351 + .2422X_2$, also shows how much weaker the black position is.

In short, the available empirical evidence indicates that blacks did indeed fare less well than the new Europeans in the highly desirable craft occupations (although one should bear in mind that the new Europeans did not do as well as whites of Northwestern European origin). To be sure, the evidence is indirect because data on union membership are not generally available for the white groups and because the available data do not deal with the population most analogous to second-generation new Europeans, northern-born blacks living in the North. But the gaps shown above are so large and so unfavorable to blacks that there is little doubt that the new Europeans were eventually less shut out by the desirable craft unions than were blacks, even if the initial disposition to the former was not particularly favorable.

TABLE 11.7
Nonfarm Male Labor Force Employed in Specified Crafts, 1960

Occupation	NWNP	Northwestern second generation	South–Central–Eastern second generation	Black	Mexican second generation
			Percentage employed		
Bakers	.20	.24	.39	.22	.59
Carpenters	3.10	2.98	1.63	1.35	1.88
Construction machinery operators	.69	.50	.64	.36	.52
Electricians and electrical servicemen	1.78	1.89	1.24	.19	.73
Foremen (NEC)	2.35	2.88	2.12	.33	.86
Machinists	1.41	1.82	1.77	.28	.34
Masons	.42	.54	.37	.68	.56
Mechanics and repairmen, automobile	2.19	1.67	1.54	1.28	1.90
Mechanics and repairmen, except automobile	3.17	3.51	3.15	1.24	2.05
Painters, paperhangers, and glaziers	1.31	1.51	.84	.85	1.09
Plumbers and pipe fitters	.87	1.03	.73	.33	.61
Printing craftsmen	.70	1.05	.84	.14	.63
Tailors and furriers	.05	.09	.23	.18	.15
Toolmakers, die makers, and setters	.35	.67	.76	.02	.15
Miscellaneous building craftsmen	.51	.57	.43	.84	1.03
Miscellaneous metal-working craftsmen	1.09	1.27	1.53	.76	1.21
Other craftsmen and kindred workers	2.80	3.09	2.36	1.09	1.99

SOURCE: Hutchinson, 1956, table A-2a.
NOTE: Percentages for Northwestern and SCE European groups are means for 10 and 11 individual groups, respectively.
NEC: Not elsewhere classified.

Why the Less Favorable Situation?

There are a number of basic forces that led to blacks enjoying a less favorable position than the new Europeans eventually did in the craft unions. Involved here, in one way or another, are the following factors: participation as strikebreakers; the general standard of living of the groups; alternative forms of employment; societal dispositions toward the groups; attitudes of employers; occupational queuing; and the orientation toward the trade union movement of the groups themselves. For analytical purposes one may distinguish between some of these causes, but they make sense when viewed in toto as a complicated nonrecursive system with numerous feedbacks.

In searching through the enormous literature on trade unions, one finds very little that directly compares blacks and the new Europeans, but from time to time there is some indication that the nation's dispositions toward these groups differed such that some forms of open discrimination against blacks were not acceptable if directed toward the new Europeans. Not that the impulse was absent, for if the unionists were motivated by a desire to restrict the labor supply, maintain wages, and a concern for unity and a common bond, then there would be much to be said for keeping out these strange European newcomers. One need only turn to DuBois's observations of the situation in Philadelphia at the turn of the century.

> Without strong effort and special influence it is next to impossible for a Negro in Philadelphia to get regular employment in most of the trades, except [that] he work as an independent workman and take small transient jobs.
>
> The chief agency that brings about this state of affairs is public opinion; if they were not intrenched, and strongly intrenched, back of an active prejudice or at least passive acquiescence in this effort to deprive Negroes of a decent livelihood, both trades unions and arbitrary bosses would be powerless to do the harm they now do; where, however, a large section of the public more or less openly applaud the stamina of a man who refuses to work with a "Nigger," the results are inevitable. The object of the trades union is purely businesslike; it aims to restrict the labor market, just as the manufacturer aims to raise the price of his goods. Here is a chance to keep out of the market a vast number of workmen, and the unions seize the chance save in cases where they dare not as in the case of the cigar-makers and coal-miners. If they could keep out the foreign workmen in the same way they would; but here public opinion within and without their ranks forbids hostile action. [DuBois, 1967, pp. 332–333]

In a certain sense, we can say that blacks were lower on the general societal queue for all rights, and therefore, if society was to accept differential access to union membership, it would be most likely to accept such restrictions if directed at blacks. As Bloch (1969, p. 79) observes, because black inferiority was socially sanctioned and embedded in the social structure and beliefs, it was possible for unions to resist blacks more aggressively.

To a certain degree, the new Europeans and blacks posed different problems for labor unions. After the demise of slavery, whites in the North feared that they might someday face competition from blacks who would be prepared to work for far lower wages than the existing level (see, for example, Drake and Cayton, 1945, p. 271). This fear after the Civil War of future competition from blacks was reflected in the presidential address in 1867 at the National Labor Congress as well as in their committee report on black labor (Bloch, 1969, p. 83). This new source of potential competition was already *in* the nation. By contrast, although new Europeans were a similar threat, in the sense that they would also work for lower wages, there were important differences. The solution was seen more in terms of restricting immigration rather than in purely restricting those already in the nation. Because potential European competitors included more than just migrants from SCE Europe but migrants from the ancestral homelands of the native American white workers, the issue was broader than a purely ethnic one and required answers that were posed more generally toward the SCE sources. However, it was true that the SCE would work for even lower wages than northwestern European immigrants and were victims of more antipathy.

To be sure, as noted earlier, the unions found that drawing in the immigrants could alienate the native white members. But still they initially opposed only the controlled or stimulated migration of foreign workers. At first they did not object to self-motivated migration in the absence of special inducements (Higham, 1955, p. 49). Toward the end of the nineteenth century, organized labor shifted toward vigorous opposition to immigration even if it was purely voluntary (Higham, 1955, pp. 70–73, 163). The restrictionism on the part of organized labor became even stronger after World War I (Higham, 1955, pp. 305–306). Despite these difficulties and although one comes across accounts of native Americans refusing to work with these newcomers, there is nothing comparable to the list of 50 strikes between 1882 and 1900 of whites opposed to working with blacks compiled by the United States Department of Labor (reported in Wesley, 1967, p. 237). One speculates that the SCE were ahead of blacks at times of expansion when there were not enough of the older stock whites to fill some of the craft positions.

Not only did the unions have a different disposition toward the new Europeans, but so too did the employers. There is no rigorous study that I know of which examines employers' attitudes toward blacks and the SCE groups, but the evidence that I have patched together seems to indicate a more favorable disposition toward the latter. Although increasing numbers of blacks were employed in the steel mills during World War I because of the absence of white immigrants—by the end of the war they were from 11 to 14 percent of the workers in Illinois, Indiana, and Pennsylvania—they were not viewed as satisfactory replacements:

> The new workers appeared poorly suited to the job demands in steel, had a very high turnover rate, and frequently clashed with whites in the mills. Management, accustomed to the solid peasantry of Eastern Europe, did not take readily to the black workers. "It would be better," the Inland Steel president said after the war, ". . . if the mills could continue to recruit their forces from [Europe]. The Negroes should remain in the South." [Brody, 1965, p. 46]

On the other hand, a vice-president of the Packard Company found the 700 blacks employed in Detroit in 1922 for both skilled and unskilled labor good workers who were "considerably better" than the average immigrant (Wesley, 1967, p. 298).

On the whole, the general dispositions of employers were less than favorable. Haynes quotes the general manager of the Detroit Employers Association in his summary of what leading employers in the city had experienced with blacks who were hired during the World War I shortage:

> He thought some employers were highly pleased with Negro workmen and some were not. He said, "There are two lines of adverse opinion about the Negro as a workman: First, nine-tenths of the complaints of employers against the Negro is that he is too slow. He does not make the speed that the routine of efficient industry demands. He is lacking in the regularity demanded by the routine of industry day by day.
>
> "Second, the Negro has been observed to be disinclined to work out-of-doors when the cold weather comes. Employers have discussed this and have not found the Negro satisfactory on this point. *Unless the Negroes overcome this practice employers will turn to other sources of supply when their present extreme needs are past.*" [Haynes, 1918, pp. 17–18, emphasis added]

A survey of Minneapolis, published jointly by the city's Urban League and a settlement house, found that the vast majority of employers surveyed indicated that they would not employ blacks if any were to apply. Of the 145 so refusing, most gave racial factors as their reason: mixing races is undesirable (72); public objects to Negroes (2); prefers white (3); not interested in Negro employment (6) [Harris, 1926, pp. 25–26]. I ignore here such other reasons as mentally incompetent or unreliable and lazy, which may be viewed as clearly stereotyped responses. In fact then there was the repeat of a simple negative disposition toward hiring blacks. Harris's survey also disclosed clear evidence of a queuing process operating to the disadvantage of blacks.

> During the war most of the industries in Minneapolis witnessed an acute labor shortage as was generally characteristic of industry throughout the country. At that time many Negroes found employment in various manufacturing and mechanical enterprises where hitherto but few Negroes had been employed. But at present some of these establishments either refuse to employ Negroes or say they will use them only in capacity of janitors or porters. The Minneapolis Steel and Machinery Company, which at the time of our investigations had about 10 Negro workers, employed upwards of a hundred during the World War. The Crown Iron Works and several other concerns, which do not now employ Negroes, employed them during the war. Two employers who were interviewed said that they would only use Negro labor during a labor shortage. It stands to reason that any employer facing a labor shortage would utilize the most available supply of labor. Employers who now shrink from "mixing" black and white workers would find means of placating the white workers' alleged aversion to Negro workers were they in dire need of labor. Of course few Negro workers would be so lacking in social sympathy as to attempt to induce employers to supplant white workers with Negro labor, or so foolishly race conscious as to request the indiscriminate employment of Negroes without regard to their qualifications. On the other hand, the very fact that employers, generally, are very much inclined toward using Negro labor during extreme business exaltation is all the more reason that Negroes should be given an even break in securing work during normal times or when depressions set in. [Harris, 1926, pp. 27–28]

A trade publication, complete with a reference to the role of "singing Negroes," reported a direct comparison between blacks and immigrants, largely to the disfavor of the former:

> It is observed that negroes are cleaner in their personal habits than some of the European aliens. They use the shower baths more often. They are of a happier disposition, easier to get along with, are less suspicious, more tractable, than those of the quiet, sullen type. Offsetting these characteristics, are a number of important indictments.

The negroes, plant managers say, are less dependable for steady work: they lay off on the slightest pretexts, especially on Mondays and Tuesday. They are less desirous of making money by getting ahead, are fond of gambling, flashy clothes; and generally are "broke."

Negroes in certain occupations show more aptitude and skill than do those of the alien white races; they are particularly good for hot and heavy work in foundries.

A "singing negro" especially is regarded as a prize in a gang of laborers, and he is paid higher wages some times for the influence he exerts over lazy comrades. The singer chuckles, "takes hold" and leads his crew in a song, that like the sailorman's "Yo heave ho!" gets work done. [Hain, 1923, p. 733)

The point, again, is not whether these are valid or objective judgments—that is irrelevant to the issue at hand—but that a definite predisposition in favor of the immigrants existed. DuBois 1967, p. 337 cites cases of employees being fired after it was discovered that they were light-skinned blacks.

Because of these employer dispositions only to hire blacks at a discount if there were sufficient white workers available, it was not uncommon for blacks who did join unions and subsequently sought union wages to be replaced. A number of examples of this were illustrated by the Chicago Commission on Race Relations' report (1922) after the Chicago race riot of 1919. The International Ladies' Garment Workers' Union in that city encountered a situation in which black women were paid less than white women.

Shortly after the union had organized them [black women] they were locked out. Later the employer was willing to settle "providing you sent us a set of white workers." The union refused to do this and called a strike.

The union claimed that in many recent cases where Negro girls were sent out on jobs the employers would refuse them when they found out that they had to pay them the same scale as white workers. [Chicago Commission, 1922, p. 415]

The Flat Janitor's Union had a similar report: "The experience of the union is that as soon as a Negro is taken into the union and demands the union scale the owner calls up the union and says, 'If I have to pay these wages I'm going to get a good white man' " (Chicago Commission, 1922, p. 415). In like fashion, the president of a Chicago local of the International Brotherhood of Firemen and Oilers observed some employers "to only use the Negro when he would want to maintain a lower standard of wages, but when compelled by force of circumstances to pay a living rate of wages, immediately a request would be made on the organization that the Negro be removed and a white man furnished" (Chicago Commission, 1922, p. 434).

As far as being strikebreakers, it is hard to determine whether one group was more often placed in that position than the other. Certainly the reputation blacks had as strikebreakers was not without truth. To a certain degree, this was a role that was forced on them; often it was the only time that they would be hired. Moreover, because the unions on strike were likely to be opposed to blacks anyway, there was little reason to avoid injuring their strike. A strike, from the black perspective, meant a rare chance to obtain a place from an employer that was ordinarily off limits. White employers were not adverse to importing blacks especially for this purpose. Franklin (1956, p. 309) refers to black ship caulkers being brought from Portsmouth, Virginia, in 1867 to break a white strike in Boston. Blacks broke the stockyards strike of 1904 in Chicago—indeed they were admitted into the union afterwards (Chicago Commission, 1922, pp. 412–413). It is estimated that more than 30,000 blacks were recruited to help break the great steel strike of 1919 (Brody, 1965, p. 162).

On the other hand, it should be noted that there were a number of instances in which new European groups were used as strikebreakers. According to Pelling (1960, p. 88), Czechs, Poles, and Italians were used as strikebreakers late in the nineteenth century. Similarly, carloads of Eastern Europeans were brought under armed guard from Pittsburgh and New York during a bloody miner's strike in 1884 in the Hocking Valley (Higham, 1955, p. 48). Italian women scabbed during the great waistmakers strike of 1909–1910 (Glazer and Moynihan, 1963, p. 191). Hourwich (1922) indicates there were many instances where Southern and Eastern Europeans were used as strikebreakers, although he notes cases where native whites also scabbed. He cites the 1904 miners' strike in the Alabama District when strikebreakers included Magyars, Slovaks, Greeks, Serbs, Italians, Finns, *and* native whites (pp. 345–346). According to Jones (1960), the use of immigrant strikebreakers helped to destroy the Knights of Labor. "Strike after strike in the Pennsylvania coalfields in the 1870's and early 1880's was smashed when employers brought in Slavic, Hungarian, and Italian labor" (p. 222).

Nevertheless, the evidence indicates that new Europeans participated more fully in unions at an earlier period. Part of this reflects historical linkages with the trade union movement that go back to Europe.

Immigrants from the Russian Empire, Poland, and Italy had particularly strong labor union backgrounds.

> Previous to the revolution of 1905, labor organizations and strikes were treated as conspiracies in Russia. . . . According to the statistics published by the Russian government, the total number of strikers in factories and mines during the year 1905 was 2,915,000. This figure does not include the railways and the postal-telegraph service, which were completely paralyzed by the strikes of 1905. . . . The total number of strikers for the year 1905 may therefore be conservatively estimated at 3,672,000. The highest number of strikers recorded in the United States for any one year between 1881 and 1905 was 533,000, in 1902. The strikes in the factories of the Russian Empire in 1905 affected 32.6 percent of all establishments under factory inspection, comprising 60 percent of all wage-earners.

> The strikes in the Russian Empire drew together wage-earners of all those nationalities which make up the bulk of our immigration from Russia: Hebrews, Poles, Lithuanians, Russians, and Ruthenians (South Russians).

> It is evident that a good many of the immigrants from Russia, Poland, and Italy bring with them an understanding of the aims of organized labor. These immigrants serve as a nucleus of organization among their countrymen. This fact has been brought to the attention of the American public in the recent strikes of the garment workers and textile mill operatives. [Hourwich, 1922, pp. 349–351]

Hourwich also reports data on the activity of industrial unions in Italy, including a rapid growth in the union movement among agricultural workers. Thus from 1901 to 1904 there were 3,000 strikes involving 620,000 workers (p. 349).

In the very same steel strike of 1919 in which blacks were scabs, the new Europeans were very active strikers and showed more staying power than some of the other whites (Brody, 1965, pp. 132, 151, 156–157). This was a pattern that was repeated in a number of other strikes. Some of the biggest ones, with the greatest examples of aggressiveness among union members, involved the new Europeans (Higham, 1955, p. 225). According to Peter Roberts, the Slavs and Italians were brought into the Pennsylvania anthracite fields because they were supposed to be docile and would help break the power of the Anglo-Saxon miners (reprinted in Handlin, 1959, pp. 68–69). But Slavs soon proved themselves to be strong union men. Indeed, they were often at the forefront of the strikers (Greene, 1968, p. 212). Hourwich has

gathered considerable evidence, albeit indirect, to support his contention that the new Europeans were strongly oriented to unions in short
order (1922, pp. 30–34, 325–328, 339–343, 373, 411–413, 446–449, 456).

Even if the new Europeans differed from blacks in their initial dispositions toward labor unions, it is safe to say that much of the gap in
participation reflects differences in the relative gains and losses that
might be achieved. After all, it is unlikely that most people would not
hop aboard a "good thing" if the trade union movement offered them a
more favorable economic situation. Not only was simply getting a job a
more critical variable for blacks—as opposed to upgrading conditions at
work—but as we have seen the union movement often meant a greater
hurdle to keeping one's job. When A. Philip Randolph organized the
Brotherhood of Sleeping Car Porters, he had to contend directly with the
distrust blacks held of the American Federation of Labor (Bloch, 1969,
p. 101). There are other examples of black suspicion of unionization. A
survey of blacks in the garment industry of New York City in the early
1930s found considerable hesitancy to join the union. They were afraid
that equal pay and working conditions would lead the employers to
substitute white for black workers and that the unions would give
preferential placement to white workers (Bloch, 1969, p. 108). As a
consequence, the unions were often seen as an instrument for whites.
Blacks felt "that the only way that they can ever make any headway in
the industry [was] to stick with the boss and then when there [was] a
strike to step in and take the jobs . . . left there" (Chicago Commission
on Race Relations, 1922, p. 429). In similar fashion, blacks were initially
fearful when the United Automobile Workers of the CIO first organized
the Ford plants in 1941, but then "supported the union enthusiastically
when they found that their conditions were actually improved under the
new contract" (Franklin, 1956, p. 532).

In short, a complicated feedback system both caused and maintained
the black disadvantage within the trade union movement. Their participation in the labor union movement was more difficult because of their
lower position in society generally and their lower position on the
employment queue specifically. In turn, the lack of opportunities for
union membership made blacks more willing strikebreakers for a longer
time and lowered the wage levels at which employment would be
accepted—characteristics that hardly improved their standing in the
eyes of white unionists. The lower level of black participation in the
union movement is both the product of other forces as much as it is an
independent force that helped to further handicap blacks and maintain
the conditions that initially led to their weak position. Although there

were important exceptions at earlier points, for example, the miners and the stockyard workers, it was not until the industrial union movement of the 1930s, which was oriented toward all workers employed in an industry rather than to specific occupations, that the major organizing efforts involving blacks as relative equals occurred.

FEEDBACKS MORE GENERALLY: EDUCATION AND OCCUPATION

It is important to recognize that the union movement and its relation to black–SCE employment are excellent examples of the "Vicious Circle" and the "Principle of Cumulation" described by Myrdal (1944, pp. 75–78; 1065–1070)—a situation confronted by blacks in a variety of domains. As Myrdal observed, the principle of cumulation could work to a group's advantage as well as its disadvantage, depending on the direction of the initial thrust. All evidence seems to indicate that new Europeans and blacks differed precisely in this regard. It is almost certain that a wide variety of feedback systems developed here. For example, the poorer occupational rewards received by blacks with a given level of educational attainment compared to those achieved by even the foreign-born affected both the groups' disposition toward education as a means for mobility as well as the economic resources available to parents who wanted their children to remain in school for longer spans.

Shown in table 11.8 is the occupational composition of white immigrants living outside the South in 1940. The first of three columns gives the actual percentage in the broad occupational category for white immigrants of a specific age and sex; the second and third columns give the expected percentage based on the educational distribution of immigrants and the linkage between occupation and education for, respectively, native whites and blacks. These figures show that the immigrants were doing far better occupationally than blacks with comparable education in the North. Consider, for example, service occupations. About a quarter of working immigrant women 25–34 years of age were employed in such jobs in 1940. This is 5 percent more than would be expected if these women were following the rates for native white women with the same levels of formal education, 26.4 as against 20.4 percent. Some discrepancy in this direction would be expected because a fair number of the immigrants were not educated in English and so the value of their education would be more limited than that for native whites. The contrast with black women is therefore all the more spectacular. Were immigrant women to have followed the same occupational pursuits as those held by black women with comparable education, three-fourths of those 25–34 would have been employed in service occupations. A massive gap exists here and elsewhere in educational rewards.[8]

Even a rapid run through the figures in table 11.8 can give the reader a feel for how much less encouragement blacks received in using the educational system as a pathway to economic opportunity. This must have had considerable consequence on the dispositions toward education and the opportunities offered. Consider nonfarm laborers among men. From 8.8 to 12.6 percent of white immigrants in different ages were so employed. In each case, this was somewhat in excess of what would have occurred if the rates for native whites with comparable educational levels had applied (from 7.8 to 10.1 percent). Nevertheless, from 22 to 25 percent would have been working as laborers if the education-by-occupation rates for blacks were operating for immigrant whites. The discrepancy for service workers among both sexes is even more spectacular. The percentage of immigrant men employed in these jobs is not trivial, roughly 10 percent, and is certainly in excess of that for native white men of comparable education, but still in all cases the immigrant percentage would have tripled if they had followed the black patterns, 30 percent instead of 10 percent.

By contrast, immigrant men are far more active as proprietors, in clerical/sales, or as craftsmen than they would be if the black linkages between occupation and education had applied to them. This is also striking for women employed in the white-collar clerical and sales occupations. If immigrant white women in the youngest age category had followed the black pattern for their levels of education, 3.9 percent of the foreign-born white women would have held these white-collar jobs. In point of fact, 27.3 percent were so employed. Again the reader is reminded that these rates are below those among native white women with comparable levels of formal education, but still the immigrant women are well ahead of blacks. The actual percentage of immigrant men employed as operatives and as nonfarm laborers, when compared with the figures expected on the basis of the black linkage between education and occupation, tends to further support the conclusion made in the Appendix of this chapter about immigrant–black differences in semiskilled and unskilled work.

It is almost certain that these differentials between blacks and new Europeans in the occupational rewards achieved with a given level of education must have had a feedback effect on new waves of blacks, both in terms of the hope that education offered them and the ability of parents to keep their children in school beyond the mandatory years.

TABLE 11.8
ACTUAL AND EXPECTED OCCUPATIONAL DISTRIBUTION OF FOREIGN-BORN WHITES IN NONSOUTH, 1940

Sex and occupational group	25—34			35—44		
		Expected based on			Expected based on	
	Actual	Native white	Black	Actual	Native white	Black
Male						
Professional and semiprofessional	6.0	6.4	6.1	4.9	5.2	4.6
Farmers and farm managers	2.5	8.4	0.5	3.3	13.4	0.6
Proprietors, managers, and officials (except farm)	9.3	6.8	2.0	13.5	10.6	3.2
Clerical, sales, and kindred workers	14.8	14.1	6.0	9.2	12.1	5.8
Craftsmen, foremen, and kindred workers	19.2	14.8	6.8	22.9	18.3	9.1
Operatives and kindred workers	24.0	27.1	20.6	23.4	22.0	20.5
Service workers	10.5	5.2	33.7	10.1	5.8	30.4
Farm laborers and foremen	4.9	7.1	2.5	2.7	4.5	1.5
Laborers, except farm and mine	8.8	10.1	21.9	10.0	8.0	24.3
Female						
Professional and semiprofessional	8.4	10.0	4.9	7.5	8.9	3.5
Farmers and farm managers	0.2	0.2	0	0.4	1.2	0
Proprietors, managers, and officials (except farm)	3.0	2.5	0.6	6.0	5.6	1.5
Clerical, sales, and kindred workers	27.3	32.8	3.9	16.1	28.4	2.3
Craftsmen, foremen, and kindred workers	1.7	1.3	0.2	2.3	1.9	0.5
Operatives and kindred workers	31.6	30.6	12.1	35.5	26.8	12.6
Service workers	26.4	20.4	77.3	30.3	25.1	78.5
Farm laborers and foremen	0.5	0.6	0.2	0.8	1.1	0.1
Laborers, except farm and mine	0.8	1.4	0.8	1.0	1.1	1.0

TABLE 11.8 (Continued)

| | 45—54 | | | 55—64 | |
| | Expected based on | | | Expected based on | |
Actual	Native white	Black	Actual	Native white	Black
3.2	3.7	3.5	3.5	3.6	4.5
6.0	19.6	1.6	11.0	25.0	3.0
14.2	11.4	4.0	13.8	11.8	5.1
6.7	10.1	5.8	6.9	9.2	5.5
22.8	19.5	8.6	22.0	17.1	7.6
22.6	17.0	17.5	17.9	12.6	11.8
9.8	6.2	31.0	9.8	7.7	36.4
2.1	4.3	2.7	2.9	5.2	3.4
12.6	8.2	25.3	12.1	7.8	22.7
7.1	8.3	2.6	8.4	8.2	2.5
1.5	2.5	0.1	3.2	4.3	0.3
8.6	7.7	1.8	9.5	8.2	2.2
10.3	19.5	1.8	8.3	14.1	1.4
2.4	2.1	0.4	2.2	1.9	0.4
30.2	22.3	9.9	19.6	16.2	6.6
37.5	35.2	82.7	46.6	45.0	85.2
1.1	1.3	0.1	1.1	0.7	0.2
1.3	1.1	0.6	1.2	1.5	1.3

CONCLUSION

This chapter started off asking about the forces and events during this century which moved new Europeans and blacks into rather different occupational paths. The gap did not widen in a steady manner during this century—indeed, at times it looked as if blacks might catch up, or at least hold their own, in the professional domain. But the gap seemed to widen especially for those whose occupational entrance occurred after the end of World War II. This widening took place at the same time as the cohorts were improving sharply in their educational levels. In the next chapter it will be important to consider the events occurring around the time of World War II which greatly improved the new European situation without similar consequences for blacks.

Blue-collar jobs were important for both black and new European immigrant men because they offered many opportunities for the vast bulk within each group who possessed minimal skills. An analysis of the relative numbers of new Europeans and blacks placed in the semiskilled and unskilled jobs within such domains indicates a progressive widening of the gap to the disadvantage of blacks. Two possible forces may have generated this pattern: queuing and/or a simple occupational ladder. The deterioration of the black position at a time when the new Europeans were no longer migrating in large numbers (and blacks were) suggests that at least part of the widening is due simply to a ladder effect. However, there is certainly enough evidence presented in the preceding chapter and in the discussion of unions here to support the proposition that blacks were also lower on the queue for good jobs.

The union analysis is of value not merely because it points to another source of the new European advantage over blacks in the occupational world, but because of the complex set of interrelationships which are found to exist between a group's societal position generally, its position in the work world, the attitudes of unions toward them, the disposition of employers, the work situation in the areas of origin before migration, and the actual behavior of the groups. Unfortunately such an analysis cannot be carried out for all domains, but there is good reason to suspect that the complex set of interactions observed with respect to unions would apply elsewhere as well. One part of this complex pattern is illuminated by analyzing the influence of education on immigrant occupations in 1940. The occupations of immigrants are compared with the patterns to be expected if the linkage between occupation and education was operating on them in the same way as it operated for native whites and for blacks. The immigrants do not do as well as the linkage between occupation and education for native whites would lead us to expect, but they do massively better than what blacks with comparable educational levels are able to attain. This must in no small way be due to the much more severe discrimination against blacks. The complex interaction is illustrated because these events affected educational incentives for the next generation of blacks in a radically different way than for the next generation of SCE whites.

APPENDIX

The analysis of semiskilled operatives and unskilled laborers in this chapter did not entail educational controls because it was impossible for the period under study. However, such a consideration can be made for 1940. Table 11.9 indicates that there was only a small difference between operatives and laborers in their median years of schooling, 8.3 and 8.0,

TABLE 11.9
MEDIAN YEARS OF SCHOOLING FOR EMPLOYED MALE SEMISKILLED AND UNSKILLED
WORKERS, 1940

Industry	Northeast		North-Central	
	Operatives	Laborers	Operatives	Laborers
All manufacturing	8.3	8.0	8.6	8.2
Food and kindred	8.3	8.1	8.5	8.4
Lumber, furniture, and lumber products	8.4	8.2	8.4	8.2
Paper, paper products, and printing	8.7	8.2	8.7	8.6
Chemicals and petroleum and coal products	8.7	7.9	8.8	8.3
Stone, clay, and glass products	8.3	7.9	8.4	8.3
Iron and steel (excluding special metal industry)	8.3	7.9	8.5	7.9
Nonferrous metals and their products	8.6	7.8	9.0	8.3
Machinery	8.9	8.2	9.0	8.6
Automobiles and automobile equipment	8.7	8.3	8.6	8.2
Transportation equipment, except auto	8.7	8.2	8.8	7.9

SOURCE: U.S. Bureau of the Census, 1943e.

respectively, for all manufacturing jobs in the Northeast and 8.6 versus 8.2 in the North-Central states. The average difference within specific types of manufacturing work in the Northeast is somewhat greater than the overall figure (0.5 years). Among the North-Central states, the average difference within the specific categories is 0.4, exactly what it is between all operatives and laborers within the region.

It is safe to conclude that operatives and laborers do not differ greatly in their educational levels. Because the European immigrants include many without an English-language education, it is unlikely that their superior position in semiskilled versus unskilled work is due to superior educational attributes. Indeed, the immigrants gain relative to blacks at a time when the foreign-born were increasingly of South–Central–Eastern European origin. Added evidence in support of this conclusion can be found in the earlier analysis of table 11.8.

PART III
Conclusions

12
Conclusions

In some cases the data analyzed in this volume directly support one of the interpretations of black–new European differences reviewed in chapter 1. In other instances, the data lead one to generate somewhat novel ways of thinking about the problem because the existing interpretations make no sense. Although these new interpretations are clearly speculative, they are not made lightly. Rather the goal has been to develop an overview that integrates the available and somewhat disparate evidence. Before closing, here are some conclusions about existing interpretations.

EXISTING INTERPRETATIONS

Cultural and Normative Explanations

It is unlikely that cultural or normative explanations can go very far in accounting for the origin of black–new European gaps. To be sure, the literature is not entirely conclusive; Featherman (1971) has shown that various aspirational factors do not go very far in accounting for ethnic differences in mobility, but elsewhere Duncan, Featherman, and Duncan (1972, pp. 167–168) have found at least some indication that motivational forces may be affecting these matters. But my reasons for underplaying this force in accounting for black–new European differences stem from the analysis of educational shifts between cohorts in chapters 6, 7, and 8 of this book. These chapters showed that blacks were as strongly oriented toward education as were the new European groups generally. Although slaves and freedmen (in many cases) could not receive an education prior to the Civil War, the early postbellum period found a strong thrust toward education among blacks with an intensity at least matching that of southern whites. Chapter 6 lists some of the structural forces that undermined this disposition in the South. It is also clear that blacks (and whites) in the South were disadvantaged vis-à-vis the new Europeans in the North with respect to the quality of school systems available to them. Nevertheless, the new Europeans were eager for their children to leave school and contribute to their hard-pressed money situation; indeed many of the school attendance laws were passed in order to keep the children in school long enough to facilitate Americanization. To be sure, black males born in the North were less educated than were the American-born offspring of SCE European immigrants. This was not as striking in comparisons between black women born in the North and second-generation SCE women. But in both instances there was progress for succeeding cohorts of blacks when compared with either the SCE groups or with native whites of native parentage. The gaps were narrowed with each succeeding cohort, but then some remarkable shifts occurred which tossed blacks far behind (chapter 7).

All of these events suggest that blacks were working to narrow their initial educational disadvantage. Whether this would apply to other arenas of aspiration, motivation, values, and the like is, of course, an open question (more about this later). But the educational data fail to show any profound gap between blacks and new Europeans in terms of their initial dispositions, despite the argument often made that this was a central difference between them. Indeed, if anything, an argument could be constructed showing that blacks were initially more favorably disposed toward education than were many of the SCE groups. I might add that the analysis of family structure in chapter 7 does not help account for lower levels of black education either. The vast bulk of black–white differences in educational attainment is not explained by black–white differences in single-parent and two-parent families but can be explained in terms of purely economic forces.

There is also a strong indication of feedback processes that worked to the black disadvantage. During the heyday of new European immigration to the United States, the levels of education were not very high among the immigrants. Yet immigrants were preferred over blacks who were in the North at the same time for all sorts of jobs requiring minimal skills (witness the analysis in chapter 11 of unskilled versus semiskilled work, table 11.5, as well as the cross-tabulation between education and occupation, table 11.8). Considering how the evidence available here on education tends to undermine aspirational interpretations, one wonders if the motivational interpretation was overdone on other dimensions as well (perhaps through the circular reasoning discussed in chapter 1).

The Legacy of Slavery

As for the legacy of slavery, little need be said here because much of the evidence shows a deterioration in the position of blacks over time in the North. This is hardly to be expected if the position of blacks was affected by slavery because, if anything, its greatest legacy should be early in the postbellum period rather than well into the twentieth century. Yet, with respect to occupational trends for semiskilled and un-skilled work and with respect to education, the biggest setback occurred to the cohort reaching adulthood shortly after World War II. These results are most consistent with similar conclusions by Gutman (1976) about the family at the time of manumission and afterwards as well as the reanalysis of slavery conditions by Fogel and Engerman (1974).

The legacy-of-slavery argument is similar to that generated in the emphasis on norms and values, except that in this case the origins of such alleged characteristics are traced specifically to the impact of slavery. Accordingly, one can repeat here that the available hard evidence leads one to conclude that at the outset the disposition of blacks was not at all less promising than was the disposition of new Europeans.

Race and Discrimination

The obstacles faced by the new Europeans were enormous and in some cases, such as the development of political power (chapters 3 and 4), comparable to the black experience in the North. However, a mas-sive body of evidence indicates that blacks were discriminated against far more intensely in many domains of life than were the new Euro-peans. Witness, for example, the disposition of both employers and labor unions discussed in chapter 11 as well as materials that appear throughout the book. This fact cannot be glossed over as it is central to any explanation of group differences in outcome. This raises two ques-tions about race. If blacks did have greater obstacles, to what degree were these due to race? Second, if race did play an important role, how does one reconcile this interpretation with the fact that such other non-white groups as the Chinese and Japanese have done so well in the United States (to be sure only after a rocky start)?

Among those recognizing the fact that other nonwhite groups did better in the United States, there are several variations of the same basic theme, namely, that these other groups had certain characteristics that blacks lacked. For example, there may have been special institutional forces and advantages that these groups had (Light, 1972). Or, we return to the speculations about norms, values dispositions, and the like. Another variation of this emphasizes the heritage of slavery and the damaging effects of slavery, obstacles that did not exist for the other nonwhite groups. In any case, it leads to conclusions that the gaps were not really due to race after all, at least as an immediate cause as other nonwhite groups did alright.

There is another way of thinking about these racial gaps, one that emphasizes differences in the social context of contact. This perspective leads one to conclude that much of the black disadvantage was due to neither race nor certain personality characteristics. Rather, it is the structure of the situation that was so radically different for blacks and these other groups.

Let us recognize at the outset that there are certain disadvantages that blacks and any other nonwhite group would suffer in a society where the dominant white population has a preference for whites over nonwhites. This disadvantage is one blacks share with Japanese, Chinese, Filipinos, American Indians, and any other nonwhite group. These groups were more visible and more sharply discriminated against than were various white ethnic groups. The disposition to apply the same levels of legal protection and rights was weaker than that directed toward white populations. (This is possibly due to white predispositions stemming from the earlier slavery period as well as the fact that the SCE groups were at least European.) However, it is not impossible that whites have a hierarchy with respect to nonwhites such that blacks and Africans generally rank lower than Asian groups. In the early 1930s 100 Princeton University undergraduates were asked to characterize various racial and ethnic groups (Katz and Braly, 1952). Consider how radically different were the characterizations of blacks, Chinese, and Japanese shown in table 12.1. Particularly impressive is the list of characteristics listed for the Japanese, almost all of which would be considered "desirable" by most Americans. By contrast, the list of black characteristics is striking both because of its almost uniform lack of any favorable attributes and also because, I suspect, the emphasis would be quite different now.

To be sure, one might argue that these stereotypes reflect real differences between these groups and hence serve to prove that the Japanese and Chinese levels of success were a reflection of important personality

TABLE 12.1

CHARACTERISTICS MOST COMMONLY USED BY 100 PRINCETON STUDENTS, 1932

Chinese		Japanese		Negroes	
Characteristic	Number of respondents agreeing	Characteristic	Number of respondents agreeing	Characteristic	Number of respondents agreeing
Superstitious	34	Intelligent	45	Superstitious	84
Sly	29	Industrious	43	Lazy	75
Conservative	29	Progressive	24	Happy-go-lucky	38
Tradition-loving	26	Shrewd	22	Ignorant	38
Loyal to family ties	22	Sly	20	Musical	26
Industrious	18	Quiet	19	Ostentatious	26
Meditative	18	Imitative	17	Very religious	24
Reserved	17	Alert	16	Stupid	22
Very religious	15	Suave	16	Physically dirty	17
Ignorant	15	Neat	16	Naive	14
Deceitful	14	Treacherous	13	Slovenly	13
Quiet	13	Aggressive	13	Unreliable	12

SOURCE: Katz and Braly, 1952, p. 70.

differences. However, given the relatively small number of Japanese in the United States and their concentration on the Pacific Coast during the 1930s, it is unlikely that the responses of these Princeton students reflect much in the way of actual contact experience. Hence these results show radical differences in the way nonwhite groups were perceived by whites.

The reader may wonder if all of this is a bit too pat; rather than simply concluding that blacks had less of the necessary characteristics for making it in the United States, it is claimed that they did not do as well as other nonwhite groups because they faced even more severe disadvantages. Why would blacks suffer more? This is the heart of the matter. In my estimation, there are two key features that distinguish blacks from other nonwhite groups in the United States and which help explain their different outcomes. First, an exceptionally unfavorable disposition toward blacks existed on the part of the dominant white society due to the slave period and the initial contact with Africans (see Jordan, 1974, chapters 1 and 2). Blacks enter into competition as free people, but they are unable to shake off easily the derogatory notions about them and the negative dispositions toward blacks which go back to the slavery era. Of course, this was not a problem for the other nonwhite groups. Second, the threat of Asian groups was not anywhere as severe because migration was cut off before their numbers were very large. The response of whites to Chinese and Japanese was of the same violent and savage character in areas where they were concentrated, but the threat was quickly stopped through changes in immigration policy. This meant that Asian groups had more time to develop special mobility niches (see the discussion below) and that they have been of less *actual* (as opposed to *potential*) threat to whites than blacks. The cessation of sizable migration from Asia for a number of decades on the one hand indicates how quickly threatened whites were by Asian groups. On the other hand, this very cessation made it possible for those who were here to avoid eventually some of the disadvantages that would occur if there were as many of their compatriots in the country as there were blacks.

For those unconvinced, have patience because the problem is too complicated to be quickly resolved by a simple data set. Rather the answer must rest on satisfactorily weaving together the various threads of evidence and theory so that they make sense from a single perspective. Later, after analyzing the consequences that follow from a cessation of immigration, it will be possible to consider further whether the main source of black disadvantage was neither race nor their internal characteristics. At the moment, one can speculate that the comparison between Asian groups and blacks in the United States, although unfavorable to the latter in recent decades, may be due to the distinctive context of their contact with whites and the incredible threat that blacks posed. However, the contrast with other nonwhites does show that being a nonwhite was not an insurmountable obstacle.

Occupational Opportunities

It is difficult to overstate the direct importance of occupation and income as well as their indirect consequences for other long-run gaps between blacks and the new Europeans. Thanks to an excellent set of 1900 occupational data from the Census Bureau, one can draw some important conclusions about the situation these groups faced in the urban North at the beginning of the century. As one might guess, neither the new Europeans nor blacks held many of the specially desirable jobs at that time so there were not sharp differences at the upper end of the scale. But there were substantial differences in some areas, particularly in the service jobs where blacks were more concentrated and in the manufacturing jobs where the new Europeans held the edge. There was some evidence, even in 1900, that the new Europeans were in a more favorable position, even if they were still lower on the queue than were the older white groups. There is also strong evidence that the black pattern in the North resembled very much the same pattern found in the urban South after compositional differences are taken into account (chapter 10).

Other data (chapter 11) also indicate that earlier in this century blacks were disadvantaged in the urban North relative to the new Europeans. The antipathy toward blacks among labor unions displayed a striking interaction between discrimination by employers, employees, and customers, lower-wage levels among blacks, and strike breaking. However, the net effect is to see much more severe discriminatory forces operating against blacks in the labor market, with important feedback consequences on other domains of black—new European differences. As noted earlier, there is just no way of avoiding the fact that blacks were more severely discriminated against in the labor market and elsewhere. By contrast, there is strong evidence that new European participation in the labor market was not greatly affected by ethnic membership after one takes into account their lower origins. At least this is the case for a number of recent generations (Featherman and Hauser, 1978, pp. 475–479). Hence, the new Europeans were close enough to the intergenerational mobility rates for whites generally, and the rates were sufficiently open, that the SCE groups could do very well in relatively short order whereas this was not the case for blacks.

Timing and Residential Segregation

Both of these issues can be discussed together because in each case the clearest conclusion is that the conventional wisdom is not of help. Regarding timing, it is painfully clear that blacks in the North even in an earlier period were not doing as well as were new Europeans in some domains even after generation is taken into account. So one must conclude that more is going on here to widen the gap between the groups than merely the fact that the new Europeans came earlier in larger numbers. On the other hand, as will be developed below where more novel interpretations are attempted, there are important consequences due to the fact that new European immigration stopped and black migration northward continued in massive numbers for a number of decades afterwards.

The facts about residential segregation are deceptively simple. At one time, some of the new European groups were more highly segregated in the urban North than were blacks (chapter 9). But this pattern changed sharply, particularly with black residential isolation increasing earlier in this century. This suggests a shift in the relative positions of the groups—if residential segregation can be reasonably viewed as such an indicator. Why did this occur? There is reason to believe that the segregation changes did not necessarily represent a shift in the disposition of whites toward blacks, but rather reflect the impact of a change in population composition on an existing predisposition. One can interpret the changing patterns of black–white segregation not as an effort by whites to *increase* their segregation from blacks but merely to *maintain* it. This is not a paradox after taking into account the consequences of changing composition for actual white–black interaction (chapter 9). Moreover, this segregation pattern suggests that race and ethnic relations operating in the United States had a latent structure such that some of the changes in such relations over time are really shifts along an existing structure due to compositional change rather than changes in the dispositions of the groups toward one another. This makes sense in terms of queuing notions about occupations and it helps to explain changes in black–white segregation. More about this below as a different perspective is offered to help account for the facts gathered in this study.

A THEORY OF INTRINSIC DIFFERENCES

Ignoring blacks and new Europeans for a moment, consider the forces generating contact between racial and ethnic groups. These can be crudely divided into voluntary and involuntary forms of contact. Blacks were brought to the New World involuntarily as slaves; American Indians were already here but their contact with the white settlers was also involuntary insofar as they were overrun. By way of contrast, the movement of the new Europeans to the United States and the later migration of blacks from the South to the North are both examples of voluntary migration, international and internal, respectively. What do we know about voluntary migration? As a general rule, we can say that it is driven by economic forces, that is, people move from areas of low opportunity to areas of better opportunity. This is all relative, to be sure, but it means that the opportunity structure for a set of voluntary migrants is more favorable in the receiving area than in the sending area.[1] Because there is a lot of ignorance in these matters, as well as other satisfactions involved, a secondary counterflow to the sending area is sometimes rather substantial. Nevertheless, a net movement on the part of a group from one nation to another, or from one subarea within a nation to another subarea, is generally due to superior opportunities in the receiving area.

We also know that a set of potential sending areas differ from one another in their levels of living and opportunity structure. This means that the residents of countries (or subareas) A, B, C . . . N will vary in their evaluation of the options available to them in the United States (or urban North for blacks in the South) because they will be affected by the different opportunity structures available in their respective homelands (or the South for potential black migrants to the North). Migrants arriving in the United States from various sources will therefore differ in what is an acceptable job, depending on the options that exist for them in their homeland for the skills that they possess. A low-level menial job that might prove an attractive income alternative to someone with minimal skills from an extremely poor country would not be a migration "pull" for someone with more attractive alternatives in another homeland either because the level of living is higher or because the person possesses skills that can command a better job. Further, insofar as nations differ in their levels of development, it means that their labor forces will vary in the levels of skill for which they are capable as well as in their average educational levels.

Two important conclusions follow from these assumptions. First, there is an inherent reason for expecting differences between groups at the initial point of contact simply because the migrant groups differ in the alternatives available to them in the areas from which they are migrating. Ignoring special situations such as famine, social unrest, and oppression, emigrants from a nation with a relatively high level of living will tend to be both qualified for better jobs and have more attractive alternatives in their homeland than will those migrating from a nation with a lower level of living. Work acceptable to one group, in the sense of being a superior alternative to the opportunities available in the homeland, will not be attractive to members of another group (or to only a much smaller segment). Hence migrants from different sources will vary in their jobs and incomes not necessarily because of discrimination or work orientation but because of the alternatives available to them at home. Such groups at the initial point of contact in the United States differ not in their aspirations, but rather in the minimum they will settle for. And they differ in how little they will accept because of the alternatives at home that they must weigh them against. The second point is one well recognized in the work of Bonacich (1972, 1976), namely, workers in the receiving country will view migrants from nations with lower levels of living as potential competitors willing to work for less because of the alternatives at home. (This is basically the point presented in the analysis of labor unions and their discriminatory patterns in chapter 11).

However, of special interest here is the first issue, namely, whether earlier in this century and late in the last one the level of living in South–Central–Eastern Europe differed from the level of living for blacks in the South. If so, then the theory leads one to expect the group living in the poorer situation to have a lower minimum standard and so to accept working conditions and jobs that the other would reject. Deriving this conclusion is easier than testing it because to my knowledge there are no solid data on wages for the groups in comparable work which also take into account the cost of living encountered in each nation and the South at that time. Moreover, I cannot find data sets for per capita GNP during those periods for each of the countries. Consequently, I am obliged to rely on a reasonably good surrogate measure of the nature of life in these places, namely, life expectancy.

Table 12.2 compares life expectancy at birth ($\mathring{e}_0$) for blacks circa 1900, 1910, and 1920 with various nations in South, Central, and Eastern Europe. In addition, the average life table values in four southern cities in 1880 are compared with those for these same European nations. In 1880, when the sources of European migration first started to shift, $\mathring{e}_0$ in SCE Europe was generally superior to that experienced by blacks in the South. The expectation of life at birth for both black men and women in 1880, respectively, 22 and 26 years, is below that for any of the new European sources listed, the closest being Russia (males, 27; females, 29). Insofar as these life table values indicate general living conditions, one can infer that there would be jobs attractive to blacks that would not be attractive to the new Europeans.

TABLE 12.2

LIFE EXPECTANCY AT BIRTH IN SOUTH, CENTRAL, AND EASTERN EUROPE AND AMONG
BLACKS IN THE UNITED STATES, 1880–1920

			Year		
Nation	Sex	1880	1900–1902	1909–1911	1919–1920
Austria	Male	32.64	39.06	41.16	47.43
	Female	35.26	41.19	43.36	50.54
Bulgaria	Male	—	41.27	44.18	45.18
	Female	—	41.85	43.70	45.39
Finland	Male	—	44.13	46.53	49.08
	Female	—	46.52	49.68	53.03
Greece	Male	36.23	41.86	44.27	46.81
	Female	37.73	43.49	45.96	48.56
Italy	Male	34.33	43.60	45.66	48.64
	Female	34.84	44.11	46.50	50.01
Russia	Male	26.69	32.05	35.86	39.36
	Female	29.36	33.74	39.10	43.53
Black	Male	22.04	32.54	34.05	40.45
	Female	26.22	35.04	37.67	42.35

SOURCES: European nations from Dublin, Lotka, and Spiegelman, 1949, tables 87 and 88
(data interpolated to correspond to years above). Black data for original registration states
in twenieth century are from Dublin, Lotka, and Spiegelman, 1949, tables 81 and 83. Data
for blacks in 1880 are based on median figures for colored in four southern cities,
Washington, D.C., Baltimore, Charleston, and New Orleans. Derived from data reported
in Billings, 1886, pp. cxliv-cxlv.

Life expectancy was higher for Austrians, Bulgarians, Finns, Greeks,
and Italians when compared with blacks in each of the four periods
(Table 12.2). The only exception were the Russians who had lower levels
in 1900–1902 and who had mixed results in the 1919–1920 comparison.[2]
Incidentally, comparisons between Northwestern European nations and
the South–Central–Eastern nations are consistent with this perspective; the former have generally more favorable mortality than do the new
European sources.

In short, if the European and black life table values represent differences in levels of living, then there is some reason to expect that the new
Europeans might start off in a more favorable position than would blacks
in the North even if there was no discrimination. Namely, if the average
level of living for southern blacks was lower than that for whites residing
in SCE Europe, then the relative attractiveness of certain job options in

the North would differ for the groups. This does not mean that the upper end of their aspirations would differ, but it does mean that there is an intrinsic reason why blacks might start off lower. Of course, this situation is exacerbated by an additional force, the existence of even more discrimination against blacks than against SCE Europeans both in their initial jobs and later mobility. The "theory of intrinsic differences" developed here is sufficient to explain why groups will start off occupying different socioeconomic niches, but it does not account for their continuation over time. Indeed, without discrimination or other factors one would expect such initial gaps to narrow progressively if there is intergenerational mobility (Lieberson and Fuguitt, 1967).[3] Accordingly, one must look elsewhere to understand why more discrimination was directed at blacks as well as why other forces have maintained these gaps.

COMPOSITION, THE LATENT STRUCTURE OF RACE RELATIONS, AND NORTH–SOUTH DIFFERENCES

Many have observed that the position of blacks started to deteriorate in this century as their numbers increased in the North. Basically two explanations for this have been offered: a shift in the "quality" of black migration and the response of whites to the radical increase in the numbers of blacks. In evaluating these explanations and offering an alternative, we should come closer to understanding the general forces that for so many decades have kept blacks from closing the initial gaps.

The quality interpretation is simply that migration northward became less selective over time, particularly after the decline in southern agriculture forced blacks to move in more or less helter-skelter fashion. There are two bodies of data that sharply challenge this thesis. Starting with the work of Bowles, Bacon, and Ritchey (1973) there is evidence to indicate that southern black migrants to the North in recent years have done relatively well when compared with northern-born blacks in terms of welfare, employment rates, earnings after background factors are taken into account, and so on. There is reason for this pattern to occur (Lieberson, 1978a), but the point here is that the results do not support the notion that the black position in the North was undermined by these migrants because of their qualities. A second data set, covering earlier decades as well, involves a comparison in each decade between the educational level of blacks living in the North in each decade with what would have occurred if there had been no migration into or out of the North during the preceding ten years. At most, the educational level of blacks in the North was only slightly different in each period from what it would have been without migration. This is due to the highly selective nature of black out-migration from the South (see Lieberson, 1978b).

As for the second explanation, namely, that changes in racial composition caused the black position to deteriorate, we know there was a massive increase in both the absolute number of blacks and their relative proportion of the population living in northern cities. The anaysis of residential segregation in chapter 9 fits in rather nicely with this perspective, with changes in the indexes accounted for by changes in population composition. But the segregation analysis involves a subtle difference from the assumption that the structure of race relations changed; it assumes that such dispositions were always present in a latent form and simply unfurl in accordance with shifts in population composition. To draw an analogy, if an automobile changes speed as we vary the pressure on the gas pedal, we do not assume that the engine changes in character with more or less gas. Rather we assume that the potential range of speeds was always there and is simply altered by the amount of gas received. In similar fashion, it is fruitful to assume that the reason for race relations changing with shifts in composition is not due to a radical alteration in the dispositions of whites, but rather that changes in composition affect the dispositions that existed all along. In other words, there is a latent structure to the race relations pattern in a given setting, with only certain parts of this structure observed at a given time. This fits in well with a long-standing ecological perspective on the influence of compositional changes on race and ethnic relations and competition (see, for example, Hawley, 1944). It also provides a rather novel perspective on North–South differences.

This way of thinking about the linkage between composition and race and ethnic relations has important consequences when approaching the deterioration in the position of blacks in the North and, indeed, the assumptions implicit to notions about the black position in various regions of the United States. How different was the situation for blacks in the South and non-South earlier in the century? Obviously there were very important historical differences between the regions. Even if there was far more to the Civil War than freeing the slaves, still the regions differed sharply in their history regarding slavery and their disposition toward the institution. Likewise, the customs were quite different in these regions with respect to such matters as poll taxes, Jim Crow laws, lynching, racial "etiquette," and the like. Some of these regional differences can probably be explained by the establishment of antiblack traditions that remain firm even after the causes have disappeared. Social events have a life of their own: once established, the customs persist long after causes vanish (see Lieberson, in press).

But these important differences should not keep one from realizing that the North and South were still part of the same nation and shared certain qualities that were hidden only because the black composition in the regions was so radically different and because of historical forces. To be sure, if the small number of blacks living in a northern city had the vote, then they were unlikely to lose it when their proportion of the population increased to the point where it was of potential consequence to elections. But the latent structure of race relations in the North was not much different from the South on a variety of features. This has not been widely appreciated (a noteworthy exception being the analysis of the black position in the North before the end of slavery in the South by Litwack, 1961). It was not appreciated by those wanting to understand the changes in race relations as either due to the changing quality of blacks living in the North or some fundamental shifts in the United States. To be sure, there are a lot of complications affecting this comparison, witness the fact that the level of living was generally higher in the North and there were a number of institutional heritages in the South which blacks could avoid elsewhere. Hence there were strong incentives for migration from the South. But it is extremely helpful to recognize that the differences between regions with respect to bread-and-butter matters were not as radical as one would think by focusing exclusively on lynchings, poll taxes, race-baiting politicians, and legally sanctioned forms of segregation.

As noted in chapter 1, normally one does not ask why blacks in the South did not do as well as South–Central–Eastern Europeans. Until recently, circumstances were incredibly difficult for blacks in the South—witness, for example, the educational situation (chapter 6). However, I believe there is reason to suspect that a substantial part of the North–South gap was really due to the much smaller proportion blacks were of the urban population in the North and their virtual absence from the rural North. As a consequence, certain similarities in disposition toward blacks and the conflict between lower and higher wage rates were concealed by these compositional factors. In other words, underlying the two regions were a large number of common dispositions. This, I might add, also helps us understand some of the shifts that have occurred in the North when the black proportion of the population began to increase.

THE FLOW OF MIGRANTS

For more than a half century immigration from Europe has not been a significant factor in the SCE groups' growth, whereas the flow of blacks from South to North has been of importance in nearly all of this period. The significance of this widely cited difference is great. There are many more blacks who are recent migrants to the North whereas the immigrant component of the new Europeans drops off over time. Hence, at the very least it is important to make sure that generational factors are taken into account when comparing the ethnic groups. This is clearly an important consideration. For example, the median education of Japanese-American men increased massively between 1940 and 1960 in the United States—from 8.8 to 12.4 years of schooling. Almost all of this was due to changes in the generational composition of the group. With no immigration of any consequence for a number of decades, the foreign-born component dropped from 80 to 27 percent of the group. The actual shift in median education within the birthplace-specific components was rather small; from 8.3 to 8.8 years for the foreign-born and from 12.2 to 12.4 years for the American-born. In other words, almost all of the changes were simply due to shifts in generational composition (see Lieberson, 1973, pp. 562–563).

It is also argued that migration patterns are of significance because minimally skilled people no longer encounter the opportunities that once existed when the new Europeans were coming. This is not too convincing because there is every indication that occupational mobility is every bit as great now as it used to be. Second, black–white gaps in education are now narrowing rapidly. Finally, there is some reason to believe that intergenerational mobility in the North was never as good for blacks even in decades past (Thernstrom, 1973, pp. 183–194). I might add that the high unemployment rates among blacks in the North are not as novel as some have suggested. This is because smaller black–white gaps in earlier periods were a reflection of the substantial concentration of blacks in the rural South and the hidden underemployment that represented (see chapter 8).

Notwithstanding the importance of drawing generational distinctions, there is another way of thinking about the end of European immigration and the continuous flow of blacks. Theoretically, such shifts have consequences of their own in a regular and orderly way. In terms of the occupational queuing notion, the increase in the black component means a rise in the median black occupational position in the community, but it will at the same time widen the gap between blacks and new Europeans. Assuming that there is an occupational queue in which blacks are at the bottom and the new Europeans are just above them, consider the hypothetical data shown in table 12.3. In the first period, 5 percent of the work force is black and 10 percent is new European. The median black job is at the 2.5 percentile because they hold the bottom 5 percent of the jobs; the median new European job is at the tenth percentile, because they hold the jobs that range from the fifth to the fifteenth percentiles. Suppose in each period the new European component of the work force remains at 10 percent whereas blacks go to 10, then 20, and finally 30 percent of the work force. In each period, the average black percentile goes up but in each period the magnitude of the absolute gain in the average new European percentile goes up even faster. For example, from time 1 to time 2, the average black percentile goes up from 2.5 to 5, but the new European percentile goes up 5 points from 10 to 15. In similar fashion the new Europeans rise more rapidly when blacks go from 10 to 20 to 30 percent of the work force. This model ignores the fact that there will be some positive feedback as their component goes up because blacks will create a market for blacks pursuing such highly prestigious jobs as, for example, physicians, lawyers, dentists, merchants geared to blacks, and the like. Also, it assumes that the queuing is perfect such that the lowest SCE European enjoys a better job than the most highly placed black. Clearly this is false. But I believe the model does give one a clear understanding of how increases in the black component would upgrade the new Europeans at a more rapid rate as long as the queuing process remains intact. In effect, this queuing notion is compatible with the long-standing ladder model that holds that increases in a lower-ranked population would tend to upgrade the populations above them. In this sense, the growing presence of blacks did indeed benefit the new Europeans—not because they were more likely to discriminate against blacks than were other segments of the white population, but because blacks were lower on the hierarchy. This all operates insofar as there are strong enough barriers through unions,

TABLE 12.3

CONSEQUENCES OF BLACK POPULATION INCREASE FOR SCE EUROPEAN JOBS
(QUEUING MODEL)

Time	Percentage of population		Median percentile of jobs held		Increase in median percentile over previous time	
	Black	SCE European	Black	SCE European	Black	SCE European
1	5	10	2.5	10	—	—
2	10	10	5	15	2.5	5
3	20	10	10	25	5	10
4	30	10	15	35	5	10

NOTE: Median job percentile held is based on assumption that blacks received the lowest jobs in the community and that SCE European groups received the next lowest.

employers, and other discriminatory forces to stave off the potential undercutting of whites through the acceptance of lower wages by blacks.

The spectacular events since World War II should be seen in the context of these changes in the flow of migrants. The continuation of black migration to the North and the cessation of new European immigration helped upgrade the SCE groups in two additional ways besides the queuing process discussed above. These are the impact that newer segments of a group have on older segments and the overloading of special niches that each group tends to develop in the labor market. (None of this is to overlook the employment opportunities generated in the 1940s due to the massive demands of the war and in the post-World War II period. Bear in mind that there was a depression prior to the war and hence these demands not only meant new opportunities for blacks but also for the SCE European groups who were still higher on the queue.)

As for special niches, it is clear that most racial and ethnic groups tend to develop concentrations in certain jobs which either reflect some distinctive cultural characteristics, special skills initially held by some members, or the opportunity structure at the time of their arrival. In 1950 among the foreign-born men of different origins there were many such examples: 3.9 percent of Italians in the civilian labor force were barbers, eight times the level for all white men; 2.5 percent of the Irish were policemen or firemen, three times the rate for all white men; more than 2 percent of Scottish immigrants were accountants, about two and one-half times the level for whites; 9.4 percent of Swedish immigrants were carpenters, nearly four times the national level; 14.8 percent of Greek immigrant men ran eating and drinking establishments, 29 times the national level; and 3.3 percent of Russian immigrant men were tailors or furriers, 17 times the rate for all white men.[4] These concentrations are partially based on networks of ethnic contacts and experiences that in turn direct other compatriots in these directions. Each group does this and, because the job hierarchy is not a perfect system, such activities help give each group certain special niches that it might not otherwise have in a pure system of queues altered only by ethnic compatriot demands. In these cases, the group develops an "export" market in the sense of being able to supply needs and wants for other groups.

When the migration of a group accelerates, the ability to develop and exploit these special niches is badly handicapped. Such specialties can only absorb a small part of a group's total work force when its population grows rapidly or is a substantial proportion of the total population. After all, not everyone of Chinese origin could open a restaurant in a city where they are a sizable segment of the population, just as not all Jews could have opened stores in New York City. By contrast, when the numbers stabilize or increase at only a moderate clip, then the possibilities due to these ingroup concentrations are more sanguine. Thus, in communities where the group is a sizable segment of the population, it is more difficult for such niches to absorb much of the group.

The cessation of immigration, whether it involved the Japanese and Chinese or the South–Central–Eastern European groups, had long-run advantages to those members of the group already in the nation. (To be sure, there were certain negative costs such as the group's own natural market for compatriots' services or the expansion of demographically based power.) But these events help explain why blacks were unable to participate with the new Europeans in the massive socioeconomic shifts experienced in recent decades. In other words, it is more difficult to overcome the negative consequences of discrimination through special niches when the group is growing rapidly and/or is a large segment of the total population.

There is another way through which newcomers have a harmful effect on earlier arrivals and longer-standing residents from the same group. Sizable numbers of newcomers raise the level of ethnic and/or racial consciousness on the part of others in the city; moreover, if these newcomers are less able to compete for more desirable positions than are the longer-standing residents, they will tend to undercut the position of other members of the group. This is because the older residents and those of higher socioeconomic status cannot totally avoid the new-comers, although they work at it through subgroup residential isolation. Hence, there is some deterioration in the quality of residential areas, schools, and the like for those earlier residents who might otherwise enjoy more fully the rewards of their mobility. Beyond this, from the point of view of the dominant outsiders, the newcomers may reinforce stereotypes and negative dispositions that affect all members of the group.

Finally, I suspect that group boundaries shift and float in multiethnic or multiracial settings more than some recognize. Antagonisms and dispositions change in accordance with the group context. In this case, the movement of blacks to the North in sizable numbers reduced the negative disposition other whites had toward the new European groups. If the new Europeans rank higher in a queue, then the negative dispositions toward them would be muffled and modified in a setting where they would be viewed as relatively more desirable as neighbors, co-workers, political candidates, and so on than blacks. Ethnic ties and allegiances float and shift in accordance with the threats and alternatives that exist. The presence of blacks made it harder to discriminate against the new Europeans because the alternative was viewed even less favorably.

Under these circumstances, the rapid growth of the black population in the urban North during the last half century or so, accompanied by the opposite trend for the new Europeans, has significantly contributed to the differences in outcome experienced by these groups. These differences would be expected even if one ignores the latent structure of race relations tapped by these demographic changes in the North.

FURTHER ANALYSIS OF RACE

Returning to a theme suggested earlier in the chapter, I believe there is further reason for speculating that race was not as crucial an issue as is commonly supposed for understanding the black outcome relative to the new Europeans. In order to avoid being misunderstood by the casual reader, let me reiterate that such a conclusion does not mean that other nonwhite groups or the new Europeans possessed certain favorable characteristics to a greater degree than did blacks. There is an alternative way of interpreting these events, namely, a substantial source of the disadvantage faced by blacks is due to their position with respect to certain structural conditions that affect race relations generally. Having been reviewed in this chapter, one should now make sense of black–new European gaps, but what about comparisons of blacks with other nonwhites? There are eight important factors to consider.

1. Although hard quantitative data are not available, there is every reason to believe that the response to Chinese and Japanese in the United States was every bit as severe and as violent initially as that toward blacks when the latter moved outside of their traditional niches.

2. There was a cessation of sizable immigration from Japan and China for a number of decades before these groups were able to advance in the society.

3. The cessation was due to the intense pressures within the United States against Asian migration, particularly by those whites who were threatened by these potential competitors.

4. This meant that the number of these groups in the nation is quite small relative to blacks. In the 1970 census there were 22,580,000 blacks recorded compared with 591,000 Japanese and 435,000 Chinese.

5. Because of factors 2 and 4 above, the opportunity for these Asian groups to occupy special niches was far greater than for blacks. Imagine

more than 22 million Japanese Americans trying to carve out initial niches through truck farming!

6. Because of factor 2 there has been less negative effect on the general position of these groups due to recent immigrants (a situation that is now beginning to change somewhat for the Chinese).

7. Ignoring situations generated by direct competition between Asians and whites such as existed in the West earlier, there is some evidence that the white disposition toward blacks was otherwise even more unfavorable than that toward Asians. This is due to the ideologies that developed in connection with slavery as well as perhaps the images of Africa and its people stemming from exploration of the continent. Whatever the reason, one has the impression that whites have strikingly different attitudes toward the cultures of China and Japan than toward those of blacks or of Africa.

8. The massive economic threat blacks posed for whites earlier in the century in both the South and North was not duplicated by the Asians except in certain parts of the West.

I am suggesting a general process that occurs when racial and ethnic groups have an inherent conflict—and certainly competition for jobs, power, position, maintenance of different subcultural systems, and the like are such conflicts. Under the circumstances, there is a tendency for the competitors to focus on differences between themselves. The observers (in this case the sociologists) may then assume that these differences are the sources of conflict. In point of fact, the rhetoric involving such differences may indeed inflame them, but we can be reasonably certain that the conflict would have occurred in their absence. To use a contemporary example, if Protestants in Northern Ireland had orange skin color and if the skin color of Roman Catholics in that country was green, then very likely these physical differences would be emphasized by observers seeking to explain the sharp conflict between these groups. Indeed, very likely such racial differences would be emphasized by the combatants themselves. No doubt such physical differences would enter into the situation as a secondary cause because the rhetoric would inflame that difference, but we can be reasonably certain that the conflict would occur in their absence. In the same fashion, differences between blacks and whites—real ones, imaginary ones, and those that are the product of earlier race relations—enter into the rhetoric of race and ethnic relations, but they are ultimately secondary to the conflict for society's goodies.

This certainly is the conclusion that can be generated from the classic experiment by Sherif and Sherif (1953) in which a homogeneous group of children at camp were randomly sorted into two groups and then competition and conflict between the groups was stimulated. The experiment resulted in each of the groups developing all sorts of images about themselves and the other group. Yet, unknown to them, the groups were identical in their initial distribution of characteristics.

In order to avoid a misunderstanding of a position that is radically different from that held by most observers, whether they be black or white, oriented toward one group or the other, let me restate this part of my thesis. There is powerful evidence that blacks were victims of more severe forms of discrimination than were the new Europeans—although the latter also suffered from intense discrimination. Much of the antagonism toward blacks was based on racial features, but one should not interpret this as the ultimate cause. Rather the racial emphasis resulted from the use of the most obvious feature(s) of the group to support the intergroup conflict generated by a fear of blacks based on their threat as economic competitors. If this analysis is correct, it also means that were the present-day conflict between blacks and dominant white groups to be resolved, then the race issue could rapidly disintegrate as a crucial barrier between the groups just as a very profound and deep distaste for Roman Catholics on the part of the dominant Protestants has diminished rather substantially (albeit not disappeared).

THE GREAT NON SEQUITUR

The data comparing blacks and the new Europeans earlier in this century lead one to a rather clear conclusion about the initial question. The early living conditions of the new Europeans after their migration to the United States were extremely harsh and their point of entry into the socioeconomic system was quite low. However, it is a non sequitur to assume that new Europeans had it as bad as did blacks or that the failure of blacks to move upward as rapidly reflected some ethnic deficiencies. The situation for new Europeans in the United States, bad as it may have been, was not as bad as that experienced by blacks at the same time. Witness, for example, the differences in the disposition to ban openly blacks from unions at the turn of the century (chapter 11), the greater concentration of blacks in 1900 in service occupations and their smaller numbers in manufacturing and mechanical jobs (chapter 10), the higher black death rates in the North (chapter 2), and even the greater segregation of blacks with respect to the avenues of eminence open to them (Lieberson and Carter, 1979). It is a serious mistake to underestimate how far the new Europeans have come in the nation and how hard it all was, but it is equally erroneous to assume that the obstacles were as great as those faced by blacks or that the starting point was the same.

Notes

1. The Problem: Black—New European Differences

1. Compare the data on Italian, Polish, and Russian education in younger ages, occupation, and income with that for Americans of British origin in *Population Characteristics* (United States Bureau of the Census, 1973, tables 6-9). The traditional basis for allocating European sources into the old and new categories is somewhat arbitrary and, in some cases, does not correspond with the period of greatest immigration. For example, several Scandinavian sources were more important between 1880 and 1920 than they were in earlier decades. In keeping with traditional analysis, Germany is an old source and included with the Northwestern European nations even though it is a central European nation (Lieberson, 1963*b*, p. 551).

2. This is a bit of an unfair comparison because these are national corporations and hence may tend to draw to some degree on the national market for executive recruitment and board members.

3. Comparisons cannot be made between the first two decades and either the 1930 or 1950 data because the spatial units are considerably different. Several discussions based on the data in this work have ignored that point.

4. Likewise, there were some cases in which new European immigrant groups were less segregated from blacks than from the native whites (this was especially the case for Russians and, to a lesser degree, Italians). A few cases of this lingered on for some decades, but by 1950 there were no exceptions, and in all instances the new Europeans were more segregated from blacks than from native whites (Lieberson, 1963*a*, pp. 130–131, table 43).

5. A rare example in which a wide variety of influences are recognized is the review by Fried (1969). Indeed, he is able to point out a number of similarities between immigrant and black conditions without ignoring sharp differences between them (see, for example, p. 150 ff.).

6. Nothing can be done about income differences between blacks and new Europeans for the decades of greatest interest because there are virtually no data for those years.

2. The Initial Conditions

1. All of these percentages are based on estimates by Gerald Shaughessy reported in Ellis (1956, pp. 42, 86).

2. See also a study of immigrants to Australia after World War II (Lieberson, 1963a).

3. Government: Black Participation and Power

1. My account of DePriest is drawn from Drake and Cayton (1945) and Gosnell (1935).

4. Government: The New European Groups

1. My discussion of Pastore in this chapter is based on the excellent account in Lubell (1956, pp. 72–79).

2. This is particularly the case for lawyers from groups such as the new Europeans and blacks who have great difficulty getting into the lucrative corporate law practices.

3. From a Mormon perspective, in effect a Jew became the first gentile governor of the state. (I am indebted to Dr. Vernon Carstensen, Professor of History at the University of Washington, for first calling this to my attention.)

6. Education

1. No inferences can be drawn about the median of 12.6 for whites classified in the "other" ethnic category because this rubric includes members of both other old and new ethnic groups. The lower rate for the Spanish ethnic group is not of primary concern here as it largely reflects educational attainment among those of Mexican, Puerto Rican, and other New World groups.

2. In order to make the data on nonwhites comparable to the second-generation means reported in Duncan and Duncan (1968) the coding procedure

reported in Duncan (1965b, p. 20) was adopted. The advantages enjoyed by the new groups are still somewhat understated because nonwhites include more than blacks. Among nonwhite males who are not black, the mean educational level is 11.6.

3. These differences are understated by the exclusion of whites attending parochial high schools as well as by the part—whole problem.

4. The harmful consequences of this pattern for white education in areas with relatively few blacks is described in Bond (1934, chapter 5).

5. An exception is Howard University, established mainly to serve those already prepared for college and professional training.

6. Bond (1966, p. 550) disputes this, claiming that Edward A. Jones graduated from Amherst College several days earlier.

7. These regional differences actually understate the black—new immigrant gap, because the data for the South conceal relatively lower expenditures and shorter school years for blacks within the region. Although some argue that school characteristics have minimum effects, evidence is now coming to light to question these conclusions (see Mare, 1978—1979; Wiley and Harnischfeger, 1974), but the problem is not fully resolved. However, it seems reasonable to assume that gaps of the magnitude observed in this chapter must have an impact even if smaller gaps do not under a linear model (see, for example, Karweit, 1976).

7. Education in the North

1. In all fairness, this need not mean that the same differential would hold between black and white women with school-age children who are heads of households. Duncan and Duncan (1969, p. 281) observe that an occupation was reported far more often for white female heads of household than for blacks in the OCG survey. In addition, they cite 1960 Census data that are compatible with their finding. "Among females who headed a non-farm family which included a child between the ages of six and 17, the proportions employed were 45 percent for non-whites and 54 percent for whites" (p. 281). A reexamination of these census data for the North, which is the area of most interest here, indicates an even greater difference with 35 and 55 percent, respectively, of nonwhite and white female heads so employed among those with children in the ages specified above. However, we should bear in mind that black women are far more likely than whites to be in families without husbands present. Among children 6 to 17 years of age in 1970, 42 percent of white children were in households with the mother in the labor force, whereas 53 percent of black children were in the analogous situation (based on data reported in Waldman and Gover, 1971, table A).

2. I am indebted to Beverly Duncan who pointed out that the Duncan and Duncan 1969 article is based on males of a nonfarm background, whereas the

Duncan 1967 article does not exclude males with a farm background. This distinction has important consequences for the results obtained in each study.

8. Further Analysis of Education in the North

1. A separate issue is the changes since 1960, but this will not be covered here as the concern is with the historical origins of these inequalities rather than the current events.

2. The median education in the oldest cohort of immigrant men from Italy, Russia, Finland, Lithuania, Poland, and Yugoslavia was barely half that of the NWNPs.

3. The data reported in table 4.1 from the monograph by Beverly Duncan (1965b) appear to indicate that the new Europeans were achieving higher levels of education at an earlier point than is indicated by the analysis of the census data reported in this study. Among those 55–59 in 1960 (and hence 57–61 in 1962 when the survey used by Duncan was taken), Central and Eastern European second-generation men had 1.1 years more schooling than native whites of native parentage (based on a comparison betwen their gross deviations from the grand mean). However, one should note that these results are based on an extremely small sample of Central or Eastern Europeans (from 40 to 100 sample cases); the delineation of Central or Eastern European leaves out Austrians and Finns; and most important the groups included are probably heavily weighted by the results for second-generation Russians and Poles. Using census data, and including as many of the Central and Eastern European groups available in the census with the necessary cross-tabulation between age and education and using the index of net difference employed elsewhere in this study rather than their arithmetic means, I also find that the ND indicates slightly higher educational levels for the Central and Eastern Europeans when compared with the NWNP males.

4. With an N of 9, the far more desirable step of treating the earlier and later educational measures as separate variables is not practical (see Fuguitt and Lieberson, 1974).

5. Comparable data for 1950 are not available.

6. Admittedly the children not born in the city include some who were born in other northern locales and hence these figures probably understate the gap in the North between southern- and northern-born black children.

7. Data limitations make it impossible to narrow the groups more closely to the specific interests of this study.

8. It is probably because of this that the census-based rates for 1940 appear so much lower than the rates for 1931 when, at the same time, the unemployment estimates derived from a more or less consistent procedure indicate that unemployment was about the same at both periods.

9. Although not discussed above, an analysis of the basic data in table 8.16

indicates that the black—native white ratios were less favorable to blacks in 1950 than 20 years earlier in all but Detroit (both sexes) and Boston (women only).

9. Residential Segregation

1. Thanks to the work of Taeuber and Taeuber (1965) and Sørensen, Taeuber, and Hollingsworth (1975), black shifts in recent decades have already been analyzed for a large number of cities. Segregation analyses are much more difficult for most white ethnic groups in recent decades because an increasingly important segment of each group is in the third or later generation, components not enumerated by ethnic origin in the census.

2. Of course, it is unlikely that the two groups would ever have exactly identical distributions even if race was irrelevant (see Cortese, Falk, and Cohen, 1976).

3. This difference in probabilities is similar to that developed theoretically by Blau (1977). Suppose, for example, that there are ten members of group X and 100 members of group Y, and five members of each group intermarry. The intermarriage rate for X is .50 (5/10), whereas the rate for Y is only .05 (5/100).

4. In the more complex situation where there are two or more additional groups, B in the equation can represent all non-As and their probability of interacting with each other, that is, their isolation from As. Of course, the degree of self-isolation will be different for each of the specific non-A groups as well as their isolation from A.

5. The correlation is based on an N of 12—four different groups in each of the three cities. For several groups in Kansas City and Indianapolis, it was necessary to use the state figures to estimate the X variable.

6. Blacks were between 9 and 9.5 percent of the population in the latter two cities, an unusually large proportion for the North in 1910, whereas the new European groups were exceptionally unimportant in both places (less than 1 percent in the former and about 2 percent in Kansas City). The differences were not as extreme in Cincinnati, but were in the same direction.

7. In order to boost the extremely small Ns available for the regressions, the Finns were included for three cities in which that was possible and the Portuguese were likewise included for Boston. It is necessary to restrict black comparisons to cities in which the black proportion of the population falls within the range for the new European groups. Otherwise, blacks could deviate above or below the expected value generated by a regression equation simply because the basic regression becomes nonlinear at that place on the X scale. However, even for the seven cities in which the white regression was inappropriate for blacks, the actual black P* index was below the level expected on the basis of the white pattern in five of these cases as well.

8. The within-city analysis is a bit less comforting. Chicago and New York are two of the four cases in which black segregation is above the level expected

on the basis of the new European regression of segregation on population composition. In the Chicago case, the deviance is strikingly high, .1512 as opposed to an expected value of .0732; whereas it is not terribly great in New York, an actual index of .0665 as against .0538 predicted on the basis of the white regression. In Philadelphia, the black index of .1566 is below the .1970 expected on the basis of the white regression.

9. There was no separate Poland in 1890. Very likely this is a heavily Jewish group.

10. This is based on a small N of only four groups, with $r^2 = .94$ when each group's segregation is regressed on its proportion of the population. Not too much should be made of this, but it does illustrate that black isolation would probably be higher if the group in 1890 had followed the pattern exhibited among the new European groups.

11. The regression lines are the more central test, although the actual 1920 data for each city help to make the shifts clearer. However, bear in mind that half of the cities should lie above the 1910 line under the usual distributional assumptions if there was no change in 1920. Hence, it is only the unusual absence in 1920 of any points above this 1910 line which is important for the other groups.

12. Data in 1900 are for servants combined with the waiter-waitress category, and hence the 1910 and 1890 data were similarly combined for comparisons with 1900. In other comparisons, including 1910–1920, the data are just for servants, as defined and reported in each census. The correlations are between later ${}_bP_b^*$ minus the earlier one and the ratio of the percentage servants in the two periods (later percentage divided by the earlier one). Milwaukee was not included in the 1900–1910 comparisons.

13. The reader should keep in mind that black occupational composition tends to change as the black proportion of the population increases. In particular, blacks show a strong tendency to concentrate in various servant occupations even when they are a relatively small proportion of the population. Hence the correlations considered here between segregation change and changes in servant employment may be spurious and simply due to the influence that increases in the black proportion have on both of these attributes. That is, a sizable increase in the black proportion of the population will generate a decline in the black segment employed as servants simply because they have already filled up nearly all the available niches. More about this in the discussion of occupations.

14. Length-of-residence data are used for 1930 because the necessary city-specific data for immigrant groups are not available for 1920. The numerator of the variable is the population arriving in 1900 or earlier and the denominator is the total who had arrived by 1920. The correlations between this timing variable and the ratio of actual over expected segregation among the foreign-born are -.62, -.43, and -.25 for the Greek, Hungarian, and Russian groups, respectively.

15. The Roumanian, Italian, and Austrian correlations, respectively, are .06, .03, and -.09.

16. Bear in mind that all of the white indexes include the small numbers from groups who are not blacks. This is a great convenience for computational purposes but does not seriously affect the results because the number of residents who are neither black nor white is generally very small in all of these cities.

10. Earning a Living: 1900

1. This is based on the nonlinear regression, $Y = -.07944 + 1.46213X^{1/3}$, where Y is the proportion of male servants and waiters who are black, and X is the proportion of the male work force who are black. The fit is fairly good, $r = .928$, with 86 percent of the variance in the black proportion of servants accounted for simply under this nonlinear compositional fit.

2. Aside from inefficiencies in the marketplace, there are several factors that prevent the curve from reaching 100 percent. Some employers will strongly prefer a nonblack regardless of costs necessary to obtain one (in the language of Becker [1957] the "taste for discrimination is virtually infinity"). Another possibility is that there will be some whites who are unable or indisposed to seek other types of jobs in cities where they work. Further, the growth of blacks may have occurred at a time after some whites obtained their jobs and hence, although virtually no new whites will obtain employment in this area, there will be some remaining from an earlier situation. Finally, the job categories are heterogenous and so there may be some jobs within the class that are more attractive to whites because of their intrinsic characteristics.

3. The intercept is very small, .00137.

4. The correlation is no doubt less than perfect. For example, group participation could be essentially nil in various occupations when they are 5 percent of the population (thus generating similar Y values at that point), but they may differ radically in the point of inflection that follows and hence where equity is reached.

5. The similarity between the NWNP and German figures does not necessarily mean identical positions in the entire queue, but rather the low level of these jobs may be insensitive to the group differences elsewhere in the hierarchy. Witness the sharp differences between them in the professional pursuits, whereas there was little black–SCE difference in those pursuits.

6. To be sure, such small gaps at the .05 and .12 level could mean sharp differences when the groups take off at some higher level of X or when the desirability of such jobs for the more dominant groups changes.

7. To be sure, these patterns could simply reflect differential propensities to migrate northward among various segments of the black population. This would then raise the question of why such differentials would have existed. It is very difficult, however, to deal with this possibility with the available data.

8. Although black representation is above unity for the South, essentially it is at the same level as in the North—a result that would not occur if there was

only a queue operating to affect their jobs and if it was the same queue in both regions (except where the figure was extremely high in the North to begin with). In this case, one would expect a big rise in the South if the black proportion was at .38 when they were .12 of the population in the North.

11. Occupational Trends Earlier in this Century

1. These figures exclude men employed as farmers and farm managers, farm laborers and foremen, or with occupation not reported. Thus the figures inflate the actual proportion of employed men with the occupations specified. However, this permits analysis in which ethnic and racial differences in farm activities are roughly taken into account in the comparisons.

2. The shifts are not an artifact of differentials between occupation groups in the propensity to retire or otherwise leave work. Among men 55−64 in 1960, for example, those with professional occupations were a far smaller proportion of the labor reserve than of the entire experienced civilian labor force, .037 as opposed to .073 (based on data reported in U.S. Bureau of the Census, 1963d, table 4; U.S. Bureau of the Census, 1966, table 10).

3. The favorable position enjoyed by the new European groups in this instance does not contradict the results described in the preceding chapter about black−SCE European differences in professionalization in 1900. This is because the oldest cohort here was born around 1900; the SCE data here are for the second generation whereas they were for both immigrant and second generations in the previous chapter; and population composition is not taken into account here—an undesirable feature in this analysis but unavoidable given the data limitations.

4. The reader should recognize that comparisons involving northern- and western-born black residents of the non-South have added problems besides those already discussed. Namely, there is the question of selective migration from the non-South which can alter the figures. If, for example, nonsouthern blacks with professional occupations were specially likely to move to the South, then the professionalization rate would be underestimated for the group.

5. ND is a measure that does take the direction of these differences into account (Lieberson, 1975). But the occupational categories are so broad that ranking them would probably introduce massive errors when the groups are compared through ND.

6. If one assumes that new Europeans were in a less-favorable position than the old European immigrants in 1910 regarding concentration in unskilled jobs, then the data for all immigrants in that year probably overstate the SCE immigrant position relative to blacks at the beginning of this period.

7. The craftsman category also includes those employed as foremen or in kindred activities. Men employed as farmers and farm managers or as farm laborers and foremen were excluded from the analysis. This provides a rough control on differences between groups in their agricultural employment.

8. These expected data are derived from the Westergaard Expected Cases form of standardization based on the cross-tabulations available between occupation and income in the non-South for blacks and for native whites (U.S. Bureau of the Census, 1947, tables 25–28). Not enough details are available to permit the more desirable separate analysis of the SCE European immigrant groups.

12. Conclusions

1. The distinction between "voluntary" and "involuntary" is sometimes not entirely clear, as in the case of starvation or political pressures in the sending country. Nevertheless, in those cases one can still argue that the motivation to move stems from more attractive conditions in the receiving country or subarea.

2. The original ten registration states used to provide data on black mortality in 1900, 1910, and 1920 were the six New England states and four elsewhere in the North. The reader may wonder if this is an appropriate measure for blacks because it is the living conditions of blacks in the South that are relevant here as an index for determining the jobs that they would accept in the North. Regional life tables, first available for 1930–1939, indicate that the three southern regions all have higher expectation of life at birth for nonwhite males than do either the North Atlantic or North-Central regions; this is also the case for two of the southern regions when compared to the Mountain and Pacific category. The gaps are not as great for nonwhite females (see Dublin, Lotka, and Spiegelman, 1949, tables 81, 83). The same sources also indicate that nonwhites in the rural South in 1939 had higher expectations of life than did nonwhites in either different regions or in different types of communities. A special adjustment that takes into account this difficulty still supports the conclusion that life expectancy at birth for South–Central–Eastern European countries was generally more favorable. Because the West-South-Central states had the highest and the North-Central region the lowest $\overset{\circ}{e}_0$, the black data shown in table 12.2 were multiplied by the ratio of West-South-Central to North-Central regional black life table values in 1930–1939. This gave the most favorable increase to black values. In all periods the majority of SCE European nations still had higher life expectancy at birth even after this adjustment.

3. Another force probably operating in the same direction stems from the fact that the South was, of course, much closer to the North than was South–Central–Eastern Europe. If it is reasonable to assume that the minimum improvement necessary to stimulate migration will vary directly with distance, expressed in time-cost factors, then this force will also work toward generating an initial difference favoring the white groups.

4. Based on data reported in Hutchinson, 1956, table A-2a. See the table for detailed titles of the occupations described in the text.

References

Adamic, Louis. *A Nation of Nations*. New York: Harper and Brothers, 1945.

Appel, John J. "American Negro and Immigrant Experience: Similarities and Differences." In *The Aliens*, edited by Leonard Dinnerstein and Frederic Cople Jaher, pp. 339–347. New York: Appleton-Century-Crofts, 1970.

Ashenfelter, Orley, and Michael K. Taussig. "Discrimination and Income Differentials: Comment." *American Economic Review* 61 (1971): 746–750.

Baltzell, E. Digby. *The Protestant Establishment*. New York: Vintage Books, 1966.

Banfield, Edward C. *The Unheavenly City: The Nature and Future of Our Urban Crisis*. Boston: Little, Brown, 1968.

Becker, Gary S. *The Economics of Discrimination*. Chicago: University of Chicago Press, 1957.

Bell, Daniel. "Crime: A Queer Ladder of Social Mobility." In *Racial and Ethnic Relations*, edited by Bernard E. Segal, pp. 177–183. New York: Thomas Y. Crowell, 1966.

Bell, Wendell. "A Probability Model of the Measurement of Ecological Segregation." *Social Forces* 32 (1954): 357–364.

Billings, John S. *Report on the Mortality and Vital Statistics of the United States, Part 2*. Washington, D.C.: Government Printing Office, 1886.

———. *Vital Statistics of New York City and Brooklyn*. Washington, D.C.: Government Printing Office, 1894.

———. *Vital Statistics of Boston and Philadelphia*. Washington, D.C.: Government Printing Office, 1895.

Blascoer, Frances. *Colored School Children in New York*. New York: Public Education Association of the City of New York, 1915.

Blau, Peter M. *Inequality and Heterogeneity*. New York: Free Press, 1977.

Blau, Peter M., and Otis Dudley Duncan. *The American Occupational Structure*. New York: Wiley, 1967.

Blauner, Robert. *Racial Oppression in America*. New York: Harper & Row, 1972.

Bloch, Herman D. *The Circle of Discrimination*. New York: New York University Press, 1969.

Boie, Maurine. "An Analysis of Negro Crime Statistics for Minneapolis for 1923, 1924 and 1925." *Opportunity* 6 (1928): 171–173.

Bonacich, Edna. "A Theory of Ethnic Antagonism: The Split Labor Market." *American Sociological Review* 37 (1972): 547–559.

———. "Advanced Capitalism and Black/White Race Relations in the United States: A Split Labor Market Interpretation." *American Sociological Review* 41 (1976): 34–51.

Bond, Horace Mann. *The Education of the Negro in the American Social Order.* New York: Prentice-Hall, 1934.

———. "The Negro Scholar and Professional in America." *The American Negro Reference Book,* edited by John P. Davis, pp. 548–589. Englewood Cliffs, N.J.: Prentice-Hall, 1966.

Bowles, Gladys K., A. L. Bacon, and P. N. Ritchey. *Poverty Dimensions of Rural-to-Urban Migration: A Statistical Report.* Washington, D.C.: Economic Research Service, U.S. Department of Agriculture, 1973.

Broderick, Francis L., and August Meier, eds. *Negro Protest Thought in the Twentieth Century.* Indianapolis: Bobbs-Merrill, 1965.

Brody, David. *Labor in Crisis: The Steel Strike of 1919.* Philadelphia: J. B. Lippincott, 1965.

Broom, Leonard, and Norval D. Glenn. *Transformation of the Negro American.* New York: Harper & Row, 1965.

Brown, Ina Corinne. *Socio-Economic Approach to Educational Problems.* Washington, D.C.: U.S. Office of Education, 1942.

Bullock, Henry Allen. *A History of Negro Education in the South.* Cambridge, Mass.: Harvard University Press, 1967.

Carmichael, Stokely, and Charles V. Hamilton. *Black Power.* New York: Vintage Books, 1967.

Carpenter, Niles. *Immigrants and Their Children.* Washington, D.C.: Government Printing Office, 1927.

Chicago Commission on Race Relations. *The Negro in Chicago.* Chicago: University of Chicago Press, 1922.

Clift, Virgil A. "Educating the American Negro." In *The American Negro Reference Book,* edited by John P. Davis, pp. 360–395. Englewood Cliffs, N.J.: Prentice-Hall, 1966.

Coleman, James S., Ernest Q. Campbell, Carol J. Hobson, James McPartland, Alexander M. Mood, Frederic D. Weinfeld, and Robert L. York. *Equality of Educational Opportunity.* Washington, D.C.: Government Printing Office, 1966.

Commissioner-General of Immigration. *Annual Report.* Washington, D.C.: Government Printing Office, 1900.

Congressional Quarterly, Inc. *Congressional Quarterly Almanac, 1960.* Washington, D.C.: Congressional Quarterly, Inc. 1960.

———. Congressional Quarterly, Inc. Congressional Quarterly Almanac, 1963. Washington, D.C.: Congressional Quarterly, Inc., 1963.

Cortese, Charles F., R. Frank Falk, and Jack K. Cohen. "Further Considerations on the Methodological Analysis of Segregation Indices." *American Sociological Review* 41 (1976): 630–637.

Crain, Robert L., and Carol Sachs Weisman. *Discrimination, Personality, and Achievement.* New York: Seminar Press, 1972.

Dahl, Robert A. *Who Governs?* New Haven, Conn.: Yale University Press, 1961.

Daniels, John. *In Freedom's Birthplace: A Study of the Boston Negroes.* Boston: Houghton Mifflin, 1914.

Davis, Jackson. "The Outlook for Negro Colleges." *The Southern Workman* 57 (1928): 129–136.

Dinnerstein, Leonard, and Frederic Cople Jaher, eds. *The Aliens*. New York: Appleton-Century-Crofts, 1970.

Drake, St. Clair and Horace R. Cayton. *Black Metropolis*. New York: Harcourt, Brace, 1945.

Dublin, Louis I., Alfred J. Lotka, and Mortimer Spiegelman. *Length of Life: A Study of the Life Table*. 2nd ed., rev. New York: Ronald Press, 1949.

DuBois, W. E. B., ed. *The College-Bred Negro*. Atlanta: Atlanta University Press, 1900.

————. *The Negro Common School*. Atlanta: Atlanta University Press, 1901.

————. *The Philadelphia Negro*. New York: Schocken Books, 1967.

DuBois, W. E. B., and Augustus Granville Dill, eds. *The Common School and the Negro American*. Atlanta: Atlanta University Press, 1911.

Duncan, Beverly. "Dropouts and the Unemployed." *Journal of Political Economy* 73 (1965a): 121−134.

————. *Family Factors and School Dropout: 1920−1960*. Ann Arbor: University of Michigan, 1965b.

————. "Education and Social Background." *American Journal of Sociology* 72 (1967): 363−372.

Duncan, Beverly, and Otis Dudley Duncan. "Minorities and the Process of Stratification." *American Sociological Review* 33 (1968): 356−364.

————. "Family Stability and Occupational Success." *Social Problems* 16 (1969): 273−285.

Duncan, Otis Dudley. "A Socioeconomic Index for All Occupations." In *Occupations and Social Status*. edited by Albert J. Reiss, Jr., pp. 109−138. New York: Free Press, 1961.

————. "After the Riots." *The Public Interest* 9 (1967): 3−7.

Duncan, Otis Dudley, and Beverly Duncan. *The Negro Population of Chicago*. Chicago: University of Chicago Press, 1957.

Duncan, Otis Dudley, David L. Featherman, and Beverly Duncan. *Socioeconomic Background and Achievement*. New York: Seminar Press, 1972.

Duncan, Otis Dudley, and Stanley Lieberson. "Ethnic Segregation and Assimilation." *American Journal of Sociology* 64 (1959): 364−374.

Easterlin, Richard A. "Long Swings in U.S. Demographic and Economic Growth: Some Findings on the Historical Pattern." *Demography* 2 (1965): 490−507.

Edwards, Alba M. *Comparative Occupation Statistics for the United States, 1870 to 1940*. Washington, D.C.: Government Printing Office, 1943.

Efron, David, and John P. Foley, Jr. "Gestural Behavior and Social Setting." In *Readings in Social Psychology*, edited by Theodore M. Newcomb and Eugene L. Hartley, pp. 33−40. New York: Henry Holt, 1947.

Ehrenhalt, Alan. "Most Members of Congress Claim Religious Affiliation." *Congressional Quarterly Weekly Report* 37 (1979): 80−81.

Elkins, Stanley M. *Slavery*. Chicago: University of Chicago Press, 1959.

Ellis, John Tracy. *American Catholicism*. Chicago: University of Chicago Press, 1956.

Essien-Udom, E. U. *Black Nationalism*. Chicago: University of Chicago Press, 1962.

Farley, Reynolds. *Growth of the Black Population*. Chicago: Markham, 1970.

————. "Family Types and Family Headship: A Comparison of Trends Among Blacks and Whites." *Journal of Human Resources* 6 (1971): 275−296.

Farley, Reynolds, and Albert I. Hermalin. "Family Stability: A Comparison of Trends Between Blacks and Whites." *American Sociological Review* 36 (1971): 1−17.

Farley, Reynolds, and Karl E. Taeuber. "Population Trends and Residential Segregation Since 1960." *Science* 159 (1968): 953−956.

Featherman, David L. "The Socioeconomic Achievement of White Religio-Ethnic Subgroups: Social and Psychological Explanations." *American Sociological Review* 36 (1971): 207−222.

Featherman, David L., and Robert M. Hauser. *Opportunity and Change*. New York: Academic Press, 1978.

Fenton, John H. *Midwest Politics*. New York: Holt, Rinehart & Winston, 1966.

Fishberg, Maurice. *The Jews*. New York: Scribner's, 1911.

Fisher, Charles W. *Minorities, Civil Rights, and Protest*. Belmont, Calif.: Dickenson, 1970.

Fishman, Joshua A., Vladimir C. Nahirny, John E. Hofman, and Robert G. Hayden. Language Loyalty in the United States. The Hague: Mouton: 1966.

Fleming, G. James. "The Negro in American Politics: The Past." In *The American Negro Reference Book*, edited by John P. Davis, pp. 414–430. Englewood Cliffs, N.J.: Prentice-Hall, 1966.

Fogel, Robert William, and Stanley L. Engerman. *Time on the Cross: The Economics of American Negro Slavery*. Boston: Little, Brown, 1974.

Folger, John K., and Charles B. Nam. *Education of the American Population*. Washington, D.C.: Government Printing Office, 1967.

Franklin, John Hope. *From Slavery to Freedom*. New York: Alfred A. Knopf, 1956.

Freedman, Ronald, and Lolagene Coombs. "Childspacing and Family Economic Position." *American Sociological Review* 31 (1966): 631–648.

Fried, Marc. "Deprivation and Migration: Dilemmas of Causal Interpretation." In *On Understanding Poverty: Perspectives from the Social Sciences*, edited by Daniel P. Moynihan, pp. 111–159. New York: Basic Books, 1969.

Fuchs, Lawrence H. *The Political Behavior of American Jews*. Glencoe, Ill.: Free Press, 1956.

Fuguitt, Glenn V., and Stanley Lieberson. "The Correlation of Ratios or Difference Scores Having Common Terms." In *Sociological Methodology, 1973–1974*, edited by Herbert L. Costner, pp. 128–144. San Francisco: Jossey-Bass, 1974.

Garfinkel, Herbert. *When Negroes March*. Glencoe, Ill.: Free Press, 1959.

Gavit, John Palmer. *Americans by Choice*. New York: Harper, 1922.

Glazer, Nathan. "Blacks and Ethnic Groups: The Difference, and the Political Difference it Makes." *Social Problems* 18 (1971): 444–461.

Glazer, Nathan, and Daniel Patrick Moynihan. *Beyond the Melting Pot*. Cambridge, Mass.: MIT Press, 1963.

Gleason, Philip. "American Catholic Higher Education: A Historical Perspective." In *The Shape of Catholic Higher Education*, edited by Robert Hassenger, pp. 15–53. Chicago: University of Chicago Press, 1967.

Glick, Clarence. "The Relation Between Position and Status in the Assimilation of Chinese in Hawaii." *American Journal of Sociology* 47 (1942): 667–679.

Good, H. G. *A History of American Education*. 2nd rev. ed. New York: Macmillan, 1962.

Gosnell, Harold F. *Negro Politicians*. Chicago: University of Chicago Press, 1935.

Greeley, Andrew M. "Ethnic Minorities in the United States: Demographic Perspectives." *International Journal of Group Tensions* 7 (1977): 64–97.

Greene, Victor R. *The Slavic Community on Strike: Immigrant Labor in Pennsylvania Anthracite*. Notre Dame, Ind.: University of Notre Dame Press, 1968.

Gutman, Herbert G. *The Black Family in Slavery and Freedom, 1750–1925*. New York: Pantheon, 1976.

Hadden, Jeffrey K., Louis H. Masotti, and Victor Thiessen. "The Making of the Negro Mayors, 1967." In *The Transformation of Activism*, edited by August Meier, pp. 91–119. Chicago: Aldine, 1970.

Hain, A. J. "Our Immigrant, the Negro." *Iron Trade Review* 73 (1923): 730–736.

Hamilton, C. Horace. "The Negro Leaves the South." *Demography* 1 (1964): 273–295.

Handlin, Oscar. *Race and Nationality in American Life*. Garden City: Doubleday Anchor, 1957.

———. ed. *Immigration as a Factor in American History*. Englewood Cliffs, N.J.: Prentice-Hall, 1959.

Harris, Abram L. *The Negro Population in Minneapolis*. Minneapolis: Minneapolis Urban League and Phyllis Wheatley Settlement House, 1926.

Hatcher, Harold. *Survey of Negro Enrollment at Indiana Colleges*. Indianapolis: Indiana Civil Rights Commission, 1964.

Hauser, Philip M. "Differential Fertility, Mortality, and Net Reproduction in Chicago: 1930." Ph.D. dissertation, University of Chicago, 1938.

———. "Demographic Factors in the Integration of the Negro." *Daedalus* 94 (1965): 847–877.

Hauser, Robert M. "Educational Stratification in the United States." *Sociological Inquiry* 40 (1970): 102–129.

———. *Socioeconomic Background and Educational Performance*. Washington, D.C.: American Sociological Association, 1973.

Hawley, Amos H. "Dispersion Versus Segregation: Apropos of a Solution of Race Problems." Papers of the Michigan Academy of Science, Arts, and Letters 30 (1944): 667–674. Adopted in *Race: Individual and Collective Behavior*, edited by Edgar T. Thompson and Everett C. Hughes, pp. 199–204. Glencoe, Ill.: Free Press, 1958.

Haynes, George E. *Negro New-Comers in Detroit, Michigan*. New York: Home Missions Council, 1918.

Herskovits, Melville J. *The American Negro*. Bloomington, Ind.: Indiana University Press, 1964.

Higgs, Robert. "Race, Skill, and Earnings: American Immigrants in 1909." *Journal of Economic History* 31 (1971): 420–428.

Higham, John. *Strangers in the Land*. New Brunswick, N.J.: Rutgers University Press, 1955.

Hodge, R. W. "Toward a Theory of Racial Differences in Employment." *Social Forces* 52 (1973): 16–31.

Hourwich, Isaac A. *Immigration and Labor*. 2nd rev. ed. New York: Huebsch, 1922.

Hoyt, Edwin P., Jr. *The Guggenheims and the American Dream*. New York: Funk & Wagnalls, 1967.

Hutchinson, E. P. *Immigrants and Their Children, 1850–1950*. New York: Wiley, 1956.

Institute of Urban Life. "Report on the Representation of Poles, Italians, Latins and Blacks in the Executive Suites of Chicago's Largest Corporations." Chicago: Institute of Urban Life, 1973.

Johnson, Charles S. *The Negro College Graduate*. Chapel Hill: University of North Carolina Press, 1938.

Johnson, M. "A Comment on Palmore and Whittington's Index of Similarity." *Social Forces* 51 (1973): 490–492.

Jones, Maldwyn Allen. *American Immigration*. Chicago: University of Chicago Press, 1960.

Jordan, Winthrop D. *The White Man's Burden: Historical Origins of Racism in the United States*. New York: Oxford University Press, 1974.

Kantrowitz, Nathan. "Ethnic and Racial Segregation in the New York Metropolis, 1960." *American Journal of Sociology* 74 (1969): 685–695.

———. *Ethnic and Racial Segregation in the New York Metropolis: Residential Patterns Among White Ethnic Groups, Blacks, and Puerto Ricans*. New York: Praeger, 1973.

Karweit, Nancy. "A Reanalysis of the Effect of Quantity of Schooling on Achievement." *Sociology of Education* 49 (1976): 236–246.

Katz, Daniel, and Kenneth W. Braly. "Verbal Stereotypes and Racial Prejudice." In *Readings in Social Psychology*, 2nd rev. ed., edited by Guy E. Swanson, Theodore M. Newcomb, and Eugene L. Hartley, pp. 67–73. New York: Henry Holt, 1952.

Katzman, David M. *Before the Ghetto: Black Detroit in the Nineteenth Century.* Urbana, Ill.: University of Illinois Press, 1975.

Kennedy, Louise V. *The Negro Peasant Turns Cityward.* New York: Columbia University Press, 1930.

Killian, Lewis M. *The Impossible Revolution?* New York: Random House, 1968.

Kiser, Clyde V. "Cultural Pluralism." In *Demographic Analysis,* edited by Joseph J. Spengler and Otis Dudley Duncan, pp. 307–320. Glencoe, Ill.: Free Press, 1956.

Kitagawa, Evelyn M. "Components of a Difference Between Two Rates." *Journal of the American Statistical Association* 50 (1955): 1168–1194.

Klezl, Felix. "Austria." In *International Migrations, Volume II,* edited by Walter F. Willcox, New York: National Bureau of Economic Research, 1931.

Kristol, Irving. "The Negro Today Is Like the Immigrant Yesterday." *New York Times Magazine* 11 (1966): 50–51, 124–142.

Kusmer, Kenneth L. *A Ghetto Takes Shape: Black Cleveland, 1870–1930.* Urbana, Ill.: University of Illinois Press, 1976.

Learsi, Rufus. *The Jews in America: A History.* Cleveland: World Publishing, 1954.

Lieberson, Stanley. "Ethnic Groups and the Practice of Medicine." *American Sociological Review* 23 (1958): 542–549.

———. *Ethnic Patterns in American Cities.* New York: Free Press, 1963a.

———. "The Old-New Distinction and Immigrants in Australia." *American Sociological Review* 28 (1963b): 550–565.

———. "The Meaning of Race Riots." *Race* 7 (1966): 371–378.

———. "Measuring Population Diversity." *American Sociological Review* 34: (1969): 850–862.

———. "An Empirical Study of Military–Industrial Linkages." *American Journal of Sociology* 76 (1971): 562–584.

———. "Generational Differences Among Blacks in the North." *American Journal of Sociology* 79 (1973): 550–565.

———. "Rank-Sum Comparisons Between Groups." In *Sociological Methodology, 1976,* edited by David Heise, pp. 276–291. San Francisco: Jossey-Bass, 1975.

———. "A Reconsideration of the Income Differences Found Between Migrants and Northern-Born Blacks." *American Journal of Sociology* 83 (1978a): 940–966.

———. "Selective Black Migration from the South: A Historical View." In *Demography of Racial and Ethnic Groups,* edited by Frank D. Bean and W. Parker Frisbie, pp. 119–141. New York: Academic Press, 1978b.

———. "Forces Affecting Language Spread: Some Basic Propositions." In *Language Spread: Studies in Diffusion and Social Change,* edited by Robert L. Cooper, in press.

Lieberson, Stanley, and Donna K. Carter. "Making It in America: Differences Between Eminent Blacks and White Ethnic Groups." *American Sociological Review* 44 (1979): 347–366.

Lieberson, Stanley, and Glenn V. Fuguitt "Negro-White Occupational Differences in the Absence of Discrimination." *American Journal of Sociology* 73 (1967): 188–200.

Lieberson, Stanley, and Christy A. Wilkinson. "A Comparison Between Northern and Southern Blacks Residing in the North." *Demography* 13 (1976): 199–224.

Light, Ivan H. *Ethnic Enterprise in America: Business and Welfare Among Chinese, Japanese, and Blacks.* Berkeley: University of California Press, 1972.

Lincoln, C. Eric. *The Black Muslims in America.* Boston: Beacon Press, 1961.

Litwack, Leon F. *North of Slavery: The Negro in the Free States, 1790–1860.* Chicago: University of Chicago Press, 1961.

Lopreato, Joseph. *Italian Americans.* New York: Random House, 1970.

Lubell, Samuel. *The Future of American Politics.* 2nd rev. ed. Garden City, N.Y.: Doubleday Anchor, 1956.

McEntire, Davis. *Residence and Race.* Berkeley: University of California Press, 1960.

McGinnis, Frederick A. *The Education of Negroes in Ohio.* Blanchester, Ohio: Curless Printing Company, 1962.

McGouldrick, Paul F., and Michael B. Tannen. "Did American Manufacturers Discriminate Against Immigrants Before 1914?" *Journal of Economic History* 37 (1977): 723–746.

Mann, Arthur. *La Guardia Comes to Power: 1933.* Philadelphia: J. B. Lippincott, 1965.

―――. "A Historical Overview: The *Lumpenproletariat*, Education, and Compensatory Action." *The Quality of Inequality: Urban and Suburban Public Schools,* edited by Charles V. Daly, pp. 9–26. Chicago: University of Chicago Center for Policy Study, 1968.

Marden, Charles F., and Gladys Meyer. *Minorities in American Society.* 2nd rev. ed. New York: American Book Company, 1962.

Mare, Robert. "Sources of Educational Growth in America." *Focus* 3 (1978–1979): 5–6, 12.

Mayer, Martin. *The Bankers.* New York: Weybright & Talley, 1974.

Meeker, Edward, and James Kau. "Racial Discrimination and Occupational Attainment at the Turn of the Century." *Explorations in Economic History* 14 (1977): 250–276.

Meier, August, and Elliott M. Rudwick. *From Plantation to Ghetto.* New York: Hill & Wang, 1966.

Metropolitan Life Insurance Company. "Mortality of the Native and the Foreign Born." *Statistical Bulletin* 42 (1961): 3–6.

―――. "Changes in State Populations by Race." *Statistical Bulletin* 50 (1969): 7–9.

―――. "Population Changes in Leading Metropolitan Areas." *Statistical Bulletin* 51 (1970): 5–7.

Middleton, Russell. "The Civil Rights Issue and Presidential Voting Among Southern Negroes and Whites." *Social Forces* 40 (1962): 209–215.

Motley, Constance Baker. "The Legal Status of the Negro in the United States." In *The American Negro Reference Book,* edited by John P. Davis, pp. 484–521. Englewood Cliffs, N.J.: Prentice-Hall, 1966.

Moynihan, Daniel P. *The Negro Family: The Case for National Action.* Washington, D.C.: United States Department of Labor, Office of Policy, Planning, and Research, 1965.

Myrdal, Gunnar with the assistance of Richard Sterner and Arnold Rose. *An American Dilemma.* New York: Harper, 1944.

National Advisory Commission on Civil Disorders. *Report of the National Advisory Commission on Civil Disorders.* Washington, D.C.: Government Printing Office, 1968.

Nelli, Humbert S. *Italians in Chicago, 1880–1930.* New York: Oxford University Press, 1970.

Newbold, N. C. "Common Schools for Negroes in the South." *Annals of the American Academy of Political and Social Science* 140 (1928): 209–223.

New York Times *Encyclopedic Almanac, 1970.* New York, 1969.

Novak, Michael. "Further Thoughts on Ethnicity." *Christian Century* 10 (1973): 40–43.

Office of Policy Planning and Research. *The Negro Family.* Washington, D.C.: United States Department of Labor, 1965.

Ogburn, William Fielding. "Social Change and Race Relations." In *Race Relations: Problems and Theory,* edited by Jitsuichi Masuoka and Preston Valien, pp. 200–207. Chapel Hill: University of North Carolina Press, 1961.

Ovington, Mary White. *Half a Man: The Status of the Negro in New York.* New York: Longmans, Green, 1911.

Pappenfort, Donnell M. *Journey to Labor: A Study of Births in Hospitals and Technology.* Chicago: Population Research and Training Center, University of Chicago, 1964.

Payne, William. "The Negro Land-Grant Colleges." *Civil Rights Digest* 3 (1970): 12—17.

Pelling, Henry. *American Labor*. Chicago: University of Chicago Press, 1960.

Raper, Arthur F. *The Tragedy of Lynching*. New York: Dover Publications, 1970.

Reid, Ira De A. *Social Conditions of the Negro in the Hill District of Pittsburgh*. Pittsburgh: General Committee on the Hill Survey, 1930.

Reisner, Edward H. *Nationalism and Education Since 1789*. New York: Macmillan, 1922.

Reports of the Industrial Commission. *Education, Volume 15*. Washington, D.C.: Government Printing Office, 1901.

Reuter, E. B. *The Mulatto in the United States*. Boston: Richard G. Badger, 1918.

Rischin, Moses. *The Promised City*. Cambridge, Mass.: Harvard University Press, 1962.

Roberts, D. F. "The Dynamics of Racial Intermixture in the American Negro—Some Anthropological Considerations." *American Journal of Human Genetics* 7 (1955): 361—367.

Roof, Wade Clark. " 'The Negro as an Immigrant Group'—A Research Note on Chicago's Racial Trends." *Ethnic and Racial Studies* 1 (1978): 452—464.

Ross, Edward Alsworth. *The Old World in the New*. New York: Century Company, 1914.

Ross, Frank Alexander. *School Attendance in 1920*. Washington, D.C.: Government Printing Office, 1924.

Rustin, Bayard. "From Protest to Politics." In *Negro Protest Thought in the Twentieth Century*, edited by Francis L. Broderick and August Meier, pp. 405—421. Indianapolis: Bobbs-Merrill, 1965.

Sewell, William H. "Inequality of Opportunity for Higher Education." *American Sociological Review* 36 (1971): 793—809.

Sherif, Muzafer, and Carolyn W. Sherif. *Groups in Harmony and Tension: An Integration of Studies on Intergroup Relations*. New York: Harper & Brothers, 1953.

Siegel, Paul M. "On the Cost of Being a Negro." *Sociological Inquiry* 35 (1965): 41—57.

Silberman, Charles. "The City and the Negro." In *The Negro in Twentieth Century America* edited by John Hope Franklin and Isidore Starr, pp. 506—524. New York: Vintage Books, 1967.

Simpson, George Eaton, and J. Milton Yinger. *Racial and Cultural Minorities*. New York: Harper, 1958.

———. *Racial and Cultural Minorities*. 3rd rev. ed. New York: Harper & Row, 1965.

Smith, Timothy L. "Native Blacks and Foreign Whites: Varying Responses to Educational Opportunity in America, 1880—1950." *Perspectives in American History* 6 (1972): 309—335.

Sørensen, Annemette, Karl E. Taeuber, and Leslie J. Hollingsworth, Jr. "Indexes of Racial Residential Segregation for 109 Cities in the United States, 1940 to 1970." *Sociological Focus* 8 (1975): 125—142.

Sowell, Thomas. *Race and Economics*. New York: David McKay, 1975.

Spear, Allan H. *Black Chicago: The Making of a Negro Ghetto, 1890—1920*. Chicago: University of Chicago Press, 1967.

Steinberg, Stephen. *The Academic Melting Pot*. New York: McGraw-Hill, 1974.

Stone, Chuck. *Black Political Power in America*. 2nd rev. ed. New York: Dell, 1970.

Swastek, Joseph V. "Polish Americans." Pp. 143—157 In *One America*. edited by Francis J. Brown and Joseph S. Roucek, pp. 143—157. New York: Prentice-Hall.

Taeuber, Alma F., and Karl E. Taeuber. "Recent Immigration and Studies of Ethnic Assimilation." *Demography* 4 (1967): 798—808.

Taeuber, Karl E., and Alma F. Taeuber. "The Negro as an Immigrant Group: Recent Trends in Racial and Ethnic Segregation in Chicago." *American Journal of Sociology* 69 (1964): 374—382.

———. *Negroes in Cities.* Chicago: Aldine, 1965.

Taft, Philip. *Organized Labor in American History.* New York: Harper & Row, 1964.

Taylor, William L. "The Immigrant Myth." In *Race, Creed, Color, or National Origin,* edited by Robert K. Yin, pp. 27–34. Itasca, Ill.: F. E. Peacock, 1973.

Thernstrom, Stephan. *The Other Bostonians: Poverty and Progress in the American Metropolis, 1880–1970.* Cambridge, Mass.: Harvard University Press, 1973.

Thomas, Brinley. *Migration and Economic Growth.* Cambridge, England: Cambridge University Press, 1954.

Thompson, Anna J. "A Survey of Crime Among Negroes in Philadelphia." *Opportunity* 4 (1926): 217–219, 251–254, 285–286.

Thompson, Charles H. "The Educational Achievements of Negro Children." *Annals of the American Academy of Political and Social Science* 140 (1928): 193–208.

Thompson, Frank V. *Schooling of the Immigrant.* New York: Harper & Brothers, 1920.

Thurow, Lester C. *Poverty and Discrimination.* Washington, D.C.: Brookings Institution, 1969.

———. *Generating Inequality: Mechanisms of Distribution in the U. S. Economy.* New York: Basic Books, 1975.

United States Bureau of the Census. *Census of Population: 1890, Part 2.* Washington, D.C.: Government Printing Office, 1897.

———. *Census of Population: 1900, Volume 2, Part 2.* Washington, D.C.: Government Printing Office, 1902.

———. *Occupations at the Twelfth Census (Special Reports).* Washington, D.C.: Government Printing Office, 1904.

———. *Illiteracy in the United States, Bulletin 26.* Washington, D.C.: Government Printing Office, 1905.

———. *Census of Population: 1910, Volume 1.* Washington, D.C.: Government Printing Office, 1913.

———. *Census of Population: 1910, Volume 4, Occupation Statistics.* Washington, D.C.: Government Printing Office, 1914.

———. *United States Life Tables, 1890, 1901, 1910, and 1901–1910.* Washington, D.C.: Government Printing Office, 1921.

———. *Census of Population: 1920, Volume 2, General Report and Analytical Tables.* Washington, D.C.: Government Printing Office, 1922.

———. *Census of Population: 1920, Volume 4, Occupations.* Washington, D.C.: Government Printing Office, 1923.

———. *Census of Population: 1930. Unemployment, Volume 1.* Washington, D.C.: Government Printing Office, 1931.

———. *Census of Population: 1930. Unemployment, Volume 2.* Washington, D.C.: Government Printing Office, 1932.

———. *Census of Population: 1930, Volume 2. General Report, Statistics by Subjects.* Washington, D.C.: Government Printing Office, 1933a.

———. *Census of Population: 1930, Volume 6, Families.* Washington, D.C.: Government Printing Office, 1933b.

———. *Census of Population: 1930. Special Report on Foreign White Families by Country of Birth of Head.* Washington, D.C.: Government Printing Office, 1933c.

———. *Census of Population: 1940, Volume 4, Characteristics by Age, Part 1.* Washington, D.C.: Government Printing Office, 1943a.

———. *Census of Population: 1940. Nativity and Parentage of the White Population, General Characteristics.* Washington, D.C.: Government Printing Office, 1943b.

———. *Census of Population: 1940. Characteristics of the Population, Volume 2, Parts 1–7.* Washington, D.C.: Government Printing Office, 1943c.

———. *Census of Population: 1940, Nativity and Parentage of the White Population, Mother Tongue.* Washington, D.C.: Government Printing Office, 1943d.

———. *Census of Population: 1940. The Labor Force, Occupational Characteristics.* Washington, D.C.: Government Printing Office, 1943e.

———. *Census of Population: 1940. Estimates of Labor Force, Employment, and Unemployment in the United States, 1940 and 1930.* Washington, D.C.: Government Printing Office, 1944.

———. *Census of Population: 1940. Differential Fertility 1940 and 1910, Women by Number of Children Ever Born.* Washington, D.C.: Government Printing Office, 1945a.

———. *Census of Population: 1940. Educational Attainment of Children by Rental Value of Home.* Washington, D.C.: Government Printing Office, 1945b.

———. *Census of Population: 1940. Educational Attainment by Economic Characteristics and Marital Status.* Washington, D.C.: Government Printing Office, 1947.

———. *Census of Population, Volume 2. Characteristics of the Population.* Washington, D.C.: Government Printing Office, 1952.

———. *1950 Census of Housing, General Characteristics. Volume 1, Part 1, United States Summary.* Washington, D.C.: Government Printing Office, 1953a.

———. *Census of Population: 1950. Special Reports, Education.* Washington, D.C.: Government Printing Office, 1953b.

———. *Census of Population: 1950. Special Reports, Nonwhite Population by Race.* Washington, D.C.: Government Printing Office, 1953c.

———. *Census of Population: 1950. Special Reports, Nativity and Parentage.* Washington, D.C.: Government Printing Office, 1954.

———. *Census of Population: 1950. Special Reports, Occupational Characteristics.* Washington, D.C.: Government Printing Office, 1956.

———. *Population Characteristics. "Educational Attainment"* Series P-20, No. 121. Washington, D.C. Government Printing Office, 1963a.

———. *Census of Population: 1960. Subject Reports, Nonwhite Population by Race. Final Report PC(2)-1C.* Washington, D.C.: Government Printing Office, 1963b.

———. *Census of Population: 1960. Subject Reports, Educational Attainment. Final Report PC(2)-5B.* Washington, D.C.: Government Printing Office, 1963c.

———. *Census of Population: 1960. Subject Reports, Occupational Characteristics. Final Report PC(2)-7A.* Washington, D.C.: Government Printing Office, 1963d.

———. *Census of Population: 1960. Subject Reports, School Enrollment. Final Report PC(2)-5A.* Washington, D.C.: Government Printing Office, 1964a.

———. *Census of Population: 1960. Subject Reports, Women by Number of Children Ever Born. Final Report PC(2)-3A.* Washington, D.C.: Government Printing Office, 1964b.

———. *Census of Population: 1960. Subject Reports, Nativity and Parentage. Final Report PC(2)-1A.* Washington, D.C.: Government Printing Office, 1965.

———. *Census of Population: 1960. Subject Reports, Labor Reserve. Final Report PC(2)-6C.* Washington, D.C.: Government Printing Office, 1966.

———. *Statistical Abstract of the United States.* Washington, D.C.: Government Printing Office, 1970a.

———. *Population Characteristics. "Voter Participation in November 1970."* Series P-20, No. 208. Washington, D.C.: Government Printing Office, 1970b.

———. *Population Characteristics. "Characteristics of the Population by Ethnic Origin, November 1969."* Series P-20, No. 221. Washington, D.C.: Government Printing Office, 1971.

———. *Population Characteristics. "Characteristics of the Population by Ethnic Origin: March 1972 and 1971."* Series P-20, No. 249. Washington, D.C.: Government Printing Office, 1973.

————. *Historical Statistics of the United States, Colonial Times to 1970.* Washington, D.C.: Government Printing Office, 1975.

United States Bureau of Labor Statistics. *Special Studies. "The Social and Economic Status of Negroes in the United States, 1970." Report No. 394.* Washington, D.C.: Government Printing Office, 1971.

United States Census Office. *Census Reports, Volume 1, Statistics of the Population of the United States.* Washington, D.C.: Government Printing Office, 1883.

United States Commission on Civil Rights. *Political Participation.* Washington, D.C.: Government Printing Office, 1968a.

————. "Roster of Negro Elected Officials." *Civil Rights Digest* 1 (1968b): 35–39.

————. "Negro Mayors: First Hurrahs!" *Civil Rights Digest* 1 (1968c): 5–6.

United States Immigration Commission. *Statistical Review of Immigration, 1820–1910.* Washington, D.C.: Government Printing Office, 1911a.

————. *The Children of Immigrants in Schools, Volumes 1–5.* Washington, D.C.: Government Printing Office, 1911b.

————. *Abstracts of Reports, Volume 1.* Washington, D.C.: Government Printing Office, 1911c.

United States Senate Committee on Banking, Housing and Urban Affairs. *Treasury Department's Administration of the Contract Compliance Program for Financial Institutions.* Washington, D.C.: Government Printing Office, 1976.

United States Treasury Department. *Annual Statement on Commerce and Navigation, Foreign Commerce.* Washington, D.C.: Government Printing Office, 1880.

————. *Annual Report on Commerce and Navigation, Foreign Commerce.* Washington, D.C.: Government Printing Office, 1884.

————. *Annual Report and Statement on Foreign Commerce and Navigation.* Washington, D.C.: Government Printing Office, 1891.

————. *Immigration and Passenger Movement.* Washington, D.C.: Government Printing Office, 1896.

van der Slik, Jack R. "Constituency Characteristics and Roll Call Voting on Negro Rights in the 88th Congress." In *Blacks in the United States,* edited by Norval D. Glenn and Charles M. Bonjean, pp. 586–597. San Francisco: Chandler, 1969.

Viteles, Morris S. "The Mental State of the Negro." *Annals of the American Academy of Political and Social Science* 140 (1928): 166–177.

Waldman, Elizabeth and Gover, Kathryn R. "Children of Women in the Labor Force." *Special Labor Force Report 134.* Washington, D.C.: Bureau of Labor Statistics, 1971.

Waskow, Arthur I. *From Race Riot to Sit-In.* Garden City, N.Y.: Doubleday Anchor, 1967.

Weaver, Robert C. *The Negro Ghetto.* New York: Harcourt, Brace, 1948.

Weber, Adna Ferrin. *The Growth of Cities in the Nineteenth Century.* Ithaca, N.Y.: Cornell University Press, 1962.

Wesley, Charles H. *Negro Labor in the United States, 1850–1925.* New York: Russell & Russell, 1967.

Weyl, Nathaniel. *The Creative Elite in America.* Washington, D.C.: Public Affairs Press, 1966.

Whyte, William Foote. *Street Corner Society.* Chicago: University of Chicago Press, 1943.

Wiley, David E., and Annegret Harnischfeger. "Explosion of a Myth: Quantity of Schooling and Exposure to Instruction, Major Educational Vehicles." *University of Chicago Studies of Educative Processes, Report No. 8.* Chicago: University of Chicago, 1974.

Wilkerson, Doxey A. *Special Problems of Negro Education.* Washington, D.C.: Government Printing Office, 1939.

Willcox, Walter F. *International Migrations, Volume 1.* New York: National Bureau of Economic Research, 1929.

————. "Immigration into the United States." In *International Migrations, Volume 2,* edited by Walter F. Willcox, pp. 85–122. New York: National Bureau of Economic Research, 1931.

Willhelm, Sidney M. *Who Needs the Negro?* Cambridge, Mass.: Schenkman, 1970.

Wilson, James Q. *Negro Politics*. Glencoe, Ill.: Free Press, 1960.

———. "The Negro in American Politics: The Present." In *The American Negro Reference Book*, edited by John P. Davis, pp. 431–457. Englewood Cliffs, N.J.: Prentice-Hall, 1966.

———. "The Negro in Politics." In *American Ethnic Politics*, edited by Lawrence H. Fuchs, pp. 217–246. New York: Harper & Row, 1968.

Wirth, Louis. *The Ghetto*. Chicago: University of Chicago Press, 1928.

Wohlstetter, Albert, and Sinclair Coleman. *Race Differences in Income*. Santa Monica, Calif.: Rand, 1970.

Woofter, T. J., Jr. *Negro Problems in Cities*. New York: Doubleday, Doran, 1928.

Work, Monroe N., ed. *Negro Year Book, 1918–1919*. Tuskegee Institute, Ala.: Negro Year Book Publishing Company, 1919.

Wright, Richard R., Jr. *The Negro in Pennsylvania: A Study in Economic History*. New York: Arno, 1969.

Yancey, William L., Eugene P. Ericksen, and Richard N. Juliani. "Emergent Ethnicity: A Review and Reformulation." *American Sociological Review* 41 (1976): 391–403.

Indexes

Author Index

409

Subject Index